THIRD EDITION

MANAGERIAL COMMUNICATION

A FINGER ON THE PULSE

PAUL R. TIMM

KRISTEN BELL DETIENNE

Brigham Young University

Prentice Hall
Englewood Cliffs, NJ 07632

Library of Congress Cataloging-in-Publication Data

Timm, Paul R.
      Managerial communication : a finger on the pulse / Paul R.Timm,
Kristen Bell DeTienne.—3rd ed.
         p.   cm.
      Includes bibliographical references and index.
      ISBN 0-13-116196-2
      1. Communication in management.   I. DeTienne, Kristen Bell.
II. Title.
HD30.3.T56   1995
658.4′5—dc20   94-35669
                                                                                           CIP

Acquisitions Editor: Elizabeth Sugg
Production Editors: Rose Kernan and Fred Dahl
Interior Designer: Sue Behnke
Cover Design: Marianne Frasco
Manufacturing Manager: Edward O'Dougherty
Managing Editor: Mary Carnis

Printed in the United States of America
10   9   8   7   6   5   4   3   2   1

ISBN 0-13-116196-2

Prentice-Hall International (UK) Limited, *London*
Prentice-Hall of Australia Pty. Limited, *Sydney*
Prentice-Hall Canada Inc., *Toronto*
Prentice-Hall Hispanoamericana, S.A., *Mexico*
Prentice-Hall of India Private Limited, *New Delhi*
Prentice-Hall of Japan, Inc., *Tokyo*
Prentice-Hall of Southeast Asia Pte. Ltd., *Singapore*
Editora Prentice-Hall do Brasil, Ltda., *Rio de Janeiro*

CONTENTS

PART TWO
ORGANIZATIONAL EFFECTS ON COMMUNICATION

CHAPTER 5
Ongoing Communication Process and Flow, 97

CHAPTER 6
Organizational Communication Climate

Fair to Partly Confused, 124

PART THREE
ORAL COMMUNICATION IN MANAGEMENT

PART FOUR
PRESENTATIONAL SPEAKING

CHAPTER 12
Delivering the Presentation

Preparation, Preparation, Preparation, 273

PART FIVE
WRITTEN COMMUNICATION IN MANAGEMENT

CHAPTER 13
Keys to Functional Writing

Letters and Memos That Get Results, 293

CHAPTER 14
Formats for Business Letters and Memos

Different Situations—Different Approaches, 311

CHAPTER 15
Planning and Producing Effective Business Reports, 337

PREFACE

Managers communicate. Communication breathes life into planning, organizing, motivating, and controlling. Communication is the way we accomplish meaningful work by coordinating the efforts of individuals and groups. Communication consumes 90 percent of a manager's workday. Yet most college programs leading to degrees in management and much organization-sponsored management training fail to develop adequately the basic communication skills managers need. In this book we bridge the gap between what has been taught and what should be taught.

Now, over a decade after the first edition of this book was published, we are more convinced than ever of the crucial role of communication in the management process. A growing body of research shows the crucial role of managerial communication. For example, in 1993 Mary Young and James Post studied how America's best companies reconcile a compelling need for organizational change with an equally compelling need, on the part of employees, for security. These researchers found a clear answer: "Effective managers strategically use communication to manage tough organizational changes." It is imperative that we teach managers how to use communication strategically.

THE THIRD EDITION

In the following 16 chapters, we will look at important ideas about managerial communication. Many of these concepts are not systematically studied in academic programs designed to train people for administrative management responsibilities. Some areas are covered in the traditional curriculum, albeit from a business communication (e.g., letters and report writing) perspective. Many of these chapters will probably be new to you unless you've had extensive interdisciplinary training. A few chapters may serve as concise reviews of material you've already covered. The following chart indicates where the themes in this book tend to be covered in the traditional university curriculum.

COMBINING SKILLS AND STRATEGIES

Themes of Third Edition	Business Curriculum Coverage	Other Disciplines' Coverage
• Definition of communication and its role in management	Discussion of communication role in organizational behavior courses	Communication theory offered through speech curriculum
• Personal communication style	Seldom covered	Sometimes covered in speech communication curriculum under "interpersonal," "nonverbal," or "general semantics" courses
• Communication media and tools	May be covered briefly in business communiations courses	Studied in journalism and advertising programs but seldom applied to internal organizational processes
• Communication climate	Not systematically covered	Seldom covered in other disciplines
• Communication process and flow within organizations	Sometimes covered in information systems courses but seldom applied to human interactions	Seldom covered in other disciplines
• One-with-one communication skills (interviewing, instruction giving, conversation, etc.)	Seldom specifically covered except for employment interviewing (for the job applicant) in business communication courses	Studied in interpersonal communication course but not focused on employer-employee situations; covered in some psychology courses
• Interactional communication: meeting and conference skills	Some coverage in organizational behavior; also discussed in preparation for case analysis activities	A popular area of study in speech communication but seldom concentrates on managerial problems
• Speaking before groups, briefings, and presentations	May be covered briefly in business communication course; usually considered secondary to written skills training	A popular area of study in speech communication although emphasis tends to be more toward public speaking
• Listening	Seldom covered	Sometimes available in speech communication or psychology curriculum

Themes of Third Edition	*Business Curriculum Coverage*	*Other Disciplines' Coverage*
• Business letters and memos	Normally covered in business communication courses	Seldom covered in other disciplines
• Business report writing	Normally covered in business communication courses	Occasionally covered in English courses
• Diagnosing communication problems	Not covered	Not covered

PRACTICAL STRUCTURE

This book cuts through the maze of traditional academic structure and brings together the communication skills that we all need as managers. And we are all managers. You need not necessarily work in an office or supervise a group of assembly line workers. You are (or will soon be) involved in the process of getting productive work done *with and through the efforts of other individuals and groups.* A homemaker is a manager when he gets the children to help wash dishes; a basketball coach is a manager when she develops teamwork among her players; and the vice-president of a college fraternity is a manager when he leads his brothers in pulling off a successful rush program. We are, of course, using the term *management* in a broad sense, essentially synonymous with *leadership.*

If you find that you fit this definition of a manager, then this book is for you. Its focus is on practical ideas and their immediate application to your leadership functions. We're willing to bet that you'll find some new ways of behaving that will have a real impact on your communication skills and managerial effectiveness. All of this presupposes that you are willing to change the way you do things if you can be shown a better way. We'll show you better ways, but you'll need to try on some new behaviors—some different ways of doing things. We only ask that you read with an open mind.

ACKNOWLEDGMENTS

Throughout the process of putting this book together, we've had a great deal of support from family, friends, and colleagues. We owe thanks to Management Communictaion 490 students for their input regarding what was useful and what should be changed. In particular, we'd like to thank Ian Holt, Brooke Pitcher, David Newman, and Blair Janis.

We would like to acknowledge the significant input we have received from Lila Prigge at the University of North Dakota, Warren Plunkett at Wilbur Wright College, James Stull from San Jose State University, Ted Stoddard from our department at Brigham Young University, Michelle Egan from Ithaca College, and Fitz Chandler at Webster University.

We're grateful for the excellent administrative support we've had. Nina Whitehead has been wonderful in helping us with our word processing. We also appreciate the efficient and dependable support we've received from Julia Bottita.

Finally, our deepest debt goes to our spouses, Helen and David, who gave us their unfailing insight and support.

PART ONE

MANAGERIAL COMMUNICATION AND YOU

MANAGERIAL COMMUNICATION

Creating Understanding in an Organized World

▼

In this chapter you will find ideas that will help you:

♦ Appreciate the importance of communication in a management career

♦ Recognize the pervasiveness of organizations

♦ Describe why organizations are formed

♦ Understand the relationships between communication and organizational effectiveness

♦ Develop a useful yet general definition of communication

♦ Cite several factors that complicate the study of communication

♦ Recognize some common misconceptions about managerial communication

♦ Recognize basic rules for effective communication and the role of expectations in the communication process

♦ Justify a receiver-oriented approach to communication

♦ Understand the importance of communication in management

♦ Note the scope and direction that this book will take

▼

Not long ago, Harriet Rubin, executive editor of the Doubleday/Currency line of business books observed that the new book crossing her desk "tell me that traditional management ideas may no longer be relevant. The marketplace says traditional ideas about business and management don't excite much passion anymore."

One book takes the form of an extended allegory in which a fictional manager is granted the opportunity to relive his life based on the five management axioms the book champions. Together they form the acronym HEART:

*H*ear and understand me. (When people feel they have been listened to and understood, they will be ready to hear what the manager has to say.)

*E*ven if you disagree, please don't make me wrong. (People resent having their self-worth questioned. If they don't get mad, they get even.)

*A*cknowledge the greatness within me. (Everyone has the potential to grow; people tend to respond positively when that potential for greatness is recognized.)

*R*emember to look for my loving intentions. (Recognize positive motivations.)

*T*ell me the truth with compassion. (Talk to people respectfully, not about them disdainfully.)[1]

Each letter of the HEART acronym reminds us of crucial communication skills. Up front, these authors concede that the role of caring and compassion in effective management is often misunderstood and burdened with misconceptions.

The new approach to management reflects the facts that we can no longer rely on technology for quick fixes, we are now a fully functioning service economy, and the road to success for twenty-first-century corporations is via relationships—with other managers, employees, customers, and even competitors. Clearly trendsetters in management are increasingly recognizing the crucial role of communication in the process of managing. Continuous improvement in communication skills may be the single most important determinant of career success in this changing world of management.

WHAT IS MANAGERIAL COMMUNICATION?

Since the subject matter of this book is managerial communication, we begin by discussing these terms.

Managerial, of course, is the adjective form of the verb *to manage.* Managing is a process of working with and through other people to accomplish certain tasks, usually within organizations. Let's look first at the kinds of tasks managers typically do. Then we'll look at the nature of organizations and the meaning of *communication.*

Some Key Management Functions

The idea that the manager's job involves certain key functions was articulated early in the twentieth century by a French mining executive and early management theorist, Henri Fayol. He classified these functions as planning, organizing, commanding, coordinating, and controlling. Remarkably, his list has endured through the years with only minor changes.

> *Key management functions have long been recognized.*

1. *Planning* is a thinking process—a sort of internal communication within one's mind. The manager looks ahead to what must be done to maintain and improve performance, to solve problems, and to develop personal competence. To plan, a manger sets objectives in each area that are to be pursued this week, this month, this year. Having set these objectives, the manager then thinks through questions such as:

   ◆ What has to be done to reach these objectives?

   ◆ How will these activities be carried out?

   ◆ Who will do them?

   ◆ When will these activities take place?

   ◆ Where will this work be done?

   ◆ How much of what kind of resources will be needed?

2. *Organizing* involves arranging the work sequence and assigning areas of responsibility and authority. Having decided the objectives and activities of the work unit, the manager must:

   ◆ Assign these responsibilities to unit staff

   ◆ Ensure that all responsibilities and supporting authority is assigned, that none is "uncovered," and that there is no overlapping of responsibilities.

3. Fayol's principles of *commanding* and *coordinating* are often summed up in the term *leading,* those actions that the manager performs that enable the unit to achieve its objectives:

   ◆ Indicating the direction in which subordinates must go

   ◆ Generating the energy (motivation) that subordinates must feel

   ◆ Providing the needed resources

4. *Controlling* is the function that ensures the manager and the work group are working toward the selected objectives. It involves comparing actual results to expected or planned-for results so as to identify any deviation from plan. Typically, any deviation from plan leads to a replanning of activities so as to close the gap, although sometimes the objectives themselves are changed so as to be more realistic.[2]

Each of Fayol's functions involves people. Herein lies the universal characteristic of the manager's job: it always includes working with other people. Only when managers accomplish work *with and through other people* are they doing the job correctly. How do we convey to other people what needs to be done? The key is communication-managerial communication.

Managers accomplish work through others.

One other factor is involved in managerial communication: it takes place within or in association with organizations. To fully understand the nature of managerial communication, we should understand some things about the nature of organizations.

Managerial communication takes place within organizations.

LET'S GET ORGANIZED HERE

In our modern world we all spend most of our lives in some sort of organized activity. At birth we are introduced to an organization called the hospital staff. Within a few days we actively join an organization called a family. For the rest of our days our needs and wants are fulfilled directly or indirectly by organizations. Manufacturing, farming, mining, and distribution organizations bring us products to satisfy our material needs. Schools, churches, clubs, and informal social groups serve our needs for information, understanding, personal growth, and affiliation. Governments are organized to provide essential services for the public good.

Ninety percent of us work in organizations.

It's been estimated that 90 percent of us who work for a living do so within organizations. Contemporary society has very few legitimate hermits. Being a recluse from organizational life is becoming ever more difficult.

When we think about organizations, we tend to picture the physical aspects such as buildings, office space, machines and tools, or the capital assets described in an annual report. But organizations can exist without any of these things so long as people are assembled (physically or figuratively) for some purpose. The key ingredient is the existence of sustained patterns of coordinated action among people. These sustained patterns lead to the development of relationships—so long as there is communication.

Leaders in an organization can have a tremendous impact on communication effectiveness. Indeed the role of managers—those who get things done through the efforts of others—is essentially one of organizing and communicating. Communication breathes life into the organization.

Why Do We Have So Many Organizations?

Organizations permit us to accomplish things we cannot do alone.

The answers to that question are both long and short. We give you a short one: people who study such things agree that organizations emerge when people need to get something done that they cannot do working alone. From the early pioneers who enlisted the help of their neighbors to build a cabin to the massive team of experts directing a space shot, organizations serve people's needs to build and accomplish.

We also organize to enjoy social relationships and gain psychological satisfaction. Bridge clubs, service organizations, and churches, for example, serve such needs.

Can We Have Effective Organizations without Effective Communication?

Hardly. When people coordinate their activities to accomplish a common goal, they must communicate. Better communication makes the organization work better. Organizational failures occur when

- Too little communication takes place
- Too much communication is attempted
- Ineffective communication is widespread

Crumbling relationships and dysfunctional families often result from too little communication. Countless marriages fail primarily because of insufficient communication. People who cannot express their feelings to each other in marriage seldom succeed as a family organization. Likewise, when people have insufficient knowledge of how the various departments within their company function, they create roadblocks for customers and confusion within the organization.

The problem of overcommunication is perhaps less commonplace than lack of communication, but can be equally serious. Managers who find themselves bombarded with enormous amounts of information may snap under the load. Executives who take home bulging briefcases full of must-do work each night feel a great deal of stress. Their organizations may fail if that stress reaches a breaking point.

Receiving excessive amounts of communication from customers or clients can be one source of overcommunication—especially when the messages are unclear. See if you can understand the ideas expressed in the following excerpts from letters written to a county welfare office.

- Unless I receive my husband's money soon, I will be forced to live an immortal life.
- Please send my money at once, as I have fallen into error with my landlord.
- I have no children yet. My husband is a bus driver and works day and night.
- In accordance with your instructions, I have given birth to twins in the enclosed envelope.

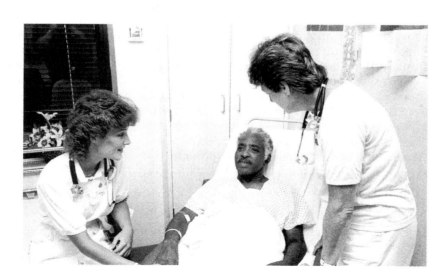

- ♦ I am happy to report that my husband, who was reported missing, now is dead.
- ♦ I am forwarding my marriage certificate and three children, one of which is a mistake as you can see.

Lest we conclude that only welfare clients have trouble communicating, here are some examples from explanations given on auto insurance claim forms:

- ♦ Coming home, I drove into the wrong house and collided with a tree I don't have.
- ♦ The guy was all over the road: I had to swerve a number of times before I hit him.
- ♦ I was on my way to the doctor's with rear end trouble when my universal joint gave way causing me to have an accident.
- ♦ I told the police that I was not injured, but on removing my hat I found that I had a skull fracture.
- ♦ The pedestrian had no idea what direction to go, so I ran over him.
- ♦ I saw the slow-moving, sad-faced old gentleman as he bounced off my car.
- ♦ The indirect cause of this accident was a little guy in a small car with a big mouth.
- ♦ The telephone pole was approaching fast. I was attempting to swerve out of its path when it struck my front end.

Although businesses can do little about the ineffective communications they *receive*, they must do a great deal about the messages they *send*. Ultimately, an organization's profitability and very existence are at stake.

People Prefer to Do Business with Organizations That Communicate Well

Think for a moment about the places where you regularly do business. Perhaps a supermarket, restaurant, convenience store, or service station comes to mind. Now think further about why you continue to patronize that place of business.

We've asked thousands of people at training sessions to think this way and then asked for specific reasons why they kept going back to the organization they were thinking of. In every group we got responses like these:

- ♦ The waitresses (or proprietors or clerks) are really friendly. They call me by name and seem genuinely interested in me.
- ♦ Old Phil at the gas station waves when I drive by.
- ♦ Mike the butcher listens to me when I ask for a special cut of meat.
- ♦ Sarah's so friendly—she's always willing to help.
- ♦ Doc Peterson's nurses are really nice. They seem to take a real interest in the kids.

> ► **Successful organizations
> communicate a sense of caring.** ◄

The words are different, but the theme is almost always the same: the organization communicates a sense of caring. Conversely, researchers from the Forum Corporation interviewed customers who had broken their relationships with particular businesses. The researchers concluded that 69 percent of those customers stopped buying, not because of product quality or cost, but because they felt *badly treated.*[3]

When asked, "Which organizations do you hate to do business with?" respondents often cite government agencies or departments within a company whose people communicate the messages: "We really don't care about you.... I hate my job and it's partly your fault.... I can't be bothered with you now."

> ► **Managers must be sensitive
> to organizational
> communication.** ◄

An obvious and significant challenge for you as a manager is to be sensitive to the ways your organization (company, division, work group), and yourself as an individual, communicate. Be alert to problems, and be willing to correct and improve communication as an ongoing management activity. This book will show you some ways to do that.

A BACK-TO-BASICS VIEW OF COMMUNICATION

We've talked briefly about management and organizations. Now let's look closer at communication. Textbook writers can and typically do offer a number of definitions of communication. Some of these are useful; some are confusing. Ours is, we think, quite simple, but still carries interesting implications.

Indeed the term *communication* is widely used in at least stress contexts. First, *communication* refers to the act of sending and receiving messages. People communicate when they talk together or write to each other. Second, when used in the expression *your recent communication,* the word describes the actual message. In a third and broader sense, communication involves the whole process of sharing meanings. It involves complex mental processes as well as outward behaviors. Some people talk to each other, thereby sending communications, but seldom seem to communicate—that is, establish an authentic understanding of each other's feelings, ideas, or values.

We use the term *communication* in all of these ways in this book. But we would like to establish a conceptual framework for viewing the most important

> ► **Communication *comes from*
> *the Latin root word meaning*
> *"to make common."*** ◄

kinds of communication that occur in most organizations. To do so, it might be useful to take a back-to-basics stance and to consider the term's Latin root word, *communicare,* which means "to make common." If we understand the word this way, we can say we have communicated when you have in your head the idea that I have in my head—that is, when we have made common our understanding. Our accuracy is determined by the degree of commonality we share.

Simple, right? Actually, in practice communication is not so simple. In fact, human communication may well be one of the most complex and difficult processes to study for several reasons.

1. Communication is often unpredictable.
2. Communication is part of our personalities.
3. Meanings are unique for each of us.

Communication Is Often Unpredictable

> *Studying our own communication is very difficult because it is a part of our personalities.*

First, the making common of meanings—or, more often, the failure to do so—comes about in many, often unpredictable ways. The numerous variables that affect communication can lead to surprising results. Although these results can be disappointing or worse, these same variables that cause frustration also provide us with "strings to pull" to improve our probability for effectiveness. Much of this book deals with improving communication by recognizing these strings and pulling them.

Communication Is Part of Our Personalities

When we study communication, we are studying something that is very hard to examine objectively. We are studying *ourselves.* The closer we get to something, the harder it is to evaluate it fairly. While others come to know us by our behaviors, our behaviors are so often automatic or unconscious that we don't recognize the way we come across. We tend to take personal pride in how we, as individuals or as organizations, have been doing or saying things all along. We resist changes in behavior and usually find it more comfortable going on as usual, getting *others* to change the ways *they* do things.

We are inextricably linked to our communication behavior. The ways we attempt to communicate are expressions of *personality,* which is the sum total of our psychological makeup.

Meanings Are Unique to Each of Us

Our psychology causes us to experience life in unique ways. People do not all see the world in the same way because their experiences and perceptions are all, in fact, different. In a fairly literal sense, people don't even *live* in the same psychological world. Each of us has a unique life. From day one, we each have individual experiences that are never exactly like anything any other person experiences. These experiences, packed into our memory banks, shape the way we attach meanings to the things of our world. Each message we receive is evaluated in terms of what we already know in order to determine whether it makes sense.

This complexity and closeness to ourselves foils many people's understanding of communication. To cope, we oversimplify the communication process to picture it like a machine: "X does something to Y" or "Mr. A. transmits a message to Mrs. B." We get preoccupied with the mechanics and techniques for perking up our speaking or writing skills, and ignore many other important dimensions of the communication situation. We begin to think that, because our message sounds better and better to us, it must be getting better for our listeners.

WHAT'S WRONG WITH A SIMPLIFIED VIEW OF COMMUNICATION?

A simple sender-does-something-to-receiver model may be adequate when we are talking about conveying simple directives or orders. But most of the things we communicate in real organizations—ideas, impressions, and feelings—are much more complex. When we back away from an emphasis on our message *sending* skills and seek to better understand the totality of what's going on, we develop a sensitivity to others that facilitates the

> *The effective communicator focuses on the receiver.*

process of making common our thoughts, feelings, impressions, goals, and policies. Being a better communicator means being a better understander. Constantly adjusting *your* message until it sounds better and better to *you* is not the ultimate communication improvement. The true communicator is concerned with thou, not I. Until we can sincerely develop a concern for understanding others, we cannot maximize our potential as communicators.

So, given the facts that communication is often unpredictable, difficult to study, and different for each of us, how should a manager define it? We contend that it is useful to view *communication as a process of establishing common understanding.* For now let's use this statement as a working definition as we explore the implications of this process, focusing on specific types of managerial communication.

SOME TROUBLESOME MISCONCEPTIONS ABOUT MANAGERIAL COMMUNICATION

A number of popular misconceptions about managerial communication can be attributed to a failure to see the broader definition we've been describing. Managers who view problems in organizational communication in terms of faulty message sending techniques without recognizing the broader view cannot realistically expect to bring about long-range, enduring improvement in the ways they communicate.

Misconception 1: Communication Is a Fringe Benefit

Some managers consider effective communication as some sort of fringe benefit for employees. They see it as a way to keep workers happy or to boost their morale. In reality, communication is the essence of the manager's job. If we accept management as a process of accomplishing tasks through people under the most economical conditions with the most profitable results, we must accept the notion that the people we manage must be communicated with. This involves instructing, guiding, and motivating. Our effectiveness depends on our sensitivity to the perceptions and expectations of those we manage, as well as the degree of involvement. Such communication involves creating conditions in which the development of mutual, two-way understanding can flourish.

> *Communicating with employees is more than a worker benefit—it is the process by which organizations are created.*

The employee who, for whatever reasons, fails to be adequately involved in an organization's communication is not just missing out on a nice corporate perquisite, In a very real sense, that individual is not a part of the sustained patterns of coordinated action and the development of relationships which *constitute* the organization. Involvement in communication cannot be viewed as some special gift awarded to employees by beneficient leaders. It is instead the very process by which people become organized.

Misconception 2: Communication Is Message Sending

Probably the most common view of communication is as an activity whereby an individual transmits information to another individual or group. This more accurately describes purposeful communication *events* or *activities* rather than the overall process. Here we are taking an "I" attitude (as opposed to a "you" orientation) and are primarily concerned with what happens when I purposefully construct a message and transmit it to others. A simple model describes the steps in this process:

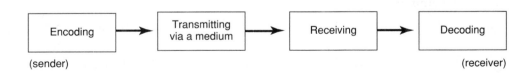

| Encoding | → | Transmitting via a medium | → | Receiving | → | Decoding |

(sender)   (receiver)

As message senders, we put thoughts and feelings or perceptions into some form of language through the encoding process. We then send off that coded message via oral or written media to someone else. Our receiver in turn decodes, or attempts to make sense of, the message he or she gets from us. Often the receiver goes through the same process in responding to us.

This is, of course, an oversimplified explanation of what happens. If we accept this at face value we might conclude that the only way to improve our commuication is to improve our message preparation skills and/or the integrity of the transmitting medium.

If we extract an isolated communication event from all that is going on in the organization, we can typically identify the activities described in the sender-to-receiver model. From a common-sense view-point, the approach seems satisfactory. If, how-ever, we accept this as *the* definitive model of communication, we are likely to run into prob-lems. Many communication processes going on in organizations cannot be realistically or accurately diagnosed from this sender-oriented approach.

> *A sender-oriented view of communication is incomplete.*

For an example of misconception 2, consider this incident: Paul Spearman, a district manager, had gone out on a limb for Dave Zaleski several times. He hired him despite the fact that Dave had no sales experience whatsoever. That decision paid off beautifully—within six months Dave was a top producer. When an opening arose, Paul pushed hard for Dave's promotion to sales manager, and made considerable effort to convince higher management. Although manage-ment was impressed with Zaleski's sales record, he had no management training, had been a sales representative only 18 months, and, frankly, had irritated more than a few people with his cocksure attitude. Nevertheless, Spearman prevailed and Dave was promoted. In the process, Paul and Dave developed a close rap-port; they appreciated their mutually supportive relationship.

During his second month as sales manager, Dave boldly announced that his team would break the company's record for new customer orders. His self-determined quota was 48 units—200 percent of the normal quota. The previous district record had been 163 percent.

The month ended and Dave's team had indeed produced an outstanding record—194 percent of quota. Paul was delighted. He immediately sent off a congratulatory note, including a good-natured "needle" about just missing the 200-percent mark:

```
To: Dave Zaleski, Sales Manager

From: Paul Spearman, District Manager

Subject: Outstanding sales month!

200 percent it ain't; but not bad for a rookie. Here's
hoping you actually accomplish what you say you're
going to do someday. Way to go, champ.
```

Dave missed the humor completely. He was personally embarrassed about not making his goal, even though his accomplishment was outstanding. When Paul later visited Dave's office he was met with an icy reception. The message's intent was to congratulate and to stimulate continued excellence. Instead, it drove a wedge between the two men.

How does a sender-to-receiver model account for this communication problem? It doesn't. Such a model simply leaves unexplained many other variables, such as personal pride, values, and sentiments which affect the communication. This concept can be tough to grasp, so one more example might help. Let's look at another situation.

Wayne Johnson, a manufacturing plant foreman, was asked to teach two new employees how to work a machine. The first employee was a young man who had been hired under a special government program to employ disadvantaged people. The foreman, whose views were not sympathetic to the hiring preference program initiated by the company, begrudgingly took the young man to the machine and instructed him how to run it: "Each time this metal part comes down this assembly line here, you pull it off, stick it under the press so that the edges line up here, and then push this foot pedal so the drill bit will come down and put the hole in the right place. Be careful to keep your hands away from the drill when you are doing it. Any moron should be able to do this. Ya got any questions?"

What could the employee say? If any moron could do this, surely asking questions would only make him look foolish to his new boss. "No, sir," he replied.

"Okay then, go to it. And good luck. If you have any problems let me know." In the foreman's mind there was little likelihood this employee would develop into a particularly effective worker. He has seen many of "these kind" of employees hired under special programs who simply couldn't seem to cut it. And frankly he didn't understand why they failed. He treated them the same as anyone else. In fact he made it a point to use exactly the same language to explain this simple procedure. In a few days this employee fell seriously behind on both the quantity and quality of his work. Johnson was not surprised.

The second new employee, a young man whom Johnson thought looked pretty sharp, was given essentially the same verbal instructions. This new worker, perhaps sensing that the foreman seemed to like him, took the "any moron should be able to do this" comment in stride and asked for a few clarifying pointers, which he got. Soon he was on his way to meeting his production quota just like the old pros who had been there for some time.

Why the different results from essentially the same message? An analysis from the sender-to-receiver model sheds little light on what happened. Other variables played a part. Perhaps the most important one is that the foreman fully *expected* the first young man to fail. And because of this, the environment of the communication event was clearly different. Perhaps at the heart of the differences illustrated here is the sense of caring.

> **To view communication as just message sending is inadequate.**

The point of both examples is that many factors affecting communication—such as expectations, receptiveness to questions, and a desire to express rapport and friendship through good-natured ribbing—are not accounted for when we view communication as mere message sending.

An Alternative to Misconception 2: Communication Is Message Receiving

Another way to look at communication is the nothing-happens-till-someone-gets-a-message approach. Theorectically this views makes a great deal of sense, but it requires adjustments in the way most of us describe communication. Let's contrast it with the more common but potentially misleading sender-oriented approach described earlier.

When people define communication as someone *sending* messages to others (or giving instructions, or directives, etc.) a couple of problems quickly arise. First, these explanations seem to imply that we are dealing with a distinct and clearly

> **People are constantly communicating.**

defined type of human activity which we can turn on or turn off as needed. It's not quite that simple. Communication doesn't start when we begin to talk or write and end when we stop. Human communication is a form of *behavior* and as long as we

behave—that is to say, as long as we live—we are *constantly* communicating—at least potentially.

> ### Communication success is determined by message receivers.

We don't determine when communication will take place, we simply provide the setting and some cues which, if we are successful, will be picked up by someone else and interpreted in a way we see as appropriate. In other words we, like a radio or TV station, are constantly transmitting signals. But until these are picked up by someone, no communication has occurred. No understanding has been created.

A second problem with the notion of communication as sending messages is that that notion implies a lot more control over the process than we may actually have. In most cases we have too long focused on talking and writing skills and have not sufficiently emphasized anticipated audience reactions. We have too long accepted the responsibility for accurate communication when our control over the communication event is really quite limited. Our success as communicators is determined by our *receivers.*

Peter Drucker, the well-known management scholar, explains it this way:

> ... it is the recipient who communicates. The so-called communicator, the person who emits the communication, does not communicate. He utters. Unless there is someone who hears, there is no communication. There is only noise. The communicator speaks or writes or sings—but he does not communicate. Indeed, he cannot communicate. He can only make it possible, or impossible, for a recipient—or rather, "percipient"—to perceive.[4]

Anytime someone sees, hears, or otherwise experiences something new and relates that experience to something already known, we have the process of perception. This is the first step in the communication process. Again quoting Drucker,

> Perception ... is not logic. It is experience. This means, in the first place, that one always perceives a configuration. One cannot perceive single specifics. They are always part of a total picture. The "silent language," that is, the gestures, the tone of voice, the environment altogether, not to mention the cultural and social referents, cannot be diassociated from the spoken language. In fact, without them the spoken word has no meaning and cannot communicate.[5]

Once perception has occurred, we attach meanings to what has been experienced. W. Charles Redding sees these mental activities as the defining characteristics of communication. He says that communication refers to those behaviors of human beings, or artifacts created by human beings, which result in messages being received by someone. A *message,* he goes on, is any kind of stimulus that arouses a response we call *meaning.*[6]

> ### Communication occurs whenever someone attaches meaning to something.

More concisely, communication is occurring whenever someone attaches meaning to objects, processes, behaviors (including intentional message behaviors), and even to hard-to-define climates or intangible events. A member of an organization has communicated, and is communicating, so long as someone is attaching meanings to what he or she does. And what one does includes words, actions, silences, and inactions. Any and all of these can and do communicate. This leads to misconception 3.

Misconception 3: Managers Control Communication in Their Organizations

Communication consultant Walter Wiesman has said,

> Whether management likes it or not, it must face the fact that all actions, by all people, on all levels, in all functions of the organization, constantly communicate; that all actions create impressions in employees, judged by each employee from his peculiar frame of reference. It makes little difference whether the employee's interpretation is correct—this is "his world" and he looks out of "his window." What he wants to see and hear is the impression he gains from the words and actions around him. The more diversified a workforce, the greater the challenge to reach all people with the maximum degree of effectiveness.[7]

We cannot always control when communication will occur.

Not only do we have relatively little control over what people pay attention to and draw meanings from, but we also cannot determine exactly *when* communication will occur. Again quoting Walt Wiesman,

> Communication takes place every time human beings use their natural facilities to listen, think, observe, be impressed (for better or worse), have doubts, feel neglected, etc. This common trouble occurs when management takes the rather naive stand that "this is not the time to talk."[8]

Messages can have ripple effects—unforeseen impact.

Another complicating factor that precludes absolute control over communication is the ever-present ripple effect. Even the simplest memo, announcement, or directive may have unforeseen impact on the organization. Here is an example:

One day a sales manager, Beth Tremont, distributed a memo with what appeared to be a simple message:

```
I am happy to announce that a member of our sales
team, Jim Hawk, has been promoted to Sales Training
Instructor. Jim will start his new duties at the
Corporate Training Center on August 1. I'm sure you
all join me in congratulating Jim.
```

If we accept a sender-to-receiver viewpoint, we have a clear message and effective communication of these few simple points of information.

- ◆ Jim Hawk was promoted.
- ◆ His new title is Sales Training Instructor.
- ◆ He'll work at Corporate Training Center.
- ◆ He starts August 1.

But there was much more to this message than meets the eyes. The manager who sent this memo was generally insensitive to ripple effects—her audience's potential reactions. If that manager had done a series of man-in-the-street interviews following this announcement, she would have been shocked. Here are some reactions:

- ◆ *Alan Travis, Sales Representative:* "I can't believe what I just read! Hawk is the biggest donkey on the entire team. He's a loudmouth backslapper who'll stop at nothing to peddle equipment—whether the customer needs it or not! He takes the same approach for every prospect: sell them the most expensive machine whether or not they need it or can afford it. He never does customer surveys to see what they would really benefit from. Sure, he's had impressive sales results, but he has a gold-mine territory. Look, I don't want to sound like sour grapes, but this promotion is a joke. Jim Hawk represents everything we are taught not to do. There are a half dozen other people that should have been promoted first—or at least given an opportunity to compete for the opening."

- ◆ *Jim Wilson, Sales Representative:* "I'd heard that there might be an opening at Corporate Training, and, frankly, I thought I had a good shot at it. When Tremont just dropped that memo on us, I was really upset. Hawk has always been one of her boys, but you'd think she'd at least talk to a few of us who should have been considered. I'll put my sales abilities up against Hawk's any day. And I know I'm more effective at customer care. I don't believe in Hawk's sell-'em-and-forget-'em approach. To make him a trainer of new sales reps is ludicrous."

- ◆ *Barbara Anderson, Sales Manager:* "It's really none of my business. Beth Tremont doesn't have to check with me when she promotes someone. But I have been a sales manager a lot longer than she has and I've seen situations like this before. The other folks on her team are fighting mad. It's not that they dislike Jim Hawk—it's just that he seems to represent the opposite of the professionalism the company is always stressing. When I face a decision like this one, I spend a lot of time talking to each of the people on my team. You can't just suddenly drop an announcement memo like that and expect that everyone will understand. The promotion situations are always tough but there's a lot you can do to smooth ruffled feathers. I think Beth has a lot to learn about managing and communicating."

♦ *LeRoy Puckett, Sales Trainee:* "I've got to be honest with you. I'm not positive I want to be a salesman in the first place. I've only been on board two months, but already I'm getting a little bit down. The company spends thousands of dollars sending me to the Corporate Training Center and stressing how important it is to be a professional representative. Then I come back here to my home office and the first guy who gets promoted is probably the least professional of them all. Frankly, I'm confused. I've seen this guy at work. He takes every short cut (ethical or not), he spends half the time flirting with the secretaries, and then feeds the customer the biggest line of baloney you've ever heard. I don't want to be like him, but I do want to get ahead. What do I do now?"

What initially appears to be a routine communication event has some very complex outcomes. For most members of the organization, Hawk's promotion was seen as a cruel joke. While the manager's memo was perfectly clear, the ripple effect was totally unpredicted. A more sensitive communicator could do much to take the sting out of such an announcement through the use of different media, allowing for more adequate explanation of management's decision criteria, and through being more in tune with the message receivers' expectations and attitudes. Although a manager cannot anticipate and control the outcome of such messages, he or she can and must be sensitive to them.

An Alternative to Misconception 3: Managers Influence the Creation of Understanding

If we don't give careful thought to the expectations and the wants and needs of those we are attempting to communicate with, we will surely fail to bring about understanding. The challenge for the manager lies in improving the *probability* that understanding will predominate in organizational relationships—by establishing and maintaining conditions under which effective communication can flourish.

THREE RULES FOR BETTER UNDERSTANDING

As we seek to develop conditions for effective communication, perhaps the three most important things we can keep in mind are the following

♦ We must expect to be misunderstood by at least some of our listeners and readers.

♦ We must expect to misunderstand others.

♦ We can strive to reduce the degree of such misunderstanding, but we can never totally eliminate it, nor can we anticipate all possible outcomes.

When we expect to be misunderstood, we are likely to respond by considering ways to make the message sending circumstances more conducive to understanding. When we expect to misunderstand others, we will be more conscientious about seeking out needed clarification. And when we recognize that we never absolutely eliminate misunderstanding or anticipate all outcomes, we are acknowledging reality.

Air traffic controllers are taught that the precise language and procedures used are clearly aimed at overcoming such problems in communication. Controllers often restate important instructions given to pilots in an attempt to reduce misunderstanding; they also request that some messages received by pilots be repeated to check for accuracy. Nevertheless, even with meticulous language and procedures, occasional accidents due to communications breakdowns do occur. Communication will never be foolproof.

We improve conditions for understanding by doing the following:

♦ *Committing ourselves to ongoing self-analysis.* We can increase our awareness of our own predispositions and expectations, and we can constantly reexamine them.

♦ *Continually evaluating the way our personality characteristics filter and distort the ways we see others.*

♦ *Learning to anticipate what our recipients expect to see and hear from us.* Only when we focus on our recipients' likely responses can we know whether we should communicate so as to utilize their expectations or whether we need to shock them with an awakening that breaks through those expectations.

A Few Words about Listener Expectations

> **Expectations play an important role in communication.**

One important implication of the receiver-oriented viewpoint is that effective communicators need to make careful guesses about receiver *expectations*. We need to anticipate receiver reactions to our messages.

We are very quick to perk up our ears any time we hear something that confirms our beliefs. We also tend literally to tune out conflicting information that does not conform to what we expect. We knew a fellow who used to test this proposition at parties he attended. Upon saying goodnight to the host and hostess he would shake their hands, smile and nod, telling them in a very serious tone that this was absolutely the worst party he had ever been to. They, in turn, would smile, nod, and thank him for the compliment. Although a number of factors account for this confusion, the social expectations of the host and hostess play an important part in tuning out the actual language of that message.

When messages are consistent with existing expectations *or* when that expectations are clarified before the message is sent, communication is more accurate.

THE MESSAGE RECEIVER DETERMINES COMMUNICATION SUCCESS

Effective managerial communication results from receiver-oriented attempts to create clear understanding, coupled with the awareness that we really can't control communication. Yet we can, and must, seek to influence it. This is a frustrating state of affairs for the manager who wants to be a better director, persuader, or motivator. We all want to get our subordinates to produce more, our peers to accept our point of view, and our bosses to be impressed with us. But that's the old sender-oriented view. The broader and more realistic perspective tells us that communication is much morfe than just getting someone to say they agree.

Real communication improvement means real sacrifices. It means developing more *understanding.* It means looking at the world through the eyes of others, walking the proverbial mile in another's moccasins. Most of us are hesitant to do this. But it is exactly through this kind of empathizing that meaningful improvement of communication occurs.

All types of human communication are enhanced by more concern for you and less for I. In many books on organizational communication, the distinction is made between upward (from subordinates to superiors) and downward (from superiors to subordinates) communication. That disctinction assumes again that the message source does the communicating, a notion of little value when we assume a receiver orientation. What we have traditionally done is try to make the manager, as message sender, a better communicator. But the only kinds of messages one can communicate downward are simple commands. We cannot "send" motivation or expectations, or understanding; these require interactive sharing between those who perceive our messages and us. When we reach out to better understand others we become the recipients, the real communicators.

Understanding begins with self-analysis.

Creation of a climate for understanding begins with self-analysis. It matures as we develop empathy for others. The process of continually creating a climate for understanding presents no small task. It requires extensive effort, and it involves giving of ourselves to an extent that many are unwilling and perhaps unable to do.

The hard reality is that life is full of failures to communicate effectively; that is, people assign inappropriate meanings to what they perceive and managers unrealistically assume that accurate meanings are being created in the minds of the people they talk and write to. We tend to expect too much from communication attempts.

Good internal communication in itself will not guarantee that your organization will profit. Internal communication is a cost of doing business. Profitability is affected to the extent that efficient and effective communication saves the organization time, effort, and resources. Whatever efforts are expended to comprehend the communication process better are likely to be worthwhile if grounded in good theory and if tempered with realistic expectations.

LEVELS OF COMMUNICATION ACTIVITY

Intrapersonal and Interpersonal Levels

Communication can be studied from several different levels, each of which introduces additional complicating factors. We communicate *intrapersonally* when our minds process informational stimuli, when we talk to ourselves, when we assign meaning to perceptions. Such internal communication is another way to describe thinking. *Interpersonally* (between two or more people), we transact or exchange thoughts to establish or maintain relationships with others. These interpersonal relationships help us gain a clearer understanding of our world by providing information from others. They also give us feedback concerning the appropriateness of our behavior or our self-image.

Groups and Organizations: The Great Complicators

Earlier we said that 90 percent of those who work do so in organizations. This is simply a fact of our complex society. As managers we need also to be concerned with *group* and *organizational* levels of communication and the behavioral effects of organizing people toward task accomplishment.

People create organizations to do things they cannot or do not want to do alone. For years organizations have been studied to try to determine why they succeed or fail and how they can be improved. As researchers studied more, they came to realize that organizational succcess seems to depend on countless variables, many of which are complex and unpredictable.

Several conclusions emerge from the development of organization theory. For one thing, we've learned that static models, like the ever-present organization chart, tell us very little about what really goes on. These charts with their boxes and lines actually create the illusion that the organization possesses a certain systematic rigidity—a rigidity that is less and less desirable as we recognize the frequent need to adapt to changing environmental pressures.

A formal organization and job specialization structure are necessary for the organization to accomplish its objectives economically, but it complicates the communication process by imposing additional restrictions on individual communicators—restrictions required by virtue of organizational positions, roles, and expectations. Inevitably, formal organizational structures also restrict the free flow of information. This is necessary to a point to prevent the organization's leadership from drowning in a sea of unneeded data. But like leaks that develop from a flow-restricting crimp in a water hose, informal channels develop and allow the information to seep out, sometimes eroding the intentions of the formal organization. Subgroups, with their own sets of objectives, roles, and procedures, emerge to further complicate things. These groups are not always detrimental to the larger organization. In fact, Redding has said that "organizations frequently get their most important work done through various kinds of coalitions, factions, or alliances." The effects of groups can be good, bad, or neutral. But in all cases they make communication more complex.

Technological Level

Technological dimensions of communication concern more than just hardware such as telephones, intercoms, copying machines, computers, and two-way radios. Lee Thayer broadly describes the technological level as

> the focus upon the technology of communication including equipment, apparatus, and/or the formalized "programs" for generating, storing, processing, translating, distributing, or displaying data—either for "consumption" by other pieces of equipment or for ultimate translation into information and consumption by human beings.

Thayer goes on to remind us that the *languages* we use, whether verbal, graphic, or gestural, are just as much a part of the technology of communication as are other devices.

So the technological level of analysis can include everything from our language usage to the frequency with which we schedule meetings, to the apparatus we use to process data. This book examines each level of managerial communication—intrapersonal, interpersonal, group, organizational, and technological.

JUST HOW IMPORTANT IS MANAGERIAL COMMUNICATION?

This question could be answered in several ways. We've already suggested that organizational success often depends on good communication. People won't continue to do business with poor communicators. Communication scholar Gerald Goldhaber says, "... we are told by management and communication consultants that more than 10 percent of U.S. business enterprises fail every year primarily due to bad management and ineffective communication."[9]

Raymond L. Hilgert, a professor of management and industrial relations with extensive consulting experience, has said.

> *Communication is often an organization's #1 problem.*

... in every organization that I have come into contact with, communication is usually the number one problem, or it is at least associated with virtually every problem the organization faces. This ranges from basic problems of human misunderstanding, all the way to major financial, marketing, and productions problems associated with the inability of people to properly communicate with one another.[10]

But there is another way of looking at the importance of managerial communication. *Importance* to the practicing manager may be defined in terms of how much time or effort one expends on a daily basis.

Henry Mintzberg's book *The Nature of Managerial Work*[11] reveals that managers are almost constantly communicating. Based on systematic observations of chief executives' work, Mintzberg calculated that verbal interaction accounted for 78 percent of managers' time and 67 percent of their activities. Although Mintzberg sees desk work as separate from communication, experience tells us that most desk work is writing and reading. The media are different, but communication is still taking place.

> *Managers communicate almost constantly.*

MANAGEMENT *Is* COMMUNICATION

Communication is what managers do. It is the essence of managerial work. All levels of management must be involved in optimizing organizational communication. Staff expertise, either in-house or consultant, should be used when necessary, but ultimately success lies with increased understanding, commitment, and effort on the part of working members of the organization.

Anything and everything that happens in the organization has potential communicative effect on everybody. Some companies have attempted to deal with communication via a single staff element or designated managers given sole responsibility for a complete communication program. Communication, however, cannot be transferred into one office. What makes sense is to "take inventory of all identifiable actions contributing to the total communication program, to phase these actions into the overall goal of the organization, to stimulate and assist segments and individuals responsible for such actions, and to have as a result a balanced, effective and timely program."[12]

> *Improvement in communication must be planned and followed up.*

As with any managerial program, communication improvement must be planned. Specific soft areas should be identified and targets established for improvement. Then we must follow up, follow up, follow up. An effective communication program is an ongoing effort. We can't apply a series of quick fixes and expect effective communication to run on perpetually.

THE STAGE IS NOW SET

A theoretical base for this book is the notion that communication occurs any time someone attaches meaning to what's going on. Intentional communication efforts are successful to the degree that common meaning develops between the message receiver and the intent of the sender. Much communication, however, is unintentional, and even seemingly simple messages have ripple effects that are unpredictable. Communication is not some distinct activity that we can turn on or off; we are constantly communicating so long as someone is around to attach meanings to cues they receive. The organizational context in which we operate greatly complicates the entire process. Although we are interdependent as members—we need each other. We are too often unaware of the kinds of things that separate us from each other and reduce the probabilities of our attaching appropriate meanings to our interactions.

This book is about ways we can experience the communication going on around us while developing a clearer understanding of why it is as it is. Such experience can be, as someone once defined it, "the transition from cocksure ignorance to thoughtful uncertainty." In a subject as complex as human communication, thoughful uncertainty is probably a healthy condition.

No one can say all there is to say about a subject as broad as managerial communication. Our job has been to choose key areas that we can investigate profitably. Although this first chapter of the book is somewhat theoretical in tone, later chapters are not. Each chapter focuses on practical information that should be immediately useful to a manager.

In short, this book is a response to a need for pragmatic interpretation and application of organizational communication theory for the working or aspiring manager.

As managers, we can profit most by establishing contexts in which understanding can germinate and blossom. Setting up such conditions requires recognizing the forces—and there are many in every organization—that work to stifle and inhibit, as well as to enhance, the development of common meanings. As one communication scholar has said, "… the best way to prepare people for communicating—like painting—is to acquaint them with the repertoire of available techniques, train their judgment, and encourage them to become what they can."[13]

A QUICK SUMMARY OF MAJOR IDEAS

- ◆ Managers fulfill key functions in organizations. Typically these functions include planning, organizing, commanding, coordinating, and controlling. But the universal characteristic of managing is accomplishing work through other people.

◆ Organizations emerge when people seek to do something they cannot or prefer not to do alone. We are constantly involved with organizations, which are sustained patterns of coordinated action among people. Communication is the glue that holds organizations together.

◆ Ineffective communication results in ineffective organizations. We seldom enjoy doing business with organizations that fail to communicate a sense of caring or understanding.

◆ A back-to-basics definition of *communication* is the creation of common understanding among two or more people.

◆ Some managers hold misperceptions about the nature and value of communication in organizations. It is more than a fringe benefit, more than just message sending, and it is not something that can be totally controlled by management.

◆ Effective managers strive to influence constructively the creation of understanding by anticipating and striving to reduce misunderstanding.

◆ The message receiver ultimately determines communication success.

◆ Management is communication.

QUESTIONS FOR FURTHER THOUGHT

1. Consider other definitions of *communication* that you have heard (or make up your own). Are these definitions sender oriented, receiver oriented, or some combination of these or others? Based on what you read in this chapter, what drawbacks do these definitions pose? What drawbacks do you see in the definition we've proposed?

2. Relate an experience in which you were given a task to perform and you felt that you were not expected to succeed. How was this expectation communicated to you?

3. Make a list of organizations you belong to. Why did you join them? What keeps you a member? Specifically, describe some tasks these organizations help you accomplish.

4. Based on your knowledge of management, argue for or against the statement, Management is communcation.

OTHER THOUGHTS ABOUT MANAGERIAL COMMUNICATION

TREAT THEM AS WINNERS ...
AND THEY WILL WIN
by Jimmy Johnson,
Former Head Coach of the Dallas Cowboys

I never tell a running back, "Don't fumble." I never tell a placekicker, "Don't miss." I say to the running back, "Protect the ball." I say to the placekicker, "Make this." You'd be surprised how few coaches understand the simple psychology I'm using here. But, in my opinion, it is vital psychology. Why?

The human mind, upon receiving the message, "Don't fumble," will record the word "fumble" and, consciously or not, worry over it. The "don't" doesn't help. If anything, it hurts—because it's a negative. And so the running back who is told, "Don't fumble," is more likely to fumble than if the coach had said nothing at all. So I try never to plant a negative seed. I try to make every comment a positive comment.

In recent years, specialists called "sports psychologists" have been collecting some nice fees from some professional athletes. For these fees, they teach the athletes to think "protect the ball" or "make this" or, in the case of baseball pitchers, "throw strikes." In my opinion, what they're doing is part of the job any coach or manager should be doing—making the player feel as good about himself as he can possibly feel.

You'd think every coach, manager and CEO in America would understand this by now. Certainly, any CEO who hired James W. Johnson as an industrial psychologist would have had it made abundantly clear to him. There's just too much scientific evidence to support positive management.

Even so, many a football coach, to start the season off, will really poor-mouth his team. Then, when the team does better than predicted, the coach comes out looking like he did a great job. At the Cowboys, we take the opposite approach.

In 1990, I came out publicly before the season and said, "I expect us to win as many as we lose." That was a bold statement, considering that we'd only won one game the year before. If our quarterback, Troy Aikman, had stayed healthy, I think we *would* have won at least as many as we lost. [Their record was 7-9.]

In 1991, my bold public statement was: "Not only will we make the playoffs, but we will have success in the playoffs." We indeed made the playoffs—and won the first playoff game.

In 1992, I said: "We will exceed what we did a year ago." [The Cowboys won the Super Bowl.]

All three times, the media looked at me like, "This guy's nuts." But all three times, our players got a message that was strong and positive about high expectations, and all three times they lived up to the expectations.

There is a saying: "Treat a person as he is, and he will remain as he is. Treat a person as if he were what he could be and should be, and he will become what he could be and should be."

There have been numerous psychological studies to support this approach. It's called the Pygmalion effect, or the psychology of self-fulfilling prophecy.

Two decades ago, a graduate student named Albert King at Texas Tech University did a study with unskilled laborers taking a welding course. To the welding instructor, King named certain students in the class who, he said, had special talents to be outstanding welders. The welding instructor did not know that King had picked those individuals at random and really had no information about their abilities.

But, as later studies have shown, because the instructor treated the students as he expected them to be, that's how they turned out to be. The ones that he was told could be outstanding welders got his individual attention and were talked to in a very positive way. They scored highest on their final exams.

Whether I'm treating the individual player as a winner, or treating the team as if it's going to win, or treating the assistant coach as if he is the brightest and hardest-working coach in the league, I do it with the scientific knowledge that if you treat people that way long enough and sincerely enough, more times than not, that's what you'll get.

Some coaches bring their rookies into training camp and—though they might know their first- and second-round picks by name—take the approach with the lower-round picks and free agents that, "Oh, I'll learn his name *if* he makes the team." What they don't understand is that *whether* a player makes the team might hinge on something as subtle as *whether* you know his name and *whether* you treat him as an individual that you care about, with talent you believe in.

You should sit with me some afternoon on the bench in the breezeway leading to our locker room during our April minicamp, when we bring the rookies in. You should see those disoriented, uncertain, anxious faces filing in. And you should see them light up over something as simple from me as, "Hey, [first name], I saw you doing some really good things out there today. We think you can play here. We like you."

And you know what? We *do* like them and we *do* think they can play here. Sincerity is the most important part of positive treatment. The only thing worse than a coach or a CEO who doesn't care about his people is one who pretends to care. People can spot a phony every time. They know he doesn't really care about them, and—worse—his act insults their intelligence.

To get the most out of my players, my teaching methods involve a combination of positive reinforcement and punishment. It has been proved in the psychology of learning that this is the most effective way to teach. We rely 90 percent on positive reinforcement, but when we do have punishment for an inaccurate response, it really makes an impact—both on our football team and on the individual. I think at times the punishment can have a short-term negative effect but give you a long-term positive reaction in that it really reinforces the learning that you want to instill.

Here's a simplified example with, say, a receiver. Nine times out of 10, when I'm talking to him, I'm saying, "Get off on the count … nice catch … super job of running your route … perfect release off the line … great attitude." And then, all of a sudden, I come down hard because he jumps offside. I may scream at him and even use some foul language. The one time that I come down hard and embarrass him really stands out, and *that* reinforces the learning in an optimum way.

Coaches who constantly scream and cuss at their players don't get much reinforcement when they really do need to come down hard. How do their players know when they're really coming down hard? How can one tirade seem more serious than another? On the occasions when I do scream and cuss, the player knows something is up. Something is wrong. Bad wrong.

Everybody says you have to coach according to your own personality. But I think you've got to take it one step further: You've got to be able to control your personality—be strong enough mentally that you can govern how positive and how sincere and how negative you are. You can't be controlled by outside situations. For example, through the 1989 season, I never chewed out a player because I was in a bad frame of mind over my divorce or the reaction I was getting from the public. I did it when I got an inaccurate football response from the player.

You never jump a player's case out of your own anger. You've got to be able to control yourself so that you're positive with that person in a sincere way. Then, when you really do occasionally jump his case, you really make an impact.

Now: How and where and when do you jump a player's case? That dependes on the individual. And you have to know the individual well enough to determine how and where and when to punish.

And there are all kinds of ways to feed positive responses to people. With one, it might be bragging about him publicly in the newspapers. With another, it might be putting my arm around his shoulder while walking off the practice field. With another, it might be saying something in a team meeting about his accomplishments. The important thing is to motivate every individual.

There seems to be a school of thought nowadays that some individuals may reach a status or income level, whether in business or sports, where they no longer need pats on the back. The notion that these highly paid athletes nowadays don't need stroking, can't be motivated and won't perform as team players—that's all bull. *Everybody* needs positive reinforcement. And *everybody* wants to win.. And, no matter the salary, players can be bonded with one another and care about one another as a team, if they're treated the right way.

When you have success, there is glory for all. With success and glory come great feelings for one another and recognition of one another's contributions. If you keep harping on that time and time again with the players and have the credibility to back you up, you can somewhat prevent the "star system." You're not just throwing the word "team" around loosely. The term is real and deeply felt. You have a team.

Adapted from "Turning the Thing Around," by Jimmy Johnson as told to Ed Hinton. Copyright © 1993 by Jimmy Johnson and Ed Hinton. Published by Hyperion.

Source: Parade, August 15, 1993, pp. 4–6.

NOTES

1. Excerpted from Jesse Cole, "Managing from the Heart," *SKY,* April 1992, pp. 18–19.

2. Adapted from David M. Hunter, *Supervisory Management* (Reston, VA: Reston Publishing Co., 1981), p. 25

3. Richard C. Whitely, *The Customer Driven Company: Moving from Talk to Action* (Reading, MA: Addison Wesley Publishing, 1991), p. 27.

4. Peter F. Drucker, *Management: Tasks, Responsibilities, Practices* (New York: Harper & Row, 1974), p. 483.

5. *Ibid.,* p. 483.

6. W. Charles Redding, *Communication within the Organization* (New York: Industrial Communication Council, 1972), p. 25.

7. Walter Wiesman, *Wall-to-Wall Organizational Communication* (Huntsville, AL: Walter Wiesman, 1973), p. 4.

8. *Ibid.,* p. 3.

9. Gerald M. Goldhaber, *Organizational Communication,* 2nd ed. (Dubuque, IA: William C. Brown, 1979), p. 3.

10. Quoted from unpublished notes of Dr. Raymond L. Hilgert, Professor of Management and Industrial Relations, Washington University, St. Louis, MO.

11. Henry Mintzberg, *The Nature of Managerial Work* (New York: Harper & Row, 1973), pp. 38–39.

12. Wiesman, *op. cit.,* p. 4.

13. W. Barnett Pearce, *An Overview of Communication and Interpersonal Relationships* (Chicago: Science Research Associates, 1976), p. 33.

PERSONAL LANGUAGE USE AND COMMUNICATION STYLES

The Way We Word

In this chapter you will find ideas that will help you:

♦ Recognize how the perception and the language we use affects us as well as those with whom we communicate

♦ Understand the functions of language and some common misconceptions about how words work

♦ See how language labels can lead to self-fulfilling expectations

♦ Identify the dilemma in attempting to enforce speech codes or politically correct language rules

♦ Understand how personality problems often arise from the misuse of language

♦ Describe the kinds of nonverbal communication that arise in managerial communication

The following opinion piece appeared in *The Wall Street Journal*. It illustrates one of the frustrations people feel in the use and misuse of language.

I want us to stop redefining things.

This is a trend that I have noticed has been escalating for many years—ever since I woke up one morning to hear Jane Pauley suggesting, on the air, that we Americans needed to redefine the word "family." Her scholarly guest at the time, as I recall, responded, "I could redefine peanut butter for you, if you wanted, Jane, but it's still peanut butter."

This is how I feel about everything else we keep trying to redefine. Over the past few months, I have heard people suggest we redefine human sexuality, child-rearing, marriage, the family (again), the arts, the budget deficit, American history, a public-school education and the American middle class.

It is much easier and more comfortable to redefine a problem as some new kind of status quo, in the name of keeping up with the times, than it is to admit that your social institutions are failing.

America needs to haul out its restoration experts to rebuild the original, long-standing definitions of our institutions.

The family is, yes, still the family. In its most desirable form, it continues to be a Mom and Dad, kids and grandparents, aunts and uncles, and cousins, with accompanying dogs and kittens and hamsters. When our families break down, we should not attempt to assuage the national guilt by calling them some new kind of family. They're broken-down families.

Surely by now the evidence is unimpeachable on the sustained trauma created by divorce and multiple marriages. Traditional families are still the norm, not the rare exception, as has been clearly demonstrated in recent studies exposing the serpentine juggling of statistics perpetrated in the name of "proving" that "anything goes" in the world of American families. Anything does not go.

No matter how convenient or soothing an idea it may be, child-rearing cannot be redefined as the responsibility of day-care workers and schools. If we now find ourselves economically forced into the position of farming America's children out to day-care institutions, we need to stop and ask what's gone wrong, and how we can fix it. Kids need their parents. They should be able to have them.

The arts are not pornography. They are the arts. In their most enduring form, our music, dance, art and theater will mirror the souls of the people. Sometimes this is elevating, and sometimes it's depressing. But if it represents the truth in a way that connects with the truth of other human beings, then it is certainly art. Pornography, on the other hand, debases and defiles the human experience in an effort to distort and beguile. We cannot "redefine" the truth of art to include the artifice and deceit of pornography. They're not the same thing.

Education is supposed to be an opportunity to inquire and to learn. Our schools are not vehicles for rearing children, or for indoctrinating them into an "accepted" set of political beliefs. A good school is there to teach kids how to think critically so they are able to make good choices and intelligent decisions in their lives.

Most recently, I heard a prominent TV newscaster suggest that journalism itself needed to be "redefined," because the American people didn't have much respect for journalists anymore. If the American people don't like what journalism has become, then we should find ways to restore higher values to the profession instead of "redefining" journalism to include the right of the press to violate the public trust.

All of this is really simple common sense.

When your washing machine breaks down, do you "redefine" it as some new kind of washing machine that is able to compensate for its reduced ability to wash the clothes with its imaginative new possibilities as a wishing well or fish tank? No. You say, "Hey, this can't wash the clothes anymore. Let's fix it."

Let's stop redefining what's wrong with America. Let's fix it.[1]

The frustrations expressed by this writer—that changing the words doesn't solve the problems—can be better understood and even resolved by considering how words work. Likewise, the ability to communicate effectively is largely based on one's understanding of how people use language and why they sometimes fail.

Our individual styles of communicating vary with our personalities. None of us is exactly like another physically or psychologically. Each person is unique. We attempt to convey our unique worlds of experiences to others through language.

Although we take the whole process pretty much for granted, the way language works is not well understood by most people. Our language affects us as well as those we talk to.

It may strike you as ironic that language—the very essence of what many view to be communication—poses one of the most common sources of misunderstandings and of failures to create understanding. The problem (and opportunity) lies in our uniqueness.

WHY PERCEPTION IS UNIQUE[2]

Each of us, from the very beginning of our lives, has had unique and individual experiences. Scientists tell us that every sensory experience—that is, everything we have ever felt, tasted, heard, and seen—is recorded in the memory banks of our brain. From the very beginning of our lives, we experience things that no other person has experienced in exactly the same way.

Each new sensory message we receive is then interpreted in terms of things that we have experienced in the past. The past events color and shade our interpretation of present events.

To make sense of all these experiences, we attach labels or words to describe them both to ourselves and to others. Your stock of usable words limits your ability to share these experiences with others. These word labels are likely to carry certain *connotations*—feelings we associated with the label. These feelings may be either positive, negative, or neutral. Here is a simple example. Suppose that as a child, you were often successful at building model airplanes. It seems very likely that the word *airplane* will have a positive connotation for you. It would recall favorable feelings.

On the other hand, if you have had a disturbing experience with airplanes as a child (say, a rocky flight that scared you badly), the term is likely to arouse a negative association.

Similarly, we may associate pleasant recollections of the term *holiday season* as we think of the many parties and festivities, while retail sales clerks may dread the hustle of crowded stores and impatient customers. Their connotation may be negative.

> *Because each of us experiences and perceives events differently, we literally live in different psychological worlds.*

People not only do not see the world in exactly the same way because of their different experiences, connotations, and perceptions, but in a fairly literal sense, people do not even live in the same psychological world.

Each new message we receive is evaluated in terms of what we already know to determine if it makes sense. What makes perfectly good sense for another person may be utter nonsense for you. In many cases, of course, the degree of our differences about terms may be only slight. However, it is highly unlikely that we will give *exactly* the same meaning to any particular event.

WHY COMMUNICATION STYLES ARE UNIQUE

We have all developed our own ways of using words (or symbols). How we process and arrange words is our personal language structure. Our perceptions of the world (ideas, thoughts, or feelings) to which we attach words and symbols can be likened to the data input for a computer. But our language structure—the way we word—is like the software, that is, the program that tells the system what to do with the data. Plugging in more and more raw data, for example, by learning more and more new words, does little good if the system program doesn't know what to do with that information.

WAYS TO IMPROVE LANGUAGE USE AND VERBAL COMMUNICATION

There are two ways to improve verbal communication skills: (1) increase a person's vocabulary so that more precise raw data can be used, or (2) improve the match between language structures and reality. Increasing someone's vocabulary is usually a far less fruitful approach than working on structure. Only when vocabulary is seriously inadequate, such as when a person is learning a new language, is emphasis on improved vocabulary significantly valuable.

> *A shared semantic code determines the clarity of communication.*

The semantic codes shared by participants—their agreement on what words mean—determine the clarity of communication. Yet these codes often go unrecognized. By deciphering the code, we unlock the power to influence others.

Recognize That We Live in Two Worlds

We need to recognize continually that we live in two worlds: a world of our experiences and a world of our words. The words that we assign to things we experience develop our unique communication personality. *We can, literally, call things anything we want to.* We can use words in any way we wish. Yet problems arise when we try to use those same words to convey an idea to another person. Or when we attempt to redefine something in a new or different way (as in our opening illustration).

Figure 2-1 shows how our world of experiences and our world of words influence the communication situation. Note that the only link between any two people is through their worlds of words or symbols.

FIGURE 2-1   Our individual worlds of words link us to other people.

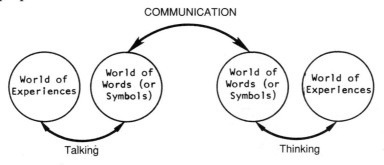

We cannot share exactly the same experiences, because of our sensory differences and our personal uniqueness. If we are careful, however, we can share our world of words to the extent that we can bring about some degree of understanding. If words are assigned in such a way that another person can gain some similar meaning from them, we can be successful in communication.

Language experts have identified a number of assumptions and misassumptions about word use that may cause serious problems in the way people communicate. Recognizing these facts and limitations of language use can help the manager become more sensitive to messages within organizations.

Understand That Words Do Not Have a "Right" Meaning

Words do not have an inherent, "right" meaning. They only have the meaning that people assign to them. And, of course, people can and do assign different meanings to the same words, as we've already discussed. Understanding this important point will help you avoid an oversimplification that can be dangerous.

Many people simplistically view communication as the transfer of meanings from one person to others. The use of the term *transfer* is misleading. It conjures up images of simply carrying a package (message) from one point to another.

> **Communication is not a transfer of meaning.**

That's not the way communication works. A sender cannot really transfer meanings; rather, the mind of the receiver creates meanings. The sender's task is to use symbols that trigger responses that accurately create meanings similar to the sender's. The creation of meaning by the receiver is a function of relating the incoming symbols to his or her total life experiences up to that point. Figure 2-2 illustrates this concept.

Twenty years ago, W. Charles Redding, a pioneer in organizational communication, taught that understanding of this viewpoint is essential to anyone who communicates in organizations, especially managers, executives, and supervisors.

FIGURE 2-2

The failure to observe the notion that the meanings are *created* in people is probably the cause of one of the most pervasive errors in everyday communication. This error has been labeled the *content fallacy*. It is the common assumption that there must be some way of so wording our messages that ... our ideas will be "transferred" to the minds of the receivers.... What happens all too often is that we keep tinkering with the contents of the message-sender's message rather than trying to find more ways of making sure that the message-receiver's responses are appropriate. This content fallacy leads us to believe that we are "getting through" to our audience merely because we are getting through to ourselves.[3]

The meanings do not reside in the words themselves but in the minds of the word's users. Associations conjured up cannot always be predicted. A cartoon in the *New Yorker* several years ago showed an alligator reading the novel Jaws and laughing so hard that tears ran down his face. Messages may create very different associations from those intended!

SEVERAL COMMON WORD USE PROBLEMS

Below is brief discussion of some of the most commonplace language use problems.[4] As you read these, think of examples you've experienced.

Confusing Facts with Opinions or Inferences

To assume that people in general, including ourselves, know an absolute fact when they see one can be dangerous.

In truth, a vast majority of information we receive is opinion or inference, not fact. An *inference* is defined as a conclusion based upon incomplete information. Something we personally observe or experience can be regarded as fact, at least for us. But just about anything else should be considered inference or opinion.

> *Language does not automatically clarify between inference and fact.*

The problem is that language does not automatically make clear the distinction between inference and facts. So we must make an extra effort to do so.

For example, under normal circumstances, we can state direct observations—"I saw Tom leave school at five o'clock—as facts. But if we take the fact about Tom leaving and elaborate on it, what we say becomes in inference. For example, when we say "I saw Tom leave school to go home," we are now adding a new dimension to the message that may or may not be true. Did Tom leave school? Yes, I saw him do so (fact). Did Tom go home? Maybe, but I cannot really be sure. I just assume that is where he went (inference).

We communicate inferences all the time. Problems arise when our listeners are unclear as to whether we are inferring or speaking of fact. Our language tends to muddy this distinction, so inferences have a way of coming out sounding very factual.

There is nothing wrong with drawing inferences. Inferences are necessary for people to make day-to-day sense of the world. The important thing is that we recognize inferences as such and that we world them in ways that will help us and our listeners avoid confusing them with facts. Failure to do so can often lead to confusion and argument.

There is an easy way to clarify an inference from a fact. Adding some reference to yourself will do it. For example, if we say, "That new policy is wrong," it sounds like a fact. It is our inference or opinion but it sounds like a fact. If we add a phrase such as "to me," or "I think," we signal our listener that this is our inference or opinion, not an absolute fact.

Think of how you would respond to the previous statements if you disagreed, if you felt the policy was a good one. In the first form, "The policy is wrong," you would be likely to argue the point since you see it otherwise. In the second form, you would perhaps disagree, but you would recognize the statement as just one person's impression of the policy.

Nobody can argue with what you like. If you say, "I do not like that decision," that is your right and other people will respect it. But if you say, "That was a rotten decision," then others may be put on the defensive if they liked (or made) the decision.

Whenever we make a statement we reveal something about ourselves. We choose what we will say, as well as how we will say it, on the basis of our personal values and attitudes. Here is an example.

If I state the opinion that "Vernon is stupid," it may appear on the surface that stupidity is some key characteristic of Vernon. But what I am really saying is that

- ◆ My personal experience has supplied me with a meaning for the word stupid.
- ◆ I have seen Vernon's behavior as fitting my view of the concept of stupidity.
- ◆ Therefore, I have concluded that Vernon is stupid.

This changing of terms often results in greater accuracy and clarity of expression. Failure to so clarify our messages can lead to considerable embarrassment, incorrect conclusions, and potential harm to our credibility. I suspect this potential breakdown was clearly in S. I. Hayakawa's mind when he said that general semantics—that is, the study of language and its behavioral effects—could be more accurately described as the study of "how not to be a damn fool."

Oversimplified Categories

Another common problem in the way we use language is the tendency to oversimplify the categories into which we mentally sort things. Often, these categories are too simple—black or white, when we really should describe shades of gray.

Many people rely too heavily on polar terms, words that force us to choose between extremes—good or bad, weak or strong, big or little—and that tend to oversimplify. In reality, most things in life are better described in fine variations among events or experiences than by either-or categories. To illustrate, simply ask yourself and others questions such as these:

1. Are you a good student or a bad student?
2. Are you big or little?
3. Are you liberal or conservative?
4. Are you attractive or ugly?
5. Are you a success or a failure?

People often ask questions just as absurd as these. The appropriate response, of course, would be *compared to what (or whom)?*

Do not let yourself get painted into a corner with someone else's oversimplified questions. If you are really interested in creating understanding—in really communicating—avoid these simplistic polar terms.

For leaders, the either-or reasoning pitfall can have serious effects. One particular problem is the tendency to classify workers as industrious or lazy or as productive or unproductive. In one company, a sales manager had a chart on his office wall with names of his salespeople boldly displayed under the headings "Heroes" and "Bums."

The problem is that when our language and thinking utilize such either-or logic, other possibilities are overlooked. If we classify a manager only as a good leader or a bad leader, we leave out a lot of other possibilities. Maybe he or she is effective in some dimensions of the job while ineffective in others.

Sales representatives and other persuaders often use this either-or orientation to their advantage. "Would you like to take delivery next Monday or Wednesday?" attempts to preclude the option of not taking delivery at all.

Our credibility can be seriously damaged when listeners recognize these kinds of oversimplified language structures. Whenever we hear ourselves or others sending either-or messages, we might be wise to consider:

♦ Are all the options covered?
♦ As compared with what (or whom)?

Words Can Lead to Self-Fulfilling Expectations

The manager who sees his or her subordinates as heroes or bums is obviously not relating to reality. It is far more realistic and hopeful to think in terms of people who can and will change their work performance. Today's hero may have been yesterday's bum if managers were able to avoid the related problem of self-fulfilling expectations—results that come true because we think they will.

> *Self-fulfilling expectations are results that come true because we think they will.*

Our minds tend to pay attention to events that "fit" what we expect. For example, a person who is biased against black workers will be more likely to notice poor behavior from a black worker. This reinforces an attitude the biased person holds. Likewise, if we expect our child to be the star of the school play, she very probably will be just that (especially in our own eyes).

What we see affects what we say. And what we say affects what we see. The filters of our mind develop over time as we label our world of experiences, and these filters determine what we select to perceive. When we can make no sense out of some thing or event—that is, if it doesn't fit our world view—we tend to reject it.

It can be quite disconcerting, for example, to find that the worker we've labeled as rebellious is suddenly vigorously defending the status quo—or to find that nice, pleasant reception person suddenly shouting angrily at a visitor. We'd prefer to reject or explain such discrepant observations because they just don't jibe with the way things are in our mental world. The way we label people leads to expectations of how those people will behave in the future.

Furthermore, expectations have a way of becoming self-fulfilling. The supervisor who labels a subordinate lazy will undoubtedly find more and more evidence to support the judgment. In all likelihood, this supervisor's attitude will be perceived by the worker, thus leading to suspicion and distrust. The overall result will be a strong potential for miscommunication. So let's keep our labels somewhat loose. Maintain some flexibility so that unanticipated changes in things, events, and people can fit into our mental worlds without throwing us off balance.

Words do not automatically allow for flexibility and change.

Words Have Emotional Loadings

Many terms carry emotional connotations that can excite, anger, offend, or create pleasant or unpleasant associations in people. An obvious example is the profane expletive, which, for example, could be extremely embarrassing or offensive to a group of worshippers, but a source of considerable amusement to a group of heavy metal music fans. The word itself doesn't change, only the receiver's associations and, in this case, the context in which the term is used.

Semanticist Stuart Chase taught about "purr" words and "slur" words. This was a catchy way of describing *euphemisms* and *dysphemisms*. A *euphemism* is a term that creates a more pleasant or less objectionable association in minds of its users. A *dysphemism* is the opposite; it conveys a more negative or unpleasant association. The degree of pleasantness or unpleasantness depends, of course, on people's attitudes.

Here are a few examples (from our point of view—your perceptions may vary):

Euphemism	Neutral	Dysphemism
Emotionally challenged	Hard-to-manage child	Brat
Luxury automobile	Standard-size car	Gas guzzler
Go powder my nose	Go to the restroom	Go to the toilet (or worse)
Passed away	Died	Croaked
Sizzling steak	Cooked meat	The flesh of a steer

Some very humorous exchanges can arise when we use euphemisms or dysphemisms in unexpected ways. A cartoon I recently saw showed a woman talking to a man who was carefully inspecting his food. She said, "That yellow scum on top happens to be Hollandaise sauce." Another illustration of slur words came from one of MacNelly's "Shoe" cartoons:

Newspaper Editor to Writer: Senator Belfry's office is complaining again about our unfair treatment of the distinguished senator in our editorials....

Writer: Baloney! I'm never unfair in any of my editorials! Which one are they talking about, anyway?

Editor: The one called, "Bozo the Clown goes to Congress."

Politically Correct Language

> *PC terminology is an attempt to override dysphemisms.*

The creation of speech codes and the encouragement of politically correct terminology is largely an attempt to override the undesirable effect of dysphemisms. Words seen as potentially offensive are proscribed and users of such terms set up for punishment, counseling, sensitivity training and the like.

While the intent to eliminate terminology that may offend other people is noble, it is simply impossible. Remember, the words do not have meaning, people assign meanings. The impact of a term varies widely depending on who says it, how it is said, and countless other variables. For example, a racially offensive term hurled at a person of another race in the heat of an argument has a totally different impact than the same term used by a fellow member of the same race in a joking, lighthearted, or teasing manner.

Attempts to enforce speech codes have come into direct conflict with first amendment rights—freedom of speech—in many universities and other organizations.[5]

The ability to anticipate how people will tend to associate meanings is a most valuable skill. Successful professionals develop a high level of sensitivity to the emotional loadings of words.

Words Sometimes Conceal
Rather Than Reveal

Sometimes we don't say what we really mean. It's shocking, but true! Actually, there are good reasons for being less than totally truthful on occasion. The situation may make us feel awkward, or we have other reasons to keep our real thoughts to ourselves. In such cases we may rely on clichés or platitudes, which are usually acceptable to those we interact with even though they convey little or no real information. Consider the following dialogue between a manager who wants to promote a worker and the employee's immediate supervisor, who would love to get rid of him.

Manager: Kim, I'm looking at your man Harrison for that programming job over on the Placebo Project. What do you think of him?

Supervisor: Harrison? Sure, he's a good dude.

Manager: Do you think he can handle it?

Supervisor: No problem. He's really with the program. He's been one of my big guns ever since he came here. He's a stand-up guy.

Manager: Thanks, Kim. I appreciate your being up front with me on this one. I'll push things along and we'll get some action on it real soon.

Supervisor: Cool.

Whatever factual information might have been exchanged here was completely muddled by the clichés. What did these people really say to each other? Not much.

Considerable skill is required to predict accurately how people associate words with meanings. For the manager processing information, one key is to reduce the emotionalism in language when clear, objective decisions and actions are required. For you, as a manager, a good starting point is to listen carefully to your own language first.

> **Carefully listen to your own language use.**

- ◆ Do you tend to use terms that may carry inappropriate associations?
- ◆ Do certain items of your terms or expressions seem to result in others getting their fur up?
- ◆ Are you sensitive to the possibilities that some of your routine expressions may be real turnoff terms to others?
- ◆ Do you generally recognize the hidden meanings in others' expressions?

It would be impossible to answer such questions accurately, of course, without getting feedback and confirmation from other people.

NONVERBAL COMMUNICATION: LOUDER THAN WORDS

As important as it is to develop sensitivity and skill in using language, remember that both verbal and nonverbal communication create meaning. Nonverbal cues, many of them very subtle, cannot be separated from the verbal aspects of received messages.

Nonverbal communication is that which does not use words or common symbols.

Just what is nonverbal communication? Describing what the category of nonverbal communication does *not* include is probably easier than specifying all that it does. Most scholars who study nonverbal communication agree that the term clearly excludes communication using words, numbers, or normal written or oral language. Instead, it focuses on all the other things that cause meanings to be created in people.

What we say cannot be extracted from the context in which we say it. Nonverbal communication defines that context and seeks to explain its effects on our word messages.

Mark Knapp, who wrote a well-known book in this area, suggested that nonverbal forms of codification can be usefully divided into the following categories:

1. *Sign language*—substitution of gestures for words, numbers, and punctuation signs
2. *Action language*—all movements not used exclusively for signals (e.g., walking, drinking, eating)
3. *Object language*—all international display of material things (e.g., implements, machines, art objects, clothing, and the human body itself)[6]

Phillip V. Lewis, in his book on organizational communication, classifies nonverbal communication as:

1. *Body motion or kinesic behavior*—gestures, facial expressions, movement posture, or body movements
2. *Paralanguage*—voice qualities, laughing, yawning, etc.
3. *Proxemics*—human use and perception of physical space
4. *Olfaction*—sense of smell
5. *Skin sensitivity*—stroking, hitting, greetings, and farewells, etc.
6. *Artifacts*—clothes, lipstick, eyeglasses, wigs, false lashes, general attractiveness, height, weight, hair color, skin color, etc.[7]

The ways we attach meanings to messages can readily be affected by any and all of these unspoken, and often unnoticed, nonverbal characteristics. The following are some nonverbal elements that frequently influence managerial communication:

Environment and Space

The variables of environment and space include any of the objects that surround us as we communicate, including size and visual dimensions of the room, lighting, and temperature.

People have a need for defining their own territorial boundaries—their personal bubble—and we define conversational distances among ourselves. From previous studies, researchers know that proximity is a potent variable in developing contact with another person. Spatial and environmental behaviors can reflect our style of leadership. The arrangement of one's office furniture can create impressions of status differences or openness. The manager who talks to an employee from behind his or her desk comes across differently than the manager who crosses the room to sit next to the employee.

In customer relations, environmental barriers can cause problems. An auto dealership removed the sales representatives' desks from their cubicles and replaced them with small round tables. The impact on sales was dramatic. Customers seemed to see the round-table environment as far less threatening.[8]

Another example of space as a nonverbal communication dimension is found in the ways we position ourselves when speaking to others.

In the American culture, people normally stand (or sit) at various distances from each other as they communicate.

Distance	Situation
Touching to about 18 inches	Lovers, close friends, or conspirators
Two to four feet	Normal social conversation
Four to twelve feet	More formal business conversation, meetings
Twelve or more feet	Public or presentational speaking

In normal conversation, a person who moves in closer than arm's length is seen as pushy or aggressive. A person who stands back a bit farther than normal conveys aloofness.

When our culturally or situationally defined space expectations are violated, we get uncomfortable. For example, observe the behavior of people crowded into an elevator. Their normal social distance is suddenly reduced to intimate distance. Most people respond by looking up at the floor indicator or otherwise distracting themselves.

Different organizational positions affect space expectations. We assume that higher level executives will have more spacious offices. Their space is also more likely to be protected via closed doors, reception rooms adjoining their office, and sometimes even their position in the building—they are often on or near the top floor.

While it's perfectly appropriate for the executive to "invade" the work area of a lower ranking organizational member, the opposite may well be seen as an act of insubordination.

Physical Appearance and Dress

If we arrive at a meeting dressed in a business suit and find the other participants in Levi's and cowboy boots, we may feel awkward. The key variable is *appropriateness* to the occasion. We'd look out of place at a funeral in casual clothing but equally out of place working in a surf shop in a tux. Dress standards vary quite widely even in the business world. California high-tech firms are often noted for casual dress, while bank employees in New York usually dress in suits.

Closely related to appearance and dress are the artifacts that people display. Expensive jewelry, elaborate office decorations, and attractive personal belongings tell others something about us. The absence of such personal artifacts may convey a different message. Either way, the impression formed from such nonverbal cues is present in the mind of the observer.

Physical Behaviors

Nonverbal physical behaviors include the positioning and movement of the arms and legs, and posture. Body language can parallel or override spoken language. Body movements often communicate unspoken messages such as:

1. Like or dislike for another
2. Status differences
3. Affective states or moods
4. Intended and perceived persuasiveness
5. Approval seeking
6. Quasi-courtship behavior
7. Need for inclusion
8. Deception
9. Interpersonal warmth[9]

Included among these physical behaviors would be nervous mannerisms, shuffling from position to position, frequent looking at one's watch, and posture or position when seated.

One type of physical behavior that ties in with spatial variables is touching behavior. While a literal pat on the back or a reassuring handshake is often appreciated, some people get a reputation for being touchy-feely. Many people feel uncomfortable with excessive touching.

Expressions of the Face and Eyes

Facial expressions and movements of the eyes are especially important ways of conveying a variety of emotions ranging from fear and anxiety to happiness, relief, or requests for additional information. Scientists have found that dilation of the pupil may indicate emotional arousal, interest, or attentiveness.

One of the key obstacles to more effective use of nonverbal communication to create clearer understanding is illustrated by the studies of face and eye expression. Paul Ekman's research in this area concludes that, with proper training, one can learn to accurately identify facial expressions with emotions and personality of the subject. He also states that there is strong evidence that some constants transcend different cultures. [10] Other researchers, such as anthropologist Ray Birdwhistell, disagree. Dr. Birdwhistell contends that "there are no universal gestures. As far as we know, there is no single facial expression, stance or body position which conveys the same meaning in all societies."[11]

Vocal Cues Accompanying Spoken Words

People stereotype others on the basis of their voices: The fellow with a lisp is a sissy. The lady with slurred speech is assumed to be drunk. The woman with a husky or breathy voice is aggressive or sexy. Although these stereotypes are often unfounded, studies have shown that a person can judge with fair accuracy the age, sex, and status of others from the sound of their voices alone. Also, people make judgments about one's trustworthiness, likability, competency, and dynamism on the basis of voice.[12]

The messages we receive are colored by these and undoubtedly other nonverbal factors. Figure 2-3 summarizes some common managerial nonverbal cues.

FIGURE 2-3   Common nonverbal cues.

NONVERBAL COMMUNICATION	SIGNAL RECEIVED	REACTION FROM RECEIVER
• Manager looks away when talking to the employee.	I do not have this person's undivided attention.	Supervisor is too busy to listen to my problem or simply does not care.
• Failure to acknowledge greeting from fellow employee.	This person is unfriendly.	This person is unapproachable.
• Omnious glaring (i.e., the evil eye).	I am angry.	Reciprocal anger, fear or avoidance depending on who is sending the signal in the organization.
• Rolling of the eyes.	I am not being taken seriously.	This person thinks they are smarter or better than I am.
• Deep sighing.	Disgust or displeasure.	My opinions do not count. I must be stupid or boring to this person.
• Heavy breathing (Sometimes accompanied by hand waving).	Anger or heavy stress.	Avoid this person at all costs.
• Eye contact not maintained when communicating.	Suspicion and/or uncertainty.	What does this person have to hide?
• Manager crosses arms and leans away.	Apathy and closed mindedness.	This person already has made up their mind; my opinions are not important.
• Manager peers over glasses.	Skepticism or distrust.	He or she does not believe what I am saying.
• Continues to read a report when employee is speaking.	Lack of interest.	My opinions are not important enough to get the supervisor's undivided attention.

Source: G. Michael Barton, "Communication: Manage Words Effectively," *Personnel Journal*, January 1990, p. 36.

The Effects of Nonverbal Communication

The sobering reality is that what we *say* is almost always overridden by what we *do*. While the language we use conveys certain objective information, our bodies convey how we *feel* about what we say. Whenever we perceive a discrepancy between the words and the nonverbal cues we receive, we usually assume that the nonverbal message is the real meaning.

To increase the probability of achieving effective understanding among people, managers must develop sensitivity to both nonverbal cues and hidden meanings in language. Our personal communication style can be refined to look beyond the obvious messages and attach accurate meanings to the enormous numbers of communication cues present in any organizational setting.

A QUICK SUMMARY OF MAJOR IDEAS

♦ The way we use language reveals much about the way we see the world. Each person relates his or her world of experiences to others through his or her world of words.

♦ Managers can be better communicators by recognizing the limitations and characteristics of language:

—Words do not have inherent meaning; they mean different things to different people.

—Words do not automatically separate facts from inferences.

—Words tend to push things into either/or categories.

—Words can lead to self-fulfilling expectations.

—Words carry emotional "loads."

—Words can sometimes conceal more than they reveal.

—Words often carry hidden meanings.

♦ Nonverbal communication conveys as much or more meaning than does verbal communication.

QUESTIONS FOR FURTHER THOUGHT

1. Consider your nonverbal communication and how you come across to others. Make a list of adjectives that describe your image. Ask several associates to make a similar list about you. How do these lists compare?

2. It has been said that language does as much to conceal as to reveal. How would you respond to that idea? Does nonverbal behavior work the same way?

OTHER THOUGHTS ABOUT LANGUAGE USE

"META-TALK"

Gerald I. Nierenberg and Henry H. Calero's popular book *Meta-Talk: Guide to Hidden Meanings in Conversations*[13] describes some functions of conversational expressions. Nierenberg and Calero categorize verbal responses as softeners, foreboders, continuers, interesters, downers, convincers, strokers, and pleaders. We have used their categories and added some examples of our own to assemble a guide to word functions Let's look at some examples of each of these.

SOFTENERS

These preface our remarks with expressions intended to influence receivers in a positive way—to soften them for the real message. Here are some examples:

Expression	*Purpose or Real Meaning*
"You're going to like what I'm about to tell you."	Prepares the receiver for what we believe will be good news for him or her.
"It goes without saying."	Attempts to get agreement by assuming it to be so.
"I venture to say," or, "off the top of my head," or, "I'm sticking my neck out," or, "at first blush."	The message sender is about to draw a conclusion based on incomplete data.
"Would you be kind enough to ..."	Flatters receiver so he or she will do what is asked.
"I'm sure someone as intelligent as you...," or, "What is your expert opinion of my...?"	Asks for concurrence, expects the listener (receiver) to indicate agreement; sets up for an exchange of compliments.
"You are right, but ..."	Attempts to avoid conflict by feigning agreement.
Use of acceptance or agreement statements followed by *but, yet, however, still,* etc.	The message sender does not feel the receiver is right but wants to soften the flow of disagreement.
"You are right."	Probably a genuine statement of fact.

FOREBODERS

We put our listeners in a negative or anxious frame of mind by using these expressions. They can lead to unpleasant encounters or psychological games.

Expression	*Purpose or Real Meaning*
"Nothing is wrong." (accompanied by a look of anxiety)	There is something wrong, but I don't want to talk about it. [or] There is something wrong and I want you to show concern and probe further.
"It really doesn't matter."	It matters.
"Don't worry about me."	Please do.
"I have nothing more to say."	I'm about to blow up and argue.
"That is all that can be said."	More could be said but it will lead to disagreements.
"I'd rather not discuss it."	I want to talk to someone about it but probably not you.
"We've beaten this dead horse enough."	There isn't much more any of us can say to improve agreement.

CONTINUERS

These expressions attempt to get listeners to disclose more of their thoughts on a matter. These are often viewed as supportive, although they can become counterproductive if people go on and on until you really need to shut them up. Here are some examples:

Expression	*Purpose or Real Meaning*
"What else is new?"	Introduce another topic for conversation.
"Go on," or, "That's very good," or, "Now you're talking," or "I like that."	Please elaborate on your point. I agree with what you say.
"Why don't you go with that line of thought?" or, "Tell us more about that idea."	You don't make much sense to me yet but this could become productive if you go on.
"If you have any further questions, do not hesitate to call upon me."	This seems like a good line to end my letter with. I sure hope I don't hear from them.

INTERESTERS

Statements and questions that attempt to arouse interest or to get the listener to say something to indicate interest are called interesters. Use of these expressions often reveals something about speakers and their prejudices. In most cases, interesters add nothing to the conversation and can become something of a verbal tick for speakers. They can also annoy your listeners. Here are some examples:

Expression	Purpose or Real Meaning
"And do you know what he said?"	Are you still listening?
"After all I've done for him, do you know what he did?"	Compliments the speaker and seeks support for the position he took.
"Guess what happened!"	The speaker is uncertain that he has anything relevant or interesting to say, so he must demand the listener's attention by getting her to say, "What?"
"Did you hear the one about…?"	Instructs the listener to conceal any knowledge of the joke that will follow. Get ready to laugh.
"What do you think of [some emotion-loaded term or expression]…?"	I hope you'll agree with my stand on this issue.
"I could say something about that!"	I don't want to cause trouble but I will anyway.

DOWNERS

These expressions are used intentionally to put the listener in a defensive state of mind. Typically, they appear when speakers see themselves in a win-lose situation and are moving in for the kill. Appropriate vocal tone and facial expression can add considerable power to the downer. The tone is often sarcastic.

Expression	Purpose or Real Meaning
"Are you happy now?"	You have just humiliated me and caused great anguish and you should feel miserable too.
"Don't make me laugh."	A mean-hearted reaction to another's request or demand.
"Don't be ridiculous."	You have said something I disagree with and I will now attack you as a person.
"Put it to music …"	I have heard your excuse and I'm not sympathetic.
"That's the way it is, pal."	I am totally unsympathetic to your plight.

CONVINCERS

Convincers are often used as substitutes for logical argument. When speakers are having trouble making a sensible case for their point of view, convincers can cause listeners to forget the logical inconsistency. Here are some examples of convincers.

Expression	*Purpose or Real Meaning*
"That's the only way we can do business in this city."	Justification of an unethical or illegal act.
"Why, anyone can do it!"	The task is so simple that even a moron could accomplish it. (This can also be a downer when the listener has just failed the task in question.)
"Anyone can follow my line of reasoning."	Persuades by intimidation; I find it simple and so should you.
"I think we all agree that ..."	Appeals for consensus or tries to smooth over conflict.
"Let me make one thing perfectly clear ..."	Introduces a conscious deception or tries to hammer home a belief.
"Everybody I know agrees ..."	Therefore, you should agree, too: [or] Therefore, it must be true.
"Believe me,..."	Please agree with me, I'm desperate for your acceptance.

STROKERS

People need verbal reassurance and approval. Sometimes such statements come naturally from others. Often, however, we feel a need to reach out and solicit some verbal-approval statements, some positive strokes. We use meta-talk to give strokes: to tell people that they are special to us and that we are willing to share feelings and information with them.

Expression	*Purpose or Real Meaning*
"How do you like my new outfit?"	I need reassurance that I look nice.
"What do you think of my plan? I didn't go too far, did I?"	Although I don't want criticism, here is a double-barreled question that invites you to praise and be critical.

Expression	*Purpose or Real Meaning*
"I shouldn't tell you this, but …" (followed by flattery)	You'll enjoy hearing this gossip, and I want to make you happy and strengthen our relationship.
"I heard some really good thing about you…."	Here are some positive strokes; be prepared to be modest.

PLEADERS

Pleaders reflect the emotions of the speaker. These emotions may be envy, uncertainty, discomfort, concealed aggression, or expressions of superiority. Here are a few examples:

Expression	*Purpose or Real Meaning*
"I certainly wouldn't parade around in a revealing dress like that." (envy)	I wish I had a figure like hers.
"He's pretty obnoxious with all his jokes." (envy)	I wish I could be the life of the party.
"I'll do my best." (uncertainty)	My best probably won't be good enough.
A fat person who says, "Watch me break the chair." (discomfort)	By anticipating disaster, I will be relieved of embarrassment if it does happen.
"Do you mind if I ask you…?" [followed by a penetrating or accusing question] (concealed aggression)	Now I've got you; my disdain is now made visible.
"That's nothing, you should see…," "Don't you know that?" or, "It may interest you to know …" (superiority)	I'm smarter, I'm more in-the-know; I'm better.

LANGUAGE MISUSE CAN BE A SYMPTOM OF PERSONALITY PROBLEMS

As suggested in this chapter, many communication problems arise from a lack of awareness of how language works. In the extreme, when people are oblivious to relationships between words and reality, they may experience serious social problems. Indeed, psychologist William Pemberton[14] suggests that maladjusted people typically exhibit tendencies such as these:

1. Assuming that, at the perceptual level, everyone is having the same experiences as themselves—that there is only one right way to look at or feel about anything
2. Assuming that if they talk long enough, loud enough, or reasonably enough, they will be able to influence others to their way of thinking
3. Assuming that the characteristic by which something is named, labeled, or judged is *in* the object, that their description is the right characteristic, the real name, the real meaning
4. Making generalized conclusions from very few experiences in such a way that new experiences have to fit old conclusions or remain ignored
5. Shutting out further consideration of a problem with, "That's all there is to it."

Note: Pemberton's list is not meant to suggest that anyone who ever exhibits such behavior is maladjusted. We are all guilty of occasional misassumptions. But maladjusted people persistently think and act as described.

NOTES

1. Excerpted from Linda Burton, "Redefinitions in a Broken-Down World," *Wall Street Journal*, December 1, 1993, p. A 14.
2. Much of this discussion is adapted from Paul R. Timm, *Basics of Oral Communication* (Cincinnati: South-Western Publishing, 1993), p. 28. Used with permission of the author.
3. W. Charles Redding, *Communication within the Organization* (New York: The Industrial Communication Council, 1972), p. 29.
4. Adapted from Timm, *op. cit.*, 1993, pp. 29–33.
5. See, for example, Sarah Lubman, "Campus Speech Codes are Being Shot Down As Opponents Pipe Up," *The Wall Street Journal*, December 22, 1993, p. 1A+.A-1, A-12.
6. Mark L. Knapp, *Nonverbal Communication in Human Interaction*, 2nd ed. (New York: Holt, Rinehart & Winston, 1978), p. 3.
7. Phillip V. Lewis, *Organizational Communication: The Essence of Effective Management*, 2nd ed. (Columbus, OH: Grid, 1980), p. 230.

8. This and other ideas on customer communication can be found in Paul R. Timm, *50 Powerful Ideas You Can Use to Keep Your Customers* (Hawthorne, NJ: Career Press, 1992), see especially page 24.

9. Knapp, *op. cit.*, p. 113.

10. *Ibid.*, p. 137.

11. Ray Birdwhistell as quoted in the *New York Times Magazine,* May 1970, pp. 8–9.

12. Knapp, *op. cit.*, p. 173.

13. This reading is excerpted from ideas discussed in Gerald I. Nierenberg and Henry H. Calero, Meta-Talk: *Guide to Hidden Meanings in Conversations* (New York: Trident Press, 1973), pp. 15–16.

14. William Pemberton, "A Semantic Approach to Counseling," ETC: A Review of General Semantics, *13*, 2 (Winter 1955–56), pp. 83–92.

CHAPTER 3

THE MEDIA AND TOOLS OF THE MANAGER-COMMUNICATOR

The Convenience-vs.-Confusion Tradeoff

▼

In this chapter you will find ideas that will help you:

♦ Recognize that the various media or communication approaches available to managers have inherent advantages and disadvantages and that these media should not be used out of habit but rather selected carefully

♦ Understand the distinction between communication efficiency and communication effectiveness

♦ Become aware of some of the unspoken ground rules associated with different communication media

♦ Carefully select appropriate media based on characteristics such as:

—Speed

—Feedback capacity

—Hard copy availability

—Message intensity and complexity

—Formality

—Relative costs

♦ Identify some ways to mix media to improve effectiveness

♦ Become aware of a variety of communication tools used successfully in other organizations

▼

Almost every manager feels the need to write a memo now and then. Unfortunately, some feel this need too often. They become memo-maniacs. They send memos to deal with the darndest things, often without considering fully the impact of their decision to use writing rather than another communication approach. Consider, for example, this blistering missive from Wilbur:

```
DATE: April 30
TO:   All Employees
FROM: Wilbur Jackson, III, Supervisor
RE:   COFFEE BREAK ABUSE

It has recently come to my attention that department
employees are taking excessively long coffee breaks
that blatantly violate company policy and impact pro-
ductivity parameters in an adverse manner. Employees
caught subsequently violating the break period limita-
tions will be terminated. Also, the management at Roach
Coach, Inc., will be told not to send their snack and
coffee truck to our plant in the future.

I trust you will all obey policy in the future regard-
ing this matter.
```

Now, suppose you work for Wilbur and you have been very careful to limit your breaks to less than ten minutes. How would you be likely to react when this memo appears in your pay envelope? We suspect you'd be pretty upset. We further suspect that you'd conclude that Wilbur isn't the brightest supervisor around.[1]

THE MEDIA THEMSELVES COMMUNICATE MEANING

As managers, we have a variety of communication media and tools at our disposal. Which ones we choose to use for a particular situation can, in itself, communicate. In other words, each form of communication—each medium or tool—conveys unspoken messages. For example, a cheap medium such as a handwritten, photocopied note might say to its recipient:

- ◆ This message isn't very important. If it were, it would be presented more formally.

- ◆ You are not important enough to receive this information from the source personally.

♦ The message source is too busy to convey this information to you in a more personal way.

♦ This matter is so urgent, the sender had to sacrifice personalism to get out the information quickly.

♦ This is routine information that you will readily understand.

Any or all of these thoughts might enter the minds of the receivers. The medium itself makes comment about the contents of the message. The results can range from confusion about the message's meaning and importance to total disregard or misunderstanding.

How information is sent adds impact to manager's messages. Communication effectiveness improves and communication costs drop when appropriate media are selected.

The term *media* is being used here in a broad sense, to include the *method, channel,* or *circumstances* under which communication takes place. Media are the tools of the manager/communicator.

Although we often associate the term *media* with radio or TV or with communications hardware such as telephone, videotape recordings, and the like, our discussion of the media of managerial communication goes beyond the mechanical aspects. We discuss various types of written, oral, and electronic media as well.

WHAT IS A MEDIUM?

A generic description of the term *medium* is "a channel or mechanism for transmitting or conveying messages from point to point." While this description may be useful in certain circumstances, consider for a moment a different working definition of the term *medium.* This proposed definition is particularly useful in the type of human interpersonal communication that managers engage in on a daily basis.

Definition: A medium is a generally accepted set of ground rules for structuring and exchanging messages.

RECOGNIZING SOME MEDIA GROUND RULES

The ground rules for use of a particular medium are usually assumed by participants rather than prescribed in advance. Here is an example from communication professor Richard Hatch. A medium called "polite conversation" usually works under the following ground rules:

♦ Whoever is talking may continue to talk until he or she appears to be finished.

♦ No speaker should talk for very long at a time; the duration may vary from a few seconds to two or three minutes, depending on the circumstances.

◆ Nobody may interrupt the speaker unless he or she agrees to be interrupted.

◆ When a silence occurs, each participant has an equal opportunity to begin talking; that is, nobody is intentionally excluded.

◆ Anybody who is talking may change the subject without getting permission from other participants.[2]

When these ground rules are violated, participants in the communication situation are thrown off. Visualize a polite conversation in which any of the rules listed is violated—let's say that interruptions abound—and you're likely to picture an ineffectual and decidedly impolite conversation.

Figure 3-1 suggests additional examples of the kinds of unspoken ground rules that generally prevail with several spoken, written, or graphic media.

Obviously we don't consciously consider these rules every time we communicate, but they are there. They've just become so familiar that we no longer notice them. These rules do, however, provide a rational basis for making decisions about what medium to use for specific messages. If, for example, we need to convey some highly technical, intricate, and complex information, we would be likely to avoid the friendly conversation medium. Such messages may involve talking for very long periods of time and listeners would be expected to refrain from changing the topic. Recognizing the ground rules in operation may alert us to potential communication failures.

Much of the success or failure of a manager's communication efforts can be attributed to media selection. Some managers, for example, use memos to convey the darndest things. Like the manger in our opening story, they fail to see the downside of their media selection. They opt for convenience and beget confusion or resentment.

> *The ground rules provide the keys to selecting a particular communication medium.*

The memo isn't the only communication medium that tends to be overused or abused. Consider the use of the infamous pink slip to inform employees abruptly that they have been terminated, or the informal chat in the restroom where the employee's work quality is critiqued in the presence of others. These communications reflect a failure to use appropriate media, and they are apt to have adverse effects on the organization.

One such adverse effect is a waste of time or money from poor media use. Here's a personal example from Paul Timm's past:

> As a business manager, I once attended a meeting called by the general manager of our large corporation. There were about 200 employees, mid-level managers, supervisors, and office staff. A meeting room was rented at a hotel near the main office, since we had no conference room large enough. The purpose of the meeting was for the general manager to explain, in a broad sense, the need to economize in our everyday operations. After stating that need and explaining how it related to the company's profit picture, the GM asked if anyone had any comments or suggestions.

Some Possible Ground Rules	Spoken Media				Written/Graphic Media		
	Conversation	Interview	Committee	Presentation	Letter/Memo	Report	Poster/Display
Receivers may interrupt and/or seek clarification	yes	yes	yes	no	no	no	no
Participants may change the subject	yes	sometimes	yes	no	no	no	no
Source may talk for extended periods of time	no	no	no	yes	no	yes	no
Participants have equal opportunity to initiate ideas	yes	sometimes	yes	no	no	no	no
Messages are presented in a standard arrangement or format	no	sometimes	no	yes	usually	yes	no
Supporting data of considerable detail are presented with conclusion	sometimes	no	no	yes	sometimes	yes	no
Artistic or aesthetic qualities are conveyed	no	no	no	somewhat	no	no	yes

FIGURE 3-1   Examples of ground rules for media.

One secretary spent approximately 10 minutes explaining how she had developed a system to save paper clips. Several others took the opportunity to impress the boss with their success stories at recycling waste paper or cutting down on photocopying.

But no one seemed to notice the cost of that meeting! By the time the people drifted back to their offices, the company had spent over 300 hours in direct labor costs alone. Then there was the cost of the meeting room, the cost of reduced efficiency back at the offices while all the supervisors were gone, and the incalculable cost of possible lost business or customer resentment created when people wanting to speak to a manager simply had to wait until our meeting ended.

What was the return on this communication investment? We learned that the company would like to make a profit, if possible (a real eye-opening notion!), and we learned how to save some paper clips. The corporation used a thousand-dollar medium to convey nickel-and-dime ideas. The point, of course, is that selection of appropriate communication media can have a considerable effect on communication costs and effectiveness.

How Can a Manager Pick the Best Media?

The first step to using media effectively is to recognize that the method we use to communicate is a signal to our receivers. It provides cues about our estimation of the audience's importance, as well as the significance and urgency of the message being conveyed. A routinely distributed photocopied memo conveys a very different immediate impression from that of a neatly typed and personally signed letter—even though the actual message may be identical.

Consider Efficiency versus Effectiveness

At the heart of media selection problems in organizations is a failure to recognize the distinction between communication efficiency and effectiveness.

> *Efficiency looks at costs compared to number of people reached.*

Efficiency is simply a ratio between the resources (including time, materials, and effort) expended in generating intentional messages and the number of people to whom the message is sent. To improve efficiency we simply increase the number of people reached or reduce the message preparation costs. The widely distributed memo or mass meeting is an efficient communication method.

$$\text{Communication efficiency} = \frac{\text{Resources (including time) expended}}{\text{Number of recipients reached}}$$

Communication *effectiveness* is quite another matter. In Chapter 1 we suggest that communication is the creation of understanding. In organizations, effective communication creates understandings which orchestrate effort in much the same way as the nervous system arranges an organism's thoughts and behaviors. Management theorist, Saul Gellerman, concludes that "organizational communication may be said to be 'effective' when a message is:

♦ *Received* by its intended audience
♦ *Interpreted* in essentially the same way by the recipients as by the senders
♦ *Remembered* over reasonably extended periods of time
♦ *Used* when appropriate occasions arise"[3]

The dilemma for the manager is that in most cases the communication methods that are most efficient are least effective and vice versa. In almost every case, face-to-face dialogue with an individual organization member is the least efficient, least convenient, and most costly method of communication. It is also the most effective. For some types of messages, face-to-face dialogue is essential.

Gellerman concludes that an unwillingness to pay the price for effectiveness in communication may well be false economy. "A very large part of the blame for ineffective communication ... falls on management's persistent efforts to communicate with the most people at the least cost. Alas, communication is one function where it does not pay to be efficient."[4]

In some cases, of course, a message is simply not important enough to transmit via individual, face-to-face interaction. In many cases, organizational complexity forbids it. The manager must then strike a balance between efficiency and effectiveness. Unfortunately, many managers make their choice of a communication method from habit, without considering the merits or drawbacks of possible alternatives.

Understand the Characteristics and Costs of Various Management Communication Media

When we describe media broadly, as a generally accepted set of ground rules, we discover that there are quite specific advantages or disadvantages to the use of different communication approaches in different circumstances. For the manager, a wise selection is based on consideration of (1) the media characteristics inherent in each, and (2) the relative costs of written versus spoken communication.

Let's look at some of the characteristics of managerial communication media that make one medium preferable to others in a given situation.

Speed.   How fast or slow a medium is depends on several factors, including preparation time, delivery time, and assimilation time (the time it takes for the receiver to comprehend the message being delivered).

A letter is generally slow getting from sender to receiver, although overnight services and facsimile transmissions have reduced the time problem. But an oral presentation of the same information may take considerably more preparation time. The time-consuming work of producing a videotape or slide presentation may be offset when repeated showings can efficiently present the same information to many employees or customers.

Normally, the spoken word is faster than a print medium, except when we are comparing a formal oral presentation with a handwritten note.

Feedback Capacity.   The amount and promptness of feedback are other media characteristics. Written media elicit no feedback from your audience while you are writing the message. Unfortunately, the usefulness of responses that come later is limited; it may be too late to adjust and clarify the original message.

Telephone conversations provide immediate feedback in the form of questions, comments, tone of voice, pauses, hesitation, and so on. Face-to-face communication situations provide all this plus other, nonverbal feedback in facial expression, body movement, and posture.

Hard-Copy Availability.   Whether or not a permanent record of the message is *normally* retained is another media characteristic. Ordinarily, interviews, informal conversation, and telephone messages leave no record. (Of course, these can be recorded, but that is not routine practice in most organizations.) E-mail messages can be printed easily but otherwise do not leave a hard copy. Written communications such as letters, reports, and most memos are often maintained on file. An informal note, however, may be discarded and therefore is usually a nonrecord medium. A nonrecord medium can have distinct advantages where candid expression off the record is called for. Putting the message in writing seems to make it more formal or official, a situation that may also call for less openness in expression.

Message Intensity and Complexity.   Some media are more appropriate for conveying complex or highly intense messages. A high-intensity message may be one that conveys unpleasant information or in some way plays on the receiver's emotions. Persuasive messages that require careful explanation of underlying reasoning are often best communicated by a medium that can carry complex data in a relatively structured format. Typically, a formal letter, a carefully planned oral presentation, or a written report would be best. Casual conversation or a brief memo would be less appropriate.

> *Putting it in writing seems to increase the formality of a message.*

Formality.   Some media are more appropriate for formal occasions, and others fit well in informal settings. A letter of congratulations to an employee seems more formal and has a rather different effect from, say, a casual, unplanned remark conveying the same information. The letter makes it official. On the other hand, a handwritten note, sent to the board of directors by a worker may be considered out of line. When the message is intended for internal consumption only (within the "family"), its format may be less formal than if it were to be publicly disseminated outside the organization.

Be Aware of the Relative Costs of Media

One further media characteristic is especially important in the business organization: costs. The cost of communicating is not easily calculated, but it clearly affects an organization's profit picture.

Many different costs should be considered in media comparisons. Usually, the highest expenditures are people costs—the wages and benefits paid to employees. There are also *technical* costs, such as paper, postage, copies, word processing equipment, E-mail networks, telephones, and videotape players. A simple face-to-face conversation between two executives involves no technical cost but considerable people cost.

The cost of sending a simple, dictated business letter today is estimated at over $9. This estimate includes technical and people costs but does not reflect unusual expenses, such as mistakes that require redoing the letter and the misuse of expensive office machinery, all of which can run the cost of a letter up to $15 or $20. Responding to such letters more than doubles the costs, so that internal letters and memos can sap organizational resources. The most expensive cost of all—the cost of *ineffective* letters that backfire, as a result of either a wrong medium choice or poor quality—is not calculated into any of these estimates. These *real* costs can only be guessed.

Figure 3-2 summarizes the characteristics and relative costs of 11 commonly used media.

Consider Media Mixing: A Sound Alternative

Communicators are certainly not limited to the use of a single medium, although many seem tied to the conventional ways "it's always been done."

Media	Fast/ Slow	Feedback (High/Low)	Record (High/Low)	Formal/ Informal	Inside/ Outside	Complex/ Simple	Cost (High/Low)
Informal conversation	*Fast*	*High*	Nonrecord	*Informal*	Either	Simple	Low
Telephone conversation	*Fast*	*Medium*	Nonrecord	*Informal*	Either	Simple	Low-Medium
Formal oral presentation	Medium	*High*	Nonrecord	*Formal*	Either	Medium	Medium
Informal note	Medium	Low	Nonrecord	*Informal*	Either	Simple	Low
Memo	Medium	Low	*Record*	*Informal*	*Inside*	Medium	Medium-High
Electronic mail	*Fast*	Low-Medium	Record	Informal	Inside	Medium	Medium-High
Directive	Slow	Low	*Record*	*Formal*	*Inside*	Medium	Medium
Fax	*Fast*	Low	Record	Either	Either	Medium	Medium
Letter	Slow	Low	*Record*	Formal	*Outside*	Complex	Medium
Formal report	Very slow	Low	*Record*	Very formal	Inside	*Complex*	High

Note: Italicized items are the specific biases that would ordinarily cause a communicator to choose that medium for his or her message.

FIGURE 3-2 Some characteristics and costs of managerial communication media.

Often a combination of several media does the job very nicely. Disadvantages of one medium can be made up by another. For example, the slow feedback characteristic of written media can be offset by accompanying the message with an oral medium. Figure 3-3 suggests some ways to combine commonly used media to offset such disadvantages.

Studies of the effects of combining media have produced rather confused results, primarily because it is difficult to keep all extraneous variables—especially nonverbal cues—constant. We cannot absolutely control what message receivers pay attention to and derive meaning from. Nevertheless, some tentative findings have emerged.

In experiments, specific factual information was transmitted using each of the following media or combinations of media:

♦ Oral only
♦ Written only

FIGURE 3-3   Combining media for effectiveness.

Medium	*Major Limitations*	*Supplemental Media*
Informal conversation	no record; deals with simple messages	informal note to acknowledge; additional written information to clarify complex topics
Telephone conversation	little nonverbal feedback; no record	informal conversation; memo or note to confirm; tape conversation
Formal oral presentation	preparation time; no record	written report of briefing (outline format) to follow up
Informal note	low feedback; deals with simple messages	telephone or conversation follow-up
Memo	low feedback	telephone or conversation follow-up
Directive	preparation time; low feedback	meeting or presentation to amplify and get feedback
Letter	preparation time and cost; low feedback	telephone follow-up to test for understanding

- ◆ Posted on a bulletin board
- ◆ The grapevine (no formal message sent)
- ◆ Both oral and written

Several days after the messages were sent, the recipients were tested to see how much content they could accurately remember. The results consistently showed that the written-plus-oral message combination resulted in the greatest retention. The oral exchange alone was second in effectiveness, followed by a written message, the bulletin board, and finally the grapevine.[4]

In another study[5], supervisors were asked to rate the effectiveness of (1) written, (2) oral, (3) written and then oral, and (4) oral and then written communication for different types of situations. In general, the oral-followed-by-written technique came out best. Supervisors saw it as most effective for situations that required immediate action, passed along a company directive or order, communicated an important policy change, reviewed work progress, called for praising a noteworthy employee, or promoted a safety campaign. The written-only technique was judged best for passing along information that required action in the future or was of a general nature. An oral-only message was suggested for reprimands or to settle a dispute among employees.[6]

Understand Media Expectations

One final point about media is that people come to expect certain types of messages to be communicated via certain media. Although these expectations differ in various organizations, habits of communicating do develop and become the norm.

To give extra impact to a message, a manager may want to use a different medium or different combination of media. If, for example, a change in work schedule is normally posted on a bulletin board, a supervisor may get better audience attention by calling a meeting or talking with each worker individually about an unusual change. Similarly, a letter sent to a worker's home will have a very different impact than will a general public address system announcement. Creativity, a consideration of media characteristics, and some educated guesses about likely effects of messages provide the manager with some real opportunities to develop an interesting and effective media mix.

TOOLS OF THE MANAGER-COMMUNICATOR

Developing creativity and communication innovation starts with a look at what's being done now. In the following pages, a number of communication tools used to promote organizational functioning and health are described. After reviewing well over one hundred internal communication tools, we have developed a classification system based on what seems to be the *primary intent* of messages generally conveyed with particular tools. These categories are:

1. Tools used to convey work directives, specific policy, and other job-related information. These are used primarily for downward communication.
2. Tools used to keep members informed of general organizational matters and provide them with for your information messages which may be of interest but not specifically necessary to their jobs.
3. Tools which develop organizational identification and loyalty. These are used to create employee pride and a sense of loyalty to the organization.
4. Tools which provide upward feedback to higher management.
5. Tools which tend to build stronger interpersonal relationships on the individual level.

Here are some examples of tools in each of these categories. This listing represents popular usage, not necessarily the optimum use of communication tools. Many of these are discussed in depth in other chapters of this book.

Tools to Convey Job-Related Information

Information that organization members must have to be effective, such as work directives and policy clarification, is frequently conveyed downward via tools such as these:

♦ *Introduction or orientation programs for new employees*
♦ *Published job descriptions*
♦ *Procedure or policy manuals*
♦ *Bulletins* (Brief announcements of something that has just happened or is about to happen, transmitted orally or via a written handout, are especially useful in "clearing the air" and stopping counterproductive rumors.)

- *Instructional interviews or briefings*
- *Performance reviews*
- *Conferences and meetings*
- *Training activities* (including on-the-job training)
- *Bulletin boards*
- *Newsletters, in-house magazines*
- *Maps or floor plans* (to direct people around the organization's plant)
- *Company reference libraries*
- *Written reports*
- *Benefits statements* (individual accountings of the value of an employee's benefit package)
- *Reprints of technical articles*
- *Subscriptions* (to magazines or journals that provide job-related information)
- *Tuition aid programs* (to provide additional job-related training)
- *Visits* (to other locations or other organizations to gather information on procedures)

Tools to Convey "For-Your-Information" Messages

For-your-information tools convey messages that are likely to be of some interest but are not crucial to the job functions of employees. These serve to keep organization members in tune.

- *Announcement folders* (used to explain personnel changes, promotions, appointments, etc.)
- *Information/reading racks* (stocked with pamphlets, how-to booklets, and magazines or journals on varying topics)
- *Bulletin boards*

Tools to Build and Strengthen Organizational Identification and Loyalty

Organizational identification and loyalty can be built by the creative use of communication tools such as these:

- *Anniversary books* (Such a book emphasizes the history and growth of the organization to convey a sense of tradition and pride. Pictures of employees are often included.)
- *Auto windshield decals, bumper stickers, or license plates*
- *Directories of employees or members* (with brief biographical sketches)
- *Open houses or family nights* (programs including tours of the plant, exhibits, demonstrations, samples, and refreshments)

◆ *Alumni or retiree activities* (systematic visits, banquets, picnics, and explanations of any changes in retirement benefits; maintaining retirees' mailing lists for company publications and annual directory of names and addresses so they can keep in touch. Many companies are also developing preretirement orientation and planning programs. Such an attitude of caring is not lost on present employees who someday will join the ranks of the retired.)

◆ *Get-well cards*

◆ *Oral and written recognitions*

◆ *Informal conversations*

◆ *Social get-togethers such as picnics and Christmas parties*

◆ *Sports or other activities*

◆ *Contests* (competition in art, photography, games or puzzles, writing—including slogans, captions for cartoons, essays, letters, model making, and, of course, sales)

◆ *Letters and cards* (sympathy, birthday, anniversary, congratulatory, etc.)

◆ *Recreational and social activities* (such as athletic leagues, picnics, and outings)

◆ *Uniforms, coveralls, hardhats, name badges, marked with company logo*

◆ *Design and appearance of work areas*

◆ *Samples or discounts on company products*

◆ *Tuition aid programs*

◆ *Training programs* (not limited to on-the-job skills, but personal and self-improvement too)

◆ *Displays and exhibits* (photos, artwork, videotape, or slide presentations accompanied by dramatic lighting and sound effects on subjects such as company history, company products, or statistical data regarding employees, management, and stockholders. Occasionally a display can be used to highlight a special problem. One company exhibited examples of broken TV sets and crushed cartons to provide dramatic evidence of results of mishandled shipping. To illustrate a theme of traffic safety, wrecked cars and mock graveyards have been used in exhibits.)

Tools to Convey Upward Feedback

Upward feedback tools provide for communication from subordinates to management.

◆ *Advisory councils on human relations* or similarly named groups provide management with feedback on employee concerns. (Employees, usually elected, serve as representatives of their departments for the purpose of better communication between all organizational levels.)

◆ *Observations* (preferably systematic observation by trained communication observers, primarily of nonverbal indicators

- *Electronic monitoring*
- *Attitude surveys*
- *Grievance interviews* (informal or via formal procedures)
- *Grapevine messages*
- *Employee focus groups to discuss concerns*
- *Exit interviews*
- *Junior board of directors programs* (where promising subordinates are given an opportunity to identify, research, and recommend strategies for solving organizational problems)
- *Readership surveys* (for company publications)
- *Reports and analyses of employee and management concerns*
- *Suggestion systems*
- *Communication audits*

Tools to Strengthen Interpersonal Relationships Within the Organization

Interpersonal relationships on the individual level can be strengthened via communication tools such as these:

- *Counseling interviews*
- *Announcements of personnel changes, accomplishments*
- *Cards sent to others on birthdays, holidays, or to mark special events for the employee or members of the employee's family*
- *Booklets* (containing subjects such as health and safety, inspirational and self-improvement topics, how-to-do-it materials)
- *Company libraries*
- *Classes or lectures* (may be on non-job-related topics such as handicrafts and self-development)
- *Company advertising awareness programs* (inform employees of upcoming promotions)
- *Posters, bulletins*
- *Letters and memos* (letters may be sent to the home rather than work location for greater impact)
- *Distribution of union contracts*
- *Visits, trips to other plants or organizations*
- *Videotape presentations* (Some companies tape a question and answer session between rank and file employees and top executives for showing in all locations. Employee questioners are free to ask about any topic).
- *Answer line columns* (in organizational publications to address employee questions or concerns)

- *Newsletters or organizational magazines*
- *Progress reports* (covering topics such as new product acceptance, plant mechanization, and civic involvement programs).

These listings represent only a sample of tools often used in organizations to communicate and create understanding. Many of the tools just described are, of course, prepared by specialized departments within an organization such as advertising, employee relations, human resources, or employee communications.

Nevertheless, the individual manager retains an important communication responsibility for determining which tools can best meet the needs of his or her organization. Such decisions should be based, not on habits of use, but on sound consideration of media characteristics, costs, and appropriateness in given situations.

A QUICK SUMMARY OF MAJOR IDEAS

- A communication medium can be viewed as a generally accepted set of ground rules for structuring and receiving messages. These ground rules play a large part in determining the medium's effectiveness in a given situation.
- Characteristics inherent in a given medium should be considered when selecting that medium. Among the salient characteristics are *speed, feedback capability, hard copy availability, message complexity, need for formality, and relative cost.*
- The media, methods, or approaches we choose when communicating can enhance or detract from our communication success.
- Communication efficiency is a simple ratio between the total costs of a message and the number of people reached by that message.
- Communication effectiveness is determined by the degree to which a message is *received by the intended audience, interpreted* correctly, *remembered* for a reasonable period of time, and used when appropriate occasions arise.
- Mixing several media can offset the disadvantages of one of them, resulting in more effective communication.
- A wide range of communication tools are available to the manager.

QUESTIONS FOR FURTHER THOUGHT

1. Describe in your own words the dilemma of communication efficiency versus communication effectiveness. Why don't we always use individual, personal media?
2. What kinds of messages can or should be transmitted by the most efficient means? Give specific examples.
3. What kinds of messages require a high degree of effectiveness regardless of efficiency? Give specific examples.

4. Recall an experience you have had in which an inappropriate medium or tool was used to convey an important message to you. Describe what happened in the form of a short case or critical incident description.

OTHER THOUGHTS ABOUT COMMUNICATION MEDIA AND TOOLS

MAKING THE MOST OF VOICE MAIL
By Carma Wadley, Deseret-News features editor

Mention voice mail, and you're liable to hear a few groans and a few stories about people who got lost in the system or totally frustrated by trying to reach a live person.

But voice mail is one of the most effective forms of business communication in the country, according to a new survey conducted by the Voice Messaging Educational Committee. The survey found that 89 percent of mailbox owners surveyed found voice mail to be an important medium for business communications, and 78 percent reported that voice mail improved their job productivity.

At the same time, voice mail can pose problems for callers. According to the survey, callers were most critical of the inability to reach a "live" person on demand. Another major caller complaint was confusing, poorly designed instructions that make callers navigate through multiple menus of options.

However, despite these concerns, many callers prefer voice mail over alternatives. Nearly 60 percent of the respondents said they prefer leaving recorded voice messages to leaving messages with administrative assistants or receptionists. Similarly, 78 percent preferred leaving detailed voice mail messages over holding for an operator or hanging up and calling back later.

But, whether you're a voice mailbox owner or a voice mail user, there are some things you can do to maximize the effectiveness of this tool. Here are some tips from the Voice Messaging Educational Committee:

FOR MAILBOX OWNERS:

Having a voice mailbox shouldn't change what your job entails, but it does mean looking at new ways of doing your job. The standard rules of business etiquette haven't changed: You simply need to apply them to how and when you use voice mail.

Most subscribers use voice mail to answer the telephone when they are not available. The most important consideration is to help the people who call feel comfortable leaving messages.

♦ Update your personal greeting regularly. Callers say they feel most comfortable leaving a message when the greeting conveys the subscriber's current status. It's best to record a new greeting on a daily basis, but if you can't do that, record a new greeting every Monday morning to let callers know your schedule for the week.

♦ In your greeting, let callers know when you'll return their call—for example, by 5 p.m. today or tomorrow—and stick to it.

♦ Include information in your greeting about how callers can reach a co-worker who can help them if you are not available. This is especially important if you are on vacation or away for an extended period of time.

♦ Tell your callers how they can easily reach someone "live" if their call is urgent—or if they prefer to leave a message with someone else.

♦ Make sure an operator or receptionist answers the line during standard business hours. His or her responsibility is to make sure callers get the assistance they need. Callers transfer to your receptionist for a reason—they should not be shunted into a second voice mailbox.

♦ If you will be away and not checking messages, let callers know. Tell them how to reach a colleague who is taking your calls.

♦ Check messages regularly, especially if you are out of the office and don't have a flashing light to remind you.

♦ Let callers know about the system and how they can use it to communicate with you. Tell your regular callers that your company is installing a system so they will be prepared.

♦ Answer your telephone when you're at your desk. Routinely screening calls is never proper business etiquette, and having a voice mailbox doesn't make it acceptable.

♦ Learn how to use the system yourself, to transfer callers into someone else's mailbox and to send messages throughout the system.

FOR CALLERS:

You will get your message across faster and better if you use guidelines that apply to everyday telephone etiquette.

♦ **If your call is urgent or you need assistance immediately, try pressing 0.** In many cases this will get you to an operator or receptionist.

♦ **Don't get trapped.** If you seem to fall into an endless cycle of menus, press 0 or the designated keys on your telephone to reach someone who can help. If that doesn't work, hang up and call back, pressing keys that get you to the operator immediately. Still no luck? Send a letter of complaint to the president of the company.

♦ **Record an effective message.** Explain why you are calling and when you need a response. Then the person can provide you with this information in their return call. Keep your message succinct and to the point.

♦ **Let the person know when it's best to call you back.** If you know you'll be in meetings from 1 until 3, ask for a call between 3 and 5. Take different time zones into consideration. Let the recipient know if it's convenient to leave a detailed message in your mailbox.

♦ **If you need information, give details.** Leave your name, full address, telephone number or fax number. Speak slowly.

♦ **If you get a receptionist and want voice mail, ask.** The person who answers your call should be able to transfer you into the system to leave a message.

Source: Reprinted from *Deseret News,* July 12, 1993, p. C1. Used with permission.

OTHER THOUGHTS ABOUT COMMUNICATION MEDIA AND TOOLS
▼

CONVERSATION WITH AL GORE
WHITE HOUSE VISION

On technological change. There's no question that this cluster of technologies will have a revolutionizing effect comparable to or exceeding the effects of any technological revolution in history, including invention of the printing press, the invention of the steam engine, or perhaps even the invention of written communication. We're enmeshed in the early stages of the transition, and it's quite difficult to perceive exactly what the nature of that impact will be. Marshall McLuhan popularized the idea that human thinking is organized in ways that accommodate the contours of the prevailing medium through which information is communicated. Something for which we do not yet have a name will emerge from these high-capacity networks—indeed, many somethings for which we do not have names. They will transform the way we communicate with one another, the way we work together, the way we perceive the world.

On the role of government. The linking of these unbelievably powerful devices during the next decade will require difficult political and social choices. But those choices must and will be made. We're making them right now. We have weekly meetings right here in this office and elsewhere in the White House to identify and pursue the best options. Government will play a catalyzing role and will set the standards and protocols to ensure interconnection and compatibility and universal access. Virtually all of the leading-edge discoveries in this field have come with government support, and government will continue to stimulate investments in the cutting-edge technologies that are beyond the investment horizons of the private sector.

The impact on citizenship. The object is not simply to create a zillion-channel cable-TV capacity. It is to empower the American people with interactive, multiway networks that allow the emergence of all these new services and products that we can't yet imagine. In a real sense, the printing press made possible the modern nation-state and representative democracy by giving citizens of a large geographic area enough civic knowledge to participate in decision making. If the printing press did that, then how much richer in spirit can our country be if our people are empowered with the knowledge that these high-capacity computer networks can distribute? It's a very exciting prospect.

Source: U.S. News & World Report, December 6, 1993.

NOTES

1. Adapted from Paul R. Timm, Supervision, 2nd ed. (St. Paul, MN: West Publishing Company, 1992), p. 188.

2. Richard Hatch, Communicating in Business (Chicago: Science Research Associates, 1977), p. 96.

3. Saul W. Gellerman, The Management of Human Resources, (Hinsdale, IL: Dryden Press, 1976), p. 61.

4. Ibid., p. 62.

5. T. L. Dahle, "An Objective and Comparative Study of Five Methods of Transmitting Information to Business and Industrial Employees," Speech Monographs, 21, 1954, pp. 21–28.

6. D. A. Level, "Communication Effectiveness: Method and Situation," Journal of Business Communication, Fall 1972, pp. 19–25.

CHAPTER 4

INTRAPERSONAL COMMUNICATION

The Voices Within

▼

In this chapter you will find ideas that will help you:

♦ Understand how the mental processes of attitudes, perceptions, and disclosure affect the way we deal with people and the world around us

♦ Describe the process of perception and explain why managers need to understand it

♦ Explain the perception/truth fallacy and how it can lead to mistaken assumptions

♦ Recognize some of the factors that affect the ways we perceive things

♦ Explain how ethical standards color our perceptions and attitudes

♦ Determine your own tendencies to be high or low in self-disclosure

♦ Understand the internal communication that goes on within your mind and its affects on attitudes and perception

♦ Recognize typical patterns of distorted perception

▼

Meet Sally and Jane, both assembly workers at Buffalo Chips Corporation (BCC), a high-technology producer of electronic circuits for microcomputers. The management at BCC has been pretty sensitive to employee needs and has made every effort to provide a pleasant working environment, good pay, and adequate benefits.

Sally sees her job as a real lifesaver. Her husband Jack is a rookie policeofficer, and her income really helps her family make ends meet. Though Sally's daily activity on the job is repetitious, she has developed a close friendship with other workers around her, and the time passes quickly as they work.

"This company's been good to me," she says. "Before I started here, I was constantly worried about our budget. And I felt that the skills I had were just being wasted. But this job is a good outlet for my skills—I'm pretty good with my hands—and a real growth experience."

Overall, Sally is a contented worker and has a positive attitude toward Buffalo Chips Corporation.

On the other hand, there's Jane. She's been with the company as long as Sally, but her attitude toward BCC is quite different.

"Working here is a real rip-off. I put in eight hours a day making chips that BCC sells for millions, and you know what I make—a lousy $213 a week take-home. Have you ever sat at a shop table doing the same thing over and over for eight hours a day, five days a week, fifty weeks a year? It'll drive you nuts! And my only diversion is the two old ladies across from my bench. They're constantly talking about their families—'My son Stanley'—or their church group or some such stuff. It drives me up a wall. I usually just tune them out. I have enough problems of my own without listening to their sob stories.

Fortunately, I'm only here temporarily. I have a real shot at becoming an actress. In fact, next week they're auditioning for summer stock theater and I'm perfect for one of the parts. I acted some in high school, you know. Was pretty good, too.

Anyway, I'll put up with this crummy company just long enough to get me to the Big Apple or California. Then I'll start living. No more Buffalo Chips for this gal."

Sally and Jane. Same job, same company but very different attitudes toward their work. Could these two people really be working in the same place?[1]

In Chapter 1, we discussed the various levels of communication readily apparent in organizations. Among these levels is one that is often taken for granted—largely ignored. That is intrapersonal communication, or that which takes place within the minds of individuals. We communicate intrapersonally when we mentally process information and glean meaning from it.

A number of personal characteristics shape the way this information processing is accomplished. Among the more critical factors are:

- ♦ Our attitudes
- ♦ Our perception skills
- ♦ Our self-concept and disclosure habits
- ♦ Our personal authenticity and internal communication

ATTITUDES AND INTRAPERSONAL COMMUNICATION

We often use the term *attitude* to refer to a person's outlook on life in general or on his or her job, school, family, and so forth. But let's take a moment and work out a more precise definition.

> *An attitude is a mental state that can cause a person to respond in a certain way to a stimulus.*

An attitude is described by psychologists as a mental state that can cause a person to respond in a characteristic manner to a given stimulus.

Some key characteristics of attitudes are that:

1. They are formed in our minds. They do not necessarily reflect reality.

2. We organize our attitudes through the experiences we've had. Since we all have unique experiences, we likewise have unique attitudes.

3. Attitudes shape our behavior as we respond to stimuli.

What Does This Have to Do with Managerial Communication?

Professor Elwood Chapman has been studying attitudes for more than forty years. He calls attitude "your most priceless possession" and encourages us to understand the mental process that creates the attitudes we hold as well as the effects attitudes have on our lives. Here are some things he teaches about attitudes:

1. On the surface, attitude is the way you communicate your mood to others. When you are optimistic and anticipate successful encounters, you transmit a positive attitude and people usually respond favorably. When you are pessimistic and expect the worst, your attitude often is negative; and people tend to avoid you. Inside your head, where it all starts, attitude is a mind set. *It is the way you look at things mentally.*

2. Think of attitude as your mental focus on the outside world. Like using a camera, you can focus or set your mind on what appeals to you. You can see situations as either opportunities or failures. A cold winter day as either beautiful or ugly. A departmental meeting as interesting or boring. It is within your power to concentrate on selected aspects of your environment and ignore others. Quite simply, you take the picture of life you want to take.

> *You choose how to respond to your world.*

3. Emphasizing the positive and diffusing the negative is like using a magnifying glass. You can place the glass over good news and feel better, or you can magnify bad news and make yourself miserable. Magnifying situations can become a habit. If you continually focus on difficult situations, the result will be exaggerated distortions of problems.

4. Attitude is never static. It is an on-going dynamic, sensitive, perceptual process. Unless you are on constant guard, negative factors can slip into your perspective. This will cause you to spend "mind time" on difficulties rather than opportunities.

5. If negative factors stay around long enough, they will be reflected in your disposition. The positive is still there, but it has been overshadowed by the negative. It is a challenge to push the negative factors to the outer perimeter of your thinking. Those who learn this "trick" will reflect it, and others will notice.

6. Of course, no one can be positive all of the time. Excessive optimism—like Pollyanna in the novels by Eleanor Porter—is not realistic. Friends and business associates will probably feel it is plastic. After all, a positive attitude is not an act; it must be genuine. Sometimes, when things get really tough, a positive attitude may be impossible or even inappropriate.

7. When things are going well, a positive attitude becomes self-reinforcing and easy to maintain. Being human, however, ensures that something will always happen to test your positive mind set. Some person or situation is always on the horizon to step on your attitude and challenge your ability to bounce back.

8. Winners are those who can regain their positive attitudes quickly. Individuals who are unable to bounce back and who drag out or dwell excessively on misfortune miss out on much of what life has to offer.

9. A positive outlook provides the courage to address a problem and take action to resolve it before it gets out of hand. Refusing to become angry or distraught can motivate you to assemble the facts, talk to others, determine your options, and then come up with the best solution. Even if there is no ideal solution, your attitude can help you live with the problem more gracefully, which will help neutralize its negative impact.

10. It may sound like an oversimplification to say you see what you want to see. Yet some individuals see beauty in a wilderness area; others do not. Some can turn a business problem into an opportunity. A few see the good that others cannot in a child, friend, supervisor, or situation. To a considerable degree, the camera is in your hands, and you see what you decide to see.[2]

Attitudes, then, arise from the ways we filter information and draw conclusions about the world around us. But before we filter information, we must perceive it, and perception is another internal communication process that is unique to each of us.

OUR PERCEPTION SKILLS

> *Perception is the way we make sense of our experiences.*

Perception is a mental process by which we take sensory stimuli (sights, sounds, smells, tastes, etc.) and attach meanings to them. It is the way we make sense out of what we experience. As we receive perceptions through seeing, hearing, feeling, tasting, and smelling, we mentally organize these sensations into something that has meaning for us. The phrase "for us" is important, because no two people perceive things in exactly the same way.

An Example of the Perception Process

Let's visualize ourselves walking down a busy city sidewalk. We see that a crowd of people is assembled near an intersection. As we get closer we hear unusual sounds—the rhythm of steel drums. Eventually, we assemble these sights and

sounds and attach meaning—there is a street band playing Jamaican music as an advertising gimmick for a travel agency. We smile and pass by.

> **We perceive when we mentally organize impressions and label them.**

First came the attention to raw information—sights and sounds. Then we mentally organized these impressions into a meaningful event and labeled it "Jamaican street band." That's perception.

Perceptions Are Not Always Accurate

Perception does not always yield truth. We can be fooled. Suppose our sensory processing was affected by our experience. Suppose you were an undercover cop and you knew of a gang of thieves that used a Jamaican band as a way of diverting attention so they could rob a nearby jewelry store. Or what if you confused the band with solicitors for a religious cult with whom you vigorously disagree? Would you still smile and walk by? Would you

> **Our perceptions are affected by our experience and are not always true.**

perceive the event in the same way? Probably not. And that fact leads to a major point: Be careful not to confuse *perceptions* with *truth*.

Beware of the Perception/Truth Fallacy

People have a strong tendency to believe that the way they see the world is closer to the truth than the way others see it. Some of us assume that people who see things differently than we do are wrong. This assumption can lead to misunderstandings, conflict, and embarrassing mistakes.

How Misperceptions Lead to Embarrassing Mistakes

Visualize this situation: You walk into the machine shop of your small and not very profitable manufacturing company. The place is quiet. Only three people are there. One man is sitting on a bench next to his machine, leaning against the wall. He has a blank look on his face. Another employee is fixing a child's bicycle. The third person is talking on the phone to someone he addresses as "Honey." It is 9:30 a.m. on a Tuesday. What do your immediate impressions tell you about this scene?

Write out two or three conclusions you could draw from this brief description.

Since this book is about management communication, you may have drawn conclusions from a management perspective. Many readers of this description respond this way:

"A bunch of goof-offs working there." "I'll bet their supervisor is away. I'd probably fire them if they worked for me!" "No wonder the company isn't very profitable."

Perhaps your perceptions are accurate. But if you act on this picture of reality without performing further investigation, you could be making a big mistake.

Here is what was really happening in that machine shop. The first employee had worked all night to get out a special rush order, an order that will result in a major profit increase for the company. He hadn't slept in over 26 hours and was taking a 15-minute break. The man on the phone had also been at work through the night. This was the first chance he's had to call his wife to see how their sick four-year-old daughter was responding to some new medication. The third worker was taking time on his normal day off to work on the company-sponsored Toys for Kids Christmas project.

> *Don't be too quick to draw conclusions based on first impressions. You may end up with egg on your face.*

Does that change your perceptions of this scene a bit? What might have happened if you had just been appointed as a new supervisor and you'd ordered everyone back to work?

> *An optimist may see a light where there is none, but why must the pessimist always run to blow it out?*
> *Michel DeSaint Pierre*

Don't take initial perceptions at face value. Get as much information as possible before you translate your perceptions into opinions that will influence your actions. A good way to avoid such misperceptions is to understand better how each of us perceives and how we engage in this process of making sense out of stimuli around us.

The Problem of Perceptual Expectancy

Magicians use it to fool people. Teachers and other professional communicators use it to preview the messages they give us. Advertisers use it to lure us into the new car showroom. *Perceptual expectancy* is the mental anticipation we experience in our everyday actions. We constantly make mental guesses about how people, events, or things will be. Sometimes we are right. Other times we are wrong. And sometimes we are deliberately misled.

> *Perceptual expectancy is the mental anticipation of future events, our guesses about what is about to happen.*

Look at the picture in Figure 4-1. Can you see the old woman? Now look again to see a young woman. Our suggestion that you'll see either an old or a young woman will create different perceptual expectations.

> *Perceptual expectations influence the way we get along with others and how we respond to them.*

The expectations that result from our perceptions influence the way we get along with others and how we respond to them.

Perceptual expectations cause us to anticipate future behaviors or events. Suppose that you work in a store where a new manager is scheduled to take over next week. The scuttlebutt has it that he has a reputation for being very energetic, very autocratic, out to make money, cold, and standoffish. We bet you can hardly wait to meet him, right? Our guess is that most people who were to be managed by this person would feel some anxiety. Their perceptual expectancy would help create a mental anticipation of a leader who would be pretty hard to work for.

What would happen if, when the new manager took over, his demeanor, behavior, and treatment of the employees was exactly the opposite of their expectations? It's likely that the workers would be a little uncomfortable. Their expectations would *not* be met. "When is he going to get mean?" they might ask. Unmet expectations (both negative or positive) can be confusing.

FIGURE 4-1   **What do you see?**

OTHER FACTORS AFFECTING OUR PERCEPTIONS AND ATTITUDES

Experience

We interpret events in the light of similar experiences we've had in the past. If your experience tells you that people smile at you because they want to flirt, you'll respond differently than if you have seen past smiles as nonsexual, friendly gestures.

Assumptions about the Way People Are

We all hold certain views of human nature. If you honestly believe that people are basically lazy and do as little work as possible or that, despite past criminal records, people can usually be trusted, your perceptions are affected by your beliefs. In addition, we often seek out examples that confirm what we assume about people. We love to tell ourselves, "I told you so."

Personal Moods

All people experience a wide range of moods. The moods affecting us at a given moment can influence our perceptions. For example, if you've just had a disagreement with another person, it can sour your outlook—and the way you see the world around you—for hours or even days.

Self-Concept: Assumptions about Me

The assumptions we hold about ourselves can affect the ways we perceive. A healthy self-concept is a realistic perception of one's self. It recognizes strengths, accomplishments, and positive attributes. But it also recognizes and intelligently deals with weaknesses, limitations, and failures. (We all have lots of each of these!) A healthy, realistic picture of our strengths helps us assume the best from others: a realistic picture of our limitations helps us recognize that no one is superhuman, at least not all the time. Our perceptions of others are more sensible when our self-concept is reasonable.

> *A healthy self-concept is one's realistic perception of strengths and weaknesses.*

Ethical Standards

Our notions of what is right and fair, or wrong and unjust, color our perceptions and attitudes. People who have a clear set of ethical standards have the advantage in building a strong-self-concept and positive attitudes.

Management writer Kenneth Blanchard and personal motivation expert Norman Vincent Peale say that

...ethical behavior is related to self-esteem. We both believe that people who feel good about themselves have what it takes to withstand outside pressure and to do what is right rather than do what is merely expedient, popular, or lucrative. We believe that a strong code of morality in any business is the first step toward success. We believe that ethical managers are winning managers.[3]

The ability to maintain an objective focus and not have perceptions distorted by outside pressure is a powerful tool. It helps one create confidence in one's ability and reduces self-doubt.

"People with self-doubt usually don't like themselves very much and they don't trust their own judgment. As a result, they are driven by a desire to be liked and accepted by others."[4] The result: distorted perception and unproductive attitudes.

OUR SELF-CONCEPT AND DISCLOSURE HABITS

Self-concept can be described simply as the mental picture a person holds of his or her self. It is closely involved with attitudes and feelings people have about themselves. If we dwell on our shortcomings (things we can't do very well), we are likely to feel inferior to others. If we have an unrealistically positive self-concept (I can fly; I am invincible!), we are likely to face a rude run-in with reality.

> **Authenticity is key to a healthy self-concept.**

Psychologists encourage people to strive for *authenticity*, the realistic understanding that we all have strengths and weaknesses, assets and liabilities. The authentic person has mastered self-acceptance. He or she no longer wastes psychic energy playing roles that are unrealistic. It's exhausting to act as if we were someone or something we are not.

Understanding our self-concept is important because doing so not only affects us psychologically, but also causes us to anticipate and react to others in different ways. For example, if we feel unsure about our ability to handle an oral presentation, it is quite likely that we will expect others to view us as doing poorly. On the positive side, if we have a strong self-concept—a healthy assessment of our ability to do a task—it can give us additional confidence and willingness to take certain risks.

How Positive Self-Concept Can Affect Work Results

Research has shown that one's self-concept can actually affect one's future behavior. If we realistically expect to be successful at something (because we have an authentic, positive self-concept), the likelihood is much greater that we *will* be successful. Likewise, if a low self-concept causes us to expect to fail, the probability of failure is greatly increased. This self-fulfilling prophecy has been shown to be a powerful influence in people's lives.

> *Our expectations of others can affect their behaviors.*

Another important consideration for supervisors is this: our expectations of others can also affect their behavior. In a sense, we can project a self-concept to others by expressing what we think they can or cannot do. Quite often people will live up to or down to our expectations.

We Reveal Our Self-Concepts and Attitudes to Others

Disclosure, or more accurately self-disclosure, is the degree to which we as individuals reveal our attitudes and feelings to others. We've already said that people's behaviors often mirror their attitudes. But, to varying degrees, people also express those attitudes vocally.

Some people are very open and expressive about how they feel. Others are far more hesitant to express feelings and opinions. Undoubtedly we can go too far in either direction. The person with a very low self-disclosure (the person who has a tough time expressing feelings) tends to leave other individuals in the dark. Those people don't exactly know what that person is thinking, which can, if that person is in a management position, create ambiguity for employees. The person who is very high in self-disclosure (speaks his or her mind openly) may run the risk of being offensive to other individuals. Sometimes we can say too much.

Evidence indicates that healthy, effective interpersonal relationships develop when there is *constructive* disclosure. The more open you are with someone else, the more open the other person will tend to be with you. Two people who share with each other their reactions to an experience are often drawn together. Giving and receiving feedback tends to lead people to more productive and useful relationships with each other. If you do not know how others feel and how much they are reacting to events, you will not be of much help to those people. Likewise, if you are too hesitant to disclose your own feelings, others may not be able to help you and you may fail to gain the advantages of that closer relationship.

There are, of course, reasonable limits to disclosure. Few people are interested in the most intimate feelings or fantasies of others, and people have limits on how much they can or will tell. In addition, it is usually a good idea for managers *not* to express their negative feelings toward management policies or about other people. The key word used in the following is *constructive*. Disclosure can reach a point where it is destructive to a relationship.

How You Can Tell if You Are High or Low in Self-Disclosure

Joseph Luft and Harrington Ingham developed a model called the Johari Window* that can help us understand our own disclosure tendencies. The Johari Window describes four areas: open, blind, hidden, and unknown (see Figure 4-2).

Open Area

Each of us has information that we know about ourselves and that is also known by others. We feel okay about sharing such information, attitudes, and feelings.

Blind Area

There is also information that others may know about us that we do not know about ourselves. Our habitual ways of reacting to certain things that our spouse or friends see, but we do not—the way the back of our head and some of our unconscious mannerisms look—may fall into this category. This unknown information is called our blind area.

Hidden Area

We all hold certain kinds of information that we know about ourselves, but because it refers to matters that are personal or sensitive, we do not want others to know about it. Everyone harbors some secrets that he or she would rather not discuss with others.

Unknown Area

Some information that we retain in our subconscious mind is obscured from both ourselves and others. This is the unknown area of the Johari Window.

Truly constructive relationships depend on the willingness of two or more persons to maintain fairly large open areas in which they share a great deal of

---

*They got the name Johari by combining their nicknames, Joe and Harry.

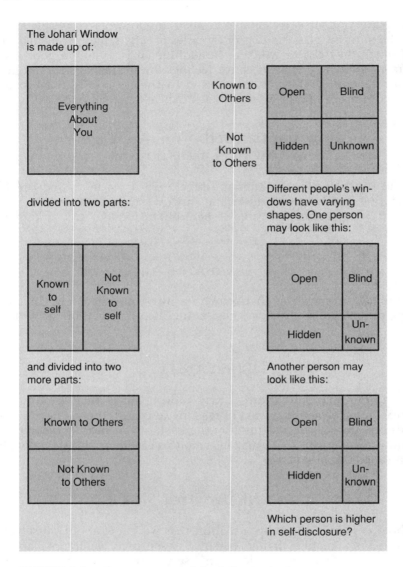

FIGURE 4-2   Components of the Johari window.

information about one another. The open area is made larger by providing supportive and useful feedback to others—honest reactions—that does not degrade or tear them down.

When we receive feedback from others, we can move information from our blind area (that which we are not aware of) to our open area by listening to and observing their reactions to us. When we give feedback, we move information from our hidden area into our open area. That is, we disclose information that others did not previously know about us. The person who has received feedback has decreased the dimensions of his or her blind area. When you disclose information from your hidden area, you give other people a better look into your attitudes and feelings.

Why Supportive Feedback Is So Important

Besides creating an open relationship, supportive feedback is useful for the following reasons:

- ◆ Supportive feedback develops from a desire to improve relationships with others because the relationships are recognized as important.
- ◆ Supportive feedback strives to create a shared understanding of a relationship so that both parties view the relationship from nearly the same perspective. Expectations are clarified.
- ◆ Supportive feedback recognizes that behaving in an open manner involves some risk of being rejected or hurt by the other person; thus, you retain the right to decide what you will reveal and what you will not reveal.

PERSONAL AUTHENTICITY AND INTERNAL COMMUNICATION[5]

Perception and attitude formation take place within our minds. There is a clear relationship between the messages we process in our minds and the world we create for ourselves. Our relationships with others depend largely on how we see the world.

Effective self-talk helps us be authentic—true to our true selves. Effective self-talk promotes helping us know who we are.

We recognize four phases in the quest for authenticity. We start the cyclical process by recognizing who we *really* are. In the first phase, the *identity* phase, we clarify our self-concepts, recognizing our strengths and shortcomings. We unconditionally accept ourselves despite any past mistakes or losses.

Next, we determine a course of action. We set goals and targets and establish a plan of action. Then we *do* what we've set out to do. With persistence and effort, we then progress into the *achieve* phase. Now, having had new and successful experiences, we find ourselves at a new starting point: the *new me*.

The cycle then repeats itself, propelling us to new plateaus. Underlying the process in our sense of authenticity—seeking ourselves and others realistically. Remember, others have their own cycles and they may differ from where you are right now. That is only natural and perfectly acceptable. We have no right to demand that others be different from what they are.

Vital to authenticity is admitting mistakes—not groveling in self-pity, remorse, or self-condemnation, but taking a realistic look at where we are now and how we got there.

In the novel *Lonesome Dove*, by Larry McMurtry, a great piece of dialogue occurs between the two lead cowboy characters, Gus McRae and Woodrow Call.

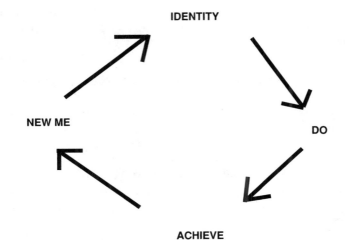

FIGURE 4-3   Personal authenticity cycle.

Call, the stereotypical strong, silent type, is a stoic leader, but almost totally lacking expressiveness—utterly incapable of voicing his emotions. McRae is his opposite, a frontier philosopher who likes nothing better than to "jaw" about almost anything. The difference between the two men leads to this conversation:

Gus: "You're so sure you're right it doesn't matter to you whether people talk to you or not. I'm glad I've been wrong enough to keep in practice."

Call: "Why would you want to keep in practice being wrong? I'd think it would be something you'd try to avoid."

Gus: "You can't avoid it, you've got to learn to handle it. If you only come face to face with your own mistakes once or twice in your life, it's bound to be painful. I face mine every day—that way, they ain't usually much worse than a dry shave."[6]

Past mistakes, real or imagined, are beyond our control. All people make mistakes, but while recognizing them and learning from them is imperative, dwelling on them is counterproductive.

A QUICK SUMMARY OF MAJOR IDEAS

- ◆ Intrapersonal communication is the creation of meaning that takes place within an individual's mind.

- ◆ Characteristics that affect intrapersonal communication include attitudes, perception skills, self-concept, disclosure habits, and our personal authenticity.

- ◆ Perception expectations lead to a mind set that causes us to anticipate future behaviors or events (sometimes inaccurately).

♦ Your interpretation of an event is influenced by
—Similar experiences
—Assumptions about the way people are
—Expectations of how things will be
—Knowledge of related events
—Personal moods
—Self-concept: assumptions about yourself

♦ Ethical standards affect our self-esteem and create a base for our attitudes.

♦ Disclosure is the degree to which people reveal their true attitudes and feelings to others.

♦ Authenticity comes from honest internal communication.

QUESTIONS FOR FURTHER THOUGHT

1. What is perception? Attitude? Disclosure?

2. Why is perception such an individual mental activity?

3. Is it possible for more than one person to have exactly the same perceptual experience? Why or why not?

4. What is meant by the perception/truth fallacy?

5. How can jumping to conclusions based on your individual, immediate perceptions result in embarrassing mistakes?

6. What are some attitudes that might influence your perceptions of the following events?

   A father slapping a three-year old child

   An order from your boss to unload a large truck load of canned goods

   A laser light show accompanying a rock concert

   A labor union leader's emotional speech on the excesses of big corporate executives

7. How might a person's self-concept affect their perceptions of other people? Give an example.

8. How can one's ethical standards affect self-esteem?

9. What are self-fulfilling expectations, and why are they important?

OTHER THOUGHTS ABOUT INTRAPERSONAL COMMUNICATION

SELF-CONCEPT AND
SELF-FULFILLING PROPHECIES ...[7]

The self-concept is such a powerful force on the personality that it not only determines how you see yourself in the present but can actually influence your future behavior and that of others. Such occurrences come about through a phenomenon called the self-fulfilling prophecy.

A self-fulfilling prophecy occurs when a person's expectation of an event makes the outcome more likely to occur than would otherwise have been true. Self-fulfilling prophecies occur all the time, although you might never have given them that label. For example, think of some instances you may have known.

♦ You expected to become nervous and botch a job interview and then did so.

♦ You anticipated having a good (or terrible) time at a social affair and found your expectations being met.

♦ A teacher or boss explained a new task to you, saying that you probably wouldn't do well at first. You did not do well.

♦ A friend described someone you were about to meet, saying that you wouldn't like the person. The prediction turned out to be correct—you didn't like the new acquaintance.

In each of these cases, there is a good chance that the event happened because it was predicted to occur. You needn't have botched the interview, the party might have been boring only because you helped make it so, you might have done better on the job if your boss hadn't spoken up, and you might have liked the new acquaintance if your friend hadn't given you preconceptions. In other words, what helped make each event occur was the expectation that it would happen.

There are two types of self-fulfilling prophecies. The first occurs when your own expectations influence your behavior. Like the job interview and the party described earlier, there are many times when an event that needn't have occurred does happen because you expect it to. In sports, you've probably psyched yourself into playing either better or worse than usual, so that the only explanation for your unusual performance was your own attitude. Similarly, you've probably faced an audience at one time or another with a fearful attitude and forgotten your remarks, not because you were unprepared, but because you said to yourself, "I know I'll blow it."

Certainly you've had the experience of waking up in a cross mood and saying to yourself, "This will be a bad day." Once you made such a decision, you may have acted in ways that made it come true. If you approached a class expecting to be bored, you most probably did lose interest, due partly to lack of attention on your part. If you avoided the company of others because you expected that they had nothing to offer, your suspicions would have been confirmed—nothing exciting or new happened. If you approached the same day with the idea that it had the potential to be a good one, this expectation probably would also have been met. Smile at people, and they'll probably smile back. Enter a class determined to learn something, and you probably will—even if it's how not to instruct students! Approach many people with the idea that some of them will be good to know, and you'll most likely make some new friends. In these cases and ones like them, your attitude has a great deal to do with how you see yourself and how others will see you.

A second type of self-fulfilling prophecy occurs when the expectations of one person govern another's actions. The classic example was demonstrated by Robert Rosenthal and Lenore Jacobson in a study they described in their book, *Pygmalion in the Classroom:*

> Twenty percent of the children in a certain elementary school were reported to their teachers as showing unusual potential for intellectual growth. The names of these 20 percent were drawn by means of a table of random numbers, which is to say that the names were drawn out of a hat. Eight months later, these unusual or "magic" children showed significantly greater gains in IQ than did the remaining children who had not been singled out for the teacher's attention. The change in the teachers' expectations regarding the intellectual performance of these allegedly "special" children had led to an actual change in the intellectual performance of these randomly selected children.

In other words, some children may do better in school, not because they are any more intelligent than their classmates, but because they learn that their teacher, a significant other, believes they can achieve.

To put this phenomenon in context with the self-concept, we can say that when a teacher communicated to a child the message, "I think you're bright," the child accepts that evaluation and changes her self-concept to include that evaluation. Unfortunately, we can assume that the same principle holds for students whose teachers send the message, "I think you're stupid."

This type of self-fulfilling prophecy has been shown to be a powerful force for shaping the self-concepts and thus the behaviors of people in a wide range of settings outside the schools. In medicine, patients who unknowingly use placebos—substances such as injections of sterile water or doses of sugar pills that have no curative value—often respond just as favorably to treatment as people who actually received a drug. The patients believe they have taken a substance that will help them feel better, and this belief actually brings about a cure. In psychotherapy Rosenthal and Jacobson describe several studies which suggest that patients who believe that they will benefit from treatment do so, regardless of the type of treatment they receive. In the same vein, when a doctor believes a patient will improve, the patient may do so precisely because of this expectation, while another person for whom the physician has little hope often fails to recover. Apparently the patient's self-concept as sick or well—as shaped by the doctor—plays an important role in determining the actual state of health.

In business the power of self-fulfilling prophecy was proved as early as 1890. A new tabulating machine had just been installed at the U.S. Census Bureau in Washington, D.C. In order to use the machine, the bureau's staff had to learn a new set of skills that the machine's inventor believed to be quite difficult. He told the clerks that after some practice they could expect to punch about 550 cards per day; to process any more would jeopardize their psychological well-being. Sure enough, after two weeks the clerks were processing the anticipated number of cards and reported feelings of stress if they attempted to move any faster.

Some time later, an additional group of clerks was hired to operate the same machines. These workers knew nothing of the devices, and no one had told them about the upper limit of production. After only three days, the new employees were each punching over 2,000 cards per day with no ill effects. Again, the self-fulfilling prophecy seemed to be in operation. The original workers believed themselves capable of punching only 550 cards and so behaved accordingly, while the new clerks had no limiting expectations as part of their self-concepts and so behaved more productively.

NOTES

1. This illustration and many of the ideas covered in this chapter are adapted from Paul R. Timm, *Supervision* 2nd ed. (St. Paul, MN: West Publishing Co., 1993), Chapter 3.

2. Adapted from Elwood N. Chapman, *Attitude: Your Most Priceless Possession* (Menlo Park, CA: Crisp Publications, 1990), pp. 3–6. Reprinted with permission of the publishers.

3. Kenneth Blanchard and Norman Vincent Peale, *The Power of Ethical Management* (New York: Ballantine Books, 1989), p. x.

4. *Ibid*, p. 51.

5. This section is adapted from Paul R. Timm, *Recharge Your Career and Your Life* (Menlo Park, CA: Crisp Publications, 1990), pp. 140–41. Reprinted with permission of the author.

6. Larry McMurtry, *Lonesome Dove*, (New York: Simon and Schuster, 1985), p. 625.

7. Reprinted with permission from Ron Adler and Neil Towne, *Looking Out, Looking In*, 2d ed. (New York: Holt, Rinehard & Winston, 1978), pp. 87–89.

PART TWO

ORGANIZATIONAL
EFFECTS ON
COMMUNICATION

CHAPTER 5

ONGOING COMMUNICATION PROCESS AND FLOW

In this chapter you will find ideas that will help you:

♦ Identify key elements of an organizational communication system

♦ Recognize the dangers posed by the serial transmission effect as messages flow through an organization

♦ Cite the distortions that can occur in the serial reproduction of messages

♦ Anticipate possible communication problems associated with:

—Individual personality characteristics

—Power, status, and roles

—Communication overload

—Communication isolation

—Participative decision making

—The informal grapevine

—The absence of feedback opportunities

♦ Recognize the effects of informational diffusion on organizational functioning

The story is told of a man who once argued with his doctor over the high cost of medical care. "After all," the man contended, "a physician's job is really no different from that of an auto mechanic. Functionally, a human being is only a complex machine that occasionally needs to be fixed. So how can you charge these astronomical fees?"

After listening patiently, the doctor retorted, "Yes, but I do my work with the engine running!"

The communication functions in an organization also need to be examined and fixed while the engine is running. To artificially stop the communication process and examine it in a static state tells us very little about the system's true health.

SOME ELEMENTS OF AN ORGANIZATION'S COMMUNICATION SYSTEM

Human organizations are comprised of components. Some of these components are:

♦ People
♦ Relationships
♦ Interactions
♦ Goals
♦ Environment

People in organizations work within *relationships,* which arise from their *interactions* as they move toward *goals* within their *environment.* Communication provides the lubrication that allows these elements to work together.

We will later look at communication environment or climate, as well as how it emerges from members' orientation to goals, roles, and policies. In this chapter we consider:

♦ How communication tends to flow in the organization, forming *networks of interactions*
♦ Message distortions that result from the "serial transmission effect"
♦ Other factors that effect the integrity of networks

FIGURE 5-1   **Key elements of an organizational communication system.**

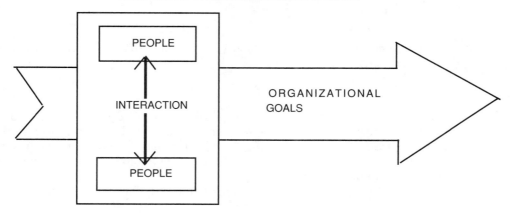

COMMUNICATION FLOW AND
NETWORKS OF INTERACTION

Information flowing through an organization provides the stimuli to which members will respond and from which they will create understanding. Ongoing message processes are fluid and often unpredictable. Communication networks serve to direct communication flow and improve the probability that understanding will develop. The effectiveness of a communication network is determined by the degree to which:

1. Messages maintain accuracy as they move through the system
2. The people who need or want the messages get them at appropriate times
3. People within the organization can avoid becoming overloaded with too many messages

Networks emerge from repetitive communication events among organizational members—that is, from habits of interaction. These repeated interactions arise from job needs, convenience, proximity, personality similarities, or any number of other factors.

For example, workers who talk together regularly to coordinate their job functions develop a network. Likewise, when two employees work side by side every day, a network emerges. Finally, workers who develop friendships (even though they may not work together directly) create a network through their interactions at lunch, on breaks, or in a car pool.

Most organizations are quite careful about defining formal communication networks, especially when task-relevant messages are to be conveyed. For a downward-flowing work directive, a plant manager gives it to section leaders who, in turn, give the message to supervisors, who give it to foremen. Similarly, with upward communication, the worker conveys information to his or her immediate boss. It is usually considered inappropriate to go over someone's head to the next level. Most organizations make the unwritten assumption that the higher-level managers get work-related information and policy changes before the rank and file workers. Similarly, the immediate supervisor receives employee suggestions or complaints before higher-level managers do. When this protocol is violated, the message timing is thrown off and the network's effectiveness (at least from the viewpoint of those who organized the network) is impeded.

Not coincidentally, we tend to see communication networks as virtually the same thing as the organization chart. Job specialization and the principle of unity of command—the notion that each employee should have only one boss—are, in part, efforts to control the flow of information. If, however, we come to believe that in our organization communication flows only through designated channels, we are living in a dream world. In reality, the flow of information is seldom as predictable as we would like. More often that not, our planned flow becomes an indiscriminate dribble.

Messages often ignore our carefully outlined network and instead take short cuts, ending up with the wrong people—or with the right people, but under the wrong circumstances. Or important information may simply be gobbled up by the system, ending nowhere. Organizational breakdowns of monumental proportions often result from communication systems that failed.

THE SERIAL TRANSMISSION EFFECT

Many of us have played the game in which one person whispers a message in the ear of the person next to him or her who, in turn, passes it on to another person, etc. After 10 or 15 people, the message which is then announced aloud is very different from the original. Something happens to it as it moves from person to person.

The game illustrates what researchers call the *serial transmission effect* on network accuracy. The distortion becomes even more pronounced when different organizational levels are involved.

Opinion Research Corporation ran a pioneer study to measure the integrity of information as it flowed from level to level in organizations. A company's top management, concerned over declining profits, sought to measure how clearly people at four levels in the organization understood the severity of the problem. The results were startling.[1]

Of the top corporate officers	91% understood
Of upper middle management	48% understood
Of lower middle management	21% understood
Of first-line supervisors	5% understood

The frightening point is that these results are probably not unusual. How do messages get distorted or lost as they flow through different levels in the organization?

Ways Messages Get Distorted

To understand how the serial transmission effect works, one point must be clarified. Despite the common use of the word *flow* when describing message movement in an organization, messages don't really flow—at least not in the same sense that water flows through a pipe.

In reality, the reproduction of the first person's message becomes the message of the second person, and the reproduction of the reproduction becomes the message of the third person. The movement of information in an organization occurs in this serial, reproductive fashion. Information itself does not flow.

Since each person participating in the movement of messages is a unique individual, his or her perspective will shade, color, or change the message originally received in some way.

A number of fairly consistent changes seem to occur during the process of serial reproduction:

1. Details are dropped out of the message (sometimes called *leveling*).
2. Details that are retained become *highlighted,* allowing them to gain in importance and meaningfulness (sometimes called *sharpening*).
3. Details are added for the purpose of embellishing the description or message.
4. Details become modified to conform to the predispositions of the reproducers (sometimes called *assimilation*).
5. Details that were previously qualified tend to become definite statements in later reproductions.
6. Details tend to be combined into a single, unitary concept—three different individuals become, in later reproductions, a "group" (sometimes called *condensation*).
7. Details of events tend to be described in the order in which one would expect them to occur rather than as they actually did occur.
8. Details are adapted so as to make the entire message or event seem plausible.
9. Details are adjusted to reflect the accepted style of expression used by the social group of the individuals involved in the reproduction process.

The following example show just how confusing things can get.[2]
A *colonel* issued the following directive to his executive officer:

"Tomorrow evening at approximately 2000 hours Halley's Comet will be visible in this area, an event which occurs only once every 75 years. Have the men fall out in the battalion area in fatigues, and I will explain this rare phenomenon to them. In case of rain, we will not be able to see anything, so assemble the men in the theater and I will show them films of it."

Executive officer to company commander:

"By order of the colonel, tomorrow at 2000 hours, Halley's Comet will appear above the battalion area. If it rains, fall the men out in fatigues. Then march to the theater where the rare phenomenon will take place, something which occurs only once every 75 years."

Company commander to lieutenant:

"By order of the colonel in fatigues at 2000 hours tomorrow evening the phenomenal Halley's Comet will appear in the theater. In case of rain in the battalion area, the colonel will give another order, something which occurs once in every 75 years."

Lieutenant to sergeant:

"Tomorrow at 2000 hours, the colonel will appear in the theater with Halley's Comet, something which happens every 75 years. If it rains, the colonel will order the comet into the battalion area."

Sergeant to squad:

"When it rains tomorrow at 2000 hours, the phenomenal 75-year-old General Halley, accompanied by the Colonel, will drive his Comet through the battalion area theater in fatigues."

OTHER FACTORS AFFECTING THE INTEGRITY OF NETWORKS

In addition to the serial transmission effect, other factors influence how well information moves through and is used by organizations. The remainder of this chapter considers eight such factors, which include:

1. Individual personality characteristics
2. Individual power, status, and roles
3. Communication overload
4. Communication isolation
5. Participation opportunities
6. Informal grapevines
7. The two-step flow of communication in organizations
8. Feedback opportunities

Individual Personality Characteristics

An important determinant of network effectiveness is the people in it. Koehler, Anatol, and Applbaum[3] discuss the ways personality characteristics shape our perception of the world around us, including the way we hear or read messages passed to us. In the organization, we tend to pay close attention to messages which we see as somehow serving our needs or wants, while we are likely to ignore less relevant information.

Some people view their roles in the organization with indifference. They see their work as a necessary evil. They have little commitment to organizational values or goals and they often depreciate the company or the products it makes. Messages passed through them may lose a great deal of enthusiasm.

Other people have authoritarian personalities and tend to be very critical. Their thinking and language is likely to be marked by many *shoulds* and *oughts* and *musts.* Research on the authoritarian personality concludes that several personality traits and "packages" of attitudes tended to occur together in the same people. The authoritarian dislikes and avoids any kind of ambiguity. He or she will reach firm conclusions, make judgments without qualifications, and stick to them. The world exists in black and white terms for this type person. Below are some characteristics considered typical in the authoritarian personality as summarized by Koehler et al.[4]

1. Conventionalism—a rigid adherence to conventional middle class values
2. Authoritarian submission—a submission to authority figures and an uncritical attitude toward idealized moral authorities of the ingroup
3. Hostility toward those who violate social norms (a form of authoritarian aggression)—a tendency to be overready to perceive, condemn, reject, and punish people who violate conventional norms
4. Dislike of subjectivity—an aversion to the subjective, the imaginative, the aesthetic, the tender-minded
5. Superstition and stereotyping—beliefs in mystical determinance of the individual's fate; the disposition to think in rigid categories
6. Preoccupation with strength, power, and toughness—concern with the dominant-submissive, strong-weak, leader-follower dimension; identification with power figures; exaggerated assertion of strength and toughness
7. Destructive cynicism toward human nature—rather generalized hostility— the vilification of the human
8. Projectivity—a tendency to project unacceptable impulses—disposition to believe that wild and dangerous and wicked things go on in the world
9. An exaggerated concern with sex and sexual goings-on

Messages passed through the authoritarian personality are likely to come out sounding considerably more emphatic and dogmatic. Value judgments of right or wrong, good or bad, are likely to be added to the message.

A Machiavellian personality type[5] is one we associate with a manipulative attitude toward others and a generally cynical view of other people's motives or character. The person with a strong Machiavellian personality (high Mach) tends to be self-centered and self-serving. Such a person's relative lack of emotional involvement in interpersonal relationships makes it easy for him or her to manipulate and control others. The high Mach also distrusts colleagues; has little faith in human nature; and tends to rate fellow workers as less interesting, less assertive, less productive, less cooperative, and less intelligent than him or herself. Since the high Mach disdains them, he or she experiences no qualms in taking advantage of them.

Such people will be less concerned with whether or not people *understand* their meanings and more concerned with how effective they have been at getting the message receivers to *do* what they want.

Recent studies of so called Type-A managers also suggest an impact of personality on communication flow.

Type-A people engage in a chronic, incessant struggle to achieve more and more in less and less time. In the extreme, this orientation leads to haste, aggressiveness, achievement impatience, competitiveness, time urgency, work involvement, and free-floating hostility.[6] While such an orientation can be useful in some kinds of high-pressure organizations, it often leads to antisocial compliance-gaining techniques or coercive communication. The negative ripple effects of such communication can be devastating to an organization.

There are, of course, many other personality types present in any complex organization. Our point here is simply that personality affects the way we receive messages and the ways we attempt to create meaning in others. As messages flow through the organizational networks, personality traits act as filters, each distilling the information and shaping the content.

Individual Power, Status, and Roles

Additional forces in communication networks further determine effectiveness. Among these are the power, status, and roles of the members/participants. The way we perceive the power of persons affects the way we pass messages to them in the network. In a series of early studies, French and Raven[7] determined that there are five types of power.

1. *Reward power* stems from the number of positive rewards, such as money, protection, and benefits, that people perceive another can muster.

2. *Coercive power* arises from perceived expectations that punishment (e.g., being fired or reprimanded) will follow if one doesn't comply with the bearer of such power.

3. *Legitimate power* develops from one's internalized values which dictate that the reference person has a legitimate right to influence and that one has an obligation to accept this influence (e.g., a police officer or organizational leader).

4. *Referent power* is based on identification with the person and wanting to be associated with him or her or what he symbolizes (e.g., a son of a president or, a secretary to the chairman of the board).

5. *Expert power* results from the reference person's social expertise, knowledge, or ability in an area where influence is attempted (e.g., the lawyer or surgeon).

Other researchers have categorized these sources as *position* power and *personal* power. Position power is bestowed upon a person from someone having organizational authority or position. Personal power comes from the perceivers' recognition of certain traits or capabilities and their decision to be influenced by these.

The way employees perceive power in others can greatly inhibit or facilitate the propensity to communicate. Perceived power affects both *whether* messages are passed and *in what condition* they are passed. This is especially true when workers see others' power as having direct influence on them. No one wants to bear bad news to the powerful.

Status often relates closely with power. One may enjoy formal and/or informal status within groups. Formal status—often taking the form of organizational position, titles, and various symbols of rank—is conferred by those in authority. Informal status may be accorded one by peers, subordinates, or bosses, but it reflects personal power dimensions, not formal position or rank within the group. It is important to keep in mind that people may have varying degrees of status in different realms. The entry-level assembly line worker (low position power) may attain recognition for pumping iron in an athletic competition that affords the worker considerable status.

Organizational roles also affect network effectiveness. Role positions are typically arranged in a hierarchy that closely relates status and power. Roles entail certain rights, duties, and obligations, which frequently call for different interaction patterns with others. Members tend to direct more messages to people they view as fulfilling important roles, such as those in organizational leadership positions.

Finally, roles prescribed by gender tend to influence the ways we communicate. Although this factor seems less important than it once was now that most organizations have both male and female workers at all levels, social norms dictate that men and women act (that is, communicate) differently. Men, for example, are often expected to be more reluctant to exhibit their feelings, preferring instead to display a toughness that suppresses the sentimental or emotionally expressive. Evidence indicates that men do conceal more about themselves from others than do women. Women, on the other hand, who traditionally are thought to express more sentiment, are now modifying this kind of communicative behavior in light of new organizational roles. Nevertheless, our organizational and socially dictated sex roles do affect the ways we communicate.

Managers wanting to reduce the potential problems associated with power, status, and roles may wish to select media that reduce the number of links (or people) in the network. This means communicating directly to target receivers and avoiding others in the organizational hierarchy. Yet such direct communication can lead to a problem of another type. When many messages flow indiscriminately to organization members rather than through a predetermined network, a major danger can result: Some people—especially the leaders—find themselves facing communication overload.

Communication Overload

With the increase in organized activities and the growing sophistication of communications technology, we are confronted with more information than we can possibly process. Managers are typically caught between the need to know and the ability to digest incoming information. People with strong upwardly mobile aspirations and those whose power and role positions put them in the middle of the information mainstream are especially susceptible: the upwardly mobile, because they recognize the value of and hunger for information, and those in the mainstream because their job responsibilities demand that they be in the know.

We have all experienced momentary overload. Driving down a city street is an exercise in handling countless messages which assault our senses. We listen to the car radio, talk to our passengers, read street signs and outdoor advertisements—all of which compete for our attention. Doing research in a large library, virtually surrounded by data, all of which could never be assimilated, can be psychologically and emotionally exhausting.

When we are overloaded, our normal response mechanisms are forced to choose among countless informational stimuli. These choices leave many messages out. Psychologists tell us that we will attend to items that best meet the conscious or unconscious needs or desires we are experiencing at that time. Yet, since our needs are constantly changing, so are our selection mechanisms.

A number of studies look at what people do when faced with communication overload at work. When overloaded, we typically cope by some combination of seven options.[8]

1. *Omission.* We simply fail to attend to or handle some incoming messages. We ignore some information.

2. *Error.* If we are overloaded we overlook or fail to correct errors that have been made. We get sloppy in our information processing.

3. *Queuing.* We let incoming messages pile up and get to them as we can. This, of course, only works when we have hard copy—written information; spoken messages cannot as readily be lined up for later attention.

4. *Filtering.* We deal with incoming messages according to some predetermined system of priorities—for example, responses to customers get first attention and the employees come next.

5. *Approximation.* We may lower our standards of precision. Instead of clearly understanding details of a message, we may become satisfied with a summary or condensed version.

6. *Multiple Channels.* We may delegate or decentralize information processing procedures to reduce the load. For example, we hire administrative assistants to handle our mail.

7. *Escape.* We simply refuse to handle any input at all or refuse to reach out for information available.

Some managers, upon taking over a new position, throw away files kept by the previous manager, except those required by law or policy. This way their minds will not be cluttered with excess historical data. This reduces potential overload and has an added employee relations benefit: by starting off with a clean slate, rather than accepting someone else's perceptions of employee behaviors, we can *assume* the best from others. Who knows, they may even live up to our expectations!

The effective communication network should reduce the probability of communication overload. Periodic analysis of who is getting what messages for what purpose should be carried out in the organization.

Communication Isolation

At the opposite end of the scale from the overload problem is isolation. When any member of the organization is cut off from the communication network, we are wasting a precious human resource. Human resources management has taught us that every member must be considered as asset and should be utilized. We no longer hire a "hand." We hire the whole man or woman. People don't want only to be *treated* well, they want to be *used* well. Their potential for sharing thoughts, ideas, and perceptions comes as part of the package. To toss that aside doesn't make much sense.

Yet, in most organizations, some individuals become isolated. There are a number of reasons for this. One may be simply a matter of geography. An individual whose work location is away from other employees and/or who is not linked up by phone or intercom may become isolated. One study found employee satisfaction to be very low among bank tellers who worked in isolated drive-in facilities compared with that of inside tellers.[9]

More subtle reasons for employee isolation also exist. Often one's role or authority position in the organization, personality characteristics, ethnic background or race, or even personal hygiene habits can cause a person to be ostracized from the larger work group. The problem is fairly widespread, but it becomes tragic for the organization when high-level leaders are the victims. One lesson learned from Watergate points out the dangers in becoming isolated from the buffetings of discrepant, yet necessary, information. Corporate leaders are no less susceptible to isolation than politicians.

Executive isolation, a situation in which a leader loses contact with what is really happening in the organization, comes about when several factors are present.[10]

1. When there is a heavy reliance on downward communication alone.
2. When leaders fail to go into the organization and observe firsthand what is going on.

3. When leaders develop a pattern of overreacting to bad news.
4. When delegating takes place without plans for follow-up.
5. When executives proclaim an open door policy but fail to recognize obstacles preventing people from coming in.
6. When leaders are fearful or they are embarrassed to ask about details of work they don't fully understand.

When we recognize any of these characteristics in our own behavior, it is time to take a hard look at just how in touch we really are. A manager can do several things when executive isolation is recognized. Although these actions often call for fundamental changes in managerial behaviors, concerned leaders should:

1. Cultivate a genuine desire to hear bad news as well as good
2. Get out of the office and personally check to see how things are going
3. Meet periodically with groups of subordinates to discuss operations and problems—meet them at their job location and demonstrate a genuine interest in what is happening. While the manager is with them, she can ask them to explain something about their job that she may not know. Develop the art of listening to the right people.

In short, the way to avoid isolation for the manager and for any other member of the work force is to reach out and *ask questions*. Don't interrogate, but do seek out employee perceptions.

Participation Opportunities

Innumerable studies have shown that when members are included in the decision making that affects them and their organizations, they tend to be more satisfied. However, it is important to recognize the limitations as well as the strengths of participative decision making (PDM).

Many managers tend to resist PDM because it

♦ Can be time-consuming and thus expensive
♦ Can be viewed as a threat to one's ego in that it redistributes leadership functions, and thus power, to subordinates in the formal organization
♦ Takes a degree of humility to accept their decisions

We must recognize that PDM is not practical in every decision situation. When emergencies arise that require quick response, there simply isn't time for participation. Similarly, the cost of PDM must be worthwhile in relation to the benefits. Assembling a group of employees on company time quickly gets expensive; a one-hour meeting of 8 or 10 individuals can cost hundreds of dollars in salaries alone. The quality of the decision outcome and/or the reductions in resistance to change must be worth the additional cost.

As a general rule, PDM has a better chance of being effective when

1. The problems or issues dealt with are seen as relevant and important to the participants. The topics should have some recognizable effect on them; they should feel some ownership in the problem.
2. The employee has some expertise in the subject being discussed. Such expertise arises from education or experience.
3. Interaction between participants is free and open. Participants are in no way threatened by active exchanges of different ideas.
4. The group is allowed the freedom to work within clearly defined limits. Off-limits areas—such as company policy, budgets, or legal responsibilities—that are not subject to change should be so stated before PDM gets under way.
5. Participants have sufficient interpersonal communication skills and a realistic understanding of the group process.
6. Organizational leadership acts from Theory Y assumptions. They recognize especially that "the capacity for creativity in solving organizational problems is widely distributed in the population." (For a quick review of Theory X and Theory Y assumptions, see page 123.)[11]

While managerial leadership styles and assumptions about human nature go far toward determining whether participation will be effective, characteristics of the employees also play an important part. Hersey and Blanchard[12] have developed a situational leadership theory that provides a model for predicting whether participation will be effective in a given situation. The key to such predictions is the "task-relevant maturity" of the participants. Such maturity is defined by the group members' ability to set effective goals, willingness and ability to accept responsibility, education and/or experience, and self-confidence.

When these ingredients are taken together and considered in relation to the specific issue under discussion, a prediction about the potential effectiveness of participation is possible. The higher the level of task-relevant maturity an individual or group shows, the higher is the probability that participation will be an effective management approach. The lower the task-relevant maturity shown by participants, the lower is the probability that participation will be useful.

When maturity is very low, PDM would simply be pooling ignorance. When the maturity of certain individuals or small groups is extremely high, however, management may defer the decision to those having obvious expertise and capabilities rather than risk diluting a high-quality decision with opinions of less-qualified participants. Robert Townsend's advice on using professional advertising agencies provides an example: "Don't hire a master to paint you a masterpiece and then assign a roomful of schoolboy-artists to look over his shoulder and suggest improvements."[13]

Informal Grapevine

Thus far we have been talking about formalized communication networks. Much of the information which flows though organizations, however, does not use formal networks or prescribed procedures. Instead it travels through the grapevine.

For many years managers were very concerned about the grapevine. The general consensus was that people should use formal channels and that we should defoliate this undesirable weed. But, as in the case of many things, when we take a close look at informal communication flow, we find it has some redeeming social value, some potentially constructive characteristics. Research by a number of people, most notable among them the management theorist Keith Davis, has revealed some rather surprising findings.

First, despite the connotation that many of us associate with the grapevine (or rumor mill or gossip chain), information transmitted through this informal network is often very *accurate*. Several researchers meticulously counted details of messages received through the grapevine and determined that they ranged from 78 to 90 percent accurate. The accuracy was especially high when the messages did not deal with highly emotional or controversial data.[14]

A second finding is that the grapevine is very *fast*. People tend to receive and pass on information very quickly. The greater the communication opportunities found on the grapevine, the faster information flows. As a manager for a telephone company, Paul Timm was astounded at how organizational associates all over the country knew the scuttlebut within hours of an event, often long before any official announcement. Easy access to long-distance phone service helped!

A third finding is that the grapevine is *active* and carries large quantities of information in almost every organization. It is a fact of organizational life. Often it serves several constructive roles:

1. It provides a network for some types of information that would be inappropriate in the formal network. Often such scuttlebut or personal information serves to strengthen relationships among organization members and helps develop a sense of comradeship.

2. It can also provide an outlet for voicing emotionally charged messages which, if not expressed, could fester into growing hostility among employees.

3. It can be useful in translating some of management's directives into language easily understood by employees.

4. It can prevent unfounded rumors or misinformation by providing clarifying details.

5. Finally, the grapevine provides feedback to management about employee sentiments and morale. Likewise, managers can use the grapevine to check how contemplated actions will be received.[15]

The kind of information flowing through an organization's grapevine tends to depend on the supply of and demand for specific messages. Caplow explains that

> The grapevine is most active when information is scarce and the demand for it is high; it is least active when the information is plentiful and the demand for it is low. If an organization's future plans are kept secret, there will be many rumors about future plans. If they are widely publicized,

there will be few such rumors and perhaps none at all. Some sorts of information, like scandalous gossip, are always in demand and usually in short supply. When information in this category becomes available, the grapevine transmits it far and wide.[16]

Perhaps the most effective way to deal with a grapevine is to feed it lots of information. When employees feel they are being kept abreast of every detail in the organization's operation—maybe even more information than they want—the thirst for additional data is quenched.

The Two-Step Flow of Communication in Organizations

Studies of information diffusion reveal other facts about the grapevine that can be useful to the manager. Beginning with the sociological studies of voting behavior by Lazarsfeld and other in the late 1940s,[17] there emerged a *two-step flow hypothesis.* Their findings indicated that the flow of mass communication messages (speeches, radio, newspaper articles, and the like) may have less direct effects on receivers than was commonly supposed. Instead, it appears, messages stemming from the mass media first reach "opinion leaders" who, in turn, "pass on what they read and hear to those of their everyday associates for whom they are influential."[18] Later studies examined the implications of this hypothesis. One line of research looked more closely at the nature of these opinion leaders, revealing several prominent characteristics. An opinion leader tends to

1. Personify certain values or attributes that his or her followers admire
2. Have competence, experience, or expertise in the area in which his or her influence is sought
3. Be in a strategic social location—a position that permits him or her to be in the know regarding an area of influence

We can all think of people whose opinion or ideas we especially value or whose behavior, appearance, or demeanor we tend to imitate. Whom would you turn to for investment advice? Whom would you go to if you had marital problems? Who could recommend a good restaurant in Chicago? The people identified in answering these questions may be our opinion leaders.

It is important to note that there is very little overlap of opinion leadership: a leader in one area is not likely to be influential in another, unrelated sphere as well. The individual we turn to for investment advice may not be the one whose opinions about clothing or hairstyles we'd value. Most of us have a number of individuals who help us make decisions about various topics.

One of the earliest studies of the effects of the two-step flow hypothesis in organizations was done by Jacobsen and Seashore.[19] Their research examined the communication patterns of 200 employees in a governmental agency. These people were asked to name individuals in the organization with whom they had communication contact, other than those they were linked to by the formal organizational structure. At all levels of the organization, the researchers discovered key persons (whom they termed *liaison members*) who served as opinion leaders within their subgroups. Jacobsen and Seashore's main purpose was to make managers aware of the opinion leaders in their organizations so that more effective organizational communication could be attained.

Phillip Tompkins[20] is another researcher who applied the two-step flow hypothesis to organizational communication. His studies suggest that, as in the case of society at large, "individual local influentials" (opinion leaders) exist within the industrial or governmental organization. Just as the influentials in the earlier Lazarsfeld *et al.* research were found to interpret the mass-media-generated information and pass it on to the remainder of the public, the organizational opinion leaders tune in to organizational media and pass information on to other members of their organizational subgroup. They also pass along their interpretations of such information.

In his doctoral dissertation, Richetto[21] combined a study of the two-step flow in an organization with the *credibility* of a message source-person. Personal leadership was investigated within three separate spheres of influence: (1) task-related influence, (2) political (grapevine) influence, and (3) social-emotional (non-job-related) influence. Using interviews and rating scales, Richetto determined to whom workers turned for information in each area and how they perceived that source-person. He concluded that:

1. Influentials were found to receive higher ratings on all measures of source credibility
2. When subjects named immediate supervisors as influentials, the credibility of these supervisors did not differ significantly from the credibility of informal (nonsupervisory) influentials
3. When credibility ratings between informal influentials and immediate supervisors (who were not cited as influentials) were compared, the *informal sources rated significantly higher*

This study indicated the importance of using informal leaders to disseminate organizational information. If employees rate opinion leaders higher on credibility than they do their own supervisors, the need for managers to be aware of and understand opinion leaders is further substantiated.

Although research concerning organizational opinion leaders has been approached in a variety of ways with a number of conclusions, one thread seems to consistently hold the research together. This thread, both stated and inferred, is that for effective communication to occur throughout the organization, managers should be aware of the role of opinion leaders and should attempt to identify and work through them.

The wise manager knows the importance of being in tune with the grapevine. Informal networks need not exclude formal organizational leaders if those leaders are sensitive to potential problems of executive isolation which inhibit messages from coming to them. Getting an ear to the ground is a worthwhile expenditure of effort. Tap into the grapevine, instead of wasting time trying to chop it down.

Feedback Opportunities

Managers need to be sensitive to two ways in which they can encourage or discourage employee feedback: *receptiveness* and *responsiveness.*

Receptiveness involves a general willingness to accept and encourage feedback *as perceived by your subordinates.* Saying you are open doesn't make it so. It's the impression your people have of you that determines your receptiveness. Responsiveness involves the degree to which you are willing and able to *do* something about the feedback you receive from subordinates. Again this is in the eye of the beholder.

While most managers tell their employees that their door is always open, often that's true only in a physical sense at best. Psychological barriers remain. The new mayor in one city dramatized his openness policy by physically removing the door to his office. While this may have had symbolic effect, in reality it was no easier to get an appointment to see His Honor than it was to see his predecessor who was roundly criticized for being aloof. Visitors still had to get by one deviously protective secretary. After a few weeks and several encounters with unsavory characters who conned their way in, the mayor developed the habit of working in a hideaway office in another part of city hall so that his secretary could dutifully report that he was not in.

An open door policy must be more than a symbolic gesture. To be open we must be aware that we're likely to be spending a certain amount of time talking about things that seem trivial or talking with people we'd rather avoid. We'll get a lot of chaff with the wheat. But under all that chaff we're likely to find valuable nuggets of information. The object of the game is to maximize the income of useful data while accepting a tolerable amount of useless verbiage.

We can't simply open the door and expect only useful information to come tumbling in. What we can do is develop patterns of behavior that convey to our subordinates our active interest in what they have to say, especially when their ideas are relevant to the organization.

A QUICK SUMMARY OF MAJOR IDEAS

- ♦ Communication provides the lubrication as people seek to establish relationships and move toward goals in organizations. As messages flow within an organization more effectively, its effectiveness grows.
- ♦ Networks emerge from repetitive communication events among organizational members. These networks arise from job needs, convenience, proximity, personality similarities, and so on.
- ♦ The serial transmission effect refers to how messages get distorted as they flow from person to person to person. Unless corrective actions are taken, distortion is inevitable.
- ♦ A wide range of personal, organizational, and environmental factors affect a communication network's integrity in organizations. The more of these factors we are familiar with, the better our chances of minimizing damaging effects.
- ♦ A willingness—even an enthusiasm—for getting feedback can be a helpful managerial trait. Seeking clear, meaningful feedback can enhance the performance of individuals and the organization as a whole.

QUESTIONS FOR FURTHER THOUGHT

1. Make a brief list of your opinion leaders. For example, whom would you ask to recommend a good course for next semester, a new stereo, a good restaurant, a good doctor? Why do you look to them?
2. Think of an organizational leader who claims to have an open door policy. What kinds of things make that policy successful or unsuccessful? Identify some nonverbal cues which may make a person hesitant to accept that openness policy at face value.
3. What accounts for the potentially damaging effects of the serial transmission problem? What actions could a manager take to minimize the problem when disseminating information in an organization?
4. How might a manager *use* the grapevine to his or her advantage? Describe a scenario where this might be the case.

OTHER THOUGHTS ABOUT THE EFFECTS OF ORGANIZATIONAL COMMUNICATION SYSTEMS ON MESSAGE CONTENT

"Why can't people get things straight?" How frequently has this questions been asked silently or out loud in an organization? Probably as often as employees get together to discuss problems with the boss, or bosses talk about misunderstandings with employees. Routine person-to-person communication is subject to a multitude of pitfalls and processes that have detrimental effects on understanding. Many of the problems stem from the way in which human beings process information. Other sources of misunderstanding are a function of the system by which messages are distributed throughout an organization. Organizational communication is subject to not only the maladies of interpersonal interaction but also the anomalies of relaying messages through human links in a communication system.

PERSONAL FACTORS THAT DISTORT MESSAGES

We shall discuss a number of principles that reflect personal factors that contribute to the distortion of messages. These factors issue naturally from our concept of communication as the act and process of assigning meaning to displays. A display is anything that activates one of our senses—seeing, hearing, tasting, smelling, feeling. At any moment we are bombarded by a limitless variety of displays originating from inside ourselves as well as from outside. Hence the first factor that contributes to the distortion of messages is related to our perception of displays.

PRINCIPLE 1: PEOPLE PERCEIVE THINGS SELECTIVELY

Our sensory receptors—eyes, ears, fingers, noses, tongues—are physically limited so that they can respond to only a few of the stimuli impinging upon them. Each of us responds to those sensations that get past our natural barriers or limitations, that seem most pertinent to our situation, and that are consistent with our own personal preferences and perspectives. The fidelity, or accuracy, of information is limited by the selective perceptions we make.

PRINCIPLE 2: PEOPLE SEE THINGS CONSISTENT WITH WHAT THEY BELIEVE

Our perceptions are effected by the way we talk about people, things, and events. What we believe changes our perceptions. If we expect to see a friend react in a negative way to a suggestion, we shall no doubt perceive him or her to react negatively. This is sometimes called the *Pygmalion effect*. If we believe that people are very smart and intelligent, we will tend to see their behavior as consistent with our belief. On the other hand, if other people see that we expect great things from them, they will try to behave consistently with our expectations.

PRINCIPLE 3: LANGUAGE ITSELF IS INACCURATE

Our perceptions of people, things, and events never correspond exactly to reality because we selectively see them and because we tend to see what we believe about people, things, and events. In communicating we use language to represent our perceptions. Our talking involves language that is supposed to portray or describe that about which we are talking. It is through language that we make our private perceptions somewhat public so that others may get some idea of what we mean. Language does not diminish the importance of nonlanguage. Nonverbal signals clue others in to what we mean. Nevertheless, we must not lose sight of the basic principle that language symbols do not accurately represent what a person means.

PRINCIPLE 4: THE MEANING OF A MESSAGE OCCURS AT BOTH CONTENT AND RELATIONAL LEVELS

A message consists of both verbal or language (oral and written) and nonverbal or nonlanguage (aural and pictorial) symbols. What a person says and how a person behaves combine to make a message-display. Each message can be analyzed at a *content* or denotative level and at a *relational* or interpretive level....

The content, or denotative, level of meaning concerns the ideas, things, people, events, and happenings to which the message literally refers. You are functioning at the content level when you respond to the information of the message—that is, when you respond to the ideas, attitudes, opinions, and facts referred to by the message, you are dealing with the message at the content level.

The relational, or interpretive, level of meaning concerns how the message is to be taken, for example, lightly or seriously. When you say, "Smile when you say that," you are dealing at the relational level because your comment tells the other person how to interpret the message and what kind of relationship you are to have. The relational level indicates how the information and the relationship is to be understood. Your attitudes toward other people are expressions at the relational level.

PRINCIPLE 5: DISTORTIONS ARE ENCOURAGED BY INCONSISTENCIES BETWEEN VERBAL AND NONVERBAL ASPECTS OF A MESSAGE

A basic axiom of communication theory is that *a person cannot behave.* Thus as [W. Charles] Reddings and [George A.] Sanborn ... have concluded, "Communication is always going on, then, whether one desires it or not—so long as there is someone to interpret what we say, or fail to say, or do, or fail to do".... It has been estimated that in a conversation involving two people, verbal aspects of a message account for less than 35 percent of the social meaning, whereas nonverbal aspects of a message account for 65 percent of the social meaning. On the other hand, [Albert] Mehrabian ... states that "a person's nonverbal behavior has more bearing than his words on communicating feelings or attitudes to others" .... He estimates that 7 percent of the total feeling is derived from verbal aspects, 38 percent from vocal aspects, and 55 percent from facial aspects, resulting in 93 percent of the feeling communicated being based on nonverbal features.

PRINCIPLE 6: MESSAGE AMBIGUITY OFTEN LEADS TO DISTORTIONS

Ambiguity may be defined as some degree of uncertainty associated with information or actions. If a statement you make seems ambiguous to me, that means that I am uncertain how to take what you say. There are three types of ambiguity that may occur in communication: ambiguity of meaning, ambiguity of intent, and ambiguity of effect....

Ambiguity of meaning concerns the uncertainty of predicting what the originator of a message means. To the extent that you cannot readily and efficiently determine what a person meant when he or she said or wrote a message, the message will have a degree of ambiguity for you. The greater the ambiguity of meaning, the greater the difficulty you will have in comprehending the message.

Ambiguity of intent concerns the uncertainty of predicting why the originator of a message said or wrote this particular message to you at this particular time in this particular way and under these particular conditions. To the extent that you cannot figure out why the person is communication with you, the message will be ambiguous to you. For example, suppose you go home and find a note pinned to your bedroom curtain with this message on it: "The president of the university called and wants to talk to you tomorrow morning." Why would the president want to talk to you? What does he or she want? The degree to which you are unable to answer such questions indicates how ambiguous the intent of the message is to you.

Ambiguity of effect concerns the uncertainty of predicting what the consequences of responding to a message might be. You may accurately interpret the meaning of the nore about the president's request for a meeting—the president wants you to arrive at his or her office in the morning; you may even predict his or her intent fairly accurately—to talk to you about your standing in the university; however, what will be the effect or consequence of understanding the message, arriving at the president's office, and engaging in a conversation about your standing in the university? Of course, nothing may come of it; on the other hand, what might be come possible consequences? The extent to which some of these questions have unclear answers is the extent to which the message involves ambiguity of effect.

PRINCIPLE 7: MEMORY PROPENSITIES TOWARD SHARPENING AND LEVELING DETAILS ENCOURAGE DISTORTION TO OCCUR

Some evidence suggests that people may have some patterns associated with their memory systems that lead to distortions in verbal communication. [P.S.] Holzman and [R.W.] Gardner ... developed a schematizing test that differentiated between *levelers* and *sharpeners*. Individuals who are levelers had fewer correct memories of an incident or story and tended to show more loss and modification of the overall structure of the story than did those who were sharpeners. Gardner and [L.J.] Lohrenz demonstrated that the serial reproduction of a story underwent different fates when transmitted through separate chains of levelers and sharpeners. Levelers lost more themes, lost more of the overall story, and showed increasingly more fragmented messages than did sharpeners. A person may be structured toward leveling information or toward sharpening information. A propensity toward stripping away the details in a verbal message is called *skeletonizing* ..., and a propensity toward the invention of details is called *importing*. Each of us may have a memory propensity that leads toward leveling, stripping away, or skeletonizing details in messages or a memory propensity that leads toward sharpening, inventing, or importing details into messages. In either case a memory propensity may contribute to distortions and lack of fidelity in communication.

PRINCIPLE 8: MOTIVATIONAL FACTORS MAY ENCOURAGE
MESSAGE DISTORTIONS

Three basic motivational factors tend to produce changes in messages that result in lack of fidelity: attitudes toward the message content; desires, self-interest, and motives of communicators; and attitudes of intended receivers.

1. *Attitudes toward the message content.* A study by [W.] Johnson and [C.B.] Wood ... demonstrated that subjects who held positive attitudes toward a racial minority tend to "abstract" the positive information about them from a passage containing both positive and negative information; on the other hand, a subject who had negative attitudes tended to abstract negative information from the same passage. The tendency for communicators to distort information in a message according to their attitudes seems to be well supported by other research....

2. *Desires, self-interest, and motives of communicators.* [Jay M.] Jackson ... suggested that people in organizations communicate or fail to communicate with others in order to accomplish some goal, satisfy a personal need, or improve their immediate situation. [Anthony] Downs ... identified four major biases that produce distortions in the communication of officials in bureaucracies: (1) They tend to distort information by exaggerating data that reflect favorably on themselves and to minimize data that reveal their shortcomings. (2) They tend to prefer policies that advance their own interests and the programs they advocate and to reject those that injure or fail to advance their interests. (3) They tend to comply with directives from superiors that favor their own interests and drag their feet or ignore those that do not. (4) They tend to take on additional work if it is directly beneficial to their own goals and avoid work that weakens their ability to achieve their own goals.

[William V.] Haney ... described three motives that encourage distortions to develop in messages: (1) The desire to convey simple messages. The communication of complex information is difficult and psychologically taxing on the individual; thus organization members tend to simplify messages before or as they pass the information along. (2) The desire to convey a "sensible" message. When a person receives a message that doesn't seem to make sense, the desire is to make sense out of it before passing it along. Most of us tend to avoid sending along messages that seem illogical, incomplete, or incoherent. (3) The desire to make message sending as pleasant (or at least as painless) as possible for the sender. Organization members tend to avoid conveying messages that are painful for them. Instead they make changes that soften the message and make it less painful.

3. *Attitudes of intended receivers.* There is evidence to support the idea that the initiator of a message will tend to distort it in the direction of the announced attitude of whoever is to receive the message. This may be a subcategory of motivational factors, since expressing ideas contrary to those held by an intended receiver may be potentially painful.

ORGANIZATIONAL FACTORS THAT DISTORT MESSAGES

Characteristics of organizations themselves tend to encourage distortions to occur in messages. We shall briefly review a number of organizational factors that contribute to message distortion in organizational communication.

1. *Occupying a position in an organization influences the way a person communicates.* By becoming a functioning member of an organization who occupies a position with duties and authority assigned to it, an individual acquires a point of view, a value system, and develops expectations and limitations that are different from a person who holds a different position or is a member of a different organization entirely. A supervisor, for example, is compelled at times to look at the functioning of the organization differently from subordinates. The supervisor must react to production problems somewhat differently from the way a particular subordinate might react to them. In fact, a supervisor must think about the organization in a different way. The person within the organization sees its operations differently from an outsider. Each position in an organization demands that the person who occupies it must perceive and communicate about things from the perspective of the position. Occupying a position tends to contribute to distortions in organizational communication messages....

2. *Hierarchical—superior-subordinate—relationships influence the way in which a person communicates.* The arrangement of positions in hierarchical fashion suggests to those who occupy the positions that one set of individuals is "superior" and another set is "subordinate." The fundamental difference is one of perceived status. People and positions located higher in the hierarchy have greater control over the lives of those who are located lower in the organization. Lower-downs find it desirable to be cautious in communicating with higher-ups. Information may be distorted because a subordinate is careful to talk about things that his or her superior is interested in hearing and to avoid topics and ways of saying things that are sensitive to the boss. The superior, on the other hand, would not wish to discuss things that tend to undermine his or her position in the organization by reflecting negatively on his or her competence and decision-making abilities. Even between friends, hierarchical relationships affect what can be discussed and the way in which things can be discussed....

3. *Restrictions in who may communicate with whom and whom may make decisions influence the way in which a person communicates.* Coordination of activities and the flow of information in an organization require some centralization of decision making. To avoid having members of the organization going in too many different directions, making contradictory decisions, and having imbalances in work loads, an organization is structured so that certain decisions are made by a limited number of individuals. We have referred to them in different ways—as liaisons, gatekeepers, people in authority, decision makers, or superiors—but in nearly all cases those individuals get information from a variety of others within and without the organization. When central decision makers receive too much information too fast or have too many decisions to make too quickly, distortions are likely to occur as a result of *overload.*

4. *Impersonalization of organizational relationships influences the way in which a person communicates.* One fundamental characteristic of formal organizations is that relationships are to be formal and impersonal. The impersonalization of relationships leads to the suppression of emotional messages. In order to hide or disown emotional expressions, individuals develop ways of keeping others from expressing their emotions. Eventually organization members avoid or refuse to consider ideas that might allow or encourage the release of feelings. The consequence, in the long run at least, is a lessened awareness of the impact of a person's feelings on others and an inability to predict accurately the emotional reactions of others. Ultimately the organization is comprised of individuals who cannot communicate their feelings and who substitute rules for solving problems.

5. *The system of rules, policies, and regulations governing thoughts and actions influences the way in which a person communicates.* As a philosophy of impersonal relationships encourages the development of a system of rules that substitutes for authentic problem solving, so the characteristic of having general but definite policies for guiding decisions leads to impersonal relationships. A rigid application of rules and policies to behavior and decisions leads to an inability to make compromises and fosters impersonality and lack of emotional communication. Rules encourage the evolution of rigid, routine, and traditional patterns of communicating. Institutionalization of behavior is the consequence, with remote and distant, rather than face-to-face, interpersonal communication. Positional relationships are reinforced, and interpersonal relationships are discouraged. Information and messages may be distorted to accommodate the rules and maintain impersonality.

6. *Task specialization narrows a person's perceptions and influences the way in which a person communicates.* Although specialization has contributed immensely to national productivity by increasing efficiency, it is also the source of many communication problems. Individuals identify with their own areas of expertise, learn entire vocabularies unknown to other employees, and often fail to integrate their efforts with other departments. The result is often a bottleneck in the flow of information or a great deal of "buck passing" from one person to another because the client's problem is not in the employee's area of specialization. To some extent specialization fosters conflicts through competition for resources to accomplish narrow objectives. Although competition may help keep employees functioning with alertness, it may lead very quickly to destructive relationships and dysfunctional communication. Specialization may be the source of much of the message distortion that occurs in organizations. Task specialization leads to what some called *trained incapacity,* or a limited ability to perform general organizational functions. Accompanying an incapacity to do varied tasks is the inability to perceive the total picture and act for the good of colleagues and the organization. Such limited perspectives reduce a person's ability to comprehend other's problems, resulting in lower levels of empathy. Without empathy, understanding may be diminished and distortion increased.

ANTIDISTORTION FACTORS

Messages in every organization are subject to a degree of distortion, but formal organizations also have forces that limit the amount of distortion that occurs in communication. Although the antidistortion forces may reduce the level of distortion below that implied by the lengthy list of personal and organizational factors contributing to distortion, they do not entirely eliminate distortion. Downs ... lists four general ways in which organization members attempt to increase the fidelity of information communicated in an organization.

1. *Establish more than one channel of communication.* When an employee (manager or operative) believes that information he or she is receiving may be distorted, one way to counter the distortion is to verify the information through multiple sources of messages.

2. *Develop procedures for counterbalancing distortions.* If we assume that those who work in organizations realize that personal and organizational factors produce distortions, then those who receive information can routinely adjust reports to counteract the distortions contained in them. To the extent that a manager, for example, has accurately identified the distortions, he or she can adjust the information more closely to the original design. When counterbalancing procedures are used throughout the organization, as they tend to be, much of the cumulative effect of personal and organizational distortion factors tends to be reduced. The main distorting effect will be the inaccurate estimate of the source and degree of distortion in the information.

3. *Eliminate the intermediary between the decision maker and those who provide information.* This can be done by maintaining a basically flat organization structure.

4. *Develop distortion-proof measures.* One way to reduce distortion is to create message systems that cannot be altered in meaning during transmission, except through direct falsification. To be distortion-proof, a message must be able to be transmitted without condensation or expansion (skeletonizing or importing) between the source and the terminating point. Obviously only a very small proportion of all messages directed to any individual in an organization can be distortion-proof. Nevertheless, carefully prepared codes and easily quantifiable information may represent messages that are less subject to distortion through selective omission of qualifiers, shifts in emphasis, ambiguous terminology, and other perceptual and language factors that affect many messages.

OTHER THOUGHTS ABOUT COMMUNICATION PROCESS AND FLOW

WHAT WE HAVE HERE IS A FAILURE BY EMPLOYERS TO COMMUNICATE

Or so many commenters say. Worker loyalty is being eroded by a failure to convey goals, says Carnegie Mellon University business Professor Robert Kelley. Nearly 70% of 400 executives he queried said their firms' leaders lacked vision. In a Foster Higgins survey of chief executives of 164 large firms, most think personal communication helps workers' job satisfaction and commitment, thereby improving earnings.

But 86% said other demands prevent them from devoting more time to communicating with underlings. Chief executives said they're doing it more than two years ago, but still not enough. Some 20% of 200 personnel chiefs, in a separate poll by the consultant, said that when they survey workers about issues like benefits, they don't feed the results back to employees.

Only 34% of over a million workers in a survey by consultant Hay Group said their firms listen to their complaints.

NOTES

1. Opinion Research Corporation, *Avoiding Failures in Management Communications, Research Report of the Public Opinion Index for Industry* (Princeton, NJ: Opinion Research Corporation, January 1963).

2. Reprinted from "Permutation Personified" in *Boles Letter.* Copyright 1962 by Edmund D. Boles & Associates.

3. Jerry W. Koehler, Karl W. E. Anatol, and Ronald L. Applbaum, *Organizational Communication: Behavioral Perspectives* (New York: Holt, Rinehart & Winston, 1976), Chapters 6–7.

4. Koehler *et al., op. cit.,* p. 93.

5. Niccolo Machiavelli (1469–1527) was an Italian statesman and writer on government whose name has come to be associated with craftiness, deceitfulness, and manipulation of people of lesser status. The Machiavellian manager would not hesitate to communicate only messages which serve his or her ends.

6. Kevin G. Lamude and Joseph Scudder, "Compliance-Gaining Techniques of Type-A Manager," *Journal of Business Communication,* Winter 1993, 30, 1, p. 63–79.

7. John R. P. French and Bertram Raven, "The Bases of Social Power," in *Group Dynamics,* 2nd ed., eds., Dorwin Cartwright and A. F. Zander (Evanston, IL: Row, Peterson, 1960) pp. 607–623.

8. Summarized by W. Charles Redding, *Communication within the Organization* (New York: Industrial Communication Council, 1972), pp. 143–157.

9. T. R. Cheatham and M. L. McLaughlin, "Effects of Communication Isolation on Job Satisfaction of Bank Tellers." Paper presented at International Communication Association annual conference, Portland, OR, 1976.

10. Adapted from Christopher J. Quartly, "Executive Isolation: Can It Be Prevented," *Personal Journal,* December, 1974, pp. 902–905.

11. Douglas McGregor contended that our assumptions about people affect the ways we deal with them. He categorized managerial assumptions into his famous "Theory X-Theory Y." The following list summarizes McGregor's assumptions as presented in Paul Hersey and Kenneth H. Blanchard, *Management of Organizational Behavior,* 3rd ed. (Englewood Cliffs, NJ: Prentice-Hall, 1977), p. 55.

Theory X	*Theory Y*
1. Work is inherently distasteful to most people.	1. Work is as natural as play, if the conditions are favorable.
2. Most people are not ambitious, have little desire for responsibility, and prefer to be directed.	2. Self-control is often indispensible in achieving organizational goals.
3. Most people have little capacity for creativity in solving organizational problems.	3. The capacity for creativity in solving organizational problems is widely distributed in the population.
4. Motivation occurs only at the physiological and safety levels.	4. Motivation occurs at the social, esteem, and self-actualization levels, as well as physiological and security levels.
5. Most people must be closely controlled and often coerced to acheive organizational objectives.	5. People can be self-directed and creative at work if properly motivated.

12. Paul Hersey and Kenneth H. Blanchard, *Management of Organizational Behavior,* 3rd ed. (Englewood Cliffs, NJ: Prentice-Hall, 1977), Chapter 7.

13. Robert Townsend, *Up the Organization* (New York: Alfred A Knopf, 1970), p. 20.

14. These studies include work by Keith Davis, *Human Behavior at Work* (New York: McGraw-Hill, 1972); Evan Rudolph, *A Study of Informal Communication Patterns within a Multi-Shift Public Utility Organizational Unit,* unpublished Ph.D. Dissertation, University of Denver, 1971; Eugene Walton, "How Efficient Is the Grapevine?" *Personal 78,* 1961, pp. 45–49.

15. Shirley Kuiper and Morris P. Wolf, *Effective Communication in Business,* 10th ed. (Cincinnati: South-Western Publishing, 1990), p. 15.

16. Theodore Caplow, *How to Run Any Organization* (Hinsdale, IL: Dryden Press, 1976), p. 77.

17. Paul F. Lazersfeld, Bernard Berelson, and Hazel Gandet, *The People's Choice* (New York: Columbia University Press, 1948).

18. Elihu Katz, "The Two-Step Flow of Communication: An Up-to-Date Report on an Hypothesis," *Public Opinion Quarterly, 21,* 1957, p. 61.

19. Eugene Jacobsen and Stanley E. Seashore, "Communication Practices in Complex Organizations," *Journal of Social Issues, 7,* 1951, pp. 28–40.

20. Phillip K. Tompkins, "Organizational Communication: A State-of-the-Art Review," *Conference on Organizational Communication,* monograph, National Aeronautics and Space Administration, MSFC Form 454, 1968.

21. Gary M. Rochetto, *"Source Credibility and Personal Influence in Three Contexts: A Study of Dyadic Communication in a Complex Aerospace Organization,"* unpublished Ph.D. Dissertation, Purdue University, 1969.

22. Excerpted from R. Wayne Pace and Don F. Faules, *Organizational Communication,* 2nd ed. (Englewood Cliffs, NJ: Prentice-Hall, 1989), pp. 148–165.

23. Reprinted with permission from *The Wall Street Journal,* Jan 20, 1990, p. A1.

CHAPTER 6

ORGANIZATIONAL COMMUNICATION CLIMATE

Fair to Partly Confused

▼

In this chapter you will find ideas that will help you:

♦ Ask key questions, the answers to which will clarify the communication climate in your organization

♦ Recognize the interplay between organizational goals, personal goals, and communication climate

♦ See the effects of expectations, reward systems, and role clarity on employees' perceptions of communicate climate

♦ Distinguish between supportive and defensive communication climates and apply techniques for improving supportiveness

♦ Recognize the crucial role played by feedback and apply techniques for improving the quality and quantity of the feedback received

♦ Respect the role played by organizational policy in determining communication climate

▼

Following and administering rules might have been dandy in the placid environments of yesteryear. Not today. Managers must create new worlds, destroy them, and then create anew. Such brave acts of creation must begin with a vision that not only inspires but encourages people to take day-to-day risks involved in testing, adapting, and extending the vision.

—Tom Peters[1]

In his book *Thriving on Chaos,* Tom Peters describes many aspects of communication climate. Communication climate can be viewed as a psychological condition established by (1) the individual's understanding of and commitment to organizational values, and (2) the individual's interpersonal relationships with other organization members. Much of this book deals with the interpersonal relationships and how they are affected by communication behaviors. This chapter focuses on the person-to-organization dimension of communication climate.

KEY QUESTIONS THAT DETERMINE COMMUNICATION CLIMATE

> *We each see climate differently, but what we perceive is real (for us).*

We each perceive climate differently—the process is highly subjective. However, the answers we receive to seven key questions go a long way toward clarifying important climate dimensions. The climate dimension is in parentheses following each of the following questions:

1. What are we doing here? (clarity of organizational goals)
2. What does the organization want from me? (clarity of tasks and expectations)
3. Where do I fit into the organization system? (understanding of roles and functions of others)
4. What rewards or punishments await me if I communicate in certain ways? (motivation to communicate or not to communicate)
5. To what degree should I take risks in communicating my ideas or feelings? (supportiveness and risk encouragement)
6. How am I treated compared with others? (fairness, trust, and equity)
7. How am I doing (feedback and candor)
8. What guidelines should I follow? (organizational policy)

CLARITY OF ORGANIZATIONAL GOALS

What Are We Doing Here?

An organization member needs to know two things about goals: (1) What are his or her personal goals, and (2) How do these coincide with the goals of the organization? Those two questions are often harder to answer than we might expect. Some background thoughts on goal setting may be helpful here.

Sometimes it's difficult for us to put our goals clearly into words, let alone communicate them to others. The question frequently asked in employment interviewee, "Where do you want to be five years from now?" has thrown many a candidate for a loss. Thinking in detail enough to define a goal is troublesome for many people. When they do try to clarify their goals, the forces of change often intervene and seem to make meaningless the whole exercise of goal setting. The authors of *The Organizational World* illustrate some of the problems involved:

> "Tell me, young man," asks your prospective father-in-law, "what are your goals in life?" You stammer something about getting a good education and serving humanity and raising a happy family and perhaps getting rich. But you don't feel comfortable about the question, and even less comfortable about your answer.
>
> "Tell me," says the senior consultant to the young new company president, "what are your company's long-range goals?" The president points to a framed document on the wall titled "The Long-Range Objectives of the Cymbeline Company." The document lists several goals: producing more and better widgets at the lowest possible price, providing the best possible service to consumers, acting as responsible citizens, making a reasonable profit in a way that is consonant with the glorious traditions of the American Free Enterprise System, and a lot of other stuff.
>
> And if the president is a bright, sensitive person he will also feel a little uncomfortable about his answer. Both he and the prospective son-in-law feel, somehow, that their words have a hollow ring. Indeed, it's very difficult for any of us to have a clear and fixed idea of where we're going, of our long-run goals. We suspect that whatever we say today may not be what we feel tomorrow. We want to hold on to an option to change our minds.
>
> On the other hand, if the prospective father-in-law or the consultant were to ask a couple of different, though closely related, questions, they could be answered much more confidently. Suppose the first question was simply the behavioral one: "What do you do?" Then the young man could answer firmly and proudly that he is a student majoring in social instability. And suppose the second was a short-term question: "What will you do next year?" He could answer that he will graduate, perhaps cum laude, at the end of next year; that he hasn't yet made up his mind whether he will go into the Peace Corps, join a commune, or work in his father's fish hatchery. And the company president could answer both questions quite clearly and confidently too: "We produce 900,000 plastic widgets a day in twenty-seven styles, thirty-nine colors. We have 19,000 people on our payroll in seven countries. Next year we will open sales offices in Peking and Murmansk." We can talk easily about what we now do—our tasks; we can talk a little less easily about our short-term objectives; and we usually have a great deal of trouble talking clearly about long-run goals.[2]

It's easier for individuals and for organizations to explain to people what they *do* (their tasks) than what they *want* (their goals). The process of setting effective goals is more complex than it may look. But the payoff is enormous.

Goal Setting and Climate

Let's look first at personal goal setting and then elaborate to the organization. Few people question that specifying personal goals, preferably in writing, is a powerful tool for success. Typically, experts offer several recommendations to maximize the power of goal setting.

1. *Goals should be established in several areas.* The individual or company who sets goals only for earnings or profits becomes awfully mercenary. As a goal-planning consultants to individuals, we suggest establishing goals in several different areas: career goals, family goals, educational goals, physical goals, spiritual goals, goals of service to others, and miscellaneous goals. The individual who attacks only career objectives and disregards all others is likely to be quite unhappy—and unhealthy.

Similarly, when an organization sets only profit targets without considering service to its community, employee well-being, and social obligation objectives, it suffers for its oversight. Goal setting should not be directed only toward the financial bottom line; it should pervade every phase of the organization.

2. *Establish short-term and long-term goals.* Individuals or organizations should begin with short-range, readily attainable targets to build self-confidence in the goal-setting process. The best way to learn to putt a golf ball is to place it only a few inches from the cup and tap it in; then move it back a few inches at a time until you become proficient from greater distances. The same applies to goal setting. Begin with easily reached targets and grow from there. Also consider long-run objectives in terms of more immediate steps of progression.

3. *Whenever possible, make goals measurable in some way so you know when you've "got it."* Try to set goals you can count—that's a common recommendation. Yet a word of caution is in order. While quantification has obvious advantages, it cannot be applied to all worthwhile goals. Many creative measures of subjective concepts such as "customer service" or "personal growth" can be developed. But good goals should not be thrown out simply because we cannot come up with a purely objective way to count our results.

> *Try to make quantifiable goals.*

4. *Look at your goals frequently and mark them off as they are achieved.* We've known successful executives who spend several hours each week—uninterrupted hours—studying their goals. The more these goals are in the forefront of your mind, the more effectively they can do their job of crystallizing thoughts and focusing your energies. As you work on the goals, the goals work on you. Writing them down one time without reviewing them later is of little value.

In the organization it is crucial that objectives are clearly understood by the membership. Merely sending out a list of targets to those who will be involved in achieving them won't do the job. Clear understanding can be achieved only through participation in goal selection, clear communication of the agreed-on objectives, and frequent repetition and exposure to these goals.

5. *Finally, build in a system of rewards—special rewards—when significant objectives are met.* For many goal-directed people, the satisfaction of crossing off an accomplishment on a list is enough. But a little extra reward—be it verbal recognition (an "atta boy!") or some tangible prize—can make goal setting and goal reaching a lot more fun. A little hoopla is in order when you or your organization meet an important target.

Getting the Horses Pulling in the Same Direction

Of course, writing down personal and organizational goals is no guarantee of success. But when people become *committed* to goals they've set, these goals provide motives for action—motivation.

The optimum situation is to have members' individual goals pulling in the same direction as the organization's objectives. This can be done with effective communication, by creating understanding. When the objectives of both the individual and the organization are clarified and accurately perceived, a determination can be made as to whether those objectives can coincide. If they are diametrically opposed, there is little sense in going on. If they appear to be at least partially compatible, further clarification and commitment to each other can be the catalyst for success.

Although individual goal setting and organizational goal setting are very similar, the process is more complicated and more political in organizations. As members of organizations, each of us has a personal viewpoint and a personal domain that we seek to protect. Like people everywhere, we tend to take "local"

> **Organizational goals are more political than personal goals.**

political issues (those affecting us personally) more seriously than distant ones (those that affect the larger organization). And, as in politics, there are factions, subgroups, and coalitions pushing for their pet priorities. Organizations also have to be concerned with the welfare of many parties, such as buyers, suppliers, stockholders, and government agencies—all of whom have varying interests in the organization. Organizational goals grow out of negotiation, compromise, and some degree of personal sacrifice.

Management Involvement in Goal Setting

Ultimately, top management must be responsible for the process of organizational goal setting. Their decisions are influenced by political give-and-take as well as their ability to digest relevant data and then to seek common understanding. The process is repeated by management at all organizational levels, representing the subgroups within the larger organization. This is all further complicated by the chicken-or-egg dilemma. Middle managers complain, "Top management doesn't establish and communicate clear goals. If we knew what they wanted and what for, we could clarify our own goals and objectives." But an equally common complaint of top managers is: "Our middle managers aren't imaginative about proposing new goals and objectives. If they told us what they want to shoot for, we could say yes or no and clear the path for them."[3]

Sounds like a communication problem! It is only through effective communication that this dilemma can be resolved and the complex process of organizational and individual goal synthesis can come about.

After this fairly extensive discussion of goals, you may have forgotten that we are still talking about communication climate. The point is that without goals—without a clear sense of direction—organizations and people within them spin their wheels.

A key dimension of organizational communication climate arises from the degree of mutual understanding about each others' goals that exists between the member and the organization. When individuals and/or the organization are sketchy about objectives, the ambiguity that exists can lead to communication difficulties and lower productivity. The effective manager will assist employees in personal goal planning while also conveying company objectives. A healthy climate is one in which each member has a pretty accurate response to the question "What are we doing here?"

CLARITY OF TASKS AND EXPECTATIONS

What Does the Organization Want from Me?

Depending on the nature of the organization, members may have similar or widely differing tasks, roles, and activities. The organization itself may exist to fulfill a clearly specified function (to manufacture automobiles) or a very vague one (to study economic indicators). How the organization goes about its work depends in part on the amount of structure provided. A manufacturing operation typically has a fairly high degree of structure; that is, the job to be done is clear (you will assemble 314 three-wheeled, fiberglass skateboards today). Also, the way the job is to be done is clear (insert wheel assembly into hole A). Training programs can clarify task structure.

A problem arises when employee behaviors not directly relevant to the work are left unclear. An example may be the skateboard assembler who produces at the desired level (task-relevant behavior) but who dresses very sloppily or has poor hygiene habits (a smelly person). Organizational standards of cleanliness may range from vague to nonexistent. When confronted, the worker may be embarrassed or upset.

Confusion about formal rules of the game and the informal customs or standards of the organization can be frustrating for the employee. The problem is further aggravated when different leaders apply different interpretations to what and how things are to be done.

One nationwide study found that nearly half of the workers interviewed were working under conditions of noticeable conflict, where they were from time to time caught between two sets of people who wanted different things from them. About 15 percent of those studied reported this to be a frequent and serious problem.[4]

An important dimension of communicative climate arises from the degree to which a member feels comfortable with his or her understanding of what is expected on the job. These expectations apply to task behaviors as well as to social norms and standards of the work environment.

UNDERSTANDING ROLES AND FUNCTIONS OF OTHERS

Where Do I Fit?

Once individuals understand and become, to some degree, committed to the organization's goals and expectations, they are likely to be interested in how their particular functions fit into the larger scheme of things. A recurring theme in the John Wayne type of war movies is the soldier who wants to "see some action" because he views his present role of, say, a mess sergeant, as unimportant. In reality, of course, the mess sergeant's job is crucial to a war effort, though less glamorous in the view of the job holder.

People in organizations want to know where they fit. Helping members understand how the many organizational tasks mesh can be difficult because the position one holds often determines one's perceptions of the organization. In other words, a mess sergeant could not perceive the army in the same way as a supply sergeant or an infantry officer or a general.

People See the Organization from Different Vantage Points

Social psychologists Daniel Katz and Robert L. Kahn say "one's role in a social system dictates his perceptions of that system." They go on to explain that "organizational roles not only structure perceptions, but that changing one's role will result in concomitant changes in his perceptions."[5] Our view of the big picture is clearly affected by our vantage point. And when our vantage point changes due to a promotion, reorganization, or other change in job responsibilities, our understanding of the complex fabric of organizational functioning also changes.

> *Perceptions of an organization are influenced by one's position.*

Every business person has encountered the employees or junior executives who have all the answers to the problems of the organization. But when it becomes their turn at bat, the problems suddenly become far more complex and solutions far more elusive.

A dramatic illustration of how organizational position colors perceptions is presented in a study by Dearborn and Simon.[6] These researchers were working with a group of executives from the same company in a training workshop. One of the exercises was to examine a fairly detailed (10,000-word) case study and write a brief statement of what they considered to be the most important problem facing the company described.

Although each trainee was instructed to respond from the vantage point of the top executive in the company, the overwhelming number of trainees responded instead from their real frame of reference. Sales executives saw the fictitious company's major problem as a sales problem 83 percent of the time. Eighty percent of the production executives saw the major problem of the case study as a production difficulty. Only 29 percent of the nonsales executives cited sales as the major problem and 20 percent of the nonproduction people saw the major problem as one of production.

Clearly, one's organizational roles affect one's perception of the big picture. Since perception is an integral part of communication, organizational position affects communicative behavior. When we attempt to create understanding, this natural differing of views must be considered.

It is an oversimplification to expect that people could be brought to share precisely the same views about anything. In many cases we can get close enough to avoid serious problems. In fact, perceptual differences are okay as long as they fall within a "zone of indifference." Chester Barnard[7] coined this term more than 50 years ago to mean a range of authoritative requests to which a subordinate is indifferent and therefore compliant without resistance. Requests falling outside this zone of indifference will receive critical consideration from the subordinate. Put another way, requests outside this zone will require either persuasion or power or both to gain compliance. People's role perceptions help determine their zone of indifference. When requests or orders overstep the zone, resistance and possible conflict are likely to arise.

So what can we do about the "where do I fit" dimension of communication climate? First, recognize and help your people recognize that the positions each of us hold in the organization cause different viewpoints and different communication behaviors. Then provide opportunities to expand their understanding of the larger context. Orientation tours and employee training that include rubbing shoulders with people in other parts of the organization can go a long way toward developing empathy and more effective communication across functional lines.

Rewards and Punishments for Communicating

What'll Happen if I Speak Up?

In most organizations there are innumerable examples of reward systems that pay off for one behavior even though the rewarder dearly hopes for other, often opposite, kinds of behavior. The fundamental idea of paying people by the hour encourages the taking up of time rather than productive use of efforts. The mechanic who fixes a machine so well that it never breaks down again finds himself out of a job. And the doctor who ostensibly is paid to make us well can make a lot more money if we stay sick and continue to visit him. This is not to say that hourly workers, mechanics, or doctors don't do their jobs well, but the system rewards some behaviors that seem irrelevant or even counterproductive to the hoped-for results. This principle can be easily applied to communication in organizations.[8]

> *Reward systems sometimes reward the wrong behaviors.*

How many times have we seen the ambitious junior executive suggest a remedy to a problem, only to be instructed to write up a report on it? For a potentially useful suggestion the reward is to do more work. A clothing store owner constantly encourages her sales force to cooperate with each other—to share ideas with each other. Yet for her Christmas sales promotion she offers an award only to *the* top producer of sales. The results—salespeople tripping over

each other to get to the customers, distrust, and conflict. At a staff meeting, the member who suggests additional study of a particular problem is inevitably nominated to do the work.

In some companies, as a part of employees' performance appraisals, they are evaluated on communication effectiveness: how well they share ideas with others; how well they keep superiors informed of activities they should know about. Yet seldom is there objective evaluation of this desirable behavior. Most appraisers don't know how to judge this kind of performance, so it becomes a gut-feeling evaluation—a guess. The employee who does nothing to open up communication channels has as good a chance of being favorably evaluated as any other.

Employee suggestion systems appear to motivate upward communication but are seldom as effective as they could be. Employees who make the effort to pass an idea up are fairly often met with rejection, either because they were unable to express fully the idea in writing (often on company forms) and/or the evaluator of the suggestion didn't understand it or could care less if it was adopted.

As a staff employee at a large corporation Paul Timm shared responsibility for evaluating employee suggestions. He had three options: accept the suggestion (in which case he would then need to see that it was implemented); reject the suggestion (he wouldn't have to do anything further); or refer the suggestion to a higher organizational level where his counterpart would have the same options. The point is, there was little or no real incentive for him to approve suggestions even if they were pretty good. If he did accept a suggestion his work had just begun. He would then have to go to all the offices and teach the new procedure, create needed forms or equipment, arrange budget expenditures, etc. A rejection avoided all that work. Finally, his work evaluation was in no way affected by the number of employee suggestions his approved. In fact, these suggestions were simply extra work piled upon his regular duties.

So, where's the motivation to communicate?

This problem may be fairly pervasive. Managers advocate employee openness—until the first person speaks up and is quickly labeled an attitude problem. We tell our people to cooperate and avoid unnecessary intergroup conflict, but we do nothing to reward cooperative behavior and often unintentionally encourage friction or "friendly competition." We offer a $100 prize for a good suggestion but provide no good reason why those who will evaluate the suggestion should accept and implement it. The suggesting employee soon learns that efforts at upward communication will be rejected. Finally, we see the stifling effect of putting members on the defensive so that their ideas must be substantiated (usually in written form) before they can be offered.

These kinds of things have profound effects on climate. The employee's response is too often likely to be, "So why bother?"

SUPPORTIVENESS AND RISK ENCOURAGEMENT

Should I Really Say What I Think?

Closely related to the motivation to communicate are support and encouragement of creativity and risk taking. Encouraging—or at least tolerating—some risk taking generally pays off in organizations. Failing to be supportive leads to defensiveness in employees.

A Defensive Climate

When people feel threatened—primarily by threats to their sense of self-esteem—a defensive climate develops. Behavioral characteristics have been studied by Jack Gibb,[9] who concludes that, when defensiveness characterizes the climate, we are likely to see the following:

1. *Frequent evaluation of people:* Organization members feel that they are being subjected to good or bad judgments.
2. *A high degree of control over member behaviors:* People feel manipulated and burdened by lots of rules, regulations, and specified rigid procedures.
3. *Leadership gimmicks or tricks:* Leaders employ strategies aimed at getting employees to think they are participating in important decisions when, in fact, the boss is making the decisions.
4. *A cold and impersonal climate:* Superiors seem to maintain their status by talking down to the "little people" in the organization, and they are often dogmatic and preachy.

A Supportive Climate

The supportive environment is differentiated by the absence of the defensive characteristics. *Descriptive* language replaces evaluative comments and leaders take a *problem orientation*, that is, not simply calling up the rule or policy to stifle a difficulty, but getting to the root of the issue and seeking out underlying causes. The supportive climate is also marked by *spontaneity, empathy* for others, a sense of *equality* and fairness, as well as the replacement of dogmatism with *provisionalism*—a sense of being not yet certain of the answer but rather engaged in a continuing search for solutions.

> **A supportive climate allows for mistakes.**

In the supportive climate, individual members have a sense of participation without threat to their ego or sense of self-worth. Risk taking and the freedom to make mistakes are accepted as normal states of affairs. Consequently, growth possibilities are broadened for the employee.

The degree of supportiveness present is a key dimension in communication climate. Without supportiveness, communication becomes a contest of power plays rather than a search for common understandings. The waste of human resources in such an organization can be enormous.

FAIRNESS, TRUST, AND EQUITY

How am I Treated Compared with Others?

The degree to which organizational leadership is willing to initiate communication has a profound effect on climate. This openness of downward communication has long been recognized as desirable. Few people would argue the wisdom of keeping members well informed. A more subtle aspect, however, is *the way* members are kept informed, the *equity* or fairness with which openness is applied to individual workers.

Some research has examined the effects of equitable distribution of communication rewards in organizations. By *communicative rewards,* we mean such valued outcomes as:

1. Receiving praise or verbal approval
2. Management's receptiveness to a worker's questions
3. Management's willingness to directly answer such questions
4. The degree to which additional questions or comments are encouraged
5. The timeliness of information given to members

If managers have markedly different communication styles with different members of their work groups, the inequities are likely to be spotted by the employees. Paul Timm tested this by setting up a series of experiments in which the supervisor responded differently to one half of the work group than to the other half.

For one-half of the employees in the work group, the supervisor

1. Answered any questions they had and encouraged them to ask more questions as necessary
2. Gave each of them a number of compliments on the work they were doing

3. Provided them, early in the project, with additional information that clarified exactly what they were to do

For other members of the same work group working in the same room, the supervisor

1. Responded to their questions by telling them to "work it out as best you can" and did not encourage additional questions
2. Did not give any compliments
3. Provided them with task-clarifying information only after they were almost finished with the project

To test whether inequities are readily perceived, Paul Timm manipulated *receptiveness, supportiveness,* and *timeliness.* Not surprisingly, these workers quickly saw that some people were being treated better than others. The communication climate was clearly marked by unfairness.

The experiments went on to examine how this perceived unfairness affected workers. Those who recognized the inequitable treatment tended to respond by downgrading their evaluations of the supervisor's effectiveness, by producing less, and by withdrawing (if not physically, at least psychologically) from participation in the task.[10] Clearly the supervisor who used sharply different communication approaches with different members of the work group was seen as unfair and was distrusted and rated lower in supervisory effectiveness.

In an ideal climate, there would be equitable distribution of communicative rewards. All members at the same organizational level would enjoy the same degree of receptiveness from the boss. Each would receive compliments for work well done and each would get new information at approximately the same time. This, of course, would be a pure ideal.

This reality is complicated by the fact that perceptions of equity or fairness, like beauty or obscenity, are in the eye of the beholder. What appears completely fair to one person may be gross miscarriage of organizational justice to someone else. Because varying degrees of paranoia are widely distributed throughout most companies, achieving a pure state of communicative equity is highly unlikely. We do need, however, to avoid at least obvious favoritism.

If we keep in mind that the ways we interact with subordinates are in themselves potentially rewarding to them, we will recognize that communication meets important needs just as do tangible rewards allocated by organizations. We don't toss around money or perks indiscriminately, yet many managers go on passing out communicative rewards without any meaningful allocation strategy.

Feedback and Candor

How Am I Doing?

Employees have a basic need to know where they stand with regard to organizational expectations. The degree to which management provides them with meaningful indicators affects climate. Formal feedback arrangements are usual-

> **Management commitment to feedback affects climate.**

ly established through management's policy for performance reviews. The degree of managerial *commitment* to such policy affects climate.

Less formal feedback also creates impressions in the employee about the organization's climate. For example, the *physical conditions under which workers receive feedback* can have diverse effects. As a rather extreme illustration, compare several contexts under which a manager could compliment a productive employee:

♦ *Situation 1:* The manager summons the employee to his plush, richly carpeted office. While seated behind the desk, the manager informs the standing employee that his good performance has been recognized and is appreciated.

♦ *Situation 2:* The manager happens to meet the employee in the restroom and informs the employee that his good performance has been recognized and is appreciated.

♦ Situation 3: The manager arranges a special visit to the employee's work location to inform him that his good performance has been recognized and is appreciated.

Although we cannot absolutely predict which of these approaches would be most rewarding to the employee, reactions to the same message delivered differently are likely to be quite different. Perhaps Situation 1 would result in some resentment because status differences would be reinforced—possibly a painful reminder to the subordinate. Situation 2 might be viewed as too casual to be sincere; the compliment seems to be an off-the-cuff remark. At any rate, it is clear that little special effort was expended to compliment the employee. Situation 3 would probably be viewed as the most sincere expression of the three since the manager made special arrangements to present the message in an appropriate context.

Candor of remarks to employees also affects climate. It's okay to be polite, but most employees want management to tell it like it is. Give people the good news and the bad news. Share concerns and problems whenever appropriate.

Attempts by managers to suppress information they don't want the employees to have can be disastrous for communication climate. And often it doesn't work. As communication consultant Walt Wiesman has said, "There is never such a thing as a 'secret' in a working organization, at least not for more than 72 hours. If management creates a vacuum through silence, the employees will apply the boldest and weirdest imagination to fill it."[11] Providing candid but supportive feedback to organization members is a key to developing a healthy communication climate.

All of the aspects of communication climate we have been discussing influence the ways people attach meaning and thus gain understanding about their organization. Each member's answers to the eight questions provide a composite view of organizational communication climate for that member. The degree to which that view coincides with some objective reality is less important than the fact that such a reality does indeed exist in the mind of the employee and affects the ways he or she will interact in the organizational system.

ORGANIZATIONAL POLICY

What Guidelines Should I Follow?

Much can be done to create a positive communication climate by developing formal communication policy. Ideally, such policy statements express

1. A set of objectives the organization wishes to achieve through communication
2. Guidelines or directives to be applied to decision making about communication-related issues

The trend in large organizations is to formalize such policy by putting it in writing. As researcher David Burhans says, "In an organization where there is no formally written employee communication policy—as well as in one in which the formal policy is ignored or violated—a situation may exist in which each individual manager or supervisor has his own personal communication policy which may conflict with that of other managers and employees with whom he interacts."[12] Ideally, clear communication policies reduce ambiguity and inconsistencies, thus stabilizing the communication climate.

> *An organization's policies toward communication should be put into writing.*

Policy That Reflects Objectives

When communication policy is expressed as a series of objectives, it usually paints with broad strokes. At times these objectives are so general they serve only to spell out underlying philosophy. Such proclamations, standing alone, do not, in our opinion, constitute a bona fide communication policy.

Below are brief excerpts from several corporate policy statements. These are taken out of context for illustrative purposes and are not intended to reflect good or bad examples. Any reference to the organizations' names has been deleted.

1. To promote a better understanding that the personal objectives of XXX employees are closely related to the success of the company, by actively providing employees with timely, direct, pertinent and appropriate information on:
   - Objectives, plans, and operations of the Corporation
   - Developments affecting our business and its employees
   - Other matters of interest or concern to employees, including the basic economics of how private business enterprise operates in a free society
2. To place on line management responsibility for maintaining at local level active and regular employee and management communication programs.
3. To insure that, whenever practicable, employees learn of important matters which affect them and their jobs through internal channels first—rather than through external sources.
4. To regard employee ideas, opinions and suggestions for the improvement of operations as an important corporate asset; to provide a uniform communication program—including specifically the establishment of a uniformly administered, formal corporate suggestion plan which will provide awards to employees for usable suggestions.[13]

This organization's policy statement goes on to provide more details on implementation.

The philosophical ideal of many policy statements are tempered by recognizing limitations, illustrated as follows:

> Some information, because of its nature, must be restricted to certain levels of management, or to certain segments of the enterprise. In such instances, the confidence placed in the selected levels or segments must be maintained.

> All members of management are urged to develop a communicative attitude so they will consistently and consciously review each item they initiate or that passes through their hands, and ask themselves "Who else needs to know about this—what is the best way to get it to them, orally or in writing?"[14]

Obviously there are limitations on what realistically can be achieved in employee communication. One ongoing area of managerial concern is just how far we can go with openness. Archie McCardell, while president and chief operating officer of Xerox Corporation, addressed this issue in an article appearing in his corporate new magazine. His conclusion was that sometimes vital decisions in the works at Xerox couldn't be talked about. The article appeared at a time when business conditions were putting unusual stress on the company and its employees. And the people wanted to know what top management was doing about it. Here are the concluding paragraphs from McCardell's article, entitled "Open Communication Is Our Policy, but Sometimes ..."

> So it comes down to this: Open communication is the policy at Xerox. I believe in it fully as a policy, even as a principle, though I realize that the more openly we communicate, the more opportunity we create for further questions. But sometimes, for good reasons, we can't answer certain questions—questions which are natural and legitimate in themselves.... Quite frankly, there has to be a point at which people accept a few things on faith.
>
> I know that accepting things on faith is not always easy, and we can't always expect it—particularly when we are fortunate to have a group of bright and articulate people whose futures are tied to a major extent to the future of Xerox.
>
> But I want you to have confidence that the management of Xerox Corporation *is* aware, *is* open to upward communication, *is* working on our problems in a priority manner—and wants *you* in on the process as early and fully as possible.[15]

In addition to the openness issue, some written policies also specify that objectives vary for communication *within management* and for communication *between management and employees.* The following excerpts from a corporation's policy statements illustrate this.

Communication within Management

The objectives of communication within management will be to foster, on the part of all management members, a complete understanding of:

1. The aims, objectives, and plans of the business, both general and specific, long-range and immediate
2. The organization of the Company and its elements, of who does what, and particularly the areas of responsibility and authority of management members
3. The policies, regulations, and procedures under which the Company operates, and the reasons for them
4. The major problems faced by the business, and specifically what each member of management and what each employee can do to aid in the solution of these problems
5. Up-to-date information on whatever lies ahead—business forecasts, contemplated changes in facilities, equipment, policies, practices, and organization

Communication Between Management and Employees

The objectives of communication between management and employees will be to:

1. Facilitate the profitable operation of the business and to promote the understanding, approval and support by employees of its objectives in the free enterprise system. Cite (the Company's) tradition of leadership, thereby spurring the pride of accomplishment and good morale.

2. Create an environment of purposeful management in the eyes of employees, which is woven into the fabric of day-to-day operations at all levels, with supervisors held directly responsible for the effectiveness of communication.

3. Provide sufficient flexibility in communication methods so that they may be tailor-made to the problems of each organization, taking into account available information, the attitudes and interests of the group.

4. Provide a spirit of forthrightness so that the management will be willing to discuss openly and in detail the vital facts about the business that are of direct concern to employees and relate to their success and welfare as members of the corporation.

5. Provide the atmosphere, opportunity, and channels for communication so that employees may submit their ideas, project their attitudes, and set forth their grievances to management.

6. Recognize employee achievement and—again—to translate the meaning of these achievements for the overall benefit of (the Company).[16]

Finally, policies that express communication objectives sometimes (although perhaps not often enough) explain *why* internal communication is important. An examination of such statements can reveal a variety of assumptions held by the policymakers. For example, policies that say the employee has a *right* to know what's going on may view communication as a legalistic necessity, perhaps begrudgingly adhered to. Keeping employees informed because they *want* to know may be based on an assumption that information is a gift we bestow on the underlings.

Internal communication viewed as a vehicle for creating cooperative effort—effective participation—reflects healthier assumptions. When people are involved in information flow, they may develop synergy—that is, they may create a whole organization that is far greater than the sum of its individual members.

Policy as What, How, and When

Communication policy should go beyond the statement of principles to provide guidelines or directives about such things as what, how, and when to attempt actively the building of understanding. Peterson and Pace feel that an effective organizational communication policy should:

1. Translate the plans and objectives of the organization into guidelines for managers and subordinates.

2. Be internally consistent—policies should develop logically and consistently with and from one another.

3. Be distinguished from rules and procedures—policies represent general statements that guide thinking and provide for discretionary action. Rules and procedures are designed to channel action and allow for little or no discretion.[17]

No one communication policy is best for any and all organizations. Our key point in discussing these is that policy affects communication climate which, in turn, affects the probability that understanding and organizational effectiveness is developing.

A QUICK SUMMARY OF MAJOR IDEAS

♦ In creating an effective organization, the climate of an organization is more critical than communication skills or techniques taken by themselves.

♦ Communication climate is a psychological condition created by a member's understanding of and commitment to organizational values, as well as by the individual's interpersonal relationships with others in the organization.

♦ Key questions can be asked to determine an individual's perceptions of communication climate. These questions focus upon the following characteristics:

—Clarity of organizational goals

—Clarity of tasks and functions

—Understanding of roles and functions of others

—Motivation to communicate or to avoid communicating

—Supportiveness and risk encouragement

—Fairness, equity, and trust

—Feedback and candor

—Organizational policy

♦ An organization's communication climate can be heavily influenced by formal policy statements regarding expected communication behaviors.

QUESTIONS FOR FURTHER THOUGHT

1. How do your personal goals coincide or conflict with your perceptions of your organization's goals? Can differences be reconciled? Are they important?

2. How well do you understand the objectives or goals of your work group, club, organization, class, etc.? Talk with someone else about these and see how your perceptions may differ.

OTHER THOUGHTS ABOUT EQUITY THEORY AS IT APPLIES TO EMPLOYEE AND CUSTOMER SATISFACTION AND RETENTION

"In the quest for quality, service is now king.... Now the pursuit of a competitive edge has shifted [from product improvement] to honing the caliber of customer care." Thus begins a November 12, 1990 article in *The Wall Street Journal* (p. B1).

The *Journal* echoes the refrain heard throughout the business community: Great customer service is good business. Today's sophisticated consumers expect to find satisfaction in both the product and the purchasing process. And they are willing to pay for it.

While virtually all businesses claim to be customer oriented, many fall short, at least in relative terms. Their competition is making inroads with what is often described as "little things" done for customers. Such little things can make all the difference when competing for a limited pool of potential customers. Indeed, demographic research shows a shrinking pool of both customers and available service personnel, creating a new battlefield for companies in the 1990s.

Without the population growth we've become accustomed to in the postwar era, companies' customers will come from two major sources: (1) from retaining repeat customers, and (2) from the competitions' unsatisfied customers.

Hence businesses face the dual challenges of creating excellent customer service and attracting the best of the available labor force.

Corporate success is an outgrowth of the satisfaction experienced by both external and internal customers. Satisfied customers return or tell others about a good business experience. Satisfied employees stay with the company and contribute to the culture of service through their example and loyalty.

The challenge is to create effective external and internal customer service activities, based in sound strategic considerations.

WHY MUCH CUSTOMER SATISFACTION TRAINING DOESN'T WORK

Although many consulting firms, training companies, and internal training departments teach "techniques for excellent customer service," the fact is these approaches alone don't work. The failure of such efforts stems from three major reasons:

1. Organizations see such training as a "program," meaning that it has a distinct beginning and end. Employees who have been around through a few such efforts quickly learn that "this too shall pass." Over time, the learning curve flattens and the program, with its recommended behaviors, soon fizzles.

2. Organizations focus too much on techniques or "smile skills" which are only a part—and a fairly small part—of customer service. By imposing some rote behaviors on employees, companies ignore the complexity of communication.

For example, a large discount store chain spent considerable effort teaching its clerks to thank the customer in a specific way. This doesn't sound so tough, they thought. But the results were unimpressive as unmotivated clerks, reminded by prominent signs on their cash registers, mouthed the words of appreciation like toneless drones.

The chain did little to enhance their image. Mouthing prescribed words ignores the fact that 90 percent of communication is nonverbal. The words themselves carry only 5 to 10 percent of the impact value, while other factors (tonality, facial expression, eye contact, timing, etc.) convey the other 90 percent.

This chain stands as a classic case of technique-based satisfaction attempts. Within the retail industry it has done nothing to improve customer perceptions and, in fact, has seen a sizable share of its market eroded by competitors.

Words without feeling fall on deaf ears. Programs without flexibility, commitment, and employee involvement accomplish little.

3. Many intervention attempts are not theory-based. Although, arguably, much of customer service is common sense, a theoretical base increases the probability of success over time. Good theory gives coherence to the effort and helps participants better understand the whys as well as the hows.

Over the past three years we have done extensive research into customer service programs. One organization,* a Utah-based tire store and service center chain tried several training seminars over a two-year period. Each of these sessions promised to improve specific customer service techniques. While improvement occurred initially following each of these sessions, employees reverted to the old ways within two weeks.

As consultants, we have seen similar results following programs in supermarkets, convenience stores, and hospitals.

In each case, the attitude of the employees toward their organization has been the catalyst for the rapid disintegration of the program. Each new program is greeted with increased cynicism (or at least skepticism) by employees who know that this is just another program.

Employees are generally willing and able to learn new ways of serving customers—unless they have been demotivated by organizational systems or negative socialization from other employees. But learning must be theory-based lest the intervention center too much on the personality and opinions of the trainer.

Leading authors and consultants (including Tom Peters, Ron Zemke, Karl Albrecht, Ken Blanchard, and others) are unanimous in recognizing the limited benefit of teaching techniques. Indeed, they caution companies against putting too much stock in quick fixes. We agree.

IF TECHNIQUE TRAINING DOESN'T WORK, WHAT DOES?

Changes in individual and organizational attitudes and predispositions offer the most promising approach for lasting enhancement of customer satisfaction.

---

*Coauthor of this proposal, Alan Hansen, was General Manager of this firm.

The intent of the proposed research is to verify preliminary findings based on the following working hypotheses:

- Success or failure of customer satisfaction efforts is directly related to employee satisfaction. To paraphrase Sam Walton, "Employees will treat their customers the way they are treated by their supervisors."

- Systems within organizations will enhance or inhibit the customer satisfaction efforts. Several consultants posit that "80 percent of customer service problems aren't caused by employees, they are caused by the system."*

- Among the "systems" cited as sources of service problems are reward distribution, internal communication, perceptions of equitable treatment, and the degree to which employee expectations are met by the company. Equity theory provides a solid theory base to explain these kinds of systemic problems.

- New employees enter organizations willing to give customers (internal and external) excellent service. Organizational systems and counterproductive subcultures often demotivate or socialize these workers toward a lesser goal. Again, equity theory provides a framework for better understanding this phenomenon.

NOTES

1. Tom Peters, *Thriving on Chaos: Handbook for a Management Revolution* (New York: Harper & Row, 1988).
2. From pp. 15–16, *The Organizational World* by Harold J. Leavitt, William R. Dill and Henry B. Eyring © 1973 by Harcourt Brace Jovanovich, Inc. Reprinted by permission of the publishers.
3. Leavitt *et al. op. cit.*, p.25.
4. Daniel Katz and Robert L. Kahn, *The Social Psychology of Organizations* (New York: John Wiley & Sons, 1966), p. 186.
5. *Ibid.*, pp. 193–195.
6. DeWitt C. Dearborn and Herbert A. Simon, "Selective Perception: The Departmental Identifications of Executives," *Sociometry, 21* (1958), pp. 140–144.
7. Chester Barnard, *The Functions of the Executive* (Cambridge, MA: Harvard University Press, 1938).
8. For elaboration on this line of thinking see Steven Kerr, "On the Folly of Rewarding A, While Hoping for B," *Academy of Management Journal*, December 1975, pp. 769–783.
9. Jack Gibb, "Defensive Communication," *Journal of Communication*, 1961, pp. 141–148.
10. Paul R. Timm, "Worker Responses to Supervisory Communication Inequity: An Exploratory Study," *Journal of Business Communication, 16,* 1 (Fall 1978), pp. 11–24.
11. Walter Wiesman, Wall-to-Wall *Organizational Communication* (Huntsville, AL: Walter Wiesman, 1973), p. 3.

*An opinion voiced recently in the *Wall Street Journal* by John Goodman, president of Tarp, a Washington, D.C. research and consulting firm.

12. David T. Burhans, Jr., "The Development and Field Testing of Two Internal Communication Measuring Instruments" (unpublished paper, California State College, Los Angeles, 1971), p. 5.

13. Geneva Seybold, *Employee Communication: Policy and Tools* (New York: National Industrial Conference Board, 1966), pp. 35–36. Reprinted by permission of The Conference Board.

14. *Ibid.*, p. 39.

15. Archie McCardell, "Open Communication Is Our Policy, But Sometimes…." *Xerox World, 21* (January 1976) p. 2.

16. Seybold, *op. cit.*, pp. 33–34.

17. Brent D. Peterson and R. Wayne Pace, "Communication Climate and Organizational Satisfaction" (unpublished paper, Brigham Young University, 1977).

18. Unpublished report by Paul R. Timm and Alan D. Hansen, 1993.

PART THREE

ORAL COMMUNICATION IN MANAGEMENT

CHAPTER 7

LOW-STRUCTURE, ONE-TO-ONE COMMUNICATION

I'm Glad We Had This Little Chat

In this chapter you will find ideas that will help you:

♦ Recognize the crucial role of low-structure, less formal, one-to-one communication in the management process

♦ Understand the importance and impact of good conversation skills

♦ Identify the need satisfaction that can result from meaningful, individual conversations

♦ Apply the power of verbal approval statements in a systematic manner to improve worker performance

♦ Anticipate the effects on worker behaviors (whether positive or negative) of withheld reinforcement

♦ Distinguish between Type 1 (ineffective or counterproductive) and Type 2 (effective) praise and criticism

♦ Recognize good telephone usage techniques for business

♦ Respect some common gender differences between male and female communicators

Carlos was attending his first company conference. The whole office staff was there at the hotel training room and the morning session had just ended. For these first three hours, he had listened to the reports given by various leaders in the company. The new product introduced was particularly interesting. Even to a new employee like Carlos, the company's future looked rosy.

Now it was time to break for lunch. The employees all went to the room next door where tables for six were set for the meal. Carlos really did not know many company people and was not sure where to sit. After stalling a few minutes, he selected an empty chair at one of the tables. It was not until after he had sat down that he discovered that one of the company vice-presidents was also seated at his table.

"Oh no. What am I going to talk about with this guy?" Carlos thought. "I really feel like a fish out of water. I am sure I will make some stupid remarks—after all, I don't even feel comfortable speaking English. Maybe I should move to another table."

But it was too late.

As the other attendees began eating their salads, Mrs. Joan Bannister, the vice-president of marketing, warmly introduced herself to Carlos. She knew Carlos was new with the company and cheerfully said, "Welcome aboard." Then the conversation went something like this:

Ms. Bannister: "So what do you think of the company so far?"

Carlos: "It's fine."

Ms. Bannister: "Are you originally from around here?"

Carlos: "No."

Ms. Bannister: "Then what brings you to the city?"

Carlos: "My girlfriend."

Ms. Bannister: "Oh, what does she do?"

Carlos: "She's looking for work. She wants to be a model or maybe an actress."

Ms. Bannister: "I see."

Carlos: "Yes, maam."[1]

Making conversation or small talk isn't as easy as it may look. Sometimes we simply can't think of the right things to initiate or maintain a conversation. Yet such conversation is often at the root of interpersonal relationships that make an organization thrive.

This chapter focuses on low-structure, one-to-one communication. Examples of this medium can range from the social talk of Carlos and Ms. Bannister to more formal, job-related tasks such as instruction giving and motivational feedback. In the next chapter we deal with the more formalized, higher-structured, one-to-one communication: interviews.

> **One-to-one communicating is not efficient.**

In Chapter 3, when we discussed communication media and tools, we concluded that talking with people in a one-to-one situation is the least *efficient* way of communicating. Yet it is also the most *effective*.[2]

This superiority in effectiveness is especially true when messages conveyed are complicated or emotionally sensitive. If, for example, you are teaching a worker a new skill, one-to-one coaching brings excellent results. Likewise, if you need to criticize a worker about a potentially sensitive matter, a one-to-one conversation is the only rational approach.

CONVERSATION: AN EXCHANGE OF PERCEPTIONS AND STROKES

People talk to each other to establish and maintain relationships, which in turn serve certain needs. Specifically these needs are:

1. To gain a better understanding of "reality" and to develop and clarify our self-image
2. To satisfy a normal hunger for affiliation with others
3. To gain support for our personal growth

Reality and Self-Image Clarification

> *Conversations build relationships which, in turn, help us understand "reality."*

We get a better picture of how things are by bouncing our perceptions off others. We develop satisfying relationships by sharing our view of the world and receiving validation or correction of that view from others. In organizations, other members fill us in on the details of the way things work as we learn the ropes—the way things really are.

But there is another type of reality that is clarified by our relationships with others. It is our self-concept. We develop a healthy self-image (or an unhealthy one) largely through our communication with others. From our earliest recollections, others—most often our parents—provided feedback to us about our personal worth. Our teachers commented that we were "bright" or "better at gym class than academics." Our peers noted that we "danced pretty good for a fat kid." Each evaluative comment could magnify or discount our self-image.

By the time we reach adulthood we have a fairly stabilized self-image; nevertheless, we continue to seek out information from others that reinforces the way we see ourselves. Among the tragic outcomes of the negative self-image is that it can be reinforced most effectively by negative "strokes"—by put-downs, humiliation, and failures.[3] The tendency is to establish relationships with those who provide the kind of self-worth confirmation we really want—positive or negative.

> *We quickly build relationships with people who reinforce our self-image—positively or negatively.*

Our Need to Satisfy a Hunger for Affiliation

People's needs for affiliation with others are met through their conversational relationships. All of us have some degree of need for social belonging. We want to identify and be identified with other individuals, groups, and organizations. Being deprived of human associations is most distressing. During the Vietnam war, servicemen who were prisoners of war suffered long periods of isolation

> **Deprivation from human contact is a form of torture.**

from all others. They later spoke of the ecstatic relief they felt on hearing even tapping on the dungeon walls by another prisoner. Periods of almost total deprivation from human interaction were broken by the primitive communication that said, "I know you are there."

Fortunately, few of us need to endure the agony of total isolation. Nevertheless, each person faces new and unusual experiences that may bring momentary deprivation of familiar forms of interaction with others. Travel to a foreign country where we do not speak the language or beginning an unfamiliar job in a strange city are examples. In such situations we are likely to gravitate toward others who seem to understand us best. Affiliation salves the discomfort of uncertainty. Relationships established by conversation satisfy this social need.

> **Affiliation with others reduces uncertainty.**

Support for Our Personal Growth

Clarifying reality, strengthening self image, and satisfying affiliation needs all contribute to our development as persons. Communicative interaction forms the stuff that holds relationships together.

Of course, interaction with employees is a key management tool as well. Touring work areas or circulating among organization members has, in recent years, been seen as an increasingly important function of the manager. Doing so increases opportunities for giving recognition and gaining insights from the people on the firing line. The payoff goes beyond mere pleasant interpersonal relations; it shows up in the maximization of human resources.

Managers can have profound effects on their employees simply by thanking or complimenting them. It sounds simplistic, but the fact remains that, as Robert Townsend said in *Up the Organization*, "Thanks [are] a really neglected form of compensation."[4]

EXPRESSING APPROVAL AND WORKER MOTIVATION

Management consultants have applied systematic approaches to expressing verbal approval that have demonstrated remarkable results. In countless corporations, such programs led to substantial cost savings and improvements in employee morale.

But what is a *systematic* approach to expressing verbal approval? The most common one is based in a psychological approach called *behavior modification*. At some companies application of this approach is called simply the *performance improvement* program.

Managers typically implement such a program first by holding a series of meetings in which managers and employees discuss mutual needs and problems as well as potential solutions. Key data are benchmarked to measure a starting point. These diagnostic sessions provide a base for determining job performance standards and how they will be met. The meetings also identify reinforcers that managers may use to modify the employees' behavior. One company held a three-day session, which revealed that what workers, such as clerk typists, wanted most was a sense of belonging, a sense of accomplishment, and a sense of teamwork. In return, for their attempts to provide these, managers asked for quicker filing of reports and fewer errors.

The second step is to arrange for worker performance to be observed with reliable follow-up; the third is to give feedback often, immediately letting employees know how their current level of performance compares with the level desired. For example, in one early attempt, an airline company with five telephone reservation offices employing about 1,800 people kept track of the percentage of calls in which callers made flight reservations. Then they fed back the results daily to each employee. At the same time, supervisors were instructed to praise employees for asking callers for their reservations. Within a few months, the ratio of sales to calls soared from one in four to one in two.[5]

> *The objective of a verbal approbation program is to reward systematically— to tie the reward to specific performance.*

Whatever the name of the program, the objective is to provide communicative rewards in such a way that they motivate performance and reduce dissatisfaction. The timing of this feedback should meet the criteria of high speed. Face-to-face conversation would normally be the best choice of media, with a phone call ranking second.

Why This Works: A Psychology of Change

At the heart of any such performance improvement effort is the premise that *future behavior is influenced by the outcomes of past behavior*. If the outcome immediately following an act is in some way rewarding, people are likely to repeat the behavior. If the response is punishing, people are likely to not do it again, unless they see punishment as preferable to other outcomes, such as simply being ignored.

Managers, then, can provide three types of responses to employee behaviors:

♦ Positive reinforcement

♦ Negative reinforcement

♦ No observable response at all

Some people question just how far we can go with verbal approval as a motivator. Theoretically, it should work indefinitely so long as appropriate *schedules of reinforcement* are used. The two main reinforcement schedules are

> *Continuous reinforcement gets quick performance results initially.*

continuous and *intermittent*. Continuous reinforcement means the individual receives reinforcement (a compliment or supportive statement) every time he or she engages in the desired behavior. This approach is useful when the person is being taught a new behavior and needs to be shored up to develop confidence in this new ability. People learn very quickly, at least initially, under continuous reinforcement.

You can readily see the results of continuing reinforcement when teaching a small child how to do something like catching a ball. If, each time the ball is caught, you praise the child, the child will develop this skill very quickly. The principle generally holds for employees working on unfamiliar tasks.

Yet the use of continuous reinforcement poses at least three problems:

1. It takes too much time, and therefore it costs a great deal in terms of supervisory effort. It is just not feasible always to be there complimenting each job done—you might at well do the job yourself!

2. It can diminish in effectiveness because of "inflation." Just as dollars lose value when too many are in circulation, verbal approval is cheapened by overuse.

3. Once continuous reinforcement is expected, it is tough to wean people away from it without certain risks. If we suddenly drop continuous reinforcement—that is, if we no longer express verbal approval for each good behavior—the message to our worker may be that the behavior is no longer appropriate and should be stopped. In short, we may extinguish the desired behavior.

The drawbacks to continuous reinforcement are largely overcome by shifting to *intermittent reinforcement*. Here, instead of expressing approval of every act, we use another system to allocate compliments. We may decide to express approval at intervals, such as each time a unit of work—say, a day's or week's quota—is completed. Most organizations use intermittent reinforcement in the payment of wages. Workers do not get paid 15¢ each time they assemble an item. Instead they are paid at the end of the week or twice a month. The same principle can apply to communicative rewards.

> *Random, intermittent reinforcement can lead to longer-term motivation.*

Another intermittent reinforcement approach is to provide rewards at completely random times. Much of the lure of slot machine gambling comes from the anticipated random windfall. The anticipation or hope of a sudden big reward keeps the players engaged in the "desired" behavior—putting money in the slot.

Under random intermittent reinforcement workers don't know exactly when they will be rewarded. So long as employees hold hope of eventually receiving a reward such as verbal approval, extinction of the desired behavior is delayed. If the rewards are too far apart, of course, workers will not continue to produce unless they are particularly good at working hard today for some far-off, but certain-to-be-worthwhile reward. Relatively few workers today are content to get their reward in heaven.

The best approach is to use continuous reinforcement when new behaviors are being developed and then gradually move to an intermittent schedule so the desired performance won't be inadvertently extinguished. In other words, shift the employees' expectations so that longer intervals between reinforcement are seen as normal.

PRAISE AND CRITICISM

Sometimes praise is downright embarrassing and so-called constructive criticism just plain makes you mad. Morrison and O'Hearne have developed an explanation of why praise and criticism seem to have such an on-again, off-again value.[6] These authors suggest that both praise and criticism can be broken down into two types. Type 1 praise consists of those statements that have little effect on the performance of the receiver. They are accepted like water on a duck's back. Type 2 praise consists of those statements that *might* have a positive effect on performance under certain circumstances. There are no guarantees, but these kinds of "attaboys" might motivate or at least build stronger authentic relationships between the giver and the receiver. Some examples of Type 1 and Type 2 praise are offered in Figure 7-1.

A similar classification of criticism is illustrated in Figure 7-2. Type 1 criticism results in defensiveness and deterioration of performance while Type 2 criticism is at least potentially constructive in that it *might* result in improved future performance.

GIVING INSTRUCTIONS

Two-way instruction giving works best.

In some organizations the most frequent communication contact managers have with employees is giving orders, directions, or instructions. Although some bosses approach this as one-way, boss-to-subordinate communication, a two-way format is usually far more appropriate.

As managers, we need to know exactly what action we want to result from instructions given. That seems self-evident. Yet this assessment is occasionally overlooked. When we give a subordinate instructions to "clean up this area," we may not have a clear picture of what the finished product will look like. And we might be disappointed. Instead we need to clarify mentally our purpose—our reason for giving the order—and then *plan* the best way of creating understanding with the employee.

Use clear, concrete terms when giving instructions.

The term "a clean area" will likely have different meanings for different people. An effective instruction giver will create a clearer image in the message receiver's mind by supplying some details.

Providing sufficient details and *repetition* are good ways to minimize misunderstandings. The journalist's "who, what, where, when, why, and how" provide a good framework for giving instructions. Be sure you know the answers to each of these before directing someone else. And be sure to encourage questions from the message receiver.

A simple "Do you have any questions?" probably isn't the best technique. The question calls for a yes-or-no response, and many people opt for no to avoid showing ignorance. By changing the wording to "What questions do you

Type 1 praise—has little effect on performance of the receiver.	Type 2 praise—may have a positive effect on performance and build an authentic relationship.
1. Generalized praise such as, "You're doing a good job, Charlie." This is meaningless and it generally rolls off the back of the individual without effect. It is often seen as a "crooked" stroke.	1. Specific praise—such as, "Charlie, you did a great job handling that unpleasant customer with a complaint this afternoon." This communicates to the receiver that the boss has actually observed or heard about the praised action ...
2. Praise with no further meaning. There is no analysis of why a praised behavior is being commended. This discounts the persons being praised by assuming they will react with higher productivity and better morale merely as a response.	2. Continuing with, "The reason I think it was such a good job is because you acted interested, asked questions, wrote down the facts, asked the customer what she thought we should do to make it right." Analysis of this kind permits the employee to internalize the learning experience ...
3. Praise for expected performance, when such praise may be questioned. Mabel, who always gets in on time and is met one morning with, "Mable, you're sure on time today, you're doing great," from her boss, may wonder what's really going on.	3. Praise for better-than-expected results ...for coming in over quota ... exceeding the target ... putting out extra effort.
4. The "sandwich" system—praise is given first to make the person be receptive to criticism (the real reason for the transaction), which is then followed by another piece of praise, hoping, thereby to encourage the person to try harder next time, feel better about the criticism.	4. Praise, when deserved, is believable if it is given by itself. When mixed with critique it is suspect. Authentic relations develop better when people talk straight. When positive conditional recognition is in order, give it; when critique is deserved, give that. Don't mix the two.
5. Praise perceived by the receiver as given in the nature of a "carrot," mainly to encourage the receiver to work even harder in the future.	5. Praise that is primarily to commend and recognize, and does not seek to put a mortgage on the future.
6. Praise handed out lavishly only when the brass or higher-ups are present. Employees soon recognize the boss is trying to impress superiors with what a good human being he or she really is in dealing with subordinates.	6. Praise given when it is deserved, not just on special occasions, when it seems to build the image of the praiser to some third party.

FIGURE 7-1   Ineffective versus effective praise.

Type 1 criticism—tends to produce a defensive reaction in the receiver and worsen performance.	*Type 2 criticism—a type of constructive criticism that may improve performance.*
1. Criticism that involves use of the personal "you," e.g., "You're having too many accidents on the lift truck, Bill. What's the matter with you anyway?" It is almost always seen as a discount or put-down by the receiver ...	1. Criticism using a situational description, e.g., "Bill, we're experiencing an increase in lift-truck accidents. dents. What's going on?" This indicates the manager is open to looking at all the facts leading to the unfavorable result.
2. Criticism that is unanalyzed. The subordinate then tends to rationalize the criticism as a personal opinion of the manager.... Or, the manager is viewed as unable to analyze the problems effectively.	2. Discussion of cause and effect with the unfavorable condition per ceived by both as the result of one or more causal factors, one of which might even be the manager!
3. If the situation has been properly assessed, some managers are at a loss to provide coaching necessary for the subordinate to improve. This may be the result of ignorance or lack of competency in deciding on the corrective steps.	3. If steps 1 and 2 above have been properly accomplished, it is important for solutions to be outlined and agreed on. If the subordinate can't do this, the manager must provide, or arrange, for a resource that can develop corrective measures.
4. Critique of an individual in public is not only regarded as humiliating by the subordinate involved, but sometimes even more so by other members of the organization.	4. Individual criticism given in private is usually more acceptable. Saving face is almost as important in Western cultures as it is in the Orient.
5. Criticism given *only* in the interests of the boss (to get the boss recognition, promotion, or raise) or the organization (more profit or status in the marketplace). These may all be legitimate interests, but *authentic* relationships are not likely to develop.	5. Criticism given *also*, or even chiefly, in the interests of the employee (to provide greater competencies, future achievements, or a more secure future with the organization).
6. The manager does all the critiquing which sets the stage for a Parent-Child [relationship].	6. The subordinate participates in the critiques, even to the point of taking the lead role in defining the unsatisfactory condition, analyzing causes, and suggesting corrective steps.
7. Criticism used as a [calculated] game to justify withholding raises or promotions.	7. Game-free criticism leading toward candor and [authentic interactions].

Adapted from James H. Morrison and John H. O'Hearne, *Practical Transactional Analysis in Management* (Reading, MA: Addison-Wesley, 1977), pp. 120–121. Reprinted with permission.

FIGURE 7-2   Destructive versus constructive criticism.

have?" you say to the employee, "It's okay to have questions" and you encourage task clarification. Be sure to pause long enough to let your listeners know you are serious about getting questions from them.

When explaining instructions, use simple, specific terms. Start with something the employee already knows and move to the new or more complex. Show how the two are related. Give reasons for what's to be done so that the task won't be seen as busywork. Demonstrate or dramatize where this could enhance understanding. And follow up to evaluate the completed job. Give the employee a sense of success and give yourself an opportunity to reinforce positive behavior.

Using the Telephone In One-To-One Communication

One final form of one-to-one communication is the telephone call. The telephone has the media advantages of speed and relatively low cost. It permits one-to-one communication when participants are geographically separated. It provides, as the telephone company ads used to say, "the next best thing to being there." In fact, the only significant drawback to the phone is that it does not permit most nonverbal communication cues.

The drawback to the telephone as a communications medium is that each telephone call creates interactions where people are operating blind—without the visual feedback that helps us assign meaning to language and events. To compensate for the lack of visual stimuli, we draw many conclusions from what we hear alone. And what we hear includes some very subtle cues such as tone of voice, work choice, pauses, and the occasional mumble. Two of the most irritating telephone use errors are the failure to respond to statements made by the other party, and cutting off the conversation.

> *With the phone, we are always flying blind.*

Place and Receive Your Own Calls

Some business people think it's a sign of status to have their secretary place telephone calls for them. It probably does convey some of that and most of us wouldn't expect it to be any other way for major corporate or governmental leaders. But when a supervisor or mid-level manager has a secretary place a call to someone at the same or higher organizational level, the call may be poorly received. One businessperson reports his experience of calling a company president this way:

I'll never forget the first time I called Jack on the telephone. I asked my secretary to get him, and when she said, "Mr. Sordoni's on the line," I picked up and said, "Hello."

"Are you calling me?" asked Jack.

"Sure," I said.

"Then how come your secretary called me?"

"I just asked her to get you on the phone," I said, beginning to squirm.

"So I could wait on the phone while you get ready to let me have the honor of hearing your voice? You're calling *me*, remember?" And he hung up.

I dialed his number again myself, and sure enough he answered. No switchboard, no secretary, just Jack Sordoni, president of the Commonwealth Telephone Co., saying, "This is Sordoni."[7]

> ◄ *Placing your own calls shows you value the other person's time.* ►

When you place your own calls, you are telling your listeners that you value their time. If you are willing personally to make the effort to contact another person, the other person is likely to feel more obligated to expend some effort and converse with you.

Individuals should be encouraged to answer their own phones unless they are engaged in a face-to-face conversation that should not be interrupted. Routine screening of calls by a secretary or reception person often creates resentment in the caller. The indiscriminate use of "May I say who's calling?" is often recognized as a dodge—an opportunity to decide whether the person wants to talk to the caller or not. Even if the call legitimately cannot be accepted, the phrase may be considered a snub.

The appropriate way to answer a business call is by simply stating your name. Use of a Mrs., Miss, Ms., or Dr. may sound a bit stand-offish. Some employees might simply use their last name, unless this would be confusing to the caller. Others prefer to state first and last names.

Use of "May I help you?" following your name is a pleasant way to start off a conversation. This approach tells your caller: (1) whom they are speaking with, and (2) that you are ready to converse with them. So let's be sure you *are* ready.

Keep Calls Efficient

> ◄ *Work to be concise without being rude or abrupt.* ►

Although small talk is sometimes useful to create a personable relationship between callers, more important organization members are generally more efficient with phone use. The real pro can make a call very concise without being curt.

When placing a business call, plan ahead, preferably in writing. What is the *purpose* of your call? What information do you want to get or give? Is this likely to be a good time to call? Jot down the key questions or items you need before you begin to dial. And be sure to identify yourself immediately—business people don't like playing guess who.

Since your voice is the only source of informational clues available to your listener, be especially careful to speak clearly into the mouthpiece. Make sure you provide verbal feedback to your caller so that he or she knows you're still there. Long pauses can be disconcerting. One good way to convey appropriate voice is to visualize the other person and then visualize yourself talking directly to that person, perhaps using a few gestures as you talk to feel more comfortable and natural.[10]

GENDER DIFFERENCES IN CONVERSATIONS[9]

Recent studies confirm that males and females may respond differently to other people—especially when people talk about their problems or personal matters.

With women, conversations often go this way: The woman tells her friend her trouble. The friend nods, "I know how you feel. The same thing has happened to me," and she tells her own matching story. They finish discussing the first woman's problem. The result is that the first woman has received a validation that she and her feelings are normal, and a sense of closeness and understanding with her friend.

When a man tells his friend his trouble, however, the friend is likely to laugh it off. "Oh, that is no big deal." The man feels comforted that his problem is not so bad after all. His friend will then offer a comparable but different problem, which the first man will in turn laugh off. The message is, "The world is tough on both of us, and we are both about equally able to deal with it." Their problems are equivalent but not shared. They both maintain their independence. It is reassuring to both men.

> *Conversation problems arise when you cross gender lines without considering what the other person needs.*

Problems between people set in when the different approaches meet. If a woman tells a man that she knows just how he feels because the same thing has happened to her, it may make him more anxious. Far from helping him laugh it off, he sees her as dwelling on it.

On the other hand, if a man tells a woman her problem is really nothing, she feels belittled and may well redouble her efforts to make him understand just how bad this problem is. Or he may want to take the male "protective" role and "solve" her problem by giving advice on what she should do.

She wants understanding. He wants to laugh it off. Neither approach is better. They are simply different mind sets. But this kind of difference can be a real source of frustration.[10]

Men: Resist the temptation to fix the problem. Do a reality check; ask if she wants ideas on what to do or is she mainly expressing frustration. Then sympathize.

Women: Do not get uptight about his lack of shared concern or his jumping on with a solution. If he expresses a problem, ask what you or he can do to solve it. He probably wants more than just a sympathetic ear or to hear you describe your similar problem.

A QUICK SUMMARY OF MAJOR IDEAS

♦ One-to-one communication between a boss and subordinates can provide important psychological benefits, as well as improve the functioning of the organization. For some messages, there is no reasonable substitute for the personal touch.

♦ Conversations serve human needs for reality clarification, self-image validation, affiliation with others, and personal growth.

♦ Verbal approval statements (positive strokes) can result in significant performance improvement in workers so long as such stroking is genuine, sincere, and systematic.

♦ Depending on how they are phrased, praise and criticism can be productive or counterproductive to relationships within an organization. Poorly phrased comments result in defensiveness and resentment. Well phrased thoughts can enhance worker performance.

♦ Instruction giving works best when two-way communication is established and communicators can seek clarification.

♦ The telephone has some unique media advantages, yet it is often misused. Suggestions for effective use were presented.

♦ Gender differences affect conversation skills at the level of psychological needs.

QUESTIONS FOR FURTHER THOUGHT

1. Think of a one-to-one communication you participated in recently. It may have been an interview such as those discussed in this chapter or a discussion with someone in your family, a friend, or a sales representative. What specific behaviors or exchanges can you recall that led to developing understanding? What things tended to turn you off to that person? Be as specific as possible.

2. Recall recent praise or criticism you received on your job or in school. How did you feel and respond? Was it Type 1 or Type 2? Give some examples.

3. How do gender differences affect the creation of meaning? Give examples of how you and the opposite sex tend to interpret messages.

4. Why is it important to minimize the screening of telephone calls? Has recent technology helped or hindered your ability to use the phone efficiently?

OTHER THOUGHTS ABOUT LOW-STRUCTURE, ONE-TO-ONE COMMUNICATION

SOME DO'S AND DON'TS OF BUSINESS AND PERSONAL CONVERSATION

Except for your closest friends, people do not normally want to hear about your personal problems. (One exception is your supervisor, if a problem affects your work.) As a TV talk show host quipped, "Eighty percent of the people don't care, and the other 20 percent are *glad* you've got problems too."

Complaints about your boss, coworkers, company, or school tend to fall on deaf ears. Everybody has relationship problems at times. Unless you are seeking advice on how to improve the situation from a close friend or trusted advisor, save your breath.

As a general rule, avoid:

♦ Criticizing or belittling others (remember the golden rule).

♦ Griping about the company, department, or class.

♦ Passing on gossip and hurtful comments about others.

♦ Being judgmental of others, as though you are in a position to pass judgment. Being different is not a crime.

♦ Using profanity.

♦ Antagonizing or stirring up bad feelings among people.

♦ Criticizing people, especially in front of others.

♦ Making racial, religious, or gender insults.

♦ Flirting or making comments with sexual overtones.

As a general rule, do:

♦ Make your comments positive and upbeat.

♦ Be supportive of other people.

♦ Give others the benefit of the doubt; do not be quick to judge.

♦ Compliment freely and often.

♦ Respectfully acknowledge people's accomplishments, birthdays, and religious holidays.

Apply these conversation skills and see how they enhance your career and your personal life.

NOTES

1. Adapted from Paul R. Timm, *Basics of Oral Communication* (Cincinnati: Southwestern Publishing, 1993), pp. 43–44.

2. Remember, efficiency is the ratio between the cost of producing a message and the number of people reached. Communication effectiveness, however, results when the message is received by the right people, interpreted correctly, remembered, and used.

3. A *stroke* is any communicated expression of recognition. Arising from transactional analysis (TA), the term is sometimes misapplied to refer only to expressions of verbal approval.

4. Frequently stated in different ways, Townsend potently reminded managers of the importance of verbal approval in his book—one of the first management books to be a best seller. Robert Townsend, *Up the Organization*, (New York: Alfred A. Knopf, 1970), p. 184.

5. "Productivity Gains from a Pat on the Back," *Business Week*, January 23, 1978, pp. 57–58.

6. James H. Morrison and John H. O'Hearne, *Practical Transactional Analysis in Management* (Reading, MA: Addison-Wesley, 1977), pp. 118–121.

7. Jim Lavenson, *Selling Made Simple* (New York: Sales Management, 1973), pp. 59–60.

8. A video program and book by Paul R. Timm, *Telephone Tips* (Chicago: JWA Video, 1994) provides additional ideas on business phone use.

9. The success of best-selling books like Deborah Tannen's *You Just Don't Understand: Men and Women in Conversation* (New York: Ballantine Books, 1990) have boosted awareness of this important aspect of communication.

10. This example is adapted from a newspaper column by Amanda Smith (Scripps-Howard Syndicate), "Men, Women Respond Differently to Others, Problems," which appeared in the *Deseret News*, Salt Lake City, March 21, 1991.

11. Paul R. Timm, *Basics of Oral Communication* (Cincinnati, OH: Southwestern Publishing, 1993), p. 54.

CHAPTER 8

HIGHER STRUCTURE, ONE-TO-ONE COMMUNICATION

Interviews

▼

In this chapter you will find ideas that will help you:

♦ Identify the key ingredients of the effective interview and know how to maximize this management medium

♦ Recognize the purposes, ideal climate and process, and potential obstacles of six specialized interview formats

♦ Apply seven different types of questions in interview situations

♦ Apply techniques for effectively handling the job search interview both as an applicant and a decision maker

▼

It was seven p.m. and the office had been closed for two hours, but Sue Fleming was still at her desk. She was finishing a report due the next morning. Although she normally enjoyed preparing such reports, she was annoyed with herself for not taking a stronger stand when information for the report was turned in half-finished by Mary Keller, one of her employees. If this had been the only time that Mary had turned in unfinished work Sue would not have been angry. The problem was that Mary did this regularly. On several occasions Sue had to delay completing a design proposal that was Mary's responsibility.

Management textbooks often call Mary's action "delegating upward" or "reverse delegation." The first step recommended by textbooks to deal with the problem is to confront the employee.[1]

164

INTERVIEWS ARE PLANNED

Effective interviewing is conversation that is *planned* and has specific *purposes.* Although we often associate interviewing with the job-getting process, it has equally important functions in the organization's internal communication program. This chapter looks at internal interviews first. We end with the selection (job-getting) format.

> ***Keep the purpose clearly in mind.***

Interviews can be an organization's most effective information-sharing activities. In many situations there is no substitute for them. Too often, though, managers sit down to interview an employee without doing homework first. The key question for the interviewer must always be: "What am I attempting to accomplish in this interview?"

The three key ingredients of the successful interview are:

♦ A clear purpose for having the interview

♦ A planned approach to maximize the value of the time spent together

♦ Ample opportunities for interaction between participants

The Interview's Purpose

Interview purposes may generally be categorized as giving and getting information, seeking attitude or behavior changes, and solving problems. Of course, many situations call for a combination of purposes.

Planning The Interview

The planning phase of the interview process involves careful consideration of the following:

1. Exactly how you hope to accomplish your purpose
2. The characteristics, needs, and motivations of the other person
3. The climate or setting in which the interview will take place
4. Specific questions and general structure of questions to be used

Creating Opportunities for Interaction

The effectiveness of interaction between participants depends in large part on purpose and planning. The overall climate of the interview situation affects the degree and quality of communication. Interaction means that both parties have ample *opportunity* to participate. If the interviewer finds herself talking uninterruptedly for as long as two or three minutes, she is likely failing to maximize this communication medium. There should be a good deal of give-and-take, even when the manager's key purpose is to give information.

Creating an environment that is "safe" for interaction is an important task. Specific techniques for soliciting and encouraging feedback are presented later in this chapter.

SIX SPECIALIZED INTERVIEW FORMATS

Six types of interviews are especially important in managerial communication: (1) *performance review,* (2) *counseling,* (3) *reprimand,* (4) *grievance,* (5) *exit interviews,* and (6) *selection interviews.* We look at each of these formats in terms of:

♦ Its primary purpose
♦ The ideal climate and a brief description of the process for success
♦ Obstacles one might expect to encounter

THE PERFORMANCE REVIEW

The performance review is an excellent tool, *if* it is used effectively. And that's a big *if.* Too often, poorly prepared or improperly conducted performance reviews undo in an hour all the good supervisor-employee relationships that have developed over months or even years. This is the down side risk. But on the positive side, an *effective* review session can go a long way toward clarifying expectations and objectives for both supervisor and worker, and can provide a base for a supportive, mutually helpful work relationship.

Most workers react well to individual one-on-one attention from their boss, so long as the conversation is constructive and nonthreatening. Indeed, management theorists agree that periodic individual performance reviews are vital to the supervision process. For newer employees, formal review sessions may be held quarterly or every six months. Annual reviews are common for more long-term employees. These reviews are, of course, in addition to less formal praising, correcting, reprimanding and instruction giving which may be

> **Most workers appreciate constructive input from their boss.**

needed. The terms *performance review* or *appraisal* refer to a *formal, carefully planned interview session* with an accompanying *written report.* Those three elements—planning, interviewing, and reporting—are crucial.

In a performance review, the manager's role is and must be that of an evaluator, but it should not be judgmental in matters going beyond the work context. "Order accuracy in your work group needs to be improved" would normally be appropriate in an appraisal interview. "You need to get a haircut and stop living with your girlfriend" would be out of line.

Telling workers how they are doing is not enough. The review really must be an interview—two-way communication—to be effective. Performance reviews are not talking to subordinates, but talking *with* them.

The Purposes of a Performance Review

Norman Maier wrote an early and still influential book on performance appraisals in which he identified eight possible purposes for a formal performance review. Managers should use the performance review to:

1. Let employees *know where they stand*
2. *Recognize* good work
3. Communicate to subordinates *directions* in which they should improve
4. *Develop* employees in their present jobs
5. Develop and *train* employees for higher jobs
6. Let subordinates know the direction in which they make *progress in the organization*
7. Serve a *record* for assessment of the department or unit as a whole and show where each person fits into the larger picture
8. *Warn* certain employees that they must improve[2]

As you can see from this list, much of what is done in performance appraisals is beneficial to the worker: recognizing achievement, giving direction, developing and training, and identifying growth opportunities. There is no need for the supervisor to be apologetic or hesitant to schedule these reviews. A positive approach to planning the review should be stressed. The performance review is really a useful way to help workers grow.

Ideal Climate and Process

> *An objective, fair climate is important, even if the interview is sometimes tense.*

The interviewer should strive for a climate of objectivity—evaluating the subordinate's work while avoiding irrelevant judgments about personal characteristics. Tact and skill are required, but touchy job-related issues should be addressed head on. Don't expect the dialogue always to be warm or pleasant. Many things discussed in the performance review are hard for most people to talk about. Occasionally confrontations will arise. These should be expected.

> *Managers must be able to support criticisms with examples and data.*

One of the truly deadly sins of performance reviews is to make unsupported statements or generalizations. To tell a worker that he has a bad work attitude or that he does shoddy work does that worker absolutely no good. Such statements don't really convey anything except the supervisor's disgust. They serve only to destroy the climate of openness necessary to help the worker improve.

The most useful kind of information compares actual results against ideal or anticipated results. Anticipated results are those that have been set as targets for the worker. In some companies these goals are stated by management, and workers are expected to strive for them. But increasingly, goal setting is becoming a joint process of management and workers. The obvious advantage in getting workers to set their own goals with their manager is that the goals become more personal. The worker is likely to feel greater commitment to targets that he or she is involved in setting.

> *Work performance (goals) should be set jointly by manager and subordinate.*

The general process for effectively communicating in a performance review includes these steps:

1. Seek the person's own opinion of his or her performance.
   - Keep the lines of communication open.
   - Encourage the employee to be candid.
2. Give honest praise.
   - As the Greek said, "Many men know how to flatter; few know how to praise."
   - Don't couple praise with criticism in the same sentence: "You did a great job on X, but your Y needs improvement."

♦ Praise for better-than-expected results, not for minimal work behaviors ("You sure do come to work on time!").

3. Allow the individual to specify areas of improvement and set goals.
  ♦ Help the worker set realistic targets.
  ♦ Gain specific commitment from the individual.
  ♦ Show the individual that you have confidence in him or her.

4. Summarize what you have previously discussed.
  ♦ Be sure you understand one another.
  ♦ Show the individual that you are in agreement with his or her goals.
  ♦ Remind the individual of commitment to agreed-on goals.

5. End on an encouraging note.
  ♦ Thank the worker for his or her efforts.
  ♦ Restate your willingness to be supportive of the worker.

Obstacles

Certain attitudes on the part of the manager can set the stage for failure. Among these are:

1. Failure to accept the subordinate unconditionally as a person. A fundamental respect for the worth of people is required for effective performance appraisals to take place. This does not mean that the manager accepts the subordinate's behavior or value system. It means, instead, that the subordinate's potential and intrinsic worth to the organization are implicitly assumed. More simply stated, a useful attitude for supervisors to hold is one of regard for their people, despite any shortcomings they may have.

> *People's intrinsic worth must never be diminished.*

2. Being overly concerned with *why* subordinates behave as they do rather than with what can be done to improve is another unproductive managerial attitude. Overemphasis on specific causes tends to lead to the making of excuses and to rationalization by the subordinate. When this approach is carried too far, we find the manager playing amateur psychologist. Diagnosing a psychological condition and giving it a label such as "poor self-image," "lack of aggressiveness," or "too hot-tempered" can lead to self-fulfilling prophecies. Once we have identified a problem in such a way we are likely to see more and more evidence that supports our diagnosis as correct. We selectively pay attention to examples of "hot temper" or apparent lack of self-assurance so we can say, "Aha—just as I thought!"

> *Focus on specific behaviors, not necessarily* **why** *the behavior is occurring.*

3. A third attitudinal problem is an underlying belief that appraisal sessions should be used to punish the employee. If you find yourself thinking,

"Wait until his performance review—I'll get that SOB then," you are missing the point. Review sessions based in confrontation are seldom productive.

Performance reviews categorize people's behaviors and make judgments about behaviors in light of organizational needs. Some people, of course, feel uncomfortable being so evaluated. Perhaps this accounts for satirical guides to appraisal categories like the one found circulating in one company (see Figure 8-1).

Probably the single most common obstacle to effective performance reviews is employee *defensiveness.* Phrasing comments in nonevaluative ways can make your employee performance reviews more effective. (See the article, "Nonevaluative Approaches to Performance Appraisals," by Les Wallace, at the end of this chapter.)

One final thought on employee defensiveness: Researcher W. Charles Redding studied the effects of such defensiveness on employee performance. In one extensive study cited by Redding,

> researchers found that the typical employee reacted defensively about 54 percent of the time when criticized. Moreover, constructive responses to criticism were *rarely* observed. Finally, and most significant of all, the actual on-the-job performance suffered on those very items to which the bosses had paid special attention.[3]

> **Create a supportive climate first.**

Managers should create a supportive interview climate conducive to information sharing as well as evaluation.

COUNSELING INTERVIEWS

When an employee is experiencing specific, personal difficulties—rather than a general pattern of performance that would be dealt with in an appraisal interview—a counseling interview may be in order. Counseling sessions can address matters such as marriage difficulties, drug or alcohol dependence, or inability to cope with stress. Although personal problems may not have directly measurable impact on work performance, they can lead to serious organizational problems if unattended. You as a manager are certainly not expected to have the solutions to these problems, but it sometimes becomes necessary to confront the more obvious situations, lend a sympathetic ear, and know the procedures for referrals to professional help where appropriate.

> **You need not have the solution to confront a problem.**

Purpose of the Counseling Interview

The counseling interview addresses and seeks resolution to employee problems, often of a personal nature, which may have negative impact on the organization if left untreated.

Performance Factors	Far Exceeds Job Requirements	Exceeds Job Requirements	Meets Job Requirements	Needs Some Improvement	Does not meet Minimum Requirements
Quality	Leaps tall buildings with a single bound	Must take running start to leap over tall buildings	Can leap over short buildings only	Crashes into buildings when attempting to jump over them	Cannot recognize buildings at all
Timeliness	Is faster than a speeding bullet	Is as fast as a speeding bullet	Not quite as fast as a speeding bullet	Would you believe a slow bullet?	Wounds self with bullet when attempting to shoot
Initiative	Is stronger than a locomotive	Is stronger that a bull elephant	Is stronger than a bull	Shoots the bull	Smells like a bull
Adaptability	Walks on water consistently	Walks on water in emergencies	Washes with water	Drinks water	Passes water in emergencies
Communication	Talks with God	Talks with the angels	Talks to himself	Argues with himself	Loses those arguments

FIGURE 8-1   A satirical guide to employee performance appraisal.

Ideal Climate and Process

Trust is the key word in describing a productive climate for counseling. The manager must assure the employee that strict confidentiality will be observed and that this counseling will have no detrimental effects on the subordinate's job opportunities. The climate should also be *permissive*—the employee should feel free to introduce any subject for discussion without fear of offending, alienating, or embarrassing the interviewer. The words and nonverbal cues of the interviewer should be *nonjudgmental* and the interview approach should be *nondirective*—that is, the employee should determine what subjects will be considered. It is important that the manager feels a sense of empathy—be able to sense the feelings and personal meaning of the interviewee as though he or she personally were experiencing them. The atmosphere should be unhurried if possible.

> **Empathy is crucial to the success of a counseling interview.**

Obstacles

Most managers are not professional counselors. Most tend to get impatient with the often time-consuming and frequently discouraging process of counseling people with problems. It costs a great deal of time and therefore money. Professional counselors are often preferable. These may be in-house psychologists in larger organizations or, in many cases, the manager can do the most good by recommending—strongly—that the troubled employee seek professional advice outside the organization. If a productive worker can be salvaged, the time and effort is, of course, justified.

REPRIMAND INTERVIEWS: THE GENTLE ART OF CHEWING OUT AN EMPLOYEE

The survival and growth of any organization requires order. Responses to members who violate norms of order determine what further behaviors will be deemed acceptable.

Purpose of the Reprimand Interview

> **Ignoring inappropriate behavior may let such behavior become the norm.**

When individuals act in ways that are blatantly destructive to organizational functioning, simply ignoring their behavior in hope that it will go away may not work. The reprimand interview can and should be regarded as an opportunity to turn around unacceptable behaviors. It must be followed by positive recognition when improvement materializes.

Ideal Climate and Process

As with the performance review, some managers hold underlying assumptions that are counterproductive to the reprimand situation. Among these are certain failures to recognize the limitations within which the manager must work. Managers go wrong when they:

1. *Fail to recognize that discipline implies rules, not personal desires.* The belief that a manager has legitimate authority to reprimand those who violate his or her personal sense of what should be, without regard to whether or not organizational rules have been violated, is a misconception. Management has no divine right to act above or around organizational law.

2. *Fail to remember that discipline implies correction of error and believe that it is unnecessary to be specific in citing violations.* Some managers mistakenly feel that all they really owe employees is to tell them they're wrong-headed.

3. *Overemphasize who's to blame rather than what's wrong.* This tends to arise from an implicit and oversimplified belief that there is a single cause for any given malady.

4. *Fail to recognize the need for equitable treatment of all subordinates.* Some managers feel they can make an example of one violator while ignoring similar behaviors of others.

5. *Believe that one's supervisory rights extend to robbing a person of dignity.* Some managers assume a legitimate right to humiliate employees.

There is probably no quicker way for a manager to open mouth, insert foot than to commit one or more of what George Odiorne lists as his time-tested "Seven Deadly Sins of Reprimanding":[4]

1. *Failing to get facts.* Be sure you have all the facts before leaping. Don't accept hearsay evidence, or go on general impressions.

2. *Acting while angry.* Don't act while you've lost your temper. Be calm in your own mind, and as objective as possible in making a decision to reprimand. Ask yourself, "Is it possibly my fault that the error or violation occurred?"

3. *Allowing the person to be unclear about the offense.* Let the person know the general charge, and the specific details of the offense. Don't allude to general complaints, or refuse to give details.

4. *Failing to get the other person's side of the story.* Always let people have their full say about what happened and the reason why they did what they did. Mitigating circumstances, conflicting orders, or even orders you gave unclearly may be at fault.

5. *Backing down when you are right.* Compromise and understanding are virtues, but once you've decided and announced your decision it is a mistake to relent. It merely indicates you were wrong in your first decision, and you'll lose the effect of your reprimand.

6. *Failing to keep records.* Disciplinary reprimands should always be recorded in the personnel folder of the person. This becomes part of the work history of the person and provides evidence in the event of further disciplinary requirements. In many cases people who were known to be unsatisfactory employees over the years have been reinstated after discharge because the company could produce no evidence that the person had ever been told of his shortcomings.

7. *Harboring a grudge.* Once the reprimand has been administered and any sanctions or punishments administered, don't carry a hostile attitude forever after. The person required discipline and received it. Assume now that the employee is starting with a clean slate and let the employee know that you consider it a thing of the past.

The effective manager who puts aside counterproductive attitudes and avoids Odiorne's deadly sins has successfully clarified the real reason for the reprimand interview.

The reprimand interview attempts to correct inappropriate behavior. Reprimands should always be handled in private. There need be no special efforts to reduce anxiety or to equalize nonverbal power positions, but conversation should be measured and unemotional. A concerted effort to avoid highly judgmental or emotion-loaded terms should be made. Keep the transactions on the adult level. Never reprimand while upset, angry, or after a three-martini lunch.

> **Work to use unemotional language.**

In the popular book, *The One-Minute Manager,* authors Kenneth Blanchard and Spencer Johnson explain how to get the most from a "one-minute reprimand." They suggest dividing the reprimand into two phases. In the first half of the reprimand, they recommend that you:

- Tell the people what they did wrong—specifically
- Tell the people how you feel about what they did wrong—in no uncertain terms
- Stop for a few seconds of uncomfortable silence to let them *feel* how you feel

In the second half of the reprimand, Blanchard and Johnson recommend that you:

- Shake hands or touch them in a way that lets them know you are honestly on their side
- Remind them (verbally) of how much you value them
- Reaffirm that you think well of them but not of their performance in this situation
- Realize that when the reprimand is over, it's over.[5]

Obstacles

Most managers hate chewing out people. This is normal. We'd prefer to maintain amiable relationships, and reprimands make that difficult. The subordinate's defensiveness—his or her need to justify what's been done—may make it hard to change behavior. Personal dislike can color the reprimand and make it unfairly harsh. There is always

> **Defensiveness is a principal roadblock to behavior change.**

the danger of counteraccusations and even coming to physical blows if a participant is unduly offended. Long-term interpersonal relationships can be unalterably damaged.

A final comment about the reprimand. Although it is sometimes necessary to rebuke others' behaviors, we should afterward show an increase in our concern for that individual so that he or she does not see us as an enemy. Be quick to reinforce performance improvements that follow the reprimand. Both you and your subordinate will then look back on the experience as a useful one.

GRIEVANCE INTERVIEWS: A REPRIMAND IN REVERSE

Although subordinates cannot generally chew out the boss, they can make known their views about organizational neglect or errors. In many organizations, the grievance procedure is formalized through labor unions or other internal employee representatives. The interview type discussed here is less formal and may logically precede the filing of a formal grievance. In this sense, if the grievance interview is well handled, it can provide an early warning of potentially more serious industrial relations problems. The grievance interview should be regarded by management as an information gathering opportunity. Don't take it as a personal affront.

Purpose of the Grievance Interview

The grievance interview provides a subordinate with a format for airing a complaint to higher management.

Ideal Climate and Process

The status and power differences between the employee and the boss may make it difficult for the subordinates to express their views. This is not likely to be comfortable for grievants. Since the information they provide can be potentially valuable to the organization, attempts to create a relaxed atmosphere are usually worthwhile. A friendly greeting or light remark may help break the ice and make the exchange more pleasant and productive. As with the reprimand, both sides should have an opportunity to air their stories. Participants should avoid blowing off steam and leveling personal attacks; they should keep their exchanges on the adult level, maintaining a problem orientation.

Obstacles

As with the reprimand, there exists the possibility of emotional blowups that can only be counterproductive. When either participant is bent on vindication or on destruction of a relationship, serious long-range problems can arise.

EXIT INTERVIEWS: MORE THAN PARTING SHOTS

One of the most frequently overlooked interview situations is the exit interview. Many people have left a number of jobs in their careers and can never remember having an effective exit interview. On a few occasions these could have provided some useful information which, if acted on, could have reduced later turnover problems.

Purpose

Often it is the exit interview that provides us with the opportunity to "get it with both barrels"—get our most candid (although perhaps not most pleasant) feedback. The mature manager will welcome this unique opportunity for data gathering.

Ideal Climate and Process

The key term for this type of interview is *receptiveness.* Be receptive to unsolicited bad news. Accept it as potentially useful, and avoid the temptation to be defensive or argue with the exiting employee.

To maximize the value of the exit interview talk in specifics. The skillful interviewer probes general comments to get past abstractions and down to concrete examples. If employees cite "supervisory methods" as a reason for leaving, be sure to find out *which* methods and *which* supervisors. Encourage them to name names and cite specific cases. You don't have to agree with what's being said, but you should bring it out into the open.

Timing of the exit interview is important. It should be near the employee's last day but not on the termination date when he or she is going through other separation procedures and paperwork.

Don't expect this interview to be particularly pleasant. It may be uncomfortable to hear negative things about your organization and maybe even yourself. But the information gathered can be of considerable value. Leave the interview on a pleasant note and thank the employee for the candid comments. In a very real sense, these people are doing the organization a favor.

One side benefit of the exit interview is that it can provide important information about labor market conditions which may help the organization remain competitive in terms of salaries, benefits, organizational opportunities for advancement, and the like. Departing employees are happy to tell you about their new position if you'll simply ask.

Obstacles

James Lahiff suggests several obstacles to successful exit interviewing:

In the exit interview the interviewer is confronted with a number of unique obstacles to frank disclosure of reasons for leaving the job. A feeling of suspicion on the part of the interviewee is one of them. It is natural for him to wonder why, all of a sudden, has the company gotten interested in his thoughts and feelings. Another obstacle is presented by the interviewee's desire, often unspoken, to get a favorable recommendation from his employer. Another possible explanation for the interviewee's hesitancy to give reasons is his wish to keep a "foot in the door" by departing on a pleasant note and hence making it possible to return to this employer should his plans for the new job go awry.[6]

SELECTION INTERVIEWS: GETTING AND GIVING THE JOB

This is one interview virtually every working person has experienced from one end or the other. We focus on the job seeker's point of view here. For the interviewer, the mirror image of these concerns will likely identify the best potential employees. Put another way, people who successfully fulfill the three phases of the job search processes as described in the following will probably be the most attractive candidates for selection—assuming, of course, that they possess the needed job skills.

Three Phases of the Job Search Interview Process

The intelligent job seeker will recognize the following three phases of the process:

1. Interview preparation
2. The interview (and any related meetings with company members)
3. Interview follow-up

Surveys show that recruiters often voice the same complaints about job applicants.

Surveys point to the most frequent complaints recruiters have about interviewees. These typical complaints provide an excellent starting point to help you prepare and accomplish a successful interview.

Complaints about Interview Preparation

Ill-Prepared for the Interview

Job candidates too often have no information about the company or the job. They have no good questions to ask and often no interview training. As a two-way communication experience, it is as important for you to have prepared questions as for the interviewer. Find out as much as you can about the company before the interview. The more you know, the more impressive you will be to the interviewer.

Vague Interests

Candidates often lack career goals—they do not know what job they want. As part of your preparation, think about career objectives and long-range plans. Where do you really want to be in the future? Have specific career goals prepared.

Unrealistic Expectations

Candidates lack flexibility, are too concerned with salary, or seem to have a "What can you do for me?" attitude. Students are seen as immature because they have unrealistic or impractical ideas of what companies can offer. Learn what to expect. Get an idea of what starting salary is realistic and how long it takes to move up in an organization.

Additional ideas for interview preparation are offered later in this chapter.

Complaints about the Interview

Lack of interviewing skills is the most frequent complaint expressed by interviewers about job candidates.

Poor Communication Skills

The candidates come across as evasive, by not answering questions directly and confidently. They seem poorly organized by giving rambling responses. They talk too little or talk too much. They seem ill at ease and are nervous.

Awareness of the ideas covered throughout this book can go a long way toward improving your interview skills.

Lack of Motivation and Enthusiasm

This is another complaint often made by interviewers. Candidates are apathetic, lack interest, do not sell self, or are too agreeable. These perceptions probably arise from the presentation skills of the interviewee. Vocal variation, effective nonverbal behaviors, and good people skills will overcome this problem.

Complaints about Follow-up

> *Many interviewees never follow up, thus wasting an opportunity to make a good impression.*

This one is simple: *Too few candidates follow up at all!* They leave the interviewer and never again speak to him or her. Often interviewers see this lack of communication as a lack of interest. Some intentionally wait to see if the candidate has the initiative to follow up.

The simplest form of follow-up is a thank-you note expressing appreciation for the interview and restating your desire to work for the company. Many applicants never do this.

The Purpose of the Selection Interview

Simply put, this process serves to create a mutually positive situation for both applicant and organization. Both should be looking for mutually beneficial fit among skills, wants, and opportunities.

Ideal Climate and Process

Although some interviewers intentionally create a stressful climate, as shown in Figure 8-2, in most cases the ideal climate is a friendly yet slightly formal one.

The process, from the applicant's perspective should include the following:[7]

Do Your Homework: Research the Organization

An interviewer can't possibly give you a complete picture of the organization he or she represents in the time that you will have together in the interview. Thus, you must come into the interview having done your homework. Get information about the company before your interview. If possible, visit the company and ask people who work there what it is all about. Most people are very cooperative in giving such information to you.

> *Learn about the company before the interview.*

Among the kinds of information you should have before the interview are the following:

♦ The nature of the organization's products or services

♦ The typical path for advancement opportunities

♦ The history of growth and potential for future growth of the company

♦ The possibilities for personal growth within the company

♦ The approximate salary range you might expect

♦ The challenges and opportunities the company is facing in the marketplace (e.g., fast growth, stiff competition)

By taking the time to gather such information, you can create accurate expectations in your mind. With this information, prepare some questions to ask the interviewer.

People normally enjoy talking about their work. Some of the best interviews result from letting the interviewer do much of the talking. Remember that a common complaint interviewers have about candidates is that they do not ask intelligent questions.

FIGURE 8-2

Take Materials with You

The interview is an opportunity to sell yourself. Take along some of your own sales literature, such as your résumé and anything else that might help your presentation. Extra copies of the résumé are especially important if you will be meeting several people.

Samples of your work can often show your abilities. If the job will involve writing, take along sample papers you have written. If you did a research project in school that may be of use to your potential employer, bring a copy to the interview.

Do not forget the little things, too. Be sure to take a pen and something to write on. Your daily planner or a calendar may be useful as well. Do not forget the list of questions you want to ask the interviewer. Have these written down and handy for reference.

Communicate Skillfully in the Interview

The personal chemistry—how well you hit it off—established between you and the interviewer comes from both verbal and nonverbal cues. Be sensitive to both forms of communication.

Be prompt and prepared for the interview. Tardiness shows a lack of respect for the other person's time as well as a lack of self-discipline. Be dressed appropriately, as you would dress after you get the job. (It helps to know the company's dress code, if any.) When you are introduced, be responsive and shake hands warmly. Respond to the introduction and be prepared to tell the interviewer who you are (even if he or she probably knows your name already).

Follow the interviewer's lead.

Follow the interviewer's lead. Do not try to take over the interview, but rather respond to the climate the interviewer sets. Such questions as the formality of address (should you call the interviewer Ms. Jones, or Christy?) can be determined by the interviewer's lead. Be sensitive to the way he or she is communicating and respond in like manner. Usually it makes sense to be a bit overly formal rather than too familiar, at first. If people want to be called by their first name, they will tell you so.

Be a good, active listener. Remember, listening is not a passive activity that you sit back and do when you are not talking. Instead, it should be an active mental process. When you listen to people actively, you listen for key ideas, arrange those ideas in your mind, and provide intelligent responses to them.

Do not forget to sell yourself in the interview. It is important to focus on your key ideas (just as you would in a stand-up presentation) and show how these relate to the company. Show the interviewer how your *features*—your experiences, education, and talents—will be *benefits* for that company—the what-this-means-to-you statements. Draw the link between features and benefits as clearly as possible. Do not assume that the interviewer will automatically see how your experience fits with the company's needs.

Here are some examples of features-and-benefits statements as they might be used in a job interview.

Feature Statement Alone	*Feature Tied to a Benefit*
I worked for a temporary help placement office for two years.	I worked in the temporary help placement office where I learned how to select employees like those your company hires.
I sold shoes in the summer.	My summer sales job in a shoe store taught me how to work with even the difficult-to-please customer—the kind of customer your employees must deal with.
I worked my way through school.	I worked my way through school so I know the importance of watching my expenses carefully, just as your employees do.

Be *assertive*—pleasantly direct—in expressing your feelings honestly and taking charge of your rights responsibly. Avoid negative comments that tear down others. Never speak unkindly or negatively about other people or other organizations you have worked for. Be objective. Be frank, honest, and consistent in your answers.

One important thought to keep in mind is that not every question requires an immediate response. Indeed, the use of silence can be valuable in a job interview.

We are familiar with one case in which a young graduate was being offered a position by a company that he was excited about working for. The recruiter concluded a series of interviews with a statement such as this one: "John, we would like to invite you to join our retailing team. We would like you to start the first of next month, and we are prepared to pay you $22,000 a year." In John's mind he was delighted to receive this offer, but on the outside, he skillfully used the technique of silence—in this case a pause of only about 30 seconds—in which he made no response at all. He merely thought it over in his mind. The interviewer, however, did make a response. After this half minute of silence, the interviewer came back and said, "Okay, okay. John, we can make that $25,000." In less than a half minute, John increased his salary by $3,000 by using that thoughtful pause.

The use of silence tends to put the burden on the other person. Many people will quickly fill the gap by providing some additional information or, as in this case, by upping the ante by $3,000!

Of course, it is not always appropriate to use silence. Some questions can be answered quickly and openly and should be handled that way. But do not hesitate to use the slower, more thoughtful responses, especially when a difficult question is being asked. Do not appear flustered, simply appear to be organizing your thoughts in your mind.

> **When preparing, ask yourself tough questions.**

In preparation, be sure to ask yourself some of the tough questions—interviewers call them *blockbuster* questions. These may be vague such as, "Tell me about yourself," or convey an implied antagonism such as, "What good are you?" If you are not prepared for something like this, it can throw you off. The questions are designed to put you under some stress. Be prepared with thoughtful, concise, and effective answers.

Anybody can handle the easy questions. Be prepared for the tough ones.

When handling any question, be sure to listen to what the interviewer is requesting. Do not hesitate to ask for clarification or to restate in your own words what you think he or she is asking. Be sure you know the question before you go off half-cocked with an answer.

The job interview can be both exciting and challenging. It is for most people an important communication activity. Keep in mind that the basic objective in an interview is to spark some positive feeling in the interviewer. This feeling is often *subjective*—not something that can be measured, but more a result of personal liking. Your close attention to the little things is essential.

By focusing on several areas of preparation for the job interview, we can greatly enhance our possibilities of successful job interviewing.

Obstacles

> **There are legal limits on what recruiters may ask.**

Illegal or inappropriate questions are sometimes asked. Laws designed to reduce unfair job discrimination are enforced in the United States by the Equal Employment Opportunity Commission. (Other countries have similar agencies.) The EEOC has determined that some questions are not to be asked of job applicants.[8]

Types of Illegal Questions

QUESTIONS ABOUT RACE OR NATIONAL ORIGIN

- Where were you born?
- Are you of the _____ race?
- Do you believe that your race will be a problem in your job performance?
- Where were your parents born?

QUESTIONS ABOUT AGE OR HANDICAPS

- What do you think about working for a person younger than you are?
- Do you have any handicaps?
- As a handicapped person, what help will you need to do your work?
- How severe is your handicap?
- How old are you?

QUESTIONS ABOUT YOUR RELIGION

- What church do you attend?
- What is your religion?
- Are you a _____?
- Do you hold any religious beliefs that would prevent you from working certain days of the week?

QUESTIONS ABOUT MARITAL/FAMILY RELATIONSHIPS

- Do you have plans for having children?
- What does your husband/wife do?
- What happens if your spouse gets transferred to another city?
- Who will take care of your children when you work?
- Are you in a relationship currently?
- How would you react to working for a man/woman?

Identifying such illegal questions is, of course, only part of the challenge. Many interviewers may not be aware that they are asking illegal questions. In fact, surveys show that interviewees face a high probability of being asked an illegal question.

Your Options When Asked an Illegal Question

When you are asked an illegal question, how do you respond? Several options are available:[9]

Answer the Question

Many job candidates simply answer the question. Unfortunately, this may encourage the interviewer to ask more illegal questions. Nevertheless, in many cases, the question is asked innocently and will not be used unfairly against the candidate.

Ask How the Question Relates to Job Qualification

Example: "I am not sure how this question pertains to my qualifications for this job. I would be happy to answer if I can understand how it pertains to my qualifications."

Direct Refusal

Examples: "I am sorry, this is not a question I am willing to answer," or "I am sorry, this is not a question I am willing to answer because this information is personal."

Acknowledge Concern and Ask for Information

Example: "I am not sure what you want to know by asking that question. Could you tell me what it is you want to know?"

Answer the Underlying Concern Expressed by the Question

Examples: "I take it that your question about my plans for child care is a concern about the likelihood that I may be absent from work when they are ill. I want to assure you that I see myself as a professional person and will behave in a professionally responsible manner when they are ill." Or, "I am married. If you are concerned about how my marital status might affect my staying with the company, I can assure you that I am a professional and intend to continue working regardless of events in my personal life."

Terminating the Interview

Example: "It is interesting that your company uses such questions as a basis for hiring. I expect to file a complaint with the EEOC because you ask illegal interview questions."

Hopefully, your interviewing experiences will not end this way. You do have legal rights, of course. But the idea is to participate successfully in the job search process—to get a job. Be somewhat tolerant of the interviewer—you may be an interviewer one day.

SPECIFIC QUESTIONING TECHNIQUES

The quality of an interview is largely determined by the kinds of questions asked. There are several types of questions, each useful under certain conditions. (The term *question* is used here to refer to any comments made to elicit responses from the other party. Sometimes these take the form of statements or commands.)

The Closed-Ended Question

This type of question allows the respondent little or no freedom in choosing a response. Typically there are only one or two possible answers. Examples: "Were you on duty last Tuesday at 11 a.m.? Have you completed the Tompkins report yet?" "Do you prefer the standard retirement program or the optional annuity?" "How long have you been on your present job assignment?"

Use of closed-ended questions permits the interviewer to exercise close control over the exchange. It is, of course, the technique most frequently used by trial lawyers or police interrogators to elicit specific information. Its drawback is that it rigidly structures the interview and, while often efficient, it may completely miss opportunities for exchanging other relevant information.

> *Close-ended questions allow more interviewer control.*

One of the major features of closed-ended questions is that they can be manipulative. Respondents often feel frustrated when they must choose between one or two possible answers without opportunity to clarify. Sometimes, however, these kinds of responses are the most useful to the questioner. Yet in most business interviews, the nondirective, open-ended question makes more sense.

The Open-Ended Question

This kind of question allows the respondent maximum freedom in responding by imposing no limitations on how it may be answered. Examples: "How do you feel about our new benefits package?" "What would be a better way to handle that job?" Open-ended questions are often in the form of statements such as, "Tell me about your experiences with the new system," or "Explain that procedure to me."

This questioning approach can produce considerable information that may not come out in closed-ended questioning. Its success depends in large part on the respondent's ability to express his or her thoughts clearly. Often it is necessary for the interviewer to seek additional clarification by using "probes" when the respondent is talking in generalities or using unfamiliar language.

The Probing Question

Frequently used with open-ended questions, the probe asks the interviewee to clarify a response for better understanding. Examples: "Could you give me an example of something he did that upset you?" "What do you mean when you say she's 'ruthless'?" "Why do you say that?" "Exactly what happened?"

Probes serve to move the language level down the ladder of abstraction toward more concrete, specific, and descriptive terms. Another function of the probe is to determine intensity of feelings. Let us say that an employee has just commented that her supervisor is "tough to get along with." How tough *is* he, you wonder. Try a sympathetic or mildly supportive probe such as: "I've heard

> *Use pauses after probing questions to put the responsibility for answering on the respondent.*

several comments like that recently." Drop your comment and wait. This often encourages the interviewee to elaborate. "I think he must be having trouble at home. He comes to work first thing in the morning grouchy as a bear." Now some useful information may be coming to the surface.

The Leading Question

While a probe leads respondents to elaborate on their own feelings, the leading question typically suggests the response desired. Occasionally this is helpful, but more often it is a block to the emergence of authentic information. Examples: "I'm interested in your work experiences over in R&D. Did you learn a lot while you were there?" (Obviously the interviewer wants the respondent to say yes.) "Don't you think it's important for our people to be informed on policy decisions?" (Of course. What else could be said?) When the question is prefaced by a remark that suggests the kind of answer the interviewer would like to hear, the range of responses is reduced. "I've always loved the exciting atmosphere of the newsroom. How do you feel about your job there?" (I love it, just like you do!)

The Loaded Question

Loaded questions also suggest the desired response to the interviewee, primarily through the use of highly emotional terms. Sometimes they are used to determine a respondent's reactions under stress—when a questioner seeks to "crack" the reluctant respondent. The interviewee who is wearing a mask or acting a role may be angry enough to let true feelings or honest answers emerge.

Loaded questions rely heavily on the use of dysphemisms—terms that conjure up negative associations. Examples: "How can you work effectively in this *filth*?" "Some of your coworkers claim you're a *racist*." "I've heard reports that you are satisfied with *slipshod* quality. How would you respond to that?" The employee will probably respond by attacking. The loaded question, like a loaded gun, occasionally goes off in the wrong direction. Avoid such questions under all but the most desperate circumstances.

The Hypothetical Question

This questioning technique can be used to see how a respondent might handle a particular situation. It is helpful in identifying creativity, prejudices, ability to conceptualize the "big picture," and other respondent characteristics. Examples: "If you were promoted to sales manager, what programs would you implement?" "Put yourself in the shoes of the production manager and suggest some approaches she might take." "Let's assume that you discovered one of your employees intoxicated on the job. What would you do?"

The hypothetical question can be useful but be careful of underlying meanings that may arise in your receiver's mind. If you ask an employee to picture himself as manager, there is bound to be some implication that he or she is being considered for promotion. If the promotion doesn't, in fact, materialize, the employee may be pretty disappointed.

> *Hypothetical questions can get you helpful information.*

The Mirror Response

This technique is useful in getting at underlying meaning that might not be clearly verbalized. It also helps to maintain the communicated exchanges on a we're-both-adults level rather than a parent-child relationship. Example: An employee says to her supervisor, "Some days I'd like to put my fist through that computer." The first reaction might be, "You do and you'll pay for it," or some other such critical response. The underlying meaning of the employee's statement would remain suppressed and antagonism toward the supervisor may emerge. Using a mirror response, the supervisor might say something like, "That computer makes you angry?" Now the opportunity is presented to explain the source of her anger. "Half the time it won't boot up into the network. It's driving me nuts." Supervisor: "You find the network hookup annoying?" Employee: "Yes, can it be fixed?" Supervisor: "Sure, I'll call the LAN technician."

Often the mirror response sounds like a rather dull statement of the obvious. But it lays the groundwork for more specific expressions of information from the interviewee. Psychologists find the mirror response especially useful in getting perplexities phrased in specific terms. The manager in the counseling interview may find this technique especially effective since it is nonevaluative and nonthreatening.

In a well-executed interview, each question is asked for a particular reason. Don't worry about pauses in the interview. It is not necessary to fill every moment with the sound of someone's voice. It makes more sense to think through each question and response rather than to babble on with ill-defined and meaningless exchanges that do little to create understanding.

When the interview is over, the manager should summarize briefly and be sure the respondent understands what to do next. There should be a clear agreement about the outcome of the discussion. Often, testing for such understanding is appropriate. We might ask, "Okay, Tom, now what did we agree must be done next?" Each participant may explain the interview's outcome as he or she sees it. Then close on an upbeat and express gratitude for the employee's participation in the interview.

A QUICK SUMMARY OF MAJOR IDEAS

♦ Interviews should be purposeful, planned, and structured in such a way as to encourage a two-way flow of information. Without these characteristics, interviews will not be effective.

♦ Different types of managerial interviews pose unique obstacles and opportunities. Attention should be paid to climate and processes as well.

QUESTIONS FOR FURTHER THOUGHT

1. What could you do to create an appropriate climate for a performance review interview? A counseling interview? A reprimand interview? An exit interview? A grievance interview? A selection interview (assume you are the interviewer)?

2. Listen to yourself in conversation with others. To what extent do you tend to use closed-ended questions? How could open-ended questions be more useful? Give some examples.

3. How would you respond to an illegal or inappropriate question in a selection interview?

4. How will you respond to the commonly asked questions at the end of this chapter?

NONEVALUATIVE APPROACHES TO
PERFORMANCE APPRAISALS[10]
by Les Wallace

For the supervisor who deals predominantly with high-quality performers, the performance appraisal process is not a frightening one. But though every supervisor would prefer to work in this type of situation, most find themselves working with employees whose performance ranges from unacceptable to exceptional and therefore having to adjust their discussion appraisals to fit each employee. For the supervisor untrained in counseling on different kinds of performance problems, adjusting his or her approach to fit the needs of high-quality and lower-quality performers can be difficult—and in some cases, disturbing.

For example, during a conversation I had recently with one production supervisor, he bragged that he thoroughly enjoyed writing and discussing the performance evaluations of his 26 subordinates. But two weeks later this same supervisor was back on the phone, frantically asking for advice on how to handle a poor performer and complaining that this difficult appraisal was taking all the fun out of the process.

So this is the most common appraisal situation for supervisors: They have employees at all levels of performance—good, poor, and mediocre—and they have personnel forms and management strategies by the dozens to follow in carrying out the appraisals. But the biggest problem for supervisors is that employees react to the appraisal on a personal level, *not* on a professional one. And unfortunately many supervisors lack the communication skills to get the essential message of an appraisal across to the employee without causing bigger problems in the process. As Douglas McGregor pointed out some 20 years ago, problems with adequate performance appraisals revolve around "a normal dislike of criticizing a subordinate and perhaps having to argue about it and a lack of skill needed to handle the interview."

QUESTIONS FOR THE SUPERVISOR

Now that we have some idea of the problems supervisors face when they enter the appraisal arena, let us ask: What communicative approaches could a supervisor use to more clearly communicate to an employee what he or she must do to improve performance? At the same time, what approaches would help reduce employee hostility and defensiveness and also generate cooperation in working to improve performance?

Most suggestions that have been made for improving the appraisal process *deal more with the theory of performance appraisal and the goals of a supportive exchange rather than with concrete skills and examples on how to achieve these goals.* Whether one looks at the problem-solving interview, the participative approach to performance improvement, or the supportive-defensive climate contrasts, these are all theories suggesting a particular approach but omitting the specifics on how to put the approach into practice. As one personnel manager remarked to me recently, "Who could disagree with such ideas? I just want my supervisors to learn how to make these theories useful."

Consequently, I want to make some specific suggestions for the supervisors who have to face their subordinates eyeball-to-eyeball during performance appraisals. By utilizing such suggestions, a supervisor should be able to get much more mileage out of the performance interview and be able to approach counseling sessions with high, medium, or low performers with the same self-assured attitude.

EVALUATIVE VS. DESCRIPTIVE

First, what are the conditions in an interview that lead to employee defensiveness rather than to the more desired cooperation? Of course, we know that when a supervisor exhibits *evaluative*—that is, blame-putting—behavior, this will almost always elicit defensive behavior from an employee. But beyond this, the more personal, negative, and accusatory the evaluation by a supervisor is, the more hostile and defensive the employee will become.

The way to avoid evoking such defensive behavior is by using *descriptive* rather than evaluative approaches to the problem. By simply stating, in a nonpersonal way, that a problem exists and then describing that problem, the supervisor makes it possible for him and the employee to arrive at a joint decision—or even an employee-initiated decision—on how to resolve the problem. Some examples of both evaluative and descriptive comments that the supervisor might make in performance appraisals are as follows:

Evaluative	*Descriptive*
"You simply can't keep making these stupid mistakes."	"We're still having a problem reducing the number of scrap parts produced."
"Bob, you're tactless and undiplomatic."	"Some people interpret your candor as hostility."
"You're too belligerent when dealing with co-workers."	"Many employees perceive your attitude to be belligerent."
"The accident was your fault. You ignored the safety regulations on that project."	"This accident appears to involve some differences in interpreting the safety regulations."

Using descriptive, nonevaluative comments in the appraisal interview, the supervisor is signaling to the employee that he wants to analyze and discuss a problem, not look for an "easy out" or demean the employee. In such a way, the interview can then move on to the more constructive elements of the appraisal process.

THE THREAT OF CONTROL

Sometimes in a performance appraisal the supervisor will make the mistake of assuming a *control* communicative stance. This stance emphasizes the superior's power over the subordinate, and it reflects an error in the supervisor's thinking because, like most of us, employees don't like to feel dominated by another person and react defensively when they do.

Opposed to the control stance is *problem orientation* which is a communicative approach designed to allay an employee's fear and increase his sense of personal control over whatever problems exist. Problem orientation conveys a respect for the employee's ability to work on a problem and to formulate meaningful answers to the problem. Examples of these approaches that could be found in many performance appraisals are:

Control	*Problem Orientation*
"John, I'd like to see you doing X, Y, and Z over the next week."	"John, what sort of things might we do here?"
"I think the only answer is to move you over by Margaret on the line."	"One possibility is to have you move over by Margaret on the line. Is that likely to help?"
"I think my suggestions are clear, so why don't you get back to work?"	"Let's think about these possibilities and get back together next week, after you've thought about them."
"Arthur, you'd better tone down your criticism of co-workers."	"Arthur, this sensitivity among co-workers requires us all to try for a bit more diplomacy."
"You've got a problem here."	"We've got a problem here."
"I've decided what you must do to reduce mistakes."	"Have you thought about what we might do to reduce mistakes?"

Problem-oriented communication will generate more options for solving the problem by encouraging the employee to make suggestions and inducing a mutual concern for controlling the problem, *not* the person. Furthermore, problem orientation can also improve the appraisal discussion by aiding both parties in truly listening to what the other is saying, by encouraging both parties to offer suggestions, and by fostering a more open climate in which disagreement is not only tolerated but invited.

NEUTRALITY AND EMPATHY

Just as inimical to the appraisal process as control is a supervisor's *neutrality,* which is usually interpreted by the subordinate to be disinterest about the outcome's impact on the employee. Like the rest of us, employees tend to be more guarded and less communicative when their superior lacks real concern over their welfare. Ironically, supervisors who display such unconcern often are very interested in their employees, but they don't realize that some of their actions are interpreted by subordinates to be indicative of a neutral attitude.

Showing *empathy,* on the other hand, signals a clear concern for the employee and his situation. But to get this message across unequivocally, the supervisor must make an overt communication attempt—one that the employee cannot help but notice. Some examples of neutral and empathetic approaches are:

Neutrality	*Empathy*
"I really don't know what we can do about it."	"At this point I can't think of anything, but I know where we might look for help."
"Well, that's one way to look at it."	"I get the feeling you don't feel confident with our original plan."
"I didn't know that."	"I wasn't aware of that. Let me make sure I understand."
"Too bad, but we all go through that."	"I think I know how you're feeling. I can remember one experience I had that was similar ..."
"You could have something there, but let's get back to the real problem."	"I'm not certain I understand how that relates to this problem. Why don't you fill me in before we go on?"

Supervisors communicate empathy best when they listen well, when the follow up on suggestions, and when they inquire how employees feel about questions and solutions raised in the appraisal. Displaying a concerned sympathy about difficult problems will also signal an understanding attitude by the supervisor and encourage the employee's cooperation.

A NEED FOR EQUALITY

In any discussion between a superior and a subordinate—whether the distinction has been brought about by legal, financial, or emotional factors—if the superior uses communicative techniques that emphasize his *superiority,* this will correspondingly induce feelings of unworthiness in the subordinate. For example, the supervisor who keeps the subordinate at arm's length by stifling feedback and overtly rejecting his help only increases the employee's need to defend himself and prove his self-worth.

However, the supervisor who tries to reduce the distance between himself and his employees encourages the employees to feel they share a certain *equality* with the supervisor. This feeling can be aided by a supervisor showing concern for sharing information with the subordinates and gaining their input in solving problems. Some characteristic differences between superiority- and equality-evoking comments can be seen in these examples:

Superiority	*Equality*
"Bob, I've worked with this problem for ten years and ought to know what will work."	"This idea has worked before. Do you think it might work in this case?"
"Well, I don't think I need to give you all the background. Why don't we just do it this way for now?"	"Arthur, you might find some of the background information helpful, so let me fill you in a bit."
"The supervisory staff thought this policy through pretty thoroughly."	"We've only discussed this policy at the supervisor's meetings and I'm interested in your reactions and thoughts."
"Oh, the rationale should be of no interest to people on the line."	"Let me go over the rationale with you. Some of you might find it helpful."
"Look, I'm being paid to make these decisions, not you."	"I'll have to make the final decision, Mary, but why don't you get your suggestions in to me right away?"

Of course, workers generally do not expect complete equality from their bosses, nor are they interested in sharing the supervisor's responsibility for decisions that are implemented. Instead, they appreciate a supervisor who shares information with them, seeks their feedback, and listens to their concerns. Such communicative approaches can easily be made part of the performance appraisal process, and the supervisor should see a more enthusiastic and less defensive attitude among employees as a result.

WHO HAS THE LAST WORD?

Supervisors who emphasize *certainty* tend to phrase everything they say as if the last word had been said and a decision could never be changed. Such a dogmatic stance makes the employee feel that there is no need to offer new ideas or different solutions to the approach already outlined by the supervisor. This in turn leads to loss of morale and a feeling of powerlessness among employees.

But a supervisor who shows *provisionalism* demonstrates that he is willing to have his own ideas be challenged in order to arrive at the best possible solution to a problem. Communication that encourages analysis and investigation can restore enthusiasm and provide a challenge for employees that might otherwise not be there. Examples of certainty and provisionalism are:

Certainty	*Provisionalism*
"I know what the problem is, Tom. I don't think I need another opinion."	"I have a view of the problem, Tom, but I'd be interested in your perception."
"This is the way we're going to do things, Period."	Let's try this for a couple of weeks, then we can reconsider, based on that experience."
"I've thought these suggestions through thoroughly, Mary, so let's not waste time arguing."	"I've tried to think these suggestions through pretty thoroughly, Mary. Can you see anything I may have left out?"

Let us add that a provisional approach does not deny the fact that decisions have to be made and policies adhered to. Instead, it suggests that decision making is an alterable process and that employee suggestions and creativity are important to and appreciated by management.

FROM APPRAISAL TO ANALYSIS

The examples of communicative approaches are all designed to help the supervisor reduce the defensiveness of employees, and as such they all share a common base: They emphasize a process of *analysis,* rather than *appraisal* of employee problems. Of course, inherent in any analysis is some evaluation of past performance, but hopefully the employee will be led to approach this evaluation from a more participative and less defensive position. Instead of being told simply that he or she failed, the employee's help is enlisted to pinpoint problems and come up with answers to problems. An analytical process should emphasize the employee's personal worth and demonstrate the confidence that management has in the employee's ability to learn from and improve on past behavior.

Unfortunately, not all employees will be able to recognize and resolve their performance problems, no matter what supervisors do. But the supervisor who validates an employee's worth through supportive, nonevaluative communicative techniques will at least find that his suggestions to the employee on improving performance are received with less defensiveness and anger. Similarly, supervisors I have talked with report several other benefits that result from using nonevaluative communicative techniques, including:

♦ Improved creativity in solving problems, due to greater employee input.

♦ Less supervisory reluctance to discuss employee performance problems.

♦ A clearer understanding by the employee of why and how he or she needs to change work behavior.

♦ The growth of a climate of cooperation, which increases individual and group motivation to achieve performance goals.

♦ Greater employee self-reliance, which improves the individual's ability to diagnose problems and react quickly with less supervisory assistance.

The supervisor who implements constructive, nonevaluative appraisal techniques becomes more of a leader and teacher to his or her employees and less of a disciplinarian. This also means that employees come to see the supervisor as more of a friend and helper who assists them when their own ideas and abilities run short and less a management representative looking for a scapegoat on whom to blame poor performances. Of course, implementing such techniques does not essentially change the performance appraisal; a supervisor's suggestions and high performance goals remain part of the process. But constructive communicative techniques, when correctly used, should make the process a little less painful and intimidating for all concerned.

OTHER THOUGHTS ABOUT SELECTION INTERVIEWS

FIFTY QUESTIONS COMMONLY ASKED IN SELECTION INTERVIEWS

There is no substitute for practice when preparing for a job interview. What follows is a list of questions frequently used by recruiters.

From the list, select 10 questions you might have difficulty with. Have a friend ask you those questions and tape record your responses. Ask others to give you feedback on the answers you give. Remember to relate your answers to the potential needs of the company (features to benefits) as discussed in this chapter.

(Note: questions with an asterisk may be illegal. Select at least two of these for practice and decide how you will handle them.)

1. In what school activities did you participate? Why? Which did you enjoy the most?
2. In what type of position are you most interested?
3. What jobs have you held? How were they obtained, and why did you leave?
4. What courses did you like best? Least? Why?
5. What percentage of your school expenses did you earn? How?
6. How did you spend your vacations while in school?
7. What do you know about our company?
8. What qualifications do you have that make you feel you would be successful in your field?
9. What are your ideas on salary?
*10. How do you feel about your family?
11. If you were starting school all over again, what courses would you take?
*12. Do you have a girlfriend/boyfriend? Is it serious?
13. How much money do you hope to earn at age _____?
14. Why did you decide to go to the school you attended?
15. What do you think determines a person's progress in a good company?
*16. Where did your family originally come from? What kind of name is yours?
17. Why do you think you would like this particular type of job?
*18. What is your father's occupation?
*19. Tell me about your home during the time you were growing up.
20. Do you prefer working with others or by yourself?
21. What kind of boss do you prefer?
*22. Can you take instructions from a woman/man without feeling upset?
*23. Do you live with your parents? Which of your parents has had the most profound influence on you?

24. How did previous employers treat you?
25. What have you learned from some of the jobs you have held?
26. What interests you about our product or service?
27. Have you ever changed your major field of interest? Why?
28. What do you know about opportunities in the field in which you are trained?
*29. How long do you expect to work before having children?
*30. Do you own any life insurance?
*31. Do you have any debts?
*32. How old were you when you became self-supporting?
*33. Do you attend church?
34. Do you like routine, repetitive work?
*35. When did you first contribute to family income?
36. What is your major weakness?
37. Will you fight to get ahead?
38. What do you do to keep in good physical condition?
*39. How do you usually spend Sunday?
*40. Have you had any serious illness, injury, or handicap?
41. What job in our company would you choose if you were entirely free to do so?
*42. Is it an effort for you to be tolerant of persons with backgrounds and interests different from your own?
43. What types of books have you read?
44. Have you plans for further education?
45. Have you ever tutored another student?
46. What jobs have you enjoyed the most? Least? Why?
47. What are your own special abilities?
*48. How would your husband/wife feel about your working here?
*49. Would your children be able to handle your overtime work?
50. Do you think that grades should be considered by employers? Why or why not?

NOTES

1. Adapted from Roger Fritz, *Personal Performance Contracts,* Revised edition (Menlo Park, CA: Crisp Publications, 1993), p. 47.

2. Norman R.. F. Maier, *The Appraisal Interview: Objectives, Methods, and Skills* (New York: John Wiley and Sons, 1958). p. 3.

3. W. Charles Redding, *Communication within the Organization* (New York: Industrial Communication Council, 1972), pp. 54–55. Redding is describing research by Herbert H. Meyer, Emanuel Kay, and J. R. P. French, Jr., "Split Roles in Performance Appraisal," *Harvard Business Review* January-February 1965, *43*, 1, pp. 123–129.

4. George S. Odiorne, *How Managers Make Things Happen* (West Nyack, NY: Parker Publishing Company, Inc., 1961) pp. 138–139.

5. Kenneth Blanchard and Spencer Johnson, *The One-Minute Manager* (New York: William Morrow & Co., 1982), p. 59.

6. James M. Lahiff, "Interviewing for Results," in *Readings and Interpersonal Organizational Communication* (Boston: Holbrook Press, 1973) p. 345.

7. Adapted from Paul R. Timm, *Basics of Oral Communication* (Cincinnati: Southwestern Publishing, 1993), pp. 224–228. Used with permission of the author.

8. Some of these sample illegal questions and possible responses to them were adapted from Gerald L. Wilson, "Preparing Students for Responding to Illegal Selection Interview Questions," *The Bulletin of the Association for Business Communication*, September 1991, pp. 47–48.

9. Adapted from Wilson, p. 48.

10. Reprinted by permission of the publisher, from SUPERVISORY MANAGEMENT, (March 1978) © 1978 by AMACOM, a division of American Management Associations. All rights reserved.

CHAPTER 9

MEETINGS AND CONFERENCES: INTERACTIONAL COMMUNICATION

We've Got To Stop Meeting Like This

In this chapter you will find ideas that will help you:

♦ Determine when a meeting is appropriate and worthwhile

♦ Identify the different types of committees that may be created by managers to meet organizational needs

♦ Recognize five major elements that determine the effectiveness of a meeting: goals, climate, leadership, decision strategies, and postmeeting follow-up

♦ Distinguish between traditional and group-centered leadership

♦ Explain four phases that constitute a decision strategy

♦ Apply *brainstorming* and the *nominal group technique* to generate and process tentative solutions in groups

♦ Identify several possible misconceptions regarding meetings

The fifty salespeople from all over the country arrived the night before; but it's 9:30 a.m. when the nine o'clock sales meeting begins. The welcome message from the president was naturally delayed until he arrived. But waiting for the president is not only polite, it's smart, and what's a half hour? Actually, for fifty salespeople it's only 25 hours or three full days of selling time.

"Gentlemen," says the president, "good morning and welcome to home base. I don't want to take any of your valuable time, but I asked Artie if I could say a few words before you get down to work. I know it will be a fruitful and busy day for you men who are, in my opinion, the most important asset this company has. Welcome! I'm sorry I can't spend time with each of you, but I've got to catch a plane." And the president leaves, smiling to the applause of the salesmen who give him a standing ovation, principally because the chairs haven't arrived yet.

"Men," says Artie the sales manager, "you've heard from our president; now let's get down to business. But to use the time until the tables and chairs arrive, I have a few housekeeping announcements. The coffee break will be at 10:30 instead of 10:00, so make a note of that on your agenda."

"I didn't get an agenda," one of the salesmen says.

"Those of you who got an agenda can share it," says Artie and continues.

"Although our president has already set the tone of this meeting, I want to add a few words before we get down to the nitty-gritty. You men represent the finest sales organization in our industry. Why? Because your company demands, and gets, selling skills and performance above and beyond the call of duty. That's why at this year's meeting there are so many new faces."

"Artie, a question please?" comes a plea from one of the salesmen.

"Sure, Joe, fire away. But before you do, for the benefit of the new men, let me tell them who you are. Men, Joe is our man in the Midwest who is doing one helluva job. Really knows the market, his customers, and the product. How long have you been knocking 'em dead for the company, Joe? Four years? Five?"

"Eight months," says Joe.

"Oh, yeah, right. Now, what's the question?"

"Are we going to talk about the competition today?"

"What the competition is doing right now, you worried about?"

"What they're doing now," says Joe.

"You tell me. What is the competition doing now?" Artie is smirking.

"What the competition is doing right now," says Joe, "is calling on our customers while we're in this sales meeting."[1]

THE OVERUSE OF MEETINGS

Perhaps the most overused phrase in business is, "Let's have a meeting." Every few hours someone wants to hold one. Meetings are called routinely to deal with everything from the momentous to the mundane. And lots of meetings are held just because it's nine o'clock, Tuesday morning, and the staff meeting has always been at 9:00 a.m. on Tuesdays.

Most managers seem to agree that group decision making (GDM), which supposedly goes on in meetings, is the most productive alternative in decision making. Managers everywhere read about the miracles wrought when everybody gets to talk through problems and get involved in decisions in meetings. The question is this: is GDM the most productive approach in decision making? Participation in groups may be beneficial, but it may not always be the best solution.

More than a few managers become very frustrated with all the meetings they must attend. They find themselves forced to do their real job in spurts between and around meetings. They reach a point where a shiver runs through their bodies when they hear someone say, "Let's get everybody together and talk that out." They may well be suffering from *consensus overkill*. Here are some of the symptoms:

♦ Day-to-day work activities are structured around frequent, time-consuming, and too often unproductive meetings.

♦ Most of the management positions in the company have been duplicated, thus allowing one person to attend meetings and the other one to do the actual work. (This problem is compounded by the fact that the one doing the work is usually titled "assistant to," and that person is too often asked by the chief to sit in on some other meetings!)

♦ Decision makers in the organization suffer from feelings of restlessness, disgruntlement, and raw boredom as they come out of their many meetings.

♦ The innocent and "brief" staff meeting has become an inefficient ritual that consumes enormous amounts of organizational time.

Consensus overkill is a costly and dangerous condition for the organization. Yet it can be avoided if managers use meetings—the so-called group process—wisely. To determine when meetings are likely to be useful, managers should be aware of the advantages and disadvantages the process offers. (*Note:* The type of meeting focused on in this chapter is the problem-solving session. Meetings called solely to dispense information are less of a problem.)

OPPORTUNITIES IN MEETINGS

A number of solutions exist for almost any organizational problem.

Since the experiences we have are individuals are-limited, it follows that several individuals working on the same problem, issue, or decision can bring a wide range of experiences and more relevant information to light. Each participant represents a unique frame of reference—an individual way of looking at the world—that may provide the key to a better remedy to the organization's problem.

Multiple points of view are available to the group so long as the group develops some systematic ways to assimilate the ideas. To be successful, the group must develop procedures for:

1. Sharing ideas and perspectives so that members may build on one another's insights
2. Resolving differences among group members, which, if left unattended, would prevent eventual consensus

In short, groups must work under conditions that foster the creation of understanding.

ADVANTAGES OF MEETINGS

The two main advantages of meetings, are:

1. Groups can reach high quality decisions when synergy is present
2. Group decisions can result in less resistance and stronger commitment to implementation of change.

Groups Reach Synergy—Sometimes

To be successful, a decision-making group must develop workable ways of expressing and sharing ideas so that others in the group can build on these thoughts. In addition the group needs to cope with people's hidden motives—ones that are not in line with what the group needs to accomplish—and to resolve destructive conflicts among group members.

If these conditions are present, the group's efforts may result in *synergy*; that is, a better decision will be reached than if the same people worked individually on the problem. This synergistic effect, of course, is the object of the game.

In addition to how well the group works together, one other factor affects synergy: the nature of the group's problem. Some kinds of problems are *not* handled better by groups.

> *Synergy means that ...*

Groups work better on some tasks than others. Studies show that groups are better at solving problems that require the making of *relative* rather than *absolute* judgments; that is, groups can better solve problems for which there is no single correct solution and for which solutions are difficult to verify objectively. This finding suggests that groups are not much better than individuals at handling certain kinds of clerical tasks (such as adding up columns of figures) or at solving logical brain teasers that require purely rational answers.[2]

In addition, groups tend to be more successful than individuals working alone when the task problem is complex, having many parts and requiring a number of steps to solve. Groups also seem better at dealing with controversial or emotionally charged problems.

When the problem is relatively simple, noncontroversial, or involves routine logical tasks, group discussion does not offer significant advantages. Other organizational problems with the opposite characteristics may best be solved using the group process.

Groups Achieve Stronger Commitment

A second significant advantage to group problem solving may be even more important than the quality-of-the-solution advantage discussed in the foregoing section. People are likely to feel a *higher degree of commitment to a group decision* and a concomitant reduction of hostility or resistance to it (at least among those who participated). Similarly, if those who participated are commissioned to execute the decision, they will do so more faithfully because they understand why and how the decision was reached.

In a classic human relations study conducted in the late 1940s, Coch and French[3] compared workers' resistance to technological changes in their jobs. They found that, when workers participated in discussions regarding the implementation of new machinery on the job, significantly less resistance to those changes arose. Among other work groups who did not participate in planning the machinery changes, more resistance to the changes emerged.

Later research has repeatedly confirmed that participation reduces resistance to changes, at least among American workers in industrial settings.

Unfortunately, today some managers use this principle in an effort to reduce employee resistance without allowing genuine participation. The manipulative manager wants workers to *feel* that they are participating and goes along with the group so long as it comes up with the same decision the manager wanted in the first place. Workers usually see through such managers.

Nonetheless, when particularly emotional decisions need to be made, such as changes that workers see as a threat to job security, meetings can dissolve the resistance if the meetings are handled well.

These advantages can lead to quality decision making. In some situations, however, these advantages can be completely negated by inept or unqualified participants and leaders, as well as by other factors discussed later.

DISADVANTAGES OF MEETINGS

Important disadvantages to the use of meetings can be categorized into these general types:

1. Meetings have become substitutes for action
2. Meetings are expensive

3. Low quality decisions are produced

4. Poor decisions result from time constraints

Meetings as Substitutes for Action

Some managers call meetings instead of making a tough decision. They confuse the appearance of activity with the hard reality that nothing substantive is happening. Consciously or unconsciously, they hope that by talking it out they can avoid the unpleasant necessity of acting. For some, it's hard to face up to the fact that filibusters are seldom a useful management technique.

> **Meetings must achieve some closure to be effective.**

Ultimately, meetings should reach a final decision. Most meetings, however, do not. When meetings lack such closure, it's likely because the problems or issues haven't been clearly defined, the participants aren't really interested in reaching a solution, or some procedural roadblocks haven't been handled well.

The meetings-as-a-substitute-for-action situation can become a bad habit. This when-in-doubt-call-a-meeting approach can result in nothing, except possibly some social satisfaction from sitting around gabbing or playing organizational games.

In some cases, the meeting *is* the action. Reaching a solution means participants have to go back to work. The meeting is a refuge from other unpleasant assignments.

By definition, an operating meeting calls for the participation, involvement, and commitment of each member. To gain commitment from members of a group, management must inspire some motivation to participate. It makes little sense to assign a person to a committee without regard to his or her values or interests. If the person has nothing personally vested in the issue, or no relevant information to contribute, then productive participation will be low. They may go through the motions, but their only real outcome is to kill some time.

Meetings Are Expensive

A second disadvantage of meetings is that they cost a great deal of money. A group decision inevitably takes more time than an executive action, and the costs of such time can really add up. If it takes a 12-member committee three hours to make a decision, and the average committee member's salary is a modest $35,000 a year (including benefits), the decision costs *at least* $605.88. And this estimate includes only direct labor costs. What needs to be considered also is the ripple of psychological costs to the individual and the organization—which can be staggering.

> **Psychological costs of poor meetings can be enormous.**

For example, work done by subordinates is often tied up while the boss is in conference; customers' needs are ignored; work piles up; phone messages stack up; papers in the in basket begin to pile up; and a half dozen people just *have to* talk to the manager about some pressing matter when the conference ends. These kinds of things sap psychic energy from people who are paid to use their minds; they add to the aggravation of the manager's job. The question is one of opportunity cost: what could meeting goers do with their time if they weren't tied up in the meeting? The manager must ask, "Is this meeting worth it?"

The three-hour committee decision could perhaps be made by one manager with access to relevant information (such as via a computer database) in say, half an hour or less. The labor cost might then be $10 or so, not $605.88.

Just how much better is the $600 decision compared to the $10 one? Maybe not much, unless the group process worked better than it often does and was particularly well-suited to the type of issue being discussed.

Too much high-powered management talent is wasted on trivial decisions. Haggling over where to put the new copier machine, where to hold the company picnic, when the cafeteria should be open, and the like have been subjects of long discussions using a very expensive medium. A simple decision, in many cases even a wrong but cheaper decision—would have been a better choice.

Low-Quality Decisions

While group synergy may result in better decisions, in many cases the group process can backfire, resulting in poor decisions. This can occur in four situations:

1. *When nobody has much hard data about the topic under discussion.* The outcome of such a group reflects pooled ignorance. If the issues require specialized expertise, go to an expert. Don't muddy the water by using a committee as well. An artist's painting cannot be improved by a bunch of novices looking over her shoulder, offering suggestions.

2. *When excessive conflict prevails within the group.* In meetings, conflict is potentially useful—up to the point that it becomes destructive. When participants get into a no-holds-barred discussion, the outcome both in terms of relationships and quality of decision can be devastating. (More about dealing with conflict later in this chapter.)

3. *When the free flow of information in the group is impeded by individual dominance and groupthink.* The term groupthink was coined by Irving Janis to describe a condition of likemindedness that tends to arise in groups that are particularly cohesive. Although cohesiveness is normally a desirable condition in groups, it can be carried so far that it becomes counterproductive. This is especially likely when the group has a high *esprit de corps* and when members' desire for consensus or harmony becomes stronger than their desire for accuracy. Under such conditions critical thinking and the independent and objective analysis of ideas are foregone in deference to a smooth-running group. The likelihood of groupthink increases if the group becomes insulated from outside influences and the fresh flow of information.

Groupthink has several symptoms.

Based on Janis's concept, VonBergen and Kirk describe eight symptoms of groupthink.[4]

a. Illusion of unanimity regarding the viewpoint held by the majority in the group and an emphasis on team play.

b. A view of the opposition as generally inept, incompetent, and incapable of countering effectively any action by the group, no matter how risky the decision or how high the odds are against the plan of action succeeding.

c. Self-censorship of group members in which overt disagreements are avoided, facts that might reduce support for the emerging majority view are suppressed, faulty assumptions are not questioned, and personal doubts are suppressed in the form of group harmony.

d. Collective rationalization to comfort one another in order to discount warnings that the agreed-on plan is either unworkable or highly unlikely to succeed.

e. Self-appointed mind guards within the group that function to prevent anyone from undermining its apparent unanimity and to protect its members from unwelcome ideas and adverse information that may threaten consensus.

f. Reinforcement of consensus and direct pressure on any dissenting group member who expresses strong reservations or challenges, or argues against the apparent unanimity of the group.

g. An expression of self-righteousness that leads members to believe their actions are moral and ethical, thus inclining them to disregard any ethical or moral objections to their behavior.

h. A shared feeling of unassailability marked by a high degree of *esprit de corps*, by implicit faith in the wisdom of the group, and by an inordinate optimism that disposes members to take excessive risks.

Each of these symptoms of groupthink damages realistic thinking and effective decisions. A combination of several or all of these can be devastating to group effectiveness.

A second type of pressure that censors the free flow of information is *individual dominance*. In many groups, certain individuals become excessively dominant by virtue of their personality, organizational position, or personal status. Other participants become reluctant to interact freely, perhaps feeling that their contributions are of lesser value.

> *Individual dominance can come about inadvertently when people of higher status participate in the group.*

While individual dominance can speed up the decision process, it does so at the cost of a potential reduction in decision quality.

Managers need to be sensitive to how differences in status and expertise as well as communication styles can put a damper on free discussion. For example, a meeting of assembly line workers brought together to discuss ways of reducing quality defects may not work well if the production manager sits in. Likewise, the newest employee, who may have some excellent ideas, may be quickly quieted by a negative comment from an old timer. Such comments typically say, "We tried that before, and it didn't work."

4. *When the group takes excessive risks.* Cartwright and Zander,[5] two researchers well-known for their studies in group dynamics, pointed out what they called the *risky shift phenomenon*. A series of widely replicated experiments showed that groups tend to make more daring or more risky decisions than individuals working alone. Again, social pressures from within the group result in potentially counterproductive behavior. Risk taking is viewed as a positive personality characteristic that we demonstrate to others as we work in groups.

> *Sometimes groups make more risky decisions than would individuals working alone.*

The potential danger in this is that some groups adopt a safety-in-numbers position and recommend extreme solutions that they wouldn't dream of taking responsibility for as individuals. You end up with a lynch mob mentality.

Poor Decisions due to Time Constraints

One final disadvantage of group decision making is simply that it is sometimes inappropriate because of time constraints imposed by the problem. A battle group in combat cannot use participative decision making while the enemy awaits their solution. Similarly, in business, some decisions must be made quickly. To delay a decision may squander a potential competitive advantage or organizational opportunity.

To Meet Or Not to Meet

Although advantages and disadvantages must be carefully considered in decisions about problem-solving meetings, many such decisions are still likely to come down on the side of continued and even expanded use. Most of the disadvantages can be overcome; they are not inevitable. As Richard Dunsing said:

> When you accept poor meetings as a fact of life, you are in collusion with many others doing the same thing. In effect, you are aiding and abetting them on clogging the system and in eroding the quality of working life. Managing means changing things that aren't what they need to be. Surprisingly often, it is merely the management of the obvious.[6]

While griping about the overuse or misuse of those miserable meetings has certain cathartic value, the real issue is how to maximize the value of meetings when they are appropriate.

A first step is to determine what kind of group is needed. Problem-solving meeting groups are normally called committees. But there are several different types of committees, each with special characteristics.

Types of Committees

Three general types of committees are frequently used in organizations: the *standing* committee, the *special* committee, and the *ad hoc* committee.

The Standing Committee

Standing committees serve to relieve the manager of administrative burdens and substitute collective judgment for individual judgment in certain recurrent, noncritical situations.[7] Since standing committees act as a form of work delegation, it would be self-defeating for the manager to act as the chair. The committee membership should be representative of the organization and should be chaired by a ranking member who can comfortably allocate work to others. The work of standing committees is ongoing so long as there is organizational need.

The Special Committee

Special committees may be assembled to deal with a single, specific issue which cannot be handled realistically via ordinary organizational procedures. Often these situations are too controversial, too complex, or deal with issues of symbolic or highly emotional significance which are simply too important to be handled in a routine manner.

When the work of a special committee is done, it should disband. Problems arise when special committees don't disband but become self-appointed standing committees. The manager should ensure that this does not happen unless there is a clear need to upgrade to standing status.

Ideally, the organizational leader should assemble the special committee, give it its charge in clear unequivocal detail, and step back to let it work. Its membership should include representatives from all factions that stand to be affected by the decision or outcome. This often means a larger-than-usual number of participants, which in turn calls for a chair who is skilled in meeting management and is reasonably high in seniority or rank.

The key to the special committee's effectiveness lies in the degree of clarification provided by the manager who calls it together. The manager's instructions should describe the task in detail, indicate clearly what the end product (usually a written report) should be like, and explain what resources are available from the organization. Deadlines and instructions about conditions of secrecy or publicity under which the group should work should also be spelled out. Equally important, once this information is presented to the group, the manager should remove him- or herself from the process except for occasional briefings or further clarification.

The Ad Hoc Committee

Ad hoc committees, like special committees, deal with nonrecurrent, special tasks. They differ, however, in that ad hoc committees typically handle relatively noncontroversial tasks, are smaller in number of participants and do not necessarily represent the views of all organization members. Members should be selected on the basis of interest in and/or competence with regard to the committee's assignment.

The group may consist of as few as two members and seldom more than five. Like the special committee, their work should be temporary and they should not develop into standing committees unless the needs of the organization clearly demand this. Typically their work is somewhat less complex than the special committee. The manager who assembles the ad hoc committee should have no regular involvement in its deliberations.

Figure 9-1 summarizes key points about consulted committees.

FIVE MAJOR ELEMENTS OF THE EFFECTIVE MEETING

Effective managers need to build some flexibility into their approaches to meetings and conferences, for there is no one best way to run all types of meetings. There are, however, five major elements on which effective meetings are built:

- The meeting goals
- The meeting climate
- Leadership and the internal workings of the meeting
- The decision strategy
- Postmeeting evaluation and follow-up

The Meeting Goals: Everyone Knows Why We're Here, Right?

Although the person who called the meeting probably has a pretty good idea of why it's been called, others are seldom so clear. If you don't believe this, try asking everyone in the group to write down specifically why the meeting is being held and compare answers.

	General Purpose of Committee	Examples of Such Committees	Ideal Type of Membership
Standing	Relieves manager of administrative burden. Substitutes collective judgment for individual judgment on recurrent non-critical situations	Safety committee. Professional school admissions committee. Loan committee of a bank. Computerization committee. Personnel committee	Widely representative of all departments that may be affected by decisions reached. Wide range of organizational rank, personal characteristics
Special	Considers particularly knotty problems too complex, too controversial, or too important to be handled in a regular way. Appointed to defer or avoid an otherwise pressing decision. To deflect the onus of an unpopular decision or to allay suspicions that have arisen in connection with a particular issue. To cope with problems that are intrinsically unimportant but have acquired symbolic significance	Committees to iron out conflicts between organizational factions. Disciplinary action committees. Decision appeals or policy review committees	Representative of all relevant shades of opinion and every important faction of the organization which is likely to be affected by the decision
Ad Hoc	Deals with some nonrecurrent, noncontroversial task	Drafting a statement. Inspecting an item for sale. Arranging convention facilities. Surveying organization needs	Compatible with each other. Competent with respect to the committee assignment. Do *not* need to be representative of organization members

FIGURE 9-1   Rules of thumb for consulted committees.

	Number of Members	Qualifications of Chairperson	Manager's Participation
Standing	5 to 9	Senior to most other members (so can comfortably allocate work to others) Not holding extreme position with respect to committee's task Not someone new to organization who does not understand its informal norms	As ex officio member
Special	10 to 30 (limited only by size of organization's largest conference table)	Manager of considerable seniority Good command of parliamentary procedures Organizational maturity	Should start the committee off with unequivocal charge; describe the group's task in detail; indicate clearly what type of report should be produced; state time interval, resources available, and conditions of publicity or secrecy under which group should work Is kept posted of progress via informants
Ad Hoc	2 to 5	Interested in the assignment	None after group's assignment is given

To clarify the group's goals, work down the ladder of abstraction from a general expression of the topic (solving the morale problem) to more concrete objectives (reducing high absenteeism rate among data input clerks). Doing so creates a clearer focus for the meeting. It's not necessary to predetermine exactly what all possible goals are before meeting, but clarifying the task should be the priority activity in the early part of the discussions. Otherwise, how will you know when the job is done?

The three key questions that must be answered early in a discussion are:

◆ What exactly are we here for?
◆ What exactly will we have when we've completed our job?
◆ How will we go about accomplishing our task?

Group goal clarification is an essential first step to successful committee work. Joan Eisenstodt, President of Eisenstodt Associates, a Washington, D.C. independent meeting planning firm stresses developing goals and sticking to them; most last minute goal changes cause more future problems. Once the goals have been clarified, groups should write the important information so everyone in the meeting knows "what, where, why, and how."[8]

> **Develop clear task goals early in the meeting or committee process.**

If the primary task objective and procedures are not clearly established, participants will never know when they are finished. In that case the likelihood of time-wasting, extended meetings increases sharply.

The Meeting Climate

Clarity of goals is a legitimate part of the climate of an organization or group, as discussed in Chapter 4. Yet several other equally important climate characteristics affect the communication of participants in committee work.

Physical dimensions include such things as room temperature and lighting; presence or absence of distracting noises; odors or interruptions; the arrangement of furniture; and the availability of tools such as chalkboard, paper and pencils, flip charts, and the like. Seating arrangements allowing participants to talk to each other comfortably and to have an unobstructed view of others and of visual aids is a must. Often the impressive, large wooden table of the board room is not the best for working meetings. People should feel free to get up, move around, and not be stuck in their chairs.

Avoid meeting in rooms with auditorium-type seating, where all the participants see is the back of others' heads. Also, be sensitive to "power positions," such as the head of a table or larger chairs. Round tables help. Planning for good physical climate is a preconference responsibility of the leader.

Leadership and the Internal Workings of Meetings

Effective leadership is a key to the success of any organization. Understanding basic leadership concepts can help the manager make better choices about when and how to apply various approaches. Although the focus continues to be on the problem-solving group, the leadership principles also apply when selecting people for advancement in management, choosing work group or team leaders, and the like.

Early Research into Leadership

For many years social scientists attempted to define specific *personal traits or characteristics* inherent in individuals who seem to be effective leaders. This research approach predominated in the studies of leadership for the first half of this century. The underlying assumption was that leaders are somehow different from other people in the population. If people could but identify what makes them different, they would be able to select the best leaders "scientifically."

Because of situational variables, most leadership studies have been ambiguous and inconclusive. However, not all of the leadership research should be considered useless. A massive review of such leadership literature was prepared by Ralph Stogdill. In his analysis of almost 300 studies, he concluded that leaders, when compared with nonleaders, tended to be more

> *Personal traits taken alone do not predict good leadership skills.*

- ♦ Goal directed
- ♦ Venturesome
- ♦ Self-confident
- ♦ Responsible
- ♦ Tolerant of stress and frustration among people
- ♦ Capable of influencing the behavior of others

Stogdill also concludes, however, that these "characteristics, considered singly, hold little diagnostic or predictive significance. In combination, it would appear that they interact to generate personality dynamics advantageous to the person seeking the responsibilities of leadership."[9]

John Geier applied what was later referred to as a "method of residues" to conclude that certain personality characteristics consistently eliminate an individual from leadership consideration in almost all situations."[10] A person was virtually disqualified from the opportunity to lead when he or she was seen as:

- ♦ Uninformed about issues important to the group
- ♦ A very low participator
- ♦ Very rigid in thinking

Some people discredit such a traits approach to leadership studies, perhaps because it seems to imply that a leader either has the desired characteristics or doesn't—an implication that questions the value of leadership training. If you have the right traits, you don't need the training. If you lack these "proven" traits, leadership training probably won't help.

While the traits studies were often marred by theoretical or methodological defects, their findings may hold some validity. As Hampton, Summer, and Webber say, "The complete denial of any [leadership] traits could be an overcorrection."[11]

A More Sophisticated Look at Leadership: The Situational Perspective

In view of the serious limitations of many of the traits studied, how can leadership success be predicted? Researchers today would contend that a complex network of factors is at work in any leadership situation. From the *situational perspective*, three classes of factors seem to work together to determine leader effectiveness:

1. The nature of the task to be accomplished by the leader's group
2. The leader's personality compared with the predominant personality characteristics of the group's members
3. The leader's power

The first two factors arise from the way people interact in groups. To understand such interactions, one must recall that two classes of activities are at work in every meeting: task activities and maintenance activities. *Task activities* have to do with *what* the group is doing; *maintenance* is concerned with *how* they do their work. For example, the process of goal clarification is primarily a task activity, while the establishment of climate is mostly a maintenance activity.

Most leaders understand their task roles. They see a job to be done and know they're responsible to see that it is accomplished. Some, however, underestimate the importance of maintenance. In all, the main goal involves guiding a group to attain the maximum realizable outcome from a meeting.[12]

Although one can go too far with either activity, the degree of emphasis is an important management judgment. While the task activities get the job done, neglect of maintenance can lead to serious dissatisfaction, which could undermine the entire process. The manager who rams through a solution may face group resentment that eventually more than offsets the short-term victory. In some cases, the maintenance activities are legitimately the most important outcome of the meeting, making participants feel good about the opportunities for affiliation and participation in group work.

> *Some maintenance activities are important so long as they are appropriately blended with task direction.*

Leaders need to be sensitive to an appropriate balance between task accomplishment and the maintenance factors that strengthen intragroup relationships and make the group experience satisfying for participants.

The third variable that affects the leadership situation is power. People bring two types of power to the group: personal power and position power. *Personal power* is power that is given to an individual based on how others perceive him or her. It usually arises when one is seen as possessing expertise, skills, ability, and other characteristics the viewer deems important. There is a natural attraction toward people with high personal power.

Position power, on the other hand, is conferred on an individual by someone in a higher level of authority. It is made known by rank, position, status, and the capability of providing others with rewards and/or punishment. Most leaders exhibit some combination of both personal power and position power.

Newly announced political candidates may run initially on their personal power (personality, appearance, experiences, etc.) until position power in the form of endorsements and party nomination is granted. After being elected, officeholders have position power (having been legitimately selected by the voters), which adds significantly to their potential for leadership effectiveness.

For more ideas on situational leadership, see the reading beginning on page 224.

Traditional versus Group-Centered Leadership

Leadership in mature groups often moves from person to person.

Current thinking on leadership supports the notion that the mature group can function effectively with very little intervention from the designated leader. They can become self-directed. The leadership process of guiding the group's activity is likely to move from person to person within the mature group rather than be centered in one individual.

As groups evolve toward higher levels of task-relevant maturity over time, leaders must be ready to adjust their behaviors accordingly. As pioneer communication scholar Franklin Haiman said back in the 1950s, "The man officially called leader performs only those tasks which the group itself is not yet mature enough, intellectually or emotionally, to handle for itself. The leader's goal is to work himself out of a job."[13]

This completes our brief overview of leadership approaches. The point is that group leadership, although only one of five keys to effective meetings, is extremely important. The more one understands about the application of leadership, the more effective the meetings can be.

The leader or leaders play a crucial role in implementing a strategy for reaching decisions. This strategy is discussed next.

The Decision Strategy

Effective groups typically work through four phases as they identify the best solution(s) to a given problem. These four phases, which constitute the decision strategy, are:

♦ Define the specific problem(s).
♦ Classify criteria or conditions that would be met by a good solution.
♦ Generate tentative solutions.
♦ Select the best solution(s) from all the tentative ones.

Define the Specific Problem

Clear problem definition is critical to effective discussion.

Group members in the early stages of discussion should try to identify, in specific terms, the nature and elements of the problem or issue at hand. This process of defining and clarifying a problem also involves defining critical terms. For example, the group called together to "do something about employee morale" should define what they mean by morale. How do they know when morale is good or bad? Often an operational definition—one that defines in terms of something clearly measurable—works well. In this case, one might say that bad morale is what is present when absenteeism, number of grievances filed, and employee turnover each reach some specified levels.

Once a problem is defined, there should be a general discussion of objectives—what the best possible outcome would be if it could be achieved. Then the group should evaluate where it stands in relation to the objectives, and what obstacles prevent it from reaching those objectives. The ideal outcome should be described in terms of what could reasonably be expected to occur; that is, an ideal solution to the perceived morale problem would:

- ♦ Reduce absenteeism to less than 2 percent per day
- ♦ Reduce grievances to one filed per quarter
- ♦ Reduce turnover to 0.5 percent per month

This statement operationally defines the objective. It also suggests a way to measure success, an important requirement to help determine whether and when a problem is solved.

Classifying Criteria and Conditions

Criteria or characteristics of good decisions are generally in the back of people's minds and must be brought into the open. Once the group agrees that any successful solution must meet certain conditions, inappropriate and time wasting discussion can be reduced.

For example, with the foregoing discussion of morale, one might classify the criteria for an ideal solution as follows. The ideal solution should:

- ♦ Not undermine the authority of the supervisor in any way
- ♦ Not cost additional money for wage or benefit incentives
- ♦ Be easily implemented
- ♦ Serve as a model prototype for future employee motivation programs
- ♦ Be based in sound management theory

Criteria should be listed on a chalkboard or chart so that everyone can refer to them as possible solutions are evaluated. Once criteria are established, ideas generated in the discussion can be weighed against them. Ideas that fit the criteria most closely are the best solutions—so long as the group developed careful, clear criteria.

Generating Quality Solutions

Once the problem has been satisfactorily defined and the criteria articulated, you can begin generating tentative solutions. Before taking this third step, however, be sure that the problem and criteria are indeed clear. Too many groups want to jump to generating solutions before the problem has been completely defined. If that happens, what may emerge is an excellent solution—but to a different problem.

Two very effective methods to generate tentative solutions are brainstorming and the nominal group technique.

Brainstorming.   Although this term is used rather loosely by many people, it refers to a specific technique developed by Alex Osborn,[14] an advertising executive, to stimulate creative and imaginative problem solving. There are four basic rules to help ensure effective brainstorming:

1. Don't criticize or evaluate any ideas.
2. Don't consider any idea too wild to be suggested.
3. Don't limit the quantity of ideas generated.
4. Seize opportunities to improve or add ideas suggested by others.

The rules of brainstorming are easier to state than to obey—especially rule 2. Unless great care is taken, nonverbal cues such as facial expression and tone of voice can discourage additional wild ideas. When brainstorming, the leader should post the rules somewhere as a constant reminder. Then let the ideas fly. And don't forget to hitchhike on each others' ideas whenever possible. Only after all the ideas are generated should the group begin to evaluate them.

Nominal Group Technique (NGT).   This technique combines the process of generating tentative solutions with selecting the best solutions. NGT may be more useful than brainstorming, especially when the group is dealing with potentially emotional or controversial issues for which brainstorming may generate more heat than light.

Instead of having group members immediately speak up and reveal their point of view (a process that may commit them to that view and make them more rigid since they've voiced it publicly), NGT includes several steps, as follows:

1. Group members privately and silently write down their ideas. This can take from 10 to 20 minutes.
2. A round robin recording process takes place, in which each member gives one idea at a time, until all the ideas are recorded in full view of the group.
3. The group discusses ideas for clarification.
4. A silent group vote takes place (several votes may be needed before a final solution is accepted).

Selecting the Best Ideas from the Tentative Solutions

From the brainstormed ideas and the solutions defined by the nominal group technique, select those that best meet the criteria for best possible decision. Then comes the acid test: *action testing*. Although the group carefully employed

> *Only action testing proves the quality of a group's decision.*

every known technique for effective decision making, only action testing tells for sure if they've succeeded.

Because solutions are seldom perfect or everlasting, rechecking them over time is important. Problems have ways of recurring in a cyclical pattern or reemerging in different variations. Seldom can a solution settle the matter once and for all. Action testing checks on implementation and should be readministered periodically.

Postmeeting Evaluation and Follow-up

> *Look back on completed meetings to evaluate their success and determine what could be improved.*

Evaluation and adjustments should be an ongoing process during any meeting. In addition, taking a retrospective look at the meeting can be very useful in overcoming problematic areas in future meetings. Let's discuss for a moment some of the elements that should be observed.

The following questions about task activities should be considered after a meeting takes place. Did the meeting participants

- ◆ State exactly what the meeting was to accomplish? Set goals and objectives, list priorities, identify clearly the problem areas to be dealt with?
- ◆ Apply a systematic, logical decision-making strategy?
- ◆ Combine useful ideas while sorting through possible solutions? Was background information gathered when needed? Were more details called for when appropriate?
- ◆ Examine potential solutions in terms of their impact on others, their costs and benefits, and the need for support from others in order to be effective?
- ◆ Seek creative and innovative approaches? Seek new relationships by linking other issues into the problems that were being evaluated?
- ◆ Delegate assignments and agree on such things as time limits and resources to be used? Determine times for follow-up sessions when necessary?
- ◆ Process the final decision into a usable form, usually a written report?

Group maintenance activities should also be reviewed. These included the ways participants thought, acted, and felt while immersed in the task. Did the meeting participants

- ◆ Interact in constructive ways through supportive speech, body language, compliments, and a sense of caring?
- ◆ Avoid patterns of excessive dominance or inactivity?
- ◆ Share in commitment to cooperate? Avoid factionalism or the hard sell of personal viewpoints?

♦ Freely express feelings as well as information?

♦ Manage disagreement and conflicting ideas in constructive ways?

♦ Mix seriousness with playfulness?

♦ Seem to enjoy the work and to feel good about being together?

The degree to which these kinds of activities are happening determines the likelihood of meeting effectiveness. Systematically diagnosing the quality of one's meetings can be a useful exercise.

After a meeting is evaluated, take follow-up action. For example, if a particular member was too dominant, the goals were too vague, or the meeting took up too much time, these are problems that should be taken care of to improve future meetings.

Follow-up does not only consist of solving problems that occurred. Important in maintaining control of a meeting is ensuring that everyone leaves the meeting with the same ideas. A follow-up memorandum should be sent to all the participants within a day or two.[15] Anyone can simply evaluate a meeting, the improvement comes through effective follow-up.

COPING WITH CONFLICT

Interactional characteristics that affect meeting climate include the effective use of conflict. This concept deserves clarification.

Traditionally, it has been assumed that we should avoid conflict in meetings. The term conjures up images of fist fights or people screaming at each other. In reality, conflict is simply a state of incompatibility, and incompatibility, by itself, is neither good nor bad. What makes incompatibility either desirable or undesirable is the participants' reaction to it. Communication professor Elliott Pood[16] suggests several responses to conflict:

1. We can attempt to avoid conflict by not expressing opposing views and by withholding even nonverbal feedback that indicates disagreement. By doing so, however, we exclude some ideas from being shared within the group. Without a free sharing of information, the group cannot maximize its potential for producing superior solutions.

2. A second response to conflict reflects the opposite view. We can engage in *unregulated confrontation*, which is traditionally characterized by a win/lose orientation, leading to no-holds-barred, open warfare among participants. Unregulated conflict becomes very personal rather than group task oriented and results in the elimination of some group members, usually by their psychological withdrawal from participation. Again, the result again is the reduction of information sharing and lower-quality group decisions.

3. A third and most beneficial response to group confrontation is what Pood calls *conflict management*. The effective management of conflict seeks to regulate but not eliminate confrontation. Recognizing that the abrasive actions of opposing views polish the final product, the skillful leader seeks free exchange of information but without the win/lose destructiveness of unregulated conflict.

Jack Kaine offers seven rules to help solve conflicts in meetings or negotiations.[17]

Rule 1:   Avoid escalating a conflict. Don't try to get in the last word.

Rule 2:   Know when to walk away (figuratively or literally). Sometimes you have to walk away from a bad deal to make a good deal.

Rule 3:   Be a careful communicator. First educate, then negotiate.

Rule 4:   Lead by questioning. A negotiation can be controlled by questioning, not talking. With questions an issue can be reframed—looked at from another perspective

Rule 5:   Wait to make counterproposals. Before making a counterproposal make sure you fully understand the initial proposal.

Rule 6:   Focus on your strongest positions. Raising weaker points tends to dilute the strength of your position.

Rule 7:   Settle on an agreement that is workable. Remember that the objective is not only an agreement, but an agreement that will work.

WHAT A GOOD MEETING IS LIKE

If a committee meeting could be described as polite, orderly, and carefully led, with each participant taking his or her turn to address the group or the leader, the meeting is probably a flop. Good, effective meetings, where people wrestle with tough problems, are likely to bear little resemblance to parliamentary discussions in hushed conference rooms among polite and scrupulously reasonable people. Some good meetings are more likely to resemble cattle auctions.

Good meetings are often noisy, with hard-thinking, challenging people talking straight and bouncing ideas off each other. Under effective leadership, which often rotates from person to person as the need arises, participants debate, discuss, and even argue about the problems before them. The meeting often looks disorderly and, in fact, the phrase "wrestling with problems" conjures up a rather accurate picture of an effective meeting. Remember that there remains method to the madness of a good meeting.

> *Good meetings can often get messy.*

The key to success is that participants never lose track of what they are doing. The objective of the meeting remains clear, and commitment to accomplishing the goal is unwavering. Sure, there will be momentary sidetracks to explore possibilities that ultimately may not prove productive, but the focus remains on the issues. When the job is done, the meeting ends, period. Even if it is way before scheduled quitting time.

These are the kinds of activities found at a good, productive conference. Many managers have never been to such a thing. Perhaps this is because most have come to expect something different. Some misconceptions about what meetings should be like, and that are actually counterproductive, include the following:

Misconception 1: Meetings Should Be Orderly, with the Leader Managing the Flow of Information

If meetings are characterized by the raise-your-hand-and-be-recognized syndrome, participation is being stifled and you're not getting the maximum benefit from the process. Rules of order are fine for large groups and formal proceedings, but not for most business conferences. If you need such tight structuring to avoid total chaos, the group probably has too many members.

The designated leader need not function as a traffic officer. According to Dunsing, tight leader control of the group's activities results in

> ...a lot of "reporting." Each member is choreographed to give his or her view of things in one blurt. "Here's how we see it down in the laboratory." No one is permitted to interrupt. Dialogue is cut off. There is no free flow. Participants need not pay close attention because they can't respond naturally to ideas as they are presented—so they cast off into dreamland or start rehearsing their big moment.

> ...a bizarre kind of human interaction results: People don't talk to each other directly—they talk to each other through the leader.[18]

Such tight control destroys the vibrant, free-flowing interaction that makes meetings work.

Misconception 2: Conflict Should Be Avoided; We Should Seek Cooperation at all Cost

If there is a free exchange of ideas, there is bound to be some conflict. One reason for the group process is to subject ideas to the abrasive action of other ideas. That's the way rough edges are smoothed out. Conflict should be managed, not discouraged. Managed confrontations remain issue oriented, not people oriented. The use of appropriate communication skills allows all the benefits of assertive information exchange without the destructiveness of unregulated, win/lose warfare.

Conflict is not only inevitable—it is useful and important to the group's success.

The real apprehension people associate with verbal conflict arises from a fear of hurt feelings—ones own or others'—from such interaction. If, however, the conflict is kept on the adult level—where issues, positions, evidence, and reasoning are attacked without the advocate's *self-worth* being questioned—it can be useful. This, of course, is easier said than done. People have skins of varying thicknesses that are penetrated when pet ideas are put down or felt to be unfairly criticized.

Most meetings usually have loudmouths, extroverts who enjoy taking charge of conversations and don't seem to notice that they are drowning other voices out.[19] They can intimidate others from speaking up, while they mop up existing time like sponges. A simple solution is for the leader simply to say

"That's interesting, can we relate that back to the agenda," or "That's interesting, but let's hear from other people, too."[20] These simple comments can avoid this unnecessary conflict.

If members go into the committee meeting knowing that such useful confrontations will take place as a normal course of events, they puncture this misconception and improve the quality of the meetings. Maybe a good handshake should take place before they come out swinging.

Misconception 3: The Leader is Totally Responsible for the Success of the Meeting

Effective communication can never be assured by one participant in the interaction. As we said in Chapter 1, communication means the creation of common meanings—understanding—among two or more parties. If a conference or meeting is to work, it will require efforts from several participants.

A designated leader does have some special responsibilities, however. He or she can: (1) set the tone and establish patterns of interaction, (2) clarify the task to be accomplished and guide participants back on track when they stray too far, (3) mediate conflicts to be sure they remain productive, (4) arrange the presession agenda and postsession follow-up, and (5) make assignments as appropriate. While these responsibilities are considerable, they do not constitute control over the outcome of the committee's deliberations.

> *Designated leaders do have special responsibilities.*

An effective committee meeting is one in which these popular misconceptions are not assumed. Overemphasis on orderliness, "correct" procedures, and elimination of conflict can only detract from the usefulness of the group process. When the leader and the led share a mutual sense of responsibility for getting the job done, then the group will succeed.

A QUICK SUMMARY OF MAJOR IDEAS

♦ Some managers overuse the meeting or conference. They tend to do so without objectively considering the advantages and disadvantages of the medium.

♦ The advantages of effective, problem-solving meetings include synergy (groups can come to better solutions than individuals working alone) and a higher degree of commitment to a group decision, especially among those who participated in the decision.

♦ Disadvantages of meetings can include the fact that meetings sometimes become a substitute for action, generate high costs, and create the potential for low-quality decisions.

♦ Decision quality is hurt when participants lack sufficient information to deal with the topic, when excessive conflict prevails in the meeting, or when the free flow of information is disrupted in the group. Such disruption results when individual dominance or groupthink is present.

◆ Three general types of committees are used in organizations: standing, special, and ad hoc. Each calls for a different set of instructions from its leaders.

◆ Five major elements determine the effectiveness of meetings: goal clarity, climate, leadership, decision strategy, and follow-up.

◆ Group-centered leadership approaches recognize that leadership is a role that may rightfully move from person to person rather than remain centered in one individual.

◆ Decision strategies typically define the problem(s), articulate criteria for proposed solutions, generate tentative solutions, and then systematically select the best solutions. Brainstorming and nominal group techniques are often useful in this process.

◆ Conflict can be potentially useful in groups unless it becomes unregulated. Allowing some conflict is important to the group process.

QUESTIONS FOR FURTHER THOUGHT

1. What are the potential advantages of traditional leadership? Name some specific situations where such an approach is likely to be effective.

2. What are the potential advantages of group-centered leadership? Name some specific situations where such an approach is likely to be effective.

3. Think about a problem or issue faced by your organization. Go through the seven steps suggested as decision strategy and write out your ideas for each. Compare them with the ideas of someone else in the same organization.

4. Try applying brainstorming to a problem your organization faces which calls for creativity. Remember the four basic rules.

5. How do you tend to respond to incompatibility (potential conflicts) on the job? Is your style of response productive?

6. What do your meetings tend to be like? Describe them in detail. Based on what you've read in this chapter, are you satisfied with this description? What would you like to see changed?

OTHER THOUGHTS ABOUT MEETINGS AND CONFERENCES

SITUATIONAL LEADERSHIP

Fred E. Fiedler has developed a leadership contingency model that focuses on the three variables we have mentioned. He refers to these as leader-member relations, task structure, and position power. His research has suggested that emphasis on task or maintenance leadership efforts should be determined by the "favorableness of a situation," which he defines as "the degree to which the situation enables the leader to exert his influence over his group."[21] The most favorable situation would be one in which:

♦ The leader is well liked by the participants.

♦ The task is clearly defined.

♦ The leader's status or position power is obvious.

An unfavorable situation would be the opposite of these conditions. Some mixture of positives and negatives would put the leader in an intermediate situation.

Fiedler's research concludes that when the situation is either very favorable or very unfavorable to the leader, he or she would do well to stress task activities and not be overly concerned with maintenance activities. When the favorableness of the situation is intermediate, the leader needs to be more concerned with maintenance activities and should emphasize the building of good relationships. Figure 9-2 illustrates shifts in leadership emphases.

A skillful leader should be aware of these two channels of activity and be capable of switching emphasis as needed. As changes appear in, say, task clarity and relationships with group participants, a marked increase in situational favorableness may call for a shift in emphasis from maintenance (building rapport, etc.) to getting down to tasks.

Management theorists Paul Hersey and Kenneth H. Blanchard have synthesized the ideas of Fiedler and a number of others to develop their situational leadership theory. According to their approach, a leader can determine an appropriate mixture of relationship-building and task-directing behaviors to increase the probability of effectiveness. "To determine what leadership style is appropriate in a given situation, a leader must first determine the maturity level of the individual or group in relation to a specific task that the leader is attempting to accomplish through their efforts."[22]

What is this maturity level? According to Hersey and Blanchard, the task-relevant maturity of a person or group can be diagnosed by considering four characteristics of the group in relation to the specific job the group is called upon to accomplish. These characteristics are:

1. The capacity to set high but attainable goals

2. The willingness and ability to take responsibility

3. Education and experience (or a combination of both) relevant to the task
4. Personal maturity on the job in combination with a psychological maturity or self-confidence and self-respect

Let's look at an example. You have been asked to lead a committee to recommend a marketing strategy for a new product line. In gathering information about those who will work on the committee you determine that

1. The participants have a good record for setting ambitious yet realistic targets for themselves.
2. The participants have shown an eagerness to work on the committee and to take responsibility for marketing this new product line in a vigorous manner. If it goes over well, they expect to get credit; if it flops, they expect to shoulder the blame.
3. Each participant has been in on the new product development from the ground floor. They know how it's made, why it's built the way it is, and, based on past experience, they have a good idea of potential markets.
4. The participants are seasoned professionals in their field. They are success-oriented people with a proven track record.

Obviously in such a scenario, we have a committee with very high task-relevant maturity. But what if our team consists of quite another group?

1. They tend to take excessive risks (they have a record of biting off more than they can chew).
2. They want credit if their plan works but won't accept blame if it fails.
3. They have never worked on a committee like this one before.
4. They are rookies in this business.

Under these circumstances, the leader's job is likely to be quite different. Hersey and Blanchard would classify the first group as high in task-relevant maturity and the second example as very low. Most groups, of course, are likely to fall somewhere in between. The figure on the following page indicates how the effective leadership style would be determined.

As shown in the figure, once the maturity level of the participants is identified (or realistically guessed at), "the appropriate leadership style can be determined by constructing a right angle (90°) from the point on the continuum that represents the maturity level of the follower(s) to the point where it intersects the [curve] in the style-of-leader portion of the model. The quadrant in which that intersection takes place suggests the appropriate style to be used by the leader in that situation with follower(s) of that maturity level."[23]

As we can see, Hersey and Blanchard recommend that leaders use a different emphasis according to their estimate of follower maturity. Specifically, they recommend the predominant communication behaviors shown in Figure 9-3.

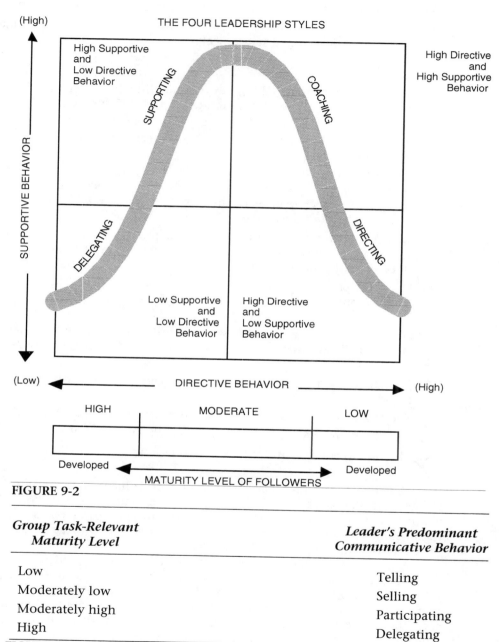

FIGURE 9-2

Group Task-Relevant Maturity Level	Leader's Predominant Communicative Behavior
Low	Telling
Moderately low	Selling
Moderately high	Participating
High	Delegating

FIGURE 9-3

Telling, selling, participating, and delegating all call for a different mix of communication skills to establish understanding. In moving from behaviors appropriate for the immature worker toward those for the more mature worker, communication skills become more important to effective leadership because of the increased complexity of communication interaction between the leader and follower(s). For example, the high-task, low-relationship quadrant of the model is characterized by one-way communication in which the leader simply gives directives—tells the follower(s) what to do and when to do it. The leadership attempt is successful to the extent that the follower does the desired thing. As workers become more mature, communication is more interactive; there is more emphasis on sharing information for mutual benefit rather than simply getting compliance.

The leadership style appropriate for highly mature employees calls for a substantial reduction in communication interaction, since the follower(s) start to run their own operation. The leader steps into the background, and the leader's function moves away from what we've viewed as traditional leadership toward less involvement and more group-centered leadership.

NOTES

1. Jim Lavenson, "Meeting the Issue," from *Selling Made Simple*. Reprinted by permission from *Sales & Marketing Management*. Copyright 1973.

2. Corwin P. King, "Decision by Discussion: The Uses and Abuses of Team Problem Solving," *S.A.M. Advanced Management Journal*, Autumn 1976, p. 33.

3. Lester Coch and John R. P. French, Jr., "Overcoming Resistance to Change," *Human Relations, 1* (1948), pp. 512–532.

4. Clarence W. Von Bergen and Raymond J. Kirk, "Groupthink: When Too Many Heads Spoil the Decision," *Management Review*, March 1978, p. 46 (New York: AMACOM, a division of American Management Associations).

5. Dorwin Cartwright and Alvin Zander, eds., *Group Dynamics: Theory and Research*, 3rd ed. (New York: Harper & Row, 1968).

6. Richard J. Dunsing, "You and I Have Simply Got to Stop Meeting This Way" (Part 1), *Supervisory Management*, September 1976, p. 9.

7. Theodore Caplow, *How to Run Any Organization* (Hinsdale, IL.: Dryden Press, 1976), p. 59.

8. Cited in Betsy Wiesendanger, "It's Always Something; Sales Meetings are Often Memorable—But Not Necessarily for the Right Reasons," *Sales and Marketing Management*, November 1993, p. 116.

9. Ralph M. Stogdill, *Handbook of Leadership* (New York: Free Press, 1974), pp. 81–82.

10. John Geier, "A Trait Approach to the Study of Leadership," *Journal of Communication, 17* (1967), pp. 316–323.

11. David R. Hampton, Charles E. Summer, and Ross A. Webber, *Organizational Behavior and the Practice of Management*, 3rd ed. (Glenview, IL.: Scott, Foresman, 1978), p. 597.

12. Ann L. Wiley, "Together We Can," *Technical Communication*, February 1993, p. 164.

13. Franklin S. Haiman, *Group Leadership and Democratic Action* (Boston: Houghton Mifflin, 1951), pp. 38–39).

14. Alex F. Osborn, *Applied Imagination: Principles and Procedures of Creative Thinking* (New York: Scribners, 1953), pp. 300–301.

15. Patricia Buhler, "The Key to More Effective Meetings," *Supervision*, September 1992, p. 19.

16. Eliott A. Pood (Assistant Professor of Communication at the University of North Carolina at Greensboro), Interview, March 1979.

17. Adapted from Jack W. Kaine, "Don't Fight—Negotiate," *Association Management*, September 1993, pp. 40–43.

18. Richard J. Dunsing, "You and I Have Simply Got to Stop Meeting This Way" (Part 2), *Supervisory Management*, October 1976, p. 12.

19. Michael Finely, "Subduing the Loudmouth—How to Keep Dominating People from Dominating Meetings," *Manage*, January 1993, p. 8.

20. Michael Finely, *ibid.* p.8.

21. Fred E. Fiedler, *A Theory of Leadership Effectiveness* (New York: McGraw-Hill, 1967), p. 13.

22. Paul Hersey and Kenneth H. Blanchard, *Management of Organizational Behavior*, 3rd ed. (Englewood Cliffs, N.J.: Prentice-Hall, 1977), p. 165.

23. *Ibid.* p. 165.

LISTENING

More Than Getting Your Ears On

▼

In this chapter you will find ideas that will help you:

♦ Describe the differences between hearing and listening

♦ Distinguish between internal, environmental, and interactional factors that complicate the listening process

♦ Explain how information overload and underuse of listening capacity can cause communication problems

♦ Describe the problems of self-centeredness and self-protection as they apply to listening

♦ Identify two behaviors to employ for better listening

▼

"You just haven't heard a word I said to you. Nobody listens to me around here. I might as well be talking to the wall." Have you ever heard such complaints? If you haven't, you must be living on another planet. The lack of effective listening may be the most common communication problem in most organizations (including families). As managers, we need to "have our ears on" regularly. We need to be particularly aware of the importance of effective listening to our organizations and to us.

Ironically, of the four basic communication skills—reading, writing, speaking, and listening—only one is not formally *taught*. Elementary schools focus heavily on the first three and assume that students are picking up listening. After all, some people reason, listening is really just a matter of sitting back and letting the talker have his or her say. Yet of all the communication skills, listening may actually be the most important. It deserves more attention than it typically gets.

> **Listening may well be the most important of all communication skills.**

In this chapter we consider the nature of listening, define some common barriers to good listening, and offer some pointers on how to become a more skillful, active listener.

THE DIFFERENCE BETWEEN HEARING AND LISTENING

Many of us confuse hearing and listening. In reality, they are two different things. The process we call *hearing* is purely physical activity by which acoustic energy in the form of sound waves is changed to mechanical and electrochemical energy that the brain can understand. All of this has little to do with listening. *Listening* refers to the psychological processes that allow us to attach meaning to the patterns of energy we hear. All the potential problems, which typically arise from differences in perception, come into play in the listening process.

> *Hearing and listening are not the same.*

The "cocktail party effect" provides a good example of the difference between hearing and listening. At a cocktail party there are usually several conversations going on simultaneously in the same room. Everyone present at the party is aware of these conversations in that they can be heard. On the other hand, we usually have to make a conscious effort to *listen* to any one of these conversations. We are physically capable of changing all or most of the acoustic energy in the room into electrochemical energy. We are much less capable of attaching meanings to all the electrochemical impulses.

WHAT CONTRIBUTES TO LISTENING?

> *Three elements complicate the listening process: internal, environmental, and interactional factors.*

Before we can begin to improve our listening skills, we need to understand the demands placed upon our listening capacities. These demands fall into three categories or elements of the listening process: internal elements, environmental elements, and interactional elements.

Internal Elements Affecting Listening

As just noted, listening involves attaching meanings to words or sounds we hear. Two preconditions must be met.

1. The words or other sounds used by the message source must be received by the hearer.

2. The listener must possess a set of meanings or referents for these sounds.

Overhearing someone speaking a strange foreign language is an obvious example of a breakdown in this second step. If the sounds have no referent, we cannot understand. Listening is the way we put sounds and their meanings together to create understanding.

Environmental Elements Affecting Listening

The second set of elements involved in the listening process includes the factors of the communication environment, which determine what we are able to listen to and what we cannot. These factors include:

- Our individual listening capacity
- The presence of noise
- The use or misuse of gatekeepers

Individual Listening Capacity

There are two ways our listening capacity can be overburdened: it can be overloaded with too much information, or it can be underutilized with too little. In both cases, listening tends to break down.

Examples of listening breakdowns caused by an exceeded listening capacity can be found in our everyday experiences. Only so many messages can be heard and responded to in any given day; only so many phone calls can be answered at one time. Once our capacity to accomplish these tasks has been reached, we develop defensive mechanisms for coping. We develop psychological strategies for selecting what we will attend to and what we will tune out.

These selection mechanisms, although often unconscious, are normally based on our individual needs, which, of course, change from time to time. When our capacity for paying attention to incoming information is exceeded, the impact on our listening behavior is difficult to predict. Only one thing is for sure: We are likely to miss some messages.

The problem is magnified for the organization as a whole. As discussed in Chapter 5, in many organizations the information load for certain people is so great that a situation of overload is created. The results are detrimental to organizational functioning.

The opposite problem, when environmental demands cause us to underutilize our listening capacity, is also widespread. Most people speak at the rate of about 120 words per minute, (except for auctioneers or disc jockeys), yet our normal capacity for listening—assigning meanings to words—is about 500 words per minute. The problem, of course, is that we listen faster than anyone can talk to us, providing ample time for our minds to wander far afield. Listening to others becomes a tedious task, forcing us to slow down our thinking to stay synchronized with those speaking to us.

> *People are capable of listening faster than others can talk.*

Noise

> *Noise may be either external—a factor of the environment—or internal—within ourselves.*

The presence of noise is another environmental element affecting listening. Noise refers to those sounds that are irrelevant to the conversation. It is important to note that noise may be either environmental (the sound of machinery, other conversations, buzzers, bells) or internal (a headache, our dislike of the person to whom we are listening, preoccupation with a meeting with the boss later in the day). Whatever the source, noise distracts us from the business of listening.

Gatekeepers

One way managers deal with the problems of exceeded listening capacity and excessive noise is through gatekeepers. The term *gatekeeper* is used in organizational communication literature to refer to one who previews incoming information to determine whether it is appropriate to the needs of the organization or an individual manager. If messages appear irrelevant, they are withheld from the system. In this sense a gatekeeper is a person whose job it is to do some of our listening for us. Almost every manager has at least one. The person may be a secretary, administrative assistant, or any other person we turn to for organizational information. In many instances, these individuals determine what needs our attention and what doesn't.

> *Gatekeepers preview incoming information before passing it on to others.*

Gatekeeping has its benefits, but it also poses problems. When we finally do get the information it has been through at least two sets of interpretations, our gatekeeper's and ours. There is no guarantee that we are listening to the message as originally intended. The serial transmission problem (as discussed in Chapter 5) may become acute. Also, our gatekeeper may accidentally filter out messages that we need to hear.

Interactional Elements Affecting Listening

In contrast to the environmental elements of the listening process, the interactional elements concern internal psychological processes that are not as easily identified. Two such psychological elements deserve careful consideration: self-centeredness and self-protection.

Effects of Self-Centeredness on Listening

Self-centeredness refers to the degree of vested interest we may have in our own point of view. When a difference of opinion arises among people, our vested interest in our ideas can create a listening barrier.

It isn't hard to understand why this occurs. When we have taken the time to formulate an idea, we usually verbalize that idea in the presence of others. In essence, we have made a public commitment to that position, and it becomes embarrassing for us to change. At the same time, the people we are interacting with have also publicly committed themselves to their opinions.

Since listening is a psychological process based in our individual needs, we think and listen from a self-centered orientation. As a result, we don't listen to *what* the other person is saying; we listen instead to how their views affect our position. In other words, we are listening through a predetermined set of biases, looking for flaws in our opponent's views rather than seeking common understanding. We develop a mind like a steel trap—closed.

Here's an example of the effects of self-centeredness on listening. In a recent training session and workshop for personnel managers, a group was split into a number of male-female pairs. Each pair was given a different conflict situation to discuss and solve.

In one discussion problem, the pair was asked to role-play the following situation as husband and wife: "The husband has a very good job in his chosen profession in the city where the couple resides. The wife has just completed her master's degree and received only one job offer in her chosen profession, but it would require the couple to move to a distant city. Although the husband has tried, he has been unable to find a job in that new city."

An analysis of the resulting interaction revealed the self-centeredness concept in action. Both participants made a valiant effort to appear to understand the other's position; however, the communication revealed that neither was as interested in listening to the other for the sake of gathering conflict-reducing information as much as to find a means of convincing the other person to his or her own viewpoint. Few of the participants developed a genuine understanding or a satisfactory solution.

The listening behaviors here are not unique. In our daily interactions we can find ourselves listening to other people solely for the purpose of finding the weaknesses in their positions so that we can formulate a convincing response.

Another example of the self-centeredness problem arises when we listen to the other person only long enough to key an answer in our own minds. At that point we stop listening and begin to plan what we'll say in response. The other person is still talking and we still hear him or her, but we are no longer listening.

Self-centered listening has a direct impact on the amount of information we receive. Since research indicates that the more information we have, the better decisions we are able to make, such blocking out of relevant information cannot help but lower the quality of our managerial decisions.

Effects of Self-Protection on Listening

A second interactional element affecting the listening process is self-protection. We protect ourselves by playing out an anticipated communication interaction in our own minds before the real interaction ever occurs, to make sure we don't get caught saying something stupid. In essence, then, we are practicing by listening to ourselves listen to others.

One example of this occurred in the office of a state agency that employed five secretaries. Four of the employees had been with the agency for several years; the fifth had recently been hired. All five secretaries were very efficient and produced superior work.

One day, one of the four veteran employees came to see the supervisor. The gist of her conversation was that all four of the employees who had been there for a number of years were unhappy with the new secretary's appearance. They didn't have any complaints about her work; they merely objected to the fact that she didn't wear a bra. The supervisor was told that unless he spoke to this woman and convinced her to wear a bra to work, the other four secretaries would quit.

The manager's behavior is a classic example of self-protection in listening. Since he valued the services of all five of the secretaries and didn't want to lose any of them, he spent the next few weeks trying to find a way to discuss the problem *tactfully* with the new employee. He began seeing their discussion in his mind, anticipating what he would say, how she would react, and practicing how he would respond to her reaction. Each time he played this scene in his mind, he would change his approach slightly to compensate for her anticipated reactions.

He finally believed he had the right way to talk with her and proceeded to do so. In their conversation he used very abstract terms, mentioning the effect of personal appearance on other people in the office and, without any reference to the embarrassing situation of bralessness, asked her to emulate her peers in the office. In this manner, she would feel more a part of the social atmosphere and be readily accepted by the other secretaries.

The young woman said she understood and promptly quit, stating that she wasn't about to replace her wardrobe of slacks with dresses just to please the other women.

The point the manager was trying to make completely eluded this employee because, in his effort to avoid offending her, the manager had not said what really needed to be said. His message was formulated in response to what he *anticipated* her reaction would be. He adjusted his communication behavior prior to establishing a need for that adjustment, and consequently, mishandled the problem.

How does this illustrate self-protectiveness? The answer to that lies in examining the manager's motives for behaving as he did. He had played the scene in his mind and adjusted his communication behavior, *not* because of his fear of hurting her feelings, although that may have been the apparent motive. In reality, he had done so because of his fear of being hurt or embarrassed himself; he was being self-protective. He was really concerned with the way she would feel *about him* if he were to say something objectionable to her.

A serious listening problem arises when we engage in conjecture by listening to ourselves listen to others, by anticipating what might be said and reacting to that instead of the actual situation.

Both of these interactional elements—self-centeredness and self-protective-ness—affect the listening process in that they tend to orient our listening behavior toward biased interpretations of messages.

These three elements of the listening process—internal, environmental, and interactional—pose potential problems requiring *active* effort. Listening must be recognized as more than something we sit back and do to kill time when we're not talking. As communication scholar Harold Janis has said, "Listening ... is not merely hearing; it is a state of receptivity that permits understanding of what is heard and grants the listener full partnership in the communication process."[1]

What can we do to improve our listening skills? A good starting point would be to recognize some bad listening habits to avoid.

SOME BAD LISTENING HABITS TO AVOID

Most of us didn't become poor listeners overnight; we learned how over a period of time. Here are four habits that most of us resort to, even though they do no good.

Faking Attention

Faking attention is an attempt to be polite to someone during a conversation and results in what someone called the "wide asleep listener." This is usually accomplished by looking directly at the speaker when you are really thinking about something else, automatically nodding responses, or even saying "yes" and "uh huh" to conversations you have mentally tuned out. When you have agreed to listen to someone, commit yourself to expending the needed effort to listen and give that conversation your active attention.

Changing Channels

A second habit to avoid is changing channels in the middle of a presentation or conversation. When something appears to be too dull, or too hard to comprehend, or too time consuming, the poor listener will tune out. Since we know there is plenty of thinking time between the speaker's thoughts, we figure we can switch back and forth between several conversations without losing any information. This assumption is often incorrect.

Listening Only for the Facts

One other habit to avoid is listening only for facts. Much of what people communicate is feelings, impressions, and emotions; factual messages are often wrapped up in these. For example, a student came to her instructor's office, and in the course of the conversation she appeared quite upset about something. When she explained to the professor that her husband had just been terminated from his job, the instructor expressed what he thought was appropriate concern and soon changed the subject. Shortly after, the student abruptly left the office, apparently angry with the instructor. He had listened to the facts of what she'd said, but completely missed her meaning.

From the instructor's perspective, these were the facts:

1. Her husband was a very capable young executive who was unhappy with his present employer and had been looking around for another company.
2. This couple was young, had no children and few financial burdens.
3. Her husband had recently been offered another comparable position which he turned down because it paid about the same as he was now making.
4. Her husband had just lost his job.

In his listening process, the instructor associated the new fact (4) with facts he already knew (1, 2, and 3) and concluded that there was no really serious problem. The husband would find a new and probably better job soon.

So why did the student storm out of the office? The instructor had listened only for the facts while the student wanted to talk about feelings and concerns she had. She wanted him to listen to what she was *not* saying. What she needed

> **Sometimes we need to listen to what people are not saying.**

was someone to share these thoughts with, and perhaps get some comfort from. Many messages convey emotion as well as information. Listening only for the facts is often not enough.

Interrupting

Don't interrupt the speaker. Interrupting in the middle of the message can disrupt both speaker and listener. Hold back on frequent use of questions like "What do you mean?" and "Why do you say that?" until you are sure the speaker is finished. Then if you need clarification, ask for it.

SOME POSITIVE STEPS TO BETTER LISTENING

Avoiding poor listening habits is only part of the process of becoming a good listener. You also need to take some positive steps to improve your listening effectiveness. Among these are:

Solicit Clarification

When a message is unclear, it is important that we let the sender know it. People who hesitate to ask for clarification usually do so because:

♦ They are afraid to appear ignorant

♦ They think they can figure the message out on their own—eventually

♦ They don't want to take the time or expend the effort to make sure they understand

By failing to ask for clarification from the sender, we force ourselves to rely too heavily on our own guesses for help in interpreting messages. When you ask questions about the meanings of a message, any implication that you lack knowledge will be more than made up for by your sincere desire to understand. This is flattering to others. It conveys a regard for people who speak to you. When you solicit clarification, ask open-ended questions.

Minimize the Number of Gatekeepers

As we noted before, gatekeepers result in our listening to someone else's version of the message. Whenever possible, avoid sending an intermediary to get the story from the source and then report back to you. Avoid requesting that people tell their story to your secretary or administrative assistant and then let that person synthesize the information for you. Avoid channeling through someone else something that will eventually end up in your office.

You'll notice we prefaced this recommendation with "whenever possible." Obviously, no manager can listen to everything everyone wants to say. To reduce the probability of information overload, managers should develop a clear policy on which information needs their direct personal attention and which can be satisfactorily handled by others in the organization. Problems that can be handled at lower levels in the organization should be. A message requiring a decision should go only as far as the lowest-ranking person authorized to make the decision. Although the policy should not be overly rigid, it should be specified in advance and widely understood.

Try Counterattitudinal Advocacy

Counterattitudinal advocacy (CAA) is a big term for a simple process. It means to take the other person's position—to advocate or express a point of view that runs counter to your own attitude. The objective of CAA is to reduce the degree to which a listener listens through his or her own biases. Counterattitudinal advocacy forces the listener to listen objectively and understand, rather than to listen only until a response is cued.

> **We can force ourselves to listen from another's point of view.**

Here is how CAA works: You, as a listener, simply make a commitment to *restate* and *defend* the position that is counter to your attitude, that is, opposite to your position. You can implement this by honestly trying to restate to others exactly what you hear them expressing. This, of course, includes both the facts and the emotions you think are being conveyed. Use your own words to express the idea you hear the other person saying. Then ask if your interpretation is

accurate. If not, restate it again until agreement is reached. What happens is this: by committing yourself to restate and defend someone else's position, you must listen more effectively to that position in order to understand what you are defending.

There are additional implications that can be especially useful in conflict management. By defending a position counter to your own, you force yourself to consider information that you avoided when advancing your own position. You have forced yourself to listen to ideas through someone else's biases. The end result is a better understanding of the entire situation, rather than just your position.

This process does not obligate you to cave in to the views of others when you honestly disagree. It simply provides one way of better understanding where those you disagree with are coming from. In some cases disagreements evaporate when we clarify each other's position. We recognize that we don't really disagree in principle; we are simply expressing similar ideas in different or confusing ways. The chart in Figure 10-1 summarizes 10 keys to effective listening.

OTHER TIPS FOR EFFECTIVE LISTENING

You can do many different things to improve your listening skills. Here are some additional tips:

10 Keys to Effective Listening	The Bad Listener	The Good Listener
1. Final area of interest	Tunes out dry subjects	Opportunizes; asks "what's in it for me?"
2. Judge content, not delivery	Tunes out if delivery is poor	Judges content, skips over delivery errors
3. Hold your fire	Tends to enter into argument	Doesn't judge until comprehension is complete
4. Listen for ideas	Listen for facts	Listens for central themes
5. Be flexible	Takes intensive notes using only one system	Takes fewer notes. Uses 4–5 different systems, depending on speaker
6. Work at listening	Shows no energy output. Attention is faked	Works hard, exhibits active body state
7. Resist distractions	Distracted easily	Fights or avoids distractions. Tolerates bad habits, knows how to concentrate
8. Exercise your mind	Resists difficult expository material; seeks light recreational-material	Uses heavier material as exercise for the mind
9. Keep your mind open	Reacts to emotional words	Interprets color words; does not get hung up on them
10. Capitalize on fact that thought is faster than speech	Tends to daydream with slow speakers	Challenges, anticipates, mentally summarizes, weighs the evidence, listens between the lines to tone of voice.

From Sperry Corporation Listening Program materials by Dr. Lyman K. Steil, Communication Development, Inc. for Sperry Corporation, Copyright © 1979. Reprinted by permission of Dr. Lyman K. Steil and Sperry Corporation.

FIGURE 10-1   10 keys to effective listening.

♦ Remember that your listeners may not process information in the same way you do.[2] Different people have different learning styles.

♦ Take notes.[3] Writing down major ideas and important facts may help you to listen and remember more effectively. However, it's important for you to be selective. Don't try to write down everything.

♦ Show your interest.[4] It is discourteous to look bored and to fidget. If you have committed to listen to the speaker, then give your full attention and show that you're listening.

THE MOTIVATION TO LISTEN BETTER

Most thoughtful managers recognize the need for careful listening. We spend more time in listening than in any other communication activity. As Phil Lewis has said, "Of all the sources of information a manager has ... listening is the most important; no tool rivals skilled and sympathetic listening. If managers were more cognizant of the needs for effective listening, they could actually increase substantially—even double—their success by controlling their tongues and really listening."

How do we motivate others to listen? A cartoon suggested a way. It showed the boss talking to employees at a meeting saying: "Now pay careful attention. I'll let you know at the end of the meeting who will write up the minutes." When everyone in the organization begins to listen as though they were going to have to write the minutes, understanding will advance in a quantum leap. But listening improvement starts at home—with ourselves.

A QUICK SUMMARY OF MAJOR IDEAS

♦ Hearing differs from listening in that hearing is a purely physiological activity while listening also involves the psychological processing of sounds.

♦ Three types of factors complicate the listening process and pose potential barriers:

—Internal elements within the listener's mind

—Environmental elements surrounding the communication

—Interactional elements which arise especially from listener self-centeredness and self-protection

♦ Communication problems can arise from information overload or from underuse of our listening capacity.

♦ Interactional elements of the listening process encompass the problems of self-centeredness and self-protection.

♦ To be a better listener, avoid poor listening behaviors such as:

—Faking attention

—Changing channels

—Listening only for facts

—Responses that turn people off

—Impatience

—Overuse of gatekeepers

♦ To improve listening effectiveness, use these behaviors (in addition to avoiding those listed above):

—Solicit clarification

—Use counterattitudinal advocacy (CAA)

—Minimize the number of gatekeepers

QUESTIONS FOR FURTHER THOUGHT

1. How do hearing and listening differ?
2. What is meant by the cocktail party effect?
3. What are the three major elements that complicate listening, as described by the authors? Give examples of each.
4. What happens when people experience communication overload?
5. What do we mean by environmental and internal noise?
6. How do gatekeepers complicate the listening process?
7. What are self-centeredness and self-protection as these terms relate to listening?
8. What is counterattitudinal advocacy and how can it be used to clarify understanding?

BARRIERS TO LISTENING IN A DIVERSE BUSINESS ENVIRONMENT
by Augusta M. Simon[5]
Cornell University

Over two years ago, *The Bulletin* presented an informative discussion about the cost to business of poor listening ability and an examination of barriers to effective listening (Hulbert, 1989). Because of significant change forces now emerging in the American workplace, high level listening ability, among other communication skills, will be required to prevent the loss of even greater amounts of dollars, if human resource management professionals are accurate in their estimate that the growth of diversity in the nation's workforce demographics is a monumentally significant development for today, the next decade and beyond. Today's and future managers are called upon to meet the diversity challenge with management skills which respond to the differences brought to the work environment by men and women of different cultures, nationalities, age groups, religions and economic and social status (Sargent, 1983).

The emerging change in workforce demographics dictates an urgent need for understanding and cooperation in the workplace—understanding and cooperation which cannot occur in the absence of developed listening ability. Through the end of the current decade and up to the year 2000 women will comprise two-thirds of new workers entering the labor force. For the same period, twenty-nine percent of new workers will be non-whites, while the presence of immigrants in the labor market will continue to grow as well. By the beginning of the next century, these three groups will contribute a net addition of more than five-sixths of new workers to the American work force (Johnston & Packer, 1987).

Thus, attention to listening is on target given these phenomenal changes on the horizon for business, industry, government, and all employment sectors in the United States. To remain vital, organizations expect and plan for change, and they implement, monitor, and assess its occurrence and impact. In any thriving organization (one in which change is successfully implemented on an ongoing basis) a climate exists in which change is viewed as natural, desirable, and, in effect, a consequence of dynamism. A critical aspect of this climate is a management culture which understands and values listening as it is used in support of effective relationships within the organization; used internally and externally for enhanced product and service delivery; and of course, used as a means for alertness to innovation arising from forces within and without the organization. The need for excellent listening skills emerges as a requirement of successful organizational change management.

Any consideration of *listening barriers* is especially relevant to business communication, given the growing diversity of the workforce. The day-to-day transactions of business communication do not occur apart from the influence of culture. The beliefs, values, attitudes, nonverbal behaviors, and linguistic structures constituting the verbal language of business communicators powerfully shape the meaning of interaction and hence relationships in the workplace as they do in all life arenas. But the estimated material cost of ineffective communication, as in the case of poor listening skills, amounts to a price tag in the billions of dollars each year for American business (Hulbert, 1989). This cost can be expected to increase if mounting cultural and social differences are left unmanaged.

LISTENING BARRIERS WHICH PREVENT THE NURTURING
OF DIVERSITY IN BUSINESS

Diversity presupposes relative degrees of dissimilarity in the language and experience of people. A diverse employment force means communicators bring different frames of reference to the workplace. Any lack, therefore, of shared meaning is exacerbated by poor listening skills. Yet, the problem is not insurmountable. Once diversity is accepted as a manageable and positive change, an entry point for improving communication skills can be established by recognizing the special barriers which interfere with listening in a culturally and socially diverse setting.

Beyond language differences, the basic challenges to listening amid diversity can be categorized as *mind set* barriers (Hulbert, 1989). These act as "noise," jeopardizing listening efficiency and distracting from the potential meaning between communicators. First, American business is typically a white male value-oriented scene with its own perceptual filter for viewing the world. Often, assumptions are characterized by homogeneity and ethnocentricism—"our way is *the* way things are done." These assumptions distance communicators and interfere with the listening process. The creation of shared frames of reference is prevented at worst and minimized at best as the message is communicated to those who are "different" that their difference does not make a difference. Other ways of seeing and doing things are simply not entertained. Ethnocentricism assumes the world is really as *we* (white males) see it. It is not *disregard,* but rather *lack of regard* for the vantage points of others and their cultural identities. Similar to the assumptions of homogeneity and ethnocentricity, egocentricity uses the self as a starting point; however, it is the individual rather than the collective self. Individual managers and employees believe others *are* or *should* be like them. In a different, yet damaging way, listening suffers when the message of disregard is sent to others in the work environment. Meaning is lost as communicators are perceived as contrasting or different in significant ways through the *worldview* (perceptual filter) or the egocentric. Differences, thus, are taken into cognition, but they are given negative evaluation.

Finally, the apparent lack of comfort which exists for many white Americans in their interaction with non-whites (Simon, 1988) is a significant barrier to listening in a diverse context. American racial and ethnic tensions are a backdrop for practically all such interaction, and they contribute to the observation that in the business communication curriculum, for example, one more often is able to find intercultural business courses which place the focus on internationals working in the United States and on the American expatriate manager rather than emphasize the American domestic multicultural/multiracial business context. White discomfort with minority individuals and related issues seems to be a product of the continuing legacy of racial tensions in the

United States. The probability exists that some white educators (the majority among American college and university professionals) and even black educators in predominantly white institutions wisely recognize that they must come to terms with their own attitudes and beliefs about racial matters before attempting to help others deal with theirs. For many people, achieving comfort with the subject is a lifelong process, whether in education, business, or any other employment sector.

SUMMARY

The dollars lost to American business because of poor listening skills are certain to mount as the employment force continues to evidence significant growth in cultural and social diversity. The chief barriers to listening and communication in a diverse work setting will, no doubt, persist; however, increasingly organizations are viewing diversity practically, responding to it as one of the many currents of change the next century will present to American business. Listening skills are a critical starting point for the management of diversity and other forces for change in business organizations.

REFERENCES

Hulbert, J. E. (1989). Barriers to effective listening. *The Bulletin, 52*(2), 3–5.

Johnston, W. B., & Packer, A. E. (1987). *Workforce 2000: Work and workers for the twenty-first century.* Indianapolis: Hudson Institution, xix–xx.

Sargent, A. G. (1983). *The androgynous manager: Blending male and female management styles for today's organization.* New York: Amacon, 77.

Simon, A. (1987–8). Toward a communication based conceptualization of interracial interaction. *Missouri Speech and Theatre Journal, 18-9,* 44–48.

NOTES

1. J. Harold Janis, *Writing and Organizational Communication,* 3rd ed. (New York: Macmillan, 1978), p. 492.

2. Kittie W. Watson and Larry L. Barker, "Training 101: Both Sides of the Platform," *Training and Development, 46,* 11, November 1992, pp. 15–17.

3. This tip, taken from a presentation by August J. Aquilla, was published in "Practice Tips: 13 Techniques to Improve Listening Skills," *The Practical Accountant, 6, 9,* September 1993, p. 13.

4. This suggestion was taken from "Careful Listening: Get the Habit," *Supervision, 54,* 5, May 1993, p. 10.

5. From *The Bulletin* of the Association for Business Communication, September 1991, p. 73.

PART FOUR

PRESENTATIONAL SPEAKING

CHAPTER 11

PREPARING THE PRESENTATION

Briefings and Oral Presentations

▼

In this chapter you will find ideas that will help you:

♦ Identify and distinguish among four types of briefings commonly used in organizations

♦ Anticipate the kinds of questions your listeners are likely to ask and conduct a systematic listener analysis

♦ Recognize and use listener expectations to improve the clarity of your presentation

♦ Plan the contents of a briefing by identifying and supporting main ideas, developing an effective introduction, organizing key points for maximum impact, conveying credibility, and presenting an effective conclusion

▼

The phone rings. It's your boss asking you to take a few minutes at Friday's staff meeting to bring everyone up to date on the program to convert the office's telecommunication system. Just as you ponder how you'll do this, one of your newer clerks comes to your office door. "I'm having a heck of a time figuring out this filing system. Where do we keep the completed orders? How can I tell if an order is complete or pending? Everybody seems to be doing things a different way. I'm confused, boss." And then there's the six-page document that arrived in this morning's mail from the corporate benefits office. "Please be sure that all affected employees understand these benefit changes," it says in capital letters.

Managers are often asked to explain job procedures, changes in policies, and progress reports. Often, the best medium for conveying such information is the oral presentation, also called the briefing. The thought of giving a talk in front of others has a way of unraveling even the most self-confident individual. Surveys have indicated that of all things people fear, giving a public speech is at the top of the list. Comedian George Jessel once said, "The human brain is a wonderful organ. It starts to work as soon as you are born and doesn't stop until you get up to deliver a speech."

While briefings are somewhat different from public speeches, they can sometimes be anxiety-producing. In this chapter we discuss tips for preparing an effective oral presentation, In the following chapter, delivery of that presentation is the focus.

THE PURPOSES OF TYPICAL BUSINESS PRESENTATIONS

Effective presentations and briefings provide people with digestible information. Information is the oxygen of a working organization; it reduces uncertainty and clarifies scope, purposes, and direction for workers. In other words, *business presentations answer questions.*

Four types of presentations are commonly used in organizations:

1. Persuasive

2. Explanatory

3. Instructional

4. Progress reports

An element of persuasion—getting agreement or action from the audience—is present in any briefing, but the first type focuses on this extensively. An attempt to sell upper management on the need for a bigger budget, more employees, or different methods is a common type of persuasive briefing. Other persuasive presentations may try to sell changes in operations, the need for additional coordination, the adoption of a new procedure, and so forth. The key feature of a persuasive briefing is that it attempts to get others to "buy" your idea, plan, or recommendation. And buying generally involves more than simply agreeing with what you say. It means getting some desired *action* from your listeners. The success of your briefing will be readily observable by how much of the desired action actually occurs.

> *Persuasive presentations seek specific action from listeners. What do you want them to DO?*

In explanatory or instructions briefings we are not trying to sell anything but are providing opportunities for the listener to gain knowledge, understanding, or skills. Explanatory briefings generally present a big-picture overview, such as for orienting new employees to the company, acquainting staff members with what is involved in opening a new branch or division in the company, or showing how each function of the organization fits in with others. Instructional briefings get more specific. They teach others how to do or use

> *Instructional presentations should include testing for listener learning.*

something such as a new machine, procedure, or paperwork system. This usually involves more audience involvement than the explanatory briefing. Testing for knowledge gained fits naturally into the instructional briefing.

The progress report brings the audience up to date on some project they are already familiar with. Examples of progress reports include reports on research and development of new products, briefings on money and manpower expenditures compared with budgets, and checking the organization's success against objectives or goals.

Regardless of the type of presentation, an important starting point in preparing the talk is to carefully consider your audience. Make educated guesses about how listeners are likely to react to your message before you even begin the briefing. Here are some ideas on listener analysis.[1]

LISTENER ANALYSIS: A STARTING POINT

Listener analysis is the process of putting ourselves in the listeners' shoes. Before preparing an oral presentation, list all possible questions your talk might provoke in the minds of your listeners. And don't just ask the obvious ones; dig a little to anticipate what else might be on the minds of your listeners. A talk that fails to address relevant listener concerns falls flat. Having all the answers, but to the wrong question, doesn't help.

Know about Your Listeners before Communicating with Them

> *Listener analysis is crucial to communication effectiveness.*

The more you know about your listeners, the more likely you will be effective. The most serious mistake any communicator can make is to fail to understand his or her audience. By making some careful judgments or guesses about the people we talk to, we can adjust our message to hit them where they live.

Listener analysis means making guesses based on as much information as we can reasonably gather. From these guesses we can determine how best to formulate our message for maximum impact. The process is not mysterious; we all make guesses about others' behaviors every day. When we walk down a busy street, we guess that others will go to one side of the sidewalk or the other. We anticipate the possibility that the person walking in front of us may suddenly stop to look in a shop window.

More to the point, when we bring a message to someone, we picture mentally how that person is likely to react. When we inform our spouse that mother is coming to visit for a month or that the kitchen sink is clogged up again, we can pretty well predict the kind of reaction we'll get. Professionally, we learn to predict responses. The orthodontist learns to anticipate the response to the announcement that Sandra needs $4,000 worth of braces. Sales representatives anticipate buyer objections ("It'll only get 16 miles to the gallon") and deliver carefully prepared responses ("But with the larger gas tank, the Speedfire V-8 can go over 500 miles between fill-ups!"). Listener analysis and the prediction of responses are normal and natural activities for people in all walks of life.

After Anticipating the Listeners' Questions, Ask Yourself a Few

The ancient philosopher Seneca said, "Our plans miscarry because they have no aim. When a man does not know what harbor he is making for, no wind is the right wind." If you don't know where you are going with an oral presentation, you'll never know whether or not you've succeeded.

Once you've anticipated your listeners' likely questions, ask yourself these questions as you plan your oral presentation:

♦ What exactly do I hope to accomplish?

♦ How will my listeners respond after I finish?

♦ What specific actions would I like to see from my listeners?

Answers to these questions define your purpose and provide an inner vision of how the presentation should be made.

HOW TO PREDICT LISTENER RESPONSES MORE ACCURATELY

You can learn to predict listener responses by carefully considering:

1. Your own experiences with situations or topics similar to the one you will be speaking about
2. Your understanding of the actions, thoughts, values, and emotions of your listeners, or other people who are similar to your listeners

Of course, since each communication situation and each person is unique, we cannot predict with 100 percent accuracy. But we can improve the prediction of likely responses with careful listener analysis.

Listener analysis is a *questioning* process. The answers aren't always clear, but the process is essential to effective communication. The following section shows four approaches that should help focus our questioning and our listener analysis.

Approach #1: What Do They Need to Know?

The following example is a case in which this approach would make sense. You've been asked to give an oral briefing to your clerical employees on a rather broad topic: technological developments in office equipment. Your purpose is to keep them posted on some of the equipment options the company is considering. Obviously, you can't say everything there is to say about listener interests and information needs. Instead, make careful guesses about the facts you think will be useful and interesting.

Don't select key ideas solely on the basis of *your* interests. Anticipate your *listeners'* interests. Base your talk on what you know about the listeners or others like them. For our example, say that in earlier presentations you've done, the strongest audience interest was in electronic mail systems. In your conversations with employees in your organization, they've expressed a need for easier access to Fax machines. You have recently attended an office-of-the-future trade show where you saw equipment that combines both Fax and E-Mail capabilities. Material you'll want to cover should obviously include these needs and interests.

Another factor of this type of listener analysis is to think about how much your listeners already know about the subject. You will lose your audience fast if you tell them what they already know; they'll feel you are insulting their intelligence. On the other hand—especially when talking about technical equipment—it is just as fatal to your presentation to talk about complex information to people who don't yet know the basics. Listeners who are, for example, totally unfamiliar with electronic technology need to be brought up to date on exactly what E-Mail systems can do before they're likely to get very excited about purchasing one.

> *Get answers or make careful guesses about listener interests, needs, and degree of detail wanted.*

Finally, anticipate how much detail your listeners want or need to know about the topic. Giving detailed information to people who just want an overview of the material may annoy or bore them. When a listener only needs to know what time it is, don't tell him how to build a watch.

Approach #2: What Do They Expect?

People often hear what they expect to hear, even if they have to distort the speaker's real message to make it fit what they anticipated. Psychologists have recognized that, whenever we encounter the unfamiliar, we instantly translate it into the familiar and thereby never see the unfamiliar.

When your message coincides with what the listener expected, your probability of communicating accurately is enhanced, unless your listener makes an "I've heard all this before" assumption. In such cases, details of your message may be lost since your listener feels he or she already knows what you are saying. If your message presents a point of view very different from what your audience expects from you, it pays to clarify early in the talk the fact that this may not be the message they anticipated.

Where Do Listener Expectations Come From?

In business a person's organizational role provides clues as the kinds of messages he or she is likely to present. For example, a sales representative is probably going to sell you something, while a labor leader will talk about employees'

needs that are not being met by management. Training directors may be expected to discuss problems unique to employee training, while the person from the computer center is expected to talk technical and often hard-to-understand computer-speak. All of these are, of course, stereotypes that may be false. The point is, a person's organizational role provides a *preview* of what we can expect them to talk about. When these expectations are not met—the hard-nosed assembly line foreman gives a humorous pitch about the company picnic or the union leader encourages sacrifices to improve productivity—the results can take us by surprise.

Personality characteristics, past behavior, personal appearance, age, sex, ethnic origin, race, and countless other factors provide clues that we translate into expectations. The leader interested in getting across ideas that vary from these expectations may need to shock her audience into a recognition that the unexpected is being presented. The sales representative may open his pitch with the sincere statements: "I'm not here to sell you anything today. In fact, I won't even accept an order from you." This is likely to cause the purchasing agent to readjust his expectations and prepare for an unusual type of presentation. Similarly, the systems analyst who announces that she's not going to talk about computers may spark curiosity and help adjust listener expectations.

It pays to ask yourself, "What does my audience expect from me?" If your topic is consistent with what they're likely to anticipate, use this to strengthen your message. If your topic is quite different, be sure to help them readjust their expectations lest they mentally distort your message and miss the point entirely.

Approach #3: The Nature of the Audience

Although the term *audience* may conjure up an image of a public speaking situation, it need not be limited to that context. When a group of listeners come together for the purpose of information sharing, we have an audience. Certain roles generally emerge in such situations. Audience members normally accept the role of listener; they are quiet and defer to the speaker. The speaker recognizes his or her role as the one speaking.

In reality there is more interaction—two-way communication—going on than may meet the eye. The alert listener carries on a mental dialogue with the speaker and with his or her own thoughts. The speaker gets nonverbal feedback from listeners in the form of facial expressions, body movements, silence, laughs, grunts, or yawns. And, finally, there is interaction between the audience members. The listener who sees others dozing off, or becoming agitated or enthusiastic may find her own reactions affected. Whispered remarks or snickers among audience members can quickly degrade the effectiveness of a serious presentation.

> **Presentational speaking is not a one-way communication process.**

The type of audience we face affects these roles. One type is the *casual* or *pedestrian* audience. An example of this type of audience may be shoppers who momentarily watch or listen to a demonstration of a product in a department store.

A second type of audience is the *passive* audience. This type is often made up of "captive" listeners, people who have been invited or perhaps required to attend.

A third type of audience is the *selected* audience. This audience is composed of people who have gathered for some purpose which they clearly understand. Usually the audience here has been invited to the meeting because they have some special interest or expertise.

A fourth audience is the *concerted* audience. This audience has an active purpose and a clear understanding of why they've come together. They are actively engaged in accomplishing clearly defined goals.

A fifth type of audience is the *organized* audience. Members of this type of audience are prepared to pay attention to the speaker. The speaker enjoys considerable control over the audience in that they recognize him or her as the leader. Examples of an organized audience are a class in school, an athletic team, a military unit, and a department within a business.

The type of audience you face determines your first priority task. If you face a pedestrian audience, your first and crucial task, is to grab your listeners'

> **Different types of audiences require different speaking approaches.**

attention. Fail in this, and they'll simply leave! The passive audience is less likely to walk out on you, but you need to gain their interest in the topic very early or they'll mentally tune you out. For selected audiences, generally some degree of interest is already established. Here, you need to make a favorable impression and establish credibility early in the process. For the concerted and organized audiences, your primary task is to elicit understanding, commitment, and specific action.

Approach #4: Demographics

The demographic approach to listener analysis requires speakers to gather as much information as possible about key characteristics of the people to whom they are speaking. These characteristics may include age, gender, socioeconom-

> *Demographic characteristics can provide important clues to the speaker.*

ic status, political viewpoint, occupation, hobbies and activities, educational level, and so forth. From these data, speakers can draw inferences about their listeners. Let's consider what these demographic characteristics might say about our listeners.

1. *Age.* A person presenting a briefing to a group of teenage employees should probably structure his message differently than one directed to older employees. A number of studies have indicated that younger people frequently tend to be more idealistic, more impatient, and more optimistic than older people. (This brings to mind the bumper sticker: "Hire a teenager while they still know it all!")

Older employees think more in terms of past experiences. They often consider new ideas in light of past failures and may be quicker to write off a suggestion with, "We've tried that before, and it didn't work." As a general rule, a young audience will respond well to challenges and exciting new ideas while an older audience will respond more favorably to appeals to tradition and to moderate changes when carefully justified.

In addition to adjusting the content of your message in the light of your audience's age, the delivery might also be adjusted. In general, older people tend to prefer a slower, more deliberate style of speaking. The younger audience will tend to prefer a faster, more lively pace. In addition, young people tend to have a higher dependence on visual aids. Having been raised in the television generation, younger people increasingly want something to look at in addition to listening. (We talk more about delivery techniques in the next chapter.)

2. *Gender.* Communication studies have shown that male and female listeners often respond differently to the same message. Although gender differences are changing, past studies have shown that women are often more easily persuaded than men. Some evidence suggests that men tend to reason more objectively while women are more responsive to emotional appeals. Women have also been shown to retain more specific information about a particular message than do men.

Deborah Tannen's best-selling book, *You Just Don't Understand: Women and Men in Conversation,*[2] reinforces the fact that males and females communicate differently. Women communicate to express themselves and ultimately to connect with other people—to create genuine understanding. Men, on the other hand, are more likely to use communication to solve problems and exert control. These are sweeping generalizations, of course.

Understanding male-female communication differences is a fruitful area for further study. Says Tannen, "if we recognize and understand the differences between us, we can take them into account, adjust and learn from each other's styles."[3]

3. *Socioeconomic status.* Good communicators must consider the capability of an audience to understand their message. People from lower socioeconomic classes are often less educated and have more difficulty understanding complex ideas. Our capabilities for understanding are based on our experiences. An individual who was raised in a socially deprived situation has probably had fewer different experiences than the educated person from a more advantageous social background.

For example, while college educated or executive-level employees may view the world as a fairly pleasant place with lots of opportunities for growth, employees in an organization's lowest-level jobs or those with poor literacy skills may see their lives less optimistically. They see the future as an endless continuation of the humdrum present.

In communicating with people who have little reason to believe that they have any opportunities, appeals to high levels of personal growth may fall on deaf ears. They'll understand your words but will reject the notion that something positive could happen to them.

The significance of such demographic characteristics as age, gender, socioeconomic class, and so forth lies in the fact that these things affect listener values and attitudes, which in turn affect the way they hear messages. New, incoming information is filtered through listener beliefs to determine whether it makes sense. If the information is deemed sensible, is it pleasant, neutral, or unpleasant to the audience? The result of this analysis is an audience that is either positive, neutral (disinterested), or negative toward the information you present.

> *Demographic characteristics affect the ways people react to our messages.*

When your listeners are neutral or indifferent to what you have to say, your primary concern is to get them interested. Indifferent listeners are likely to ask themselves, "What's in this for me?" or "Why do I need to know this?" In such situations, the presenter takes on the role of an instructor; he or she must teach the audience how this information is of value to them.

When dealing with hostile listeners—people who strongly disagree with you or dislike you for some reason—another problem arises. The speaker talking to such an audience should be aware that attitude changes come about slowly, and that the speaker should be realistic about the goals for the presentation. In dealing with a potentially hostile audience, it is useful to establish some sort of common ground on which the audience and the speaker can agree.

Socialist politician Norman Thomas faced many hostile audiences. He offers some good advice for handling such situations:

"You don't insult your audience, but you may kid it; you don't patronize it or talk down to it; you don't apologize to it for your convictions; you don't whine about being "misunderstood"; you don't beg for favor. You assume and may occasionally appeal to an audience's spirit of fair play, its sporting instinct, its desire to know what you think. You seek a point of contact—sometimes by sharp challenge to rouse attention, sometimes by beginning with partial agreement with what you assume is majority sentiment and then on that basis developing your divergence in thinking. You try—but not too often or too hard—to appeal to your audience's sense of humor even in divergence of opinion. If the facts warrant it, and you have led up to it, you may denounce specifically and vigorously ideas and action with which large sections of your audience have been in accord. But be sure of your facts and be very sparing in imputing to your opponents base motives. In the minds of some men, honest, well-supported, denunciation may stick and bring forth later fruit."[4]

The potentially hostile audience calls for special sensitivity—and courage. Some research has shown that if the communication is only slightly better than expected by the audience, hope may dominate and the message may be shaped in the listener's mind in an overly favorable way. In other words, if your hostile audience sees your message as less negative than it expects, you may come out with a favorable audience response.

Listener Analysis Is Not Something To Do Only Before the Presentation

The effective communicator makes listener analysis an *ongoing process* before, during, and after the presentation. The sensitive speaker will receive a great deal of information from his or her listeners as the talk is given. Often such information is nonverbal. Apparent attentiveness; facial expressions; a general sense of restlessness, excitement, passiveness, or apathy can convey to the speaker whether he or she is coming across effectively. The trick, of course, is to adapt and adjust to this feedback so that you hold your audience's interest. Such things as physical movement, gestures, and voice changes can do a great deal to animate and make your presentation more lively. In addition, and more importantly, gaining audience involvement through mental or physical participation is crucial to communication success.

> *Effective speakers work to get and interpret listener feedback accurately.*

Build flexibility into any presentation. We can never predict exactly the reactions of our listeners, so be prepared to take a different tack if the feedback you get tells you the audience needs a change.

Planning the Content of Your Talk: Identifying Main Ideas

Once your purpose is clear and your listeners have been analyzed, you need to sort out the main ideas of your presentation. Main ideas are the concepts that your listeners must understand for your talk to succeed. These ideas should be stated in the form of conclusions you want your listeners to reach. For example, the following list of main ideas supports the thesis, "We need to hire a plant safety inspector."

1. It is essential that the company get the expertise needed to cope with its increasing accident rate and more frequent government inspections.
2. The costs of hiring a safety expert would be offset by reduced lost-time injuries and avoidance of government penalties.
3. This company cares about its employees' well-being and is committed to creating a safe and pleasant place to work.
4. A search committee must be appointed to find a qualified safety inspector.

> *Some presentations have just one major idea, but most have several.*

For some presentations, there is only one main idea that will be approached from several directions. A progress report may simply stress that "We are on target," or "We will meet our objectives in spite of certain temporary setbacks."

When developing these main ideas or concepts—those the audience *must* understand if you are to be successful—be sure to:

1. State the main ideas as conclusions, preferably in complete sentences.
2. Be sure each idea leads to a specific objective such as securing agreement, convincing, or gaining a desired action. (In the example above, the first three ideas aim at getting agreement or inducing belief. The fourth seeks action.)
3. Express ideas in thought-provoking ways.
4. Use only a few main ideas. Three is an ideal number; listeners can't remember more than five.

Since we are still in a planning stage at this point, don't be overly concerned with the supporting details of the talk. Do be sure that you have focused on main ideas. The main ideas of the safety inspector briefing just mentioned might be identified like this:

1. Company records showing increased accident rate and increased number of government inspections.
2. Estimate of cost of employing a safety inspector.
3. Amount of fines levied by government inspectors in similar industries.
4. Description of company policy and programs that indicate high concern for employees' well-being.

Using a preliminary plan as a guide will help focus your energy toward the goal of your presentation. It also helps reduce wasted time and results in a more cohesive briefing.

Once your preplanning is complete, it is time to assemble the contents of your briefing. The three major parts of the presentation are the introduction, body, and conclusion. Transitions tie each of these together.

If your introduction fails to gain sufficient attention and interest, your message will not be received. Typically, audiences are alert as a speaker begins to talk. Their attention span curves downward as the presentation goes on and then perks up as the speaker gives his concluding remarks. If your conclusion is not effective, audience retention of what has been said suffers. For these reasons, special emphasis should be placed on preparing strong introductions and conclusions.

INTRODUCTIONS: GAINING ATTENTION AND INTEREST

The introduction that gets attention does only part of the job. You can get attention by pounding on the desk, tapping a water glass with a spoon, shouting obscenities, or telling an off-color joke. Yet none of these devices does what an introduction should do. An effective introduction creates appropriate expectations in the minds of listeners. It prepares them to receive your message.

Sometimes a simple statement of the topic is sufficient. Sometimes as a presenter you would be wise to use techniques of the public speaker to grab the audience and get their minds on what you'll be covering. Among the techniques effectively used by speakers are the startling statement or statistic, the rhetorical question, a quotation, a definition, a short narrative, or audience participation.

Startling Statement or Statistic

"The river behind our assembly plant has been declared a fire hazard." ... "By the year 2000—less than five years from now—we will run out of the primary materials we use to manufacture our products." These kinds of straightforward statements can get your listeners' attention if they are interestingly worded and not too complicated. The natural reaction is to perk up and mentally ask for more information.

Likewise, statistics can often be worded in ways that grab our attention. "Today more than 64 percent of our female employees utilize day-care facilities for their children at a cost of more than $90,000 per year." "Today, on May 10, you begin working for yourself and your family. Since the first of the year, you've been working to pay your taxes." Statistics can be expressed in many ways to make them sound smaller ("only 93¢ per day") or larger ("over its contract life the service will cost $75,000"). Your wording depends on your intent.

Rhetorical Questions

This is the use of thought-provoking questions for which you don't expect an answer. "Just how much more government interference can our company take?" ... "How would you feel if you were turned down for a promotion because you had a physical handicap?" Sometimes a whole series of these is effective:

- ♦ What will you do when there is no gasoline to drive you car?
  —when there is no fuel to heat your home?
  —when our electrical generators go silent?
  —when the oil supply is shut off?
- ♦ What will you do?

Be careful not to overwork this approach. And remember that there is always the danger that some smart aleck will *answer* your question and completely deflate your introduction. "How many more people do we have to lose to the competition before we wake up?" If someone in the audience deadpans, "Eleven," your intro may fizzle.

Quotation, Definition, or Short Narrative

Often a short story, quote, or light remark can effectively lead into the body of your talk. A briefing advocating expenditures for additional training might build on a quote from Benjamin Franklin: "If a man empties his purse into his head, no man can take it away from him." If a man invests in learning, he has made the greatest investment.

Everybody loves to hear a story. So it's no surprise that the narrative or short anecdote, especially if a personal example, often works beautifully. Simply relate your interesting experiences as though you were telling a friend. Strive for a conversational note. Don't drag out the story; use it only as a lead-in to the meat of your talk.

> A man went into a clothing store to buy a suit. The sales associate asked him his name, age, religion, occupation, college, high school, hobbies, political party, and his wife's maiden name.
>
> "Why all the questions?" the customer asked. "All I want is a suit."
>
> "Sir, this is not just an ordinary tailor shop," the salesman said. "We don't merely sell you a suit. We find a suit that is exactly right for you."
>
> "We make a study of your personality and your background and your surroundings. We send to the part of Australia that has the kind of sheep your character and mood require."
>
> "We ship that particular blend of wool to London to be combed and sponged according to a special formula. Then the wool is woven in a section of Scotland where the climate is most favorable to your temperament. Then we fit and measure you carefully."
>
> "Finally, after much careful thought and study, the suit is made. There are more fittings and more changes. And then ..."
>
> "Wait a minute," the customer said. "I need this suit tomorrow night for my nephew's wedding."
>
> "Don't worry," the salesman said. "You'll have it."[5]

"Now *that's* customer service!" the speaker concluded. The audience enjoyed it and the speaker had their attention.

A word of caution: always *practice* a joke or story *out loud* several times to be sure it *sounds* as good as it reads.

Audience Participation

Asking a few key questions of specific listeners or having the group take a "quiz" or participate in a simple activity may be a good way to get them in tune with your talk.

"I'd like to ask for your candid remarks about the new building proposals. Martha, what concerns do you have?" Be sure you don't put people on the spot. Be sensitive to your tone of voice in asking the questions. Don't do anything that's likely to embarrass your listeners or make them uncomfortable. In short, use this approach with discretion. Don't drag it out too long, and be sure to show your listeners how this relates to your theme and purpose.

Statement of Topic or Reference to Occasion

If your audience is already interested in what you'll be saying, a simple statement of your topic may be sufficient. "I am going to outline the new sales representative compensation program." Reference to the occasion may sound like this: "As you know, Tom has asked me to take a few minutes at each staff meeting to update you on new software available."

There are, of course, other introductory approaches and combinations that will work. There are also a few sure-fire ways to flop, some of which are discussed in the next section.

> *A simple statement of the theme is seldom an effective introduction. Be more creative than that.*

The key word in developing effective introductions is *creativity*. Resist the path of least resistance—the simple statement of your purpose—if there are any more interesting ways open to you. Usually there are.

Some Sure-Fire Ways to Flop

An inadequate introduction can seriously damage your talk by failing to gain attention, setting an inappropriate theme, or destroying your credibility. Here are some sure-fire ways to fall on your face.

The Apologetic Beginning.   The unaccustomed-as-I-am-to-public-speaking type of remark has no place in a briefing. Neither do opening statements such as, "I'm here to bore you with a few more statistics" or "I'm pretty nervous, so I hope you'll bear with me." If you haven't prepared well enough to be effective, it will become obvious to your audience soon enough. You accomplish nothing by announcing it.

The Potentially Offensive Beginning.   An off-color joke, a ridiculing statement, or use of the same, standard opening remark regardless of the audience or occasion will eventually get you in trouble.

The story is told of a rather timid governor who spoke to the inmates of a men's penitentiary. He began conventionally with "Ladies and …," but there was laughter before he could get out the word "gentlemen." After he recovered, he began a second time with "Fellow inmates," and again there was a burst of laughter. A moment later he blundered on with "Glad to see so many of you here." Undoubtedly, more planning should have gone into the governor's opening remarks to make them appropriate to his audience.[6]

Other openings may be inappropriate because they are trite or excessively flattering, or just plain phony: "I am filled with a deep sense of personal inadequacy when I presume to speak authoritatively in the presence of so many knowledgeable men."

The Gimmicky Beginning.   Resist the temptation to blow a whistle, sing a song, role-play a violent scene from a play, or write the word *SEX* on the blackboard saying, "Now that I have your attention ..." These just don't work. They tend to put your audience on the spot—they don't know how they should respond. It's embarrassing and distracting.

In summary, your introduction should be brief and direct. It should get the audience's attention and prepare them for what is to follow. Just ask yourself, would this introduction get my attention? If not, rework it. The introduction is probably the single most important segment of your talk, so plan it carefully.

THE BODY: NOW THAT I HAVE YOUR ATTENTION

If your introduction has been effective, it sets the stage for the body of your presentation. The body presents your main points, elaborates on them, clarifies, and summarizes so the audience will remember what you've said. The number of main points should be limited to as few as will cover the material adequately. With too many main points, your listener's retention will suffer. Research shows that most people's short-term memory is limited to about five items. To be safe, try to keep main points to three or four if possible. If you must cover more than that number, provide listeners with a written list or outline.

Organizing Your Main Points

The arrangement of main points will vary depending on your purpose. But before we recommend specific arrangements for different purposes, let us see what options are commonly available.

Direct Plan.   This arrangement begins with the main idea or the general conclusion of the briefing followed by supporting information. It uses *deductive* logic, that is, a general statement followed by explanatory details. Here is an example:

> The coming year should be our most profitable year since 1991. (main point) In the last 6 months, orders for our solar collectors have increased by 86 percent; costs of raw materials have remained stable and are projected to increase by not more than 2 percent in the coming year; and our recent contract with the union freezes wages and benefits at present levels for the next 18 months. (supporting details)

The direct order may be used to organize details under their main points and/or to arrange the entire body of the presentation. When used in the latter way, the main points should be prioritized so that the most important or dramatic or significant point comes first. The selection of these priorities may be a judgment call for the presenter, but it should be based on audience needs and interests.

The direct organization is appropriate for most briefings. It is efficient and hits the high point immediately while the audience's attention level is still high.

Indirect Plan.   The indirect or *inducive* order starts with details or supporting information and builds up to the main point. Main points are arranged in ascending order of importance so that the *big idea* or major conclusion comes last. Here is how the example above would look if arranged inductively:

> Our recent contract with the union freezes wages and benefits at present levels for the next 18 months. Costs of raw materials for our products have remained stable and are projected to increase by not more than 2 percent in the coming year. And, in the last 6 months, orders for our solar collectors have increased by 86 percent. *The coming year will be our most profitable year since 1991.*

The indirect arrangement works best when the speaker sees the need to be persuasive, when the briefing's purpose is to get the listeners to believe or to do something they are not likely otherwise to believe or do. If the conclusion were presented first as in the direct plan, the listener may be defensive or even argumentative, tuning out the evidence that supports that conclusion. The indirect plan avoids this by putting the evidence first, using convincing detail to lead to the general conclusion. Much resistance can be overcome with skillful use of indirect arrangement of ideas. Many speakers also choose the indirect plan when they are delivering bad news.

Problem-Solution Plan.   Another arrangement especially useful in persuasive situations is the problem-solution approach. Here, extensive effort and time are dedicated to the clarification and amplification of some felt need. The objective is to get the listener to recognize and be concerned about the problem in personal terms. Once this point is reached, introduction of your solution is welcomed and acceptance is likely.

Television advertisements often use an abbreviated form of this plan. They introduce a problem (an upset stomach, unreliable phone equipment, or that embarrassing dandruff) and then solve the dilemma by introducing their product.

Even commercials on TV years ago may stick in your mind because of this approach. We remember the guy who backs his trailer into his neighbor's porch (problem) because we know how difficult steering a trailer can be. Then we're relieved to hear that his insurance company will pick up the tab for the damage, if not the embarrassment (solution). We've related to the headache and stomach ailments of the late-night party-goer on a personal level (problem) and sigh with relief at the appearance of "plop, plop, fizz, fizz" (solution). This persuasive approach is seen dozens of times each day on TV. Here's an example of how a business presentation using a similar pattern of arrangement might be organized:

In the past six months our use of long-distance telephone service has increased by 71 percent with no noticeable decrease in the use of letters or teletype. As a result of this increase, our monthly phone bills now exceed $1,850 per month. Even if the usage could be held at this level, that's $22,200 per year for long distance—as much as we'd spend on an extra, desperately needed clerical employee. While the increase is alarming, the prospect of not being able to put a lid on it is what really bothers me. Without better control, our profit picture and our individual earnings are going to be hurt. (need development and personalization of problem)

There is a way we can deal with this that I think you'll like. A telecommunications company representative has been talking to me about installing a new long-distance calling system. Here are some cost figures…. (solution)

Cause-Effect Plan. This approach simply develops the relationship between two events. By clarifying how one causes the other, the speaker can recommend changes in one to bring about corresponding changes in the other. This arrangement can be useful in either explanatory or information briefings or, when followed by a call for action, in persuasive presentations. A *chain of events* pattern simply links together a series of cause-and-effect relationships.

Chronological Order. This organization plan simply arranges points as they occur in time. A briefing on the company's financial history based on fiscal periods would use this plan.

Topical or Spatial Order. Points in the presentation dealing with different but related topics or examples are arranged so that each supports the main conclusion, which may be stated either before or following the evidence. Space order typically moves from examples which are near to those far away or vice versa. For example, a progress report on computerization may begin with the local branch and move to outlying branches or to other cities.

Increasing Magnitude of Difficulty Pattern. A briefing on the effects of the economy on a business may develop from relatively local, temporary factors over which the organization maintains some control, to the more complex national or worldwide conditions that are beyond its control. For example, a slowdown in sales in a downtown shoe store may be attributed to:

- Fewer sales made per employee
- Increased competition from newer stores in outlying shopping malls
- A higher crime rate in the vicinity of the store
- A higher unemployment rate due to a layoff at a major local employer
- Delays in getting high-demand shoes from distributors
- A worldwide shortage of quality leather

Each of these points represents increasing difficulty for the local businessperson.

This order of arrangement may also be used to instruct listeners. The speaker could begin with something familiar or already known by the listener and move to the unknown or more complex. For example, training on the use of a new machine could begin by first reviewing the operation of an already familiar machine, then pointing out basic similarities of the steps in using the unfamiliar new machine.

Order of Importance Plan.   Particularly useful in the progress report, this arrangement presents the most significant or noteworthy point first, with other developments following in descending order of importance. For example, main ideas may be:

- The wind tunnel test of the missile tail assembly was successful.
- The electronic malfunction problem in the sensing device has been narrowed down to two possible causes.
- The engineers are considering the use of a different coating that will be more resistant to wear.

Figure 11-1 summarizes the ways of arranging the body of your oral presentation.

DEVELOPING AND SUPPORTING MAIN POINTS

Most main points take the form of simple declarative statements. Few of these can stand alone. Support, elaboration, clarification, and proof can shore up these themes and result in audience acceptance and agreement. Several types of support are discussed in the following.

Specific details or explanations of the main point are probably the most common though not always the most effective way to build support. Here we simply explain in other words what we have asserted. This support may be prefaced by remarks such as "Let me explain why I've said that" or "Another way to say this might be ..." In our experience, speakers rely too heavily on this type of support when other, more interesting approaches could be used.

Comparisons or analogies often result in strong support. Frequently these take the form of a narrative. Here is a recent example overheard at a convention. A young professor asked an older, well-established author how long it took him to complete his recent book. The author responded with a narrative about a wartime experience in Europe in 1945. The author, who was then a soldier in recently liberated Paris, approached a sidewalk artist whom he had observed painting. He asked if the painting was for sale and the artist responded, "Yes." When informed of the price, the soldier replied, "But it only took you an hour to paint that!" The artist responded indignantly, "But I have prepared all my life." The young professor got the point of the analogy and felt a bit embarrassed for even asking the question.

Think about what a different impact this narrative had. It communicated very clearly and went far beyond anything else that could have been said in a

Type of Briefing	General Objective	Organization of Body
Persuasive	Get audience to accept ideas and/or do something ("sell" them something)	Inductive pattern: Show several specific cases or lines of reasoning which lead up to general conclusion/action step. (Use when audience resistance to your key idea is expected to be strong.)
		Problem-solution pattern: Describe a problem vividly and in a way that your audience feels the need. Then offer your solution/action step.
		Cause-effect pattern: Develop relation between two events and show how a change in one will affect the other.
Explanatory or instructional	Inform audience (teach them something)	Deductive pattern: Present the conclusion and explain how it was arrived at. (May also be used in persuasive talks when the key idea is not likely to turn off your listeners.)
		Chronological pattern: Show how events developed over time.
		Topical or spatial pattern: Give examples from different places or categories which relate to the topic.
		Increasing difficulty pattern: Starting from something already known, add to it to explain more complex or unusual concepts.
		Chain of events pattern: Show how different steps or procedures lead to a certain conclusion.
Progress report	Inform or update knowledge	Chronological or chain of-events pattern: (as above).
		Order of importance: Present the most significant development first.

FIGURE 11-1 Arranging the body of a presentation.

direct response to the question. The parables taught by Jesus are, of course, analogies told in narrative form. They provide long-lasting and thought-provoking support to His teachings.

Examples, especially those of a personal nature, add support to main points and also lend credibility to the speaker. Some speakers are unduly hesitant about using personal experiences. These provide support of a first-hand nature and can be very convincing.

Be certain that your example is typical of and pertinent to the point being supported. An isolated incident or fluke occurrence will be obvious to your audience and should not be presented as illustrative of a general condition. For example, let's say that our main point is, "Morale in the plant is low." Yet we do not support it with a single example of one employee's complaints about working conditions. If, however, we string together a series of isolated examples, we develop support for our theme.

- *Main point:* Employee morale is low.
- *Supporting examples:* Six different workers have complained about the excessive heat in the plant.
- Absenteeism is up 20 percent over last month.
- Three workers quit, citing unbearable shop conditions.
- Four grievances have been filed with the union.

Statistics provide support when they are used ethically. There are many well-known ways to distort information using statistics but, of course, there are many ways to lie, period. The problem is that some speakers don't really understand how statistics are derived or what they have when they get them.

There are two general types of statistics: descriptive and inferential. *Descriptive* statistics can take a large quantity of numbers and make another, much smaller set of numbers out of it with the essential information remaining intact. In other words, they condense or describe the original mass of data to make it more intelligible. *Inferential* statistics predict conclusions based on evidence provided by samples and mathematically calculate probabilities that a given conclusion is so.

Sometimes statistics confuse more than they clarify or support. In briefings, speakers should determine what level of statistical expertise their audience has before relying heavily on more sophisticated statistics. Most people can readily grasp descriptive statistics but are rather confused by inferential statistics. We recently heard a speaker misusing actuarial data compiled by an insurance company to project life span based on health habits. He told his audience such things as "If you smoke more than two packs of cigarettes a day, subtract 8 years from your life, if you live in the country, add 2 years to your life." By the time he finished, half his audience figured they'd live forever and the other half wondered why they weren't already dead. The point is that actuarial data on life expectancies are very complex statistics. If you don't thoroughly understand the implications of complex statistics, don't use them.

Four things will help you develop an idea using statistics:

1. Round out large numbers so your listeners can digest them.
2. Interpret the numbers in some meaningful way. Percentages seem to be the easiest for most of us to cope with.
3. Be sure to compare apples to apples. Paul Timm heard a speaker express relief that our unemployment rate was only 6 or 7 percent, whereas in Israel, "one person in 18 is unemployed!" Those percentages, of course, are virtually the same.
4. Use charts and graphs to help your audience understand the statistics.

Use statistics sparingly. They should not be considered the only type of support but should be part of an assortment of developmental approaches.

Formal Quotations are less frequently used in business briefings than in public speeches. But they can be effective if we choose to quote an authority who is:

1. A recognized expert
2. In a position to know about the specific point we are trying to support
3. In general agreement with other authorities on the subject
4. Free from prejudice that would distort his or her view

The person quoted need not be a world-renowned expert; he or she may well be someone within the organization with considerable experience or training in the area being discussed. In deciding whether an authority is free of prejudice, consider what the person quoted may stand to gain or lose. You would probably not quote a TV advertising salesperson's views on the relative merits or newspaper versus broadcast promotions.

Audiovisual Aids may be used in conjunction with several other types of support. There is an increasing awareness of the importance of supplementing the spoken word with another medium. Many employees in organizations have been raised in the "television age" and have been conditioned to audio and visual communication techniques. As was mentioned in Chapter 3, communications effectiveness frequently is enhanced by use of more than one medium. Visuals can range from a simple chalkboard or flip chart to highly sophisticated multimedia productions involving slides, movies, special lighting effects, and elaborate sound systems. In most business presentations we can use a wide variety of devices such as charts, graphs, overhead projectors, slides, movies or videotapes, tape recordings, and models. Proper use of audiovisual aids is discussed in Chapter 12.

Transitions, Summaries, and Conclusions

Transitions are statements or questions that help provide coherence in the talk by connecting separate thoughts or parts of the presentation.

Transitional words and phrases help your listeners shift gears, readjust expectations and mentally recap what has been covered. Without adequate transitions it is almost impossible for listeners to follow even a moderately complex line of thought. But you as the speaker also get important advantages from the liberal use of transitions. They give you extra moments to check your notes, change physical position, reestablish eye contact with your audience, check for listener feedback, or adjust a visual aid.

Likewise, summaries and conclusions serve to help your listener remember important information. Four things should be accomplished as you end most presentations. (The exception may be the simple progress report.) You should:

1. Summarize key points
2. Restate your central theme
3. Point to the listeners' need to know what you've just told them and remind them of the urgency (or at least importance) of that information
4. Provide them with a clear action step, a prescribed behavior or mental activity they should *do*

Summaries are especially useful to recap the main *ideas* (but not too many details) of your talk. Repetition helps us remember, so use this important tool as you lead into your close. Avoid introducing any new material at this point. It may confuse your listeners.

Everything you have done to develop this presentation comes to a climax at the conclusion. So a most important question goes back to your conceptual planning—what was your specific intent? Picture yourself as a listener and ask the tough question: "What does this all mean to me?" Your talk should have provided a clear answer.

INCLUDE AN ACTION STEP

Action steps are appropriate for all kinds of briefings. The action step tells your listener what you want them to *do* or think (preferably, *do*). Your audience has a right to expect and receive guidance from all your research and preparation. And if you don't provide such guidance in the form of a clear, action-oriented conclusion, you have probably let your listeners down. The actions you advocate should, of course, be ones you can realistically request from your listeners. Your conclusions need not be elaborate or drawn out. If the rest of the talk is well done, the conclusion will be self-evident and you need only restate and bring a sense of finality. An effective presentation begins with a creative introduction that gains attention and binds your listeners to you. The liberal use of transitions ties together what you are saying and leads up to a strong conclusion. These are crucial to getting your thoughts across.

At first glance, this way of organizing may appear formal and boring, but listeners are more bored when they cannot figure out the thesis, do not know the main points, and do not know where the presentation is heading. Creative transitions can help the presentation not sound "boxed in" and boring. If you follow these guidelines, your presentations will never sound unorganized and the audience will retain more of your message.

A QUICK SUMMARY OF MAJOR IDEAS

♦ The general purpose of any business presentation is to answer questions— to provide usable information.

♦ Analyzing your listeners (audience) before developing the presentation increases your chance of communication success. This analysis calls for making educated guesses about your listeners.

♦ Four approaches to audience analysis are particularly useful for managers: the what-do-they-need-to-know approach, the what-do-they-expect approach, the nature-of-the-audience approach, and the demographics approach.

♦ Listener analysis should be an ongoing process that is done before, during, and after the presentation.

♦ The presentation model will increase message retention in our listeners by presenting the information in an organized fashion.

QUESTIONS FOR FURTHER THOUGHT

1. What is listener analysis? How can it improve a talk?

2. How do listener expectations of the speaker affect the messages they receive?

3. How can a speaker accomplish ongoing listener analysis?

4. What are the three key elements of any talk and how can you make the most of these?

5. Discuss the importance of an effective introduction. How can you make the most of this part of a presentation?

6. What demographic characteristics will affect the way a listener responds to your talk?

OTHER THOUGHTS ABOUT ...

PLANNING YOUR PRESENTATION[7]

Part of planning a presentation means that you must ask yourself why, not what. The "what" part will be answered when you begin to organize your thoughts. In the beginning you should concern yourself with *why* you are giving a presentation to a particular audience. The answer to this question should help you plan your presentation.

For example, you have been asked to give a presentation to a group of managers in your company on next year's departmental budget. Don't start writing down what you expect to say. Instead, ask yourself what you want to accomplish with your presentation. Will you be asking for a budget increase, or presenting a plan showing how you can operate on less money? Think about your specific objectives in relation to your audience before preparing your presentation. Can you imagine building a house without a set of plans? Before anyone can build a house, he or she needs plans to guide the purchase of the materials and to show how these materials will be used. In the same way, a plan for your presentation will make the actual work of putting it together much more efficient. A two-step process—developing objectives and analyzing your audience—will help.

STEP #1—DEVELOP OBJECTIVES

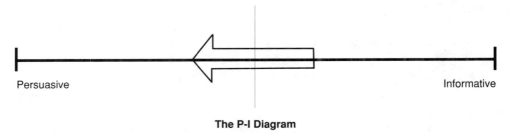

Persuasive
Informative

The P-I Diagram

This diagram describes the relationship between Persuasive and Informative presentations. They are not separate types but rather exist on a continuum. An example of an informative presentation at the far end of the diagram would be a status report or a project update. All informative presentations contain elements of persuasion (although they may be very subtle; i.e., I want everyone to feel that I am knowledgeable on this topic).

Heading in the direction of the arrow, presentations become more and more persuasive. When the vertical line in the center is crossed, in the direction of the arrow, the speaker tells the audience what change is requested; this in part is the definition of a persuasive presentation. Presentations on the Informative side of the line *imply* that some action should be taken, in a stronger and stronger manner, as the center line is approached.

USING P-I DIAGRAM:

To help determine your objective, mark the place on the diagram where your presentation falls. Is it persuasive or informative?

STEP #2—ANALYZING YOUR AUDIENCE

PUT YOURSELF IN THE SHOES OF THE PEOPLE WHO WILL BE LISTENING TO YOUR PRESENTATION!

When analyzing your audience, you have four items to consider:

1. **Values**—What is important to the group? Different organizations have different value systems. Giving a presentation outside your organization is probably very different from presenting internally. Even different departments within an organization can have different values.

2. **Needs**—It is important to find out in advance of the presentation what the group thinks they need—this may be quite different from what you thought they needed. The speaker then must find a way to resolve the discrepancy.

3. **Constraints**—These are things that might hold the audience back from doing what you want them to do or from knowing what you want them to know. They include the following areas:

   A. **Political:** Internal politics can be a constraint. If you must get support from competing factions, you must take that into consideration when organizing your presentation. In addition, personality clashes and other forms of conflict may interfere with your success.

   B. **Financial:** Whenever you ask for anything that is going to cost money, you will encounter resistance. You must factor this resistance into your presentation and find ways to overcome it.

   C. **Knowledge:** All of us have our own area of specialization. We must be careful not to use technical language, abbreviations, acronyms, buzz words, etc. that people in the audience might not understand. If in doubt, ask the audience if they are familiar with the terminology and define if necessary.

4. **Demographic Information**—Things like the size of the audience, location of the presentation, etc. may also influence the organization.

NOTES

1. Some of the information in this section is adapted from Paul R. Timm, *Basics of Oral Communication* (Cincinnati: South-Western Publishing Co., 1993), Chapter 5.

2. Deborah Tannen, *You Just Don't Understand: Women and Men in Conversation* (New York: Ballantine Books, 1990).

3. Peggy Taylor, "Can We Talk?" an interview with Deborah Tannen in *New Age Journal*, November–December 1990, p. 32.

4. Norman Thomas, *Mr. Chairman, Ladies and Gentleman* ... (New York: Heritage House, 1955), p. 116.

5. Myron Cohen, *More Laughing Out Loud* (Secaucus, NJ: Citadel Press, 1960), pp. 169–170.

6. Edward S. Strother and Alan W. Huckleberry, *The Effective Speaker* (Boston: Houghton Mifflin, 1968), p. 167.

7. Excerpted from Steve Mandel, *Effective Presentation Skills* (Menlo Park, CA: Crisp Publications, Inc., 1993), pp. 17–19. Reprinted with permission of the publisher.

DELIVERING THE PRESENTATION

Preparation, Preparation, Preparation

▼

In this chapter you will find ideas that will help you:

♦ Overcome speaker anxiety (stage fright)
♦ Deliver an oral presentation using effective nonverbal techniques
♦ Use visual aids effectively
♦ Handle the question and answer session after a briefing

▼

The well-known author Louis L'Amour published a biography called *Education of a Wandering Man* in which he talks of his experiences in developing his excellent communication skills. In the excerpt below, L'Amour speaks of the challenge of becoming an effective speaker, even for the well-read and successful.[1]

Shortly before World War II, I was invited to attend a lecture at the University of Oklahoma. Two quite gifted speakers were each to talk for a few minutes, and the feature of the evening was to be an address by George Milburn.

An Oklahoman who had made a name for himself in the short story field, Milburn ... was a gifted writer. But George was a writer, not a speaker, and this was his first time as the latter. Obviously, he had written a good speech, but he just could not put it together. He fumbled and floundered and we all suffered with him. Finally, he seemed to get started, and then a train whistle blew somewhere outside and it might as well have cut his throat.

All present were in sympathy with him, but sitting there I suffered as much as he did, I believe, for I could see myself in the same position. At the time I did not have the courage to stand up and say my name in public. What I had seen happen to George Milburn could happen to me, and because I was confident that I was going to "make it," I knew it would happen.

What to do? I knew I would never attend a class, as I would avoid even trying to speak, so I decided the thing to do was to take the bull by the horns and just start speaking. I let the word get around that I was open for speaking engagements, knowing that sooner or later I would be challenged and have to make a good... It came about just that way.

The night before the speech I did not sleep. The day of the lecture I decided I could not go through with it. A lady was driving some distance to pick me up and I called her to beg off. It was too late. She was already on her way.

All I wanted now was to get out of it, any way I could. I was sure I would make an unholy fool of myself trying to speak to any sort of crowd, yet I could think of no way out. With a dreadful sinking feeling, as of a man going to his execution, I got in the car and we turned to leave. I thought of jumping out. I thought of everything....

There was no way out. I had gotten myself into this fix and must see it through. On stage I reached into my pockets for my notes and they were not there.... So I began to talk without them, and somehow the evening passed and everyone seemed pleased. Especially me, as I was off the hook.

That was the beginning, and many years ago, but I firmly believe that if I could become a speaker, anybody can do anything if he or she wants to enough. Since that time I have appeared on the platform with a former President of the United States, a Supreme Court Justice, and many others. Education takes many forms and this was an important part of my education. Of course, if one is to speak, one must have something worth saying, and say it intelligently. The important lesson to be learned is that one's principal enemy in such cases is oneself.

A thing to remember is that the audience wants you to be good. No matter whether they know you or not, they do not want to be bored, so whether you realize it or not, they are pulling for you.

This is an age of communication. At one time or another, nearly everyone will have to stand up and sell his bill of goods, whatever it may be.

All young men and women owe it to themselves to be able to write a letter on not more than one page, to set forth an idea or possible plan. That same young person should, in a few brief spoken words, be able to deliver that idea orally.

No needs for details, for if the idea is expressed well, there will be questions, and the details can come later.

That day back in Oklahoma when I decided to become a public speaker was one of the most important in my life.

OVERCOMING NERVOUSNESS WHEN SPEAKING BEFORE GROUPS

As the Louis L'Amour excerpt shows, almost everyone is concerned about speaker anxiety, also known as stage fright. If we have any self-regard, we are concerned about how others see us and respond to us. This concern quite naturally leads to some nervousness. The skillful speaker seeks to *control* this nervous energy, not eliminate it. As the Toastmaster's handbook says, effectiveness training in speech "won't completely eliminate those butterflies in the stomach, but it will keep them flying in formation."[2]

We can do a number of things to cope with stage fright. Communication professors Harold Zelko and Frank Dance talk about developing your "coping quotient" by reducing the number of things you must give conscious attention to. In other words, as different aspects of presentational speaking become natural and spontaneous, we can channel our concentration toward the specific purpose of our briefing. It's like typing or playing a musical instrument. So long as we must consciously think about how each finger should be positioned to print a letter or produce a note, we will never be effective in putting together the entire composition.

The following are several ways to reduce the number of specific things that call for your attention in order to bring the presentation comfortably within your coping quotient.[3]

Prepare!

There is absolutely no substitute for adequate preparation. If you are well prepared, your capacity to cope with problems rises significantly. Nothing reduces anxiety like being well prepared to the point of being overprepared—that is, totally confident of your grasp of the subject matter. Preparation should go beyond the content and delivery of the presentation to include practice in handling anticipated questions. At this point, the high cost of the presentation medium comes in. A rule of thumb is that you should spend up to one hour of preparation for each minute of speaking.

Be Idea Conscious, Not Self-Conscious

Having your specific purpose in mind helps reduce overconcern for irrelevant details. The principle of the unconscious success mechanism enters here. We are most effective when we don't think of each step or each procedure needed to complete a task but instead focus on the desired result and let our subconscious mind help us get there. The baseball outfielder going after a high fly ball doesn't consciously think, "I'll take six steps to my left, two steps forward, raise my glove with my left hand and shield my eyes from the sun with my right hand." Instead he fixes his eye on the ball and visualizes the desired result of catching it. His unconscious success mechanisms go through the mechanics of bringing that to pass and free him from concerns about tripping over his shoelace, taking the wrong-sized steps, or raising his glove too late.

The same principle applies in presentation speaking. Overconcern with mechanics at the point of doing the briefing can only be distracting and anxiety producing. Zelko and Dance give this example:

> Self-consciousness tends to be self-destructive. If you are overly worried about the way you look, you often overcompensate and this draws to

yourself attention that would not ordinarily be centered on you. It's when you are trying to walk nonchalantly that you walk stiffly or affectedly. It is when you are trying to smile naturally ("Say cheese") that your smile tends to look artificial. If you care caught up in a conversation or in telling a story and the conversation or the story causes you to smile, you are usually unaware of the smile itself, and it is at that point that the smile is, and appears, most natural. Similarly with speaking in public. When you are caught up in the message of your speech, when you are interested in communicating the ideas of the speech to the listeners, you are not usually uncomfortable or noticeably concerned with how you look or how you sound—it's the idea that is at center stage, not the self. Simple remedies include: be audience centered; be message centered, not self-centered.[4]

Relax

If you are well prepared and idea conscious, not self-conscious, you are raising your coping quotient to a level where anxiety should not be a problem. If you still feel that flush of nervousness just as you're being introduced, don't worry about it. It's perfectly natural and seldom visible to your audience. When you get up to speak, take a moment to arrange your notes, look at your audience and smile, and take a few slow, deep breaths.

Once you've had a few successful speaking experiences, your coping quotient quickly increases. You may even get to the point where you welcome the opportunity to stand up before a group with your well-prepared talk.

Use Your Background and Experience

Every speaker talks from a wide background of thought and experience. We each bring unique experiences, attitudes, and ideas to any presentation we do; yet for some reason, speakers tend to depreciate the value of such experience and ideas and instead turn to other, more "authoritative" sources. There are, of course, situations where it's important to cite recognized authorities on a topic, but don't hesitate to add your own ideas too. We are usually more comfortable as we bring more of ourselves into the talk. We can better explain and answer questions about *personal* experiences. Your preparation for this briefing makes you a bona fide authority in your own right.

Recognize That Your Listeners
Want You To Succeed

Your audience does not want your presentation to flop. When people have taken the time to assemble for the purpose of hearing what you have to say, they don't want to feel the time has been wasted. Even hostile listeners want you to explain yourself clearly, if for no other reason than that they can then attempt to shoot down your ideas. Let's face it—a poor presentation can be just as embarrassing and uncomfortable for the listeners as it is for the speaker. Your audience wants you to succeed.

PROPER USE OF AUDIOVISUAL AIDS

Studies have repeatedly indicated that audiovisual materials reinforce virtually any oral presentation. Clearer understanding and retention of ideas result from the use of several media in combination.

The most common approach is to develop graphic illustrations such as posters or flip charts, overhead transparencies, or slides. Here are a few thoughts to keep in mind when using such illustrations.

1.   Each aid should be planned to drive home a *single* point. The quickest way to lose the effectiveness of an audiovisual aid is to overcomplicate it or try to convey too much information. This is especially true with charts or illustrations. Keep them simple and concise. Never display a chart or graph that your audience cannot comprehend in 30 seconds. You can accomplish this by sticking to one key point and removing any superfluous information.

2.   Be sure you know exactly *when* to present your illustration so it coincides with your oral briefing. Keep the chart or illustration covered until you are ready to present it. Otherwise it will distract your audience's attention.

3.   If you use slides or overhead transparencies that require dimming the lights, keep in mind that you are losing some important speaker-to-audience variables. Some communication experts discourage the general use of slides for this reason. Physical presence has a great deal to do with psychological motivation. When the lights go out, you lose eye contact with your audience. You become an impersonal voice in the dark—at best a mere narrator. Of course, there are many strong arguments in favor of using such visuals, especially if you can maintain eye contact.

4.   Be sure you know how to work all equipment you may use. Slide projectors, tape recorders, videotape playback units, and the like all have their own idiosyncracies. For example, more than a few users of videotape playback are unaware that each time they hit the stop button, the tape rewinds several feet. When the tape is started again the audience gets a distinct sense of *déjà vu,* the illusion of having previously had a given experience. The pause control in this case is a better choice than the stop control. But machines differ, so be sure to check out the features in advance.

Another common equipment problem is bulb burnout on an overhead or slide projector. Most machines have a backup bulb, but speakers are wise to check both bulbs before the presentation.

By and large, flip charts, posters, and overhead transparencies are the simplest types of visual aids, giving good value for the money. An added benefit is that any of them can easily be transformed into a printed handout and given to your audience after the presentation. Computers can easily be used to produce graphics that can be converted into simple visuals.

Software presentation programs are widely available. Some examples of such software are *WordPerfect Presentations,* Aldus *Persuasion,* and Microsoft's *Powerpoint.* These can prepare computer-generated visuals and sound clips that can be projected onto a large screen.

If computer projectors are not available, these programs can print out color images on paper (which can be made into transparencies via a color photocopier) or on a disk that can be taken to a copy service that will transfer the images directly onto slides or overheads. Today, anyone can create professional-quality visuals quickly and fairly easily with such software. Most such programs allow you to add sound and, in some cases, motion video clips. These can greatly improve professionalism and hold audience interest.

A few cautions: Don't let the visuals drive the whole presentation and don't get so clever that they overwhelm the message.

CONVEYING YOUR CREDIBILITY

One more factor crucial to your effectiveness in articulating your messages should be considered. Although this is not a specific technique, nor is it something you use only in the body of the briefing, it is probably the single most important factor in determining overall effectiveness. We are speaking of your *credibility*.

Credibility arises from personality characteristics that permeate all our interactions with others. In organizations, where we are likely to have repeated communication opportunities with the same people, what we said or did yesterday or last month may well have bearing on our credibility today.

Aristotle's treatise, *The Rhetoric,* was probably the first book on communication theory. In it, he explains three types of arguments one may use to convince an audience: logical appeals (*logos*), emotion appeals (*pathos*) and ethical appeals (*ethos*). And of these three, *ethos* is the strongest.

Over time the concept of ethos has come to refer to the *credibility* of the message source. People who are held in high esteem because of perceived intelligence or ethical standards are far more likely to be effective communicators.

Most of the considerable research into what creates credibility has concluded that four factors determine our perceived credibility in a given situation:

1. *Expertise.* How well informed we are about a given topic affects credibility. The highly credible source is likely to be one who has experience and/or training relevant to the topic *and* who effectively conveys this competence to the audience. Demonstration of understanding of the issues discussed and use of firsthand experience or personal examples is one way to build this expertise factor.

2. *Trustworthiness.* When a speaker is seen as being sincere and unbiased, credibility will be enhanced. One way to convey such an impression is by using facts and reasoning carefully and avoiding overuse of emotionalism in language. Also, recognizing and presenting opposing points of view can demonstrate the propensity to weigh alternatives carefully and examine issues judiciously. Of course, the absence of secret motives such as personal gain or special advantages for the individual's work group will also strengthen trust in the speaker.

3. *Composure.* Whether a person is seen as poised, relaxed, and confident—as opposed to nervous, tense, or uncomfortable—affects credibility. These perceptions arise from our audience's awareness of cues, most of which are nonverbal. Appearance, posture, mannerisms, and purposefulness of movements combine to create an impression of personal composure. There is, of course, such a thing as being *too* composed. The meticulously groomed, carefully rehearsed, and precisely choreographed presentation might be a bit suspect. Being too perfect may cause others to question your trustworthiness. The image created by looking sharp and acting confidently—with an added dash of humility—seems to be the kind most of us prefer.

4. *Dynamism.* A fourth factor believed to affect source credibility is a sense of personal dynamism: the tendency to be active, outgoing, talkative, or bold. The very introverted, shy, or apprehensive individual is usually seen as less credible. But, as with composure, this can be carried too far. The stereotyped hotshot used car salesman or the loud-mouthed jokester may be dynamic but not credible. In many situations, the soft-spoken voice of quiet reasoning is welcomed. Research showing a relationship between dynamism and high credibility has been less convincing than that relating high credibility to expertise, trust, and composure.

Credibility permeates all the activities of a communicator. In many cases, it arrives before you do in the form of others' past impressions. The speaker whose credibility is not yet established must make a conscious effort to demonstrate these characteristics to the audience. The speaker who is already high in credibility must reinforce that view. And the speaker with low credibility must expend considerable effort to create more favorable images. These changes in attitudes toward the low credibility speaker take time and usually repeated demonstrations of change.

The organization of a presentation can do much to build credibility as well as improve audience comprehension and retention. Studies have shown that the speaker who is well organized in his or her presentation is regarded as a more credible source than a speaker who is disorganized. This was determined by measuring audience attitudes toward the speaker after presenting essentially the same speech in either organized or disorganized fashion.[5]

Specific Delivery Techniques

No matter how well you've planned and prepared the presentation, your success will still depend in large part on the delivery. Delivery is a combination of many factors that collectively produce a total impression on your audience. Overcoming excessive anxiety and developing credibility are important. In addition, here are some techniques to apply:

Eye Contact

Never trust a person who won't look you in the eye. It is a cultural expectation for most of us that when we communicate we look into the eyes of our receiver. When addressing a large group this can become a problem. The best bet seems to be to look at one individual for a few seconds and then move on to another. Don't just scan over the crowd—really look *at* individuals. Be sure you get to almost everyone in the room at some point. Be aware of tendencies to look too much at one particularly attractive or attentive person while ignoring the bored person in the back of the room.

Gestures and Movement

Our sense of personal dynamism or self-confidence comes across via such body language as gestures, posture, and mannerisms. Gestures can be useful to punctuate what is being said. They should be spontaneous and natural, yet used purposefully. We all have different tendencies to use or avoid gestures. For some, it feels uncomfortable to point or raise hands in exclamation. For others it may be said that if you tied their hands they'd be speechless.

There are several common mistakes people make with gestures:

1. They fail to use them where they can be very useful for emphasis.
2. They use the same gesture over and over to the point that it becomes monotonous or even distracting.
3. They use gestures that cannot be seen clearly; a hand motion hidden from audience view by a podium is of no value.

Body movement is another important way to bring life to a talk. Pausing between points in the briefing and physically moving to another place in the room helps your listeners know that you have completed one point and are now ready to address another. This pause helps your listeners follow your logical development. If you cannot freely move around because you must speak into the microphone, you may still use the pause and a shift in position, or a change in the direction you're looking, to indicate the same things. Physical movement is the preferred approach. Whenever possible, avoid the speaker-behind-the-podium format. If a mike is needed, a portable microphone around the neck will allow you more freedom of movement.

Pronunciation

Being careful not to mispronounce words may be more important than you think. As with other distractions, such goofs may not seriously change meaning but will reflect on your credibility. One audience at a large university was unsettled to hear a professor mispronounce the word library as "liberry." We have heard data processing people mispronounce "satistics" and supervisors explain "pacific" examples. A man lost a lot of credibility when he commented about the unusually rainy weather. He hoped that the "moon-san" season was soon to end. He apparently meant *monsoon.* Folklore at an air force training school relates how pilots were surprised to hear that "humid air" is responsible for a large number of plane crashes. The culprit was really "human error."

Voice

Speakers' voices reflect their personalities. A clear, strong voice increases the probability of audience understanding. Clear articulation of the language is important, but other voice characteristics such as variation in pitch, loudness, and rate of speech have as much or more impact. The range of pitch one uses may be wide, allowing for effective vocal emphasis; or very narrow, resulting in what is commonly called a monotone voice. Over time, a committed monotone can, as the sleeping aid commercial used to say, "Help you relax, feel drowsy so you can fall asleep."

The key word to keeping listener attention is *variation.* We have seen two common voice variation problems come up over and over again. First, male speakers seldom have enough variation in pitch. Men seem to think that it sounds macho to talk only in a deep tone and they do so continuously. Tremendous emphasis can be made by raising and lowering the pitch, yet many speakers don't want to risk it.

Second, some female speakers have a different problem: they tend to lose the conversational tone in their voice when addressing a group. Their voice sounds theatrical, artificial, and forced. Occasionally this comes out sing-songy. This latter problem results from habitual pitch-change patterns that become monotonous and distracting. It also arises from overdoing voice *intensity,* perhaps in an effort to sound assertive.

We've all encountered people who are overly loud as well as some who are so soft-spoken we want to tell them, "Speak up!" Most business presentations can be made at a conversational level although additional emphasis can be achieved by variation. Don't assume always that a louder voice commands more attention. Often that still small voice—the one we have to lean toward and work to hear—is the most powerful.

One recent phenomenon in vocal use is what is called up-talk. Here, the speaker raises intonation at the end of a statement to make it sound like a question. Try saying the following sentences using up-talk—raising your intonation on the italicized word:

♦ She's very good at everything she *does.*

♦ The management is concerned about the *costs.*

♦ I'm interested in getting some information about your *vacation plans.*

Notice how up-talk creates a note of uncertainty in what is spoken. Unfortunately, some people habitually use up-talk without noticing how it can undermine their assertiveness and make them consistently sound tentative.

Verbalized Pauses

Few things can drive your audience up the wall like the liberal use of verbalized fillers such as "ah," "um," "uh," and (the popular favorite) "ya know." Some intelligent and apparently rational men and women salt their every utterance with these expressions until their listeners want to scream at them, ya know?

The human talker abhors a vacuum. And when the detested monster, silence, raises its ugly head, we beat it to death with ah, uh, um, or ya knows. Do yourself a favor; ask others you speak with to point out when you are drifting into this habit. Commit yourself to listening for and eliminating your own filler words. Rid yourself of the fear of silence.

Emphasis

Putting more stress on certain words can have interesting effects on meaning. Think of the different inflections you could give the question "What do you mean by that?"

♦ *What* do you mean by that?

♦ What *do* you mean by that?

♦ What do *you* mean by that?

♦ What do you *mean* by that?

♦ What do you mean by *that?*

Professional communicators are very sensitive to these kinds of differences. Listen carefully to the words emphasized by the radio announcer. "*Big Jim wants* to sell you a car" is likely to come across quite differently from, "Big Jim want to sell *you* a car" or, better yet, "Big Jim wants to sell you a *car.*" The last of these three examples focuses your attention on the product while the first one focuses on what Big Jim wants. Who cares what Big Jim wants?

AFTER THE BRIEFING: HANDLING QUESTIONS

For most business presentations there is a considerable amount of audience give-and-take, often in the form of a question and answer session following the talk. Sometimes a great deal of meaningful information is exchanged in such sessions. When, however, the audience is very large or your topic is unusually controversial and you don't want to risk undermining your presentation, you may want to avoid the question and answer session altogether. If you do accept questions from the audience, keep in mind that the fundamentals of handling questions are simply: (1) be prepared to handle them, and (2) keep control of yourself and control the audience.

Preparing for questions should not be a serious problem if the briefing is well planned. In each step of the preliminary plan and content development, you should put yourself in the shoes of your listeners and anticipate likely questions or reactions. Many anticipated responses will, of course, be addressed as a logical development of the briefing. There may, however, be other issues or sticky questions that you've chosen not to discuss in the talk. These are the kinds of questions you need to be prepared to handle. Brainstorm all such possible objections with the help of others, and work out the best possible answers. Then have an associate fire the tough questions at you and practice your responses.

Keeping control of the situation requires some effort when you face hostile or surprising questions. Don't get paranoid about the question asked. What may at first sound like a real zinger may simply be a listener's way of testing you under fire or even confirming his or her *agreement* with your view. If you don't know the answer, say so. Don't try to fake it. Remember how important trustworthiness is to your credibility.

When hostile or loaded questions arise, take them in stride and don't heckle back—maintain your dignity and good appearance.

GENERATING LISTENER PARTICIPATION

Often it is desirable to get your listeners involved. Rather than being apprehensive about questions we're likely to face, we may well want to generate discussion. Such discussions can take several forms. In smaller groups, you may find it useful to encourage your listeners to ask questions *as you present your talk*. For some topics and audiences, you may prefer that listeners hold their questions until *after* you've presented your talk. In some cases you may want to ask questions to check for understanding and gain commitment as you go.

How can you encourage questions from listeners so you'll know they got the message? The tone you set in handling the first few questions will have an impact on future question and answer interaction. Here are a few tips on how to maximize this give and take:

♦ Avoid embarrassing listeners by putting them on the spot with one of your questions.

- Avoid expressing negative evaluations of questions received—verbally or nonverbally. All questions asked should be regarded as requests for more information. Such requests show listeners are interested in gaining an understanding of what you have to say. That's the same goal you have! Accept the old dictum that the only stupid question is the one you don't ask.

- Restate the question for the rest of your audience before answering it, especially when all listeners may not have heard it originally.

- When a listener makes a statement, react to it (even if it doesn't require an answer). Don't just let a remark hang there in dead air. Say something to indicate agreement, disagreement, or at least appreciation for sharing the thought. A simple "thanks for sharing that idea with us, Sue," or "good point, Chris," can go a long way toward encouraging additional participation.

- Don't let a single questioner dominate. Encourage everyone who has questions or comments to speak up. If you have one person who persists in overparticipating, you may suggest that you'll get together with him or her after the presentation to clarify things.

- In some cases you may want to plant one or two questions to ensure that the question session will get off the ground. Prearrange to have a few important questions asked, preferably questions that will stimulate further comments from others.

- Don't let the questions get too far afield of your topic. If they do, you may wind up spending too much time on irrelevant issues.

- Answer questions directly and candidly. If you don't know an answer, say so. Don't try to bluff. If it's an important enough question, offer to find out and get back to the questioner.

- Be patient. Some of your listeners won't grasp the message as quickly as you think they should. Keep trying to help them understand.

One final thought. When you feel you have presented your talk as effectively as possible and you've handled a reasonable number of questions—quit. Don't drag it out. As an anonymous wag once said, "No speech can be entirely bad if it is short."

A QUICK SUMMARY OF MAJOR IDEAS

- Some anxiety is perfectly natural in people speaking before groups. We should expect it and strive to make it work for us, not against us.

- You can bring the level of speaker anxiety within a manageable range (improving your coping quotient) by being well prepared and idea conscious, by learning to relax, and by not being self-conscious.

- Your listeners want you to succeed.

♦ Gestures and body movements convey dynamism. They also provide emphasis and work as nonverbal transitions indicating to the listener the flow of your message.

♦ Facial expression and eye contact may be the most important nonverbal communicators. People expect eye contact when communicating with others.

♦ Our personal characteristics project a total image as we speak to others. Much of this image comes across through our voices. Avoid annoying vocal mannerisms such as lack of variation, verbalized pauses, and up-talk.

♦ Audience participation, question and answer sessions being the most common form, leads to the creation of better understanding. The speaker often sets the tone and climate for such give and take.

QUESTIONS FOR FURTHER THOUGHT

1. What is a coping quotient? How can we expand it so that we'll be more relaxed as speakers?

2. What is meant by the statement, "Self-consciousness tends to be self-destructive"?

3. How do nonverbal aspects of delivery affect our listeners? Give examples.

4. How can you encourage questions from your listeners?

OTHER THOUGHTS ABOUT DELIVERING A PRESENTATION

WHAT A BORE![6]
by Perry W. Buffington, Ph.D.

> *What makes some people so fascinating and others, well … so dull? It's a question that has several answers.*

Why are boring people boring? What traits do they possess that make other people avoid them so? And most important of all, can a dull person be revitalized into one who is adored instead of bored? The answers, based on boring, penetrating research, are surprising.

Social scientists have known for years that most people have no trouble identifying, labeling, and avoiding a potential bore. However, this is done so automatically that people have only a vague idea of the criteria they use to define "boring." Nevertheless, psychologists have discovered that a specific rudimentary checklist is employed before the dubious distinction is designated.

This checklist has been identified by the dean of boring research—Mark R. Leary, Ph.D., associate professor of psychology at Wake Forest University in Winston-Salem, North Carolina. Over the past ten years, Leary has identified "ways to be boring," studied how the average man or woman interacts with boring people, and evaluated the perceptions held toward dull individuals. "I was initially interested in social anxiety and shyness," he says. "What dawned on me, at a point in my studies, was that all shy people are concerned with how they are coming across. That is a central component in shyness. One thing that they are often concerned with is that they are going to be perceived as boring."

Leary points out that he does not equate shyness and dullness, but rather that shy people's "belief that they would be perceived as not interesting led me into a different line of work on 'interpersonal boredom.'"

Although there is a great deal of research on why workers grow tired of their jobs or why kids become bored with school, there has been very little inquiry into what makes one person consider another boring. As a result, it was necessary for Leary to both coin the term "interpersonal boredom" and define it. He explains, "This subset of study seeks a better understanding of why people become bored with one another."

Leary and his associates have completed three studies which have received attention in both scientific and popular circles. Why are people interested in psychological research on boredom? "I think we have a certain degree of confidence concerning our appearance or our ability to be a good friend, but a lot of people, down deep, want to know if they bore people when they talk to them," says Leary. "We all know boring people, and we look at ourselves and wonder if we are one of those boring folks."

Leary defines "boring" in terms of the amount of effort one must exert in order to pay attention to something. He explains, "Sometimes it is not effortful to pay attention, like watching an exciting football game. It pulls our attention out of us. Sometimes, it is *so* effortful to pay attention … The amount of effort one exerts is directly proportional to the degree of boredom an individual experiences." In other words, if one must work in order to pay attention to another's behaviors, then that person is likely to be evaluated as boring. Leary has identified those behaviors that require effort, even to observe.

Leary explains, "The first thing we did in our research was identify that there were several ways to be boring. After factor-analyzing a large number of boring situations, nine areas emerged as the most boring set of behaviors."

Leary has identified those areas in descending order of importance. He refers to the first as "negative egocentrism." Individuals who typify this set of behaviors are constantly complaining. Their conversation is not only self-centered, but also negative. It is easy to understand that interacting with this type of person requires effort and is designated as boring.

The second effortful behavior concerns banality and triteness. The individuals who tell the same story again and again or can only discuss one topic will require effort to indulge. As a result, they, too, may be designated as boring.

The third Leary refers to as "low affectivity," or little emotion. Those individuals who exhibit minimal emotional expression are interpreted as boring. "They are boring because they show that the person is not involved in the interaction. A monotonous voice, no facial expression, little eye contact—they imply disengagement. Perhaps they are bored with us," Leary adds.

If little emotional expression may be interpreted as boring, so will tedious behaviors, the fourth category. A person who talks too slowly, takes a long time to tell a story, takes five minutes to make a 15-second point, or digresses frequently will be viewed as boring.

Fifth is passivity, and refers to the individual who will not hold up his or her end of the conversation. Leary adds, "We normally think of boring people as dominating, but in fact it is just as likely that a boring person is one who doesn't contribute enough."

Self-preoccupation is the sixth category. This is egocentrism, although not necessarily negative. Individuals who fall under this heading may talk about their own abilities, their own problems, or their pasts.

Add to this self-preoccupation a degree of seriousness, and the seventh category emerges. The person who takes everything too seriously and is extremely task-oriented and rarely smiles.

The eighth factor is ingratiation. This is the individual who tries too hard to impress and to be nice. The result is, as Leary says, "They're just boring."

Finally, the last category is, as Leary explains, "a hodgepodge of things"—which basically center around individuals who are unable to keep a conversation going. They get side-tracked and often exhibit bizarre body language.

To observe, deal with, and relate to any of the above nine behaviors for any period of time takes effort. And according to Leary, "If attention requires significant effort, boredom may result."

After identifying the nine multidimensional behaviors most associated with boring people, the focus of Leary's research shifted. "We now were interested in finding out: how do boring and nonboring people differ in terms of their verbal interactions?" He explains, "To do this, we evaluated a number of tape-recorded conversations—52 to be exact. Subjects listened and rated them."

Boring and nonboring people do differ in the way they verbally interact with people. Boring people talk less than interesting people do. "Again we tend

> *As the lack of emotional expression is considered boring, so are tedious behaviors.*

to think of boring people as dominating conversations," Leary reiterates. And again, the research shows the opposite to be true. "People who did not hold up their end of the conversation were evaluated as boring."

Two other factors separated boring individuals from more adept conversationalists. Simply, boring people: (1) ask more questions and (2) engage in more acknowledgement—offering little information about themselves. While self-preoccupation is a turnoff, apparently so is a complete lack of self-disclosure.

Finally, the researchers investigated the listeners' reactions to boring people. Leary adds, "Specifically, we wanted to know: what inferences do listeners draw about the boring person?"

Using the same 52 conversations, those rated as most interesting or most boring were re-evaluated. Leary interprets the findings: "I was overwhelmed at how negative their impressions were of boring people. I expected them [boring people] to be devalued, but they were derogated on every dimension. Boring people were evaluated as less competent, less secure—virtually less everything."

To complicate matters, most boring people may not know just how boring they really are. Leary explains, "This is an area people don't tell us about. It is easier to tell others that they are gaining weight than it is to tell them they are boring. As a result, most people just wonder if they are boring, and really never know. People don't get much feedback on this issue, your best friends will not tell you." To that point, the entire problem of being boring stems from a communication problem—one that can, fortunately, be resolved.

Leary explains, "If you really believe that you are boring, then social-skills training is in order. That is what boring comes down to: social skills, specifically communication-skills training."

Here's where to start:

(1) Seek confirmation. Determine whether what you perceive to be your own boring behavior is founded in your interpersonal relations or is an irrational fear. The easiest way to do this is to ask a good friend, "Do I come across as boring?" Listen carefully to the answer, and be prepared.

(2) Analyze your own behavior. Leary explains, "We can each analyze our own behavior to some extent. What is it that I am doing which is boring? What are the things which I tend to do which are boring? Compare your behaviors to the list of nine most boring behaviors. Do your conversations focus on negative self-complaints? Do you focus only on one topic, unable to discuss a wide range of issues? Are you unable to become emotionally involved in a conversation?"

(3) Interact as if the social interaction were a contract. Involving yourself is tantamount to holding up your end of the conversational agreement. Leary adds, "Being boring is a violation of the contract." To contribute to the contract, offer more facts relevant to the discussion; express smiles and negative emotions when appropriate, but avoid expressing either constantly; avoid excessive questioning; and appropriately praise and acknowledge another's remarks.

(4) Seek middle ground. Leary explains, "The objective in a social interaction is not to be fascinating… but to seek a middle ground that is acceptable. We do not have to be the life of the party all the time to avoid being perceived as boring."

> *"The objective in a social interaction is not to be fascinating... but to seek a middle ground that is acceptable."*

(5) Finally, expect occasionally to be perceived as boring. As Leary explains: "All of us are boring sometimes."

REFERENCES:

Bakers, S. (1987). Boring research. *Omni, 9,* 29.

Larry, M.R., Rogers, P.A., Canfield, R., & Coe, C. (1986). Boredom in interpersonal encounters: Antecedents and social implications. *Journal of Personality and Social Psychology, 51,* 968–975.

Psychologist Perry Buffington, a contributing editor of SKY, *is based on Amelia Island, Florida. Dr. Buffington's book,* Your Behavior Is Showing, *is distributed by Peachtree Publishers, Atlanta, Georgia.*

NOTES

1. Louis L'Amour, *Education of a Wandering Man* (New York: Bantam Books, 1990), pp. 184–186.

2. Toastmaster's International is an excellent organization aimed at improving members' communication and leadership skills. For more information about their programs, consult your local phone directory.

3. This discussion is adapted from Paul R. Timm, *Basics of Oral Communication* (Cincinnati: Southwestern Publishing Co., 1993), Chapter 2. The coping quotient idea is found originally in Harold P. Zelko and Frank E. X. Dance, *Business and Professional Speech Communication,* 2nd ed. (New York: Holt, Rinehart & Winston, 1978), pp. 77–79.

4. Zelko and Dance, *op. cit.,* p. 78.

5. Larry L. Barker, *Communication* (Englewood Cliffs, NJ: Prentice-Hall, 1978), p. 241.

6. Reprinted with permission of SKY magazine, January 1990.

Written Communication in Management

CHAPTER 13

KEYS TO FUNCTIONAL WRITING

Letters and Memos That Get Results

▼

In this chapter you will find ideas that will help you:

- ♦ Recognize the *functional* nature of business communication
- ♦ Organize a message appropriately using the BIF or BILL approaches
- ♦ Help your reader get the message by applying *content set* and *access* techniques for emphasis
- ♦ Create a conversational and efficient tone in your writing by using simple, familiar wording, concrete nouns, active verbs, and avoiding unnecessary repetition
- ♦ Recognize common failures in wording messages

▼

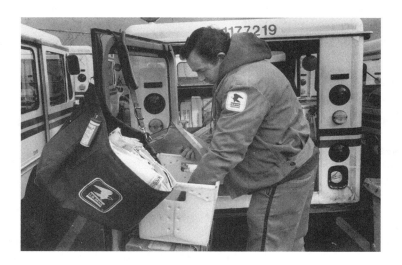

The difference between literature and business writing is like the difference between culture and agriculture. In business we're concerned with the yield.

Functional writing gets results. It causes readers to *do* something or to *think* in some way they would not if the message were not received.[1]

Two important questions for you to ask about business writing are:

1. Is this letter really necessary?
2. Is this letter efficient?

IS THIS LETTER REALLY NECESSARY?

The major advantages of the letter medium are its permanent record, relative formality, and capability of conveying fairly complex data. Disadvantages include high cost, low speed, and lack of immediate feedback.

If a given communication situation is likely to require an extensive two-way exchange of information in order to create understanding, don't write. Call or visit. There are times when flying across the country for a face-to-face conversation can be "cheaper" than a letter. Such trips would be worthwhile to save a major customer or to influence legislation affecting your business.

> *Communicate complex and critical information in person.*

If, however, you do need to convey fairly complex but not highly emotional information (say, a list of costs and serial numbers of parts, for example) or if it is important to have a permanent record of what was said (such as a proposal for services with prices quoted) or if a somewhat formal message would be useful to convey a contractual agreement, go with a letter.

When the case is not so clear cut, we may consider another alternative to a costly, formal letter. We could handwrite a note, send a form or preprinted document, or—when responding to someone else's written message—simply write a brief reply on the original letter and return it, keeping a photocopy for our own records. This latter alternative to the formal letter has become more widely used in recent years. An example is shown in Figure 13-1.

IS THIS LETTER EFFICIENT?

Once you have decided that a letter is the best medium for your message, you need to decide the most efficient method for writing the document. The primary considerations for efficient organization are choosing the best pattern of organization, selecting an effective content set and access techniques, and determining the appropriate writing style.

Patterns of Organization

The first question writers should ask as they prepare letters or memos is, "What's the big idea?" In functional writing, the *big idea* can be defined as:

January 17, 19__

Mr. William Astor, President
Plainville Supply, Inc.
1881 Western Way
Baldwin, N.Y. 14001

Dear Bill:

Please send me your updated price lists
for the Aramco Fasteners. I have been
using last year's list and I suspect there
will be an increase this year.

Thanks for your usual fine service and
have a happy New Year.

Harvey: Good
News! No price
increase is planned
until at least second
quarter. Your old price list is still
current. You have a happy
New Year too!
Best,
Bill

Sincerely,

Harvey

Harvey Supply Co.
Harvey W. Banger

FIGURE 13-1   Quick reply format.

♦ What you want the reader to *do* as a result of reading this message
♦ What you want the reader to think or feel as a result of reading this message

If the big idea is unclear to the writer, a functional message cannot be developed. Once you know what your big idea is, you need to decide whether you want to use the BIF or the BILL approach.

What's a BIF Approach?

BIF is an acronym that stands for *Big Idea First.* Good news and routine messages can be most efficient using a BIF approach.

> *By saying your idea first, your reader knows right away your purpose in writing.*

In such writing situations, there is no sense in beating around the bush. Your reader will be glad to get your message (good news) or interested in what you have to say (routine). So why not say it—and say it first?

Remember, the big idea is what you want the reader to *do* with the information in your message—your purpose for writing. The big idea is the bottom line of the message. If your reader accepts or acts on the big idea as you wish, your letter or memo has been successful. All the rest of the words used in the writing are just packaging around which you wrap the big idea, or provide additional, clarifying details.

Letters or memos set up in this fashion are generally direct, brief, and to the point. The main idea is presented first. Then supporting details are inserted, followed by a closing thought.

What are the advantages to BIF? There are several:

♦ Since readers are tipped off right away to the purpose of the message, BIF saves them valuable time.

♦ The direct beginning often attracts readers' attention. For example, it is easy to keep on reading when the first word in the letter is *Congratulations.*

♦ Writers using BIF don't waste time getting started on the letter or memo. Once we know what the big idea is, we can write it with little hesitation. The supporting details will follow naturally.

For all its advantages, BIF presents some dangers. If you anticipate that a message will be emotionally damaging (that is, disappointing) to the reader, don't put the bad news in the first line. Likewise, if your message is persuasive and you need to present convincing evidence before your conclusion, avoid BIF. A sales letter that begins, "You should buy some insurance," has little chance of succeeding.

What's a BILL Approach?

The BILL approach puts the *Big Idea a Little Later.* The effect of positioning the big idea a little later is to prepare the reader for the action or conclusion you are requesting. In emotionally sensitive or persuasive situations, we run the risk of turning the reader off if the big idea is presented too soon. When conveying bad news or a persuasive appeal, show your reasoning first.

HELPING YOUR READER GET THE MESSAGE: CONTENT SET AND ACCESSING

Of all the tips on better writing available to managers, the two discussed in this section may be the most useful. Repeatedly, we have seen mediocre to poor writers make dramatic improvements in their letters, memos, and reports by applying *content set* and *accessing.*

Content Set: A Preview

When we pick up a report, letter, or other document, we immediately begin to form expectations as to what this writing is about; we make guesses about the message even before we receive it. We also make guesses about the source of the message—the speaker or writer—and what that person's motives, intentions, and the like may be.

> **Our expectations affect how we receive a message.**

Psychologists tell us that expectations have a very strong influence on what we hear or read. In other words, what we expect is often what we get—even when we have to change our reception of the real message to fit our preconceived ideas. It makes sense, then, for the writer to create the most appropriate and positive expectations early in the communication.

One of the most effective ways to set the right expectations is simply to tell the reader what the message is about. An adage of public speaking says, "Tell them what you are going to tell them, tell them, and then tell them what you just told them." The first part of that three-step advice is what we are calling *content set*.

Content set can be general or specific. The general preview sets the stage for what will follow. Specific content set gets down to details. For example, a table of contents gives us a detailed preview of the material; the last paragraph in a report's introduction is often a description of the specific items that will be coming up.

A colleague of ours uses the following game in the classroom to illustrate how content set works—how we can *create* expectations in others.[2] You may want to try this on someone.

The instructor asks a question and requests the whole class to say the answers three times out loud. He then quickly asks a follow-up question.

Instructor: There was a U.S. president whose name rhymes with "folk." Who was he?

Students: Polk.

Instructor: OK, let's say it aloud three times: Polk; Polk; Polk. What do you call the white of an egg?

Students: Yolk.

Instructor: OK, together: yolk; yolk; yolk. There were certain structures that the pioneers built to protect themselves from Indian attacks. What do you call such a structure?

Students: Fort.

Instructor: OK, let's say it aloud three times: fort; fort; fort. What do you eat your soup with?

Students: A fork.

Instructor: A forest is made up of a whole bunch of what?

Students: Trees.

Instructor: OK, let's say *tree* aloud three times: tree; tree; tree. How many of each animal did Moses take into the ark with him? [By now the students feel they've caught on to the game. About half the group will say "three," while others will say "two."] The correct answer is that Moses didn't have an ark; it was Noah.

The exercise (which, by the way, has worked perfectly every time we've tried it) points out how mental set can be established and how it can affect listener responses. People will hear what they expect to hear unless a speaker is very careful to create awareness that something different is going to be said.

The easiest way to create content preview is by simply telling the reader what's coming up next. This works well when the message can be direct and to the point (BIF approach). Some examples of content preview:

♦ The following report recommends relocating the warehouse to the Westside Industrial Park.

♦ Enclosed is my contribution to the University Alumni Fund.

♦ This performance review cites three incidents of substandard performance.

♦ In response to your request for a transfer, I am sending you this description of the procedures you'll need to follow.

♦ Four small business computers are evaluated in this report.

Using clear content preview is a simple way of communicating. Strengthening content preview is one of the simplest ways for a writer to improve the chances that the reader will get and use the message. Content preview helps create realistic expectations in the reader's mind. Doing so reduces misconceptions and improves the accuracy of communication.

Accessing: Here's What's Important

In any message, there are certain ideas or bits of information that are more important than others. One common mistake made in functional writing is failing to point out which bits of information are, in fact, more important. Important information should receive a position of prominence—that is, the more the reader will need to understand that information—the more accessible you should make it. You should point to key ideas in your message.

One of the major differences between literary writing and functional business writing is this notion of pointing. In literature, a reader is expected to read through the whole story to find the important points. The author doesn't normally help the reader to do that efficiently. In business communication, key ideas are asserted more obviously. Ideally, a management report, letter, or memo should be written so that it need not be read word for word, but can actually be skimmed. The key bits of information should jump out at the reader.

Three types of emphasis in writing are: verbal, visual, and psychological. Each of these can be used to point to the key ideas of the message.

Verbal Emphasis

An important use of verbal emphasis is to provide *word cues* indicating that a key idea is coming up. For example, the writer might say, "The most important aspect is...," or, "This last part is particularly important...," or, "Please read these instructions carefully...," and so on. These overt cues can be used in either written or spoken communication. They simply provide guidelines for the reader.

A second type of verbal emphasis is the use of *repetition*. When a key idea is repeated several times (preferably phrased a little differently each time), the reader gets the idea that this is in fact an important bit of information. Repetitious phrases can also be used to help organize a message. Perhaps the first few words of a series of headings might be repetitious to show how these headings fit together. In a business report, for example, we may say:

- The first important reason for ...
- The second important reason for ...
- The third important reason for ... etc.

Visual Emphasis

Several types of visual emphasis can be used to help the reader skim through the message and get the important ideas in it. These visual techniques include:

- Enumeration—1, 2, 3, or I, II, III, or a, b, c
- Listing—such lists are put in columns and can have these notations:
  1. Numerals
  A. Letters
  * Asterisks or stars

- - Hyphens
- • Bullets
- ◆ CAPITALIZING—the word in CAPS gets the emphasis
- ◆ Underlining—with <u>one</u> or <u>two</u>
- ◆ Borders— such as
- ◆ Type variation—word processors have different FACES, *styles,* and SIZES
- ◆ Graphics—a picture is worth how many words?
- ◆ Shading or highlighting—with color marker or a color print out
- ◆ The attention-getting power of w h i t e space (including short paragraphs) and wide margins

Psychological Emphasis

> *Make the letter psychologically pleasing.*

Pointing by means of psychological principles entails the arrangement of information in the message. Three ways to achieve psychological emphasis are order, space, and freshness.

The *order of information*—when clearly pointed out to the reader—can help the reader anticipate what is coming next and remember what has been said. This form of psychological emphasis helps separate the key ideas from the extraneous.

When we talk about *space* in terms of psychological emphasis, we are referring to the relative amount of space devoted to a particular topic. If, for example, an advertisement for a washing machine spends several paragraphs explaining how reliable the machine is and only one short line indicating something about its "ease of operation," we psychologically determine that reliability is more important than ease of operation.

Finally, psychological emphasis can be achieved through *freshness* by suggesting that the message is a new approach, a catchy idea, or a particularly innovative notion. Imaginative wording such as identifying a problem by a clever phrase can give psychological emphasis to it.

SOME IDEAS FOR CHOOSING AN APPROPRIATE WRITING STYLE

Everyone's writing style is unique. Developing your own writing style comes naturally with practice. As you are developing your writing style, here are a few, simple pointers that will help your writing to be clear and straightforward.

Building Efficient Sentences

Long, complex, and/or compound sentences hurt message efficiency. They slow down both reader and writer.

Sentences should convey bite-size pieces of information that can be digested by your reader one piece at a time. The rule of thumb is that, for most adult

American readers, sentences should *average* about 16 to 18 words in length. Of course, some sentences may have only two or three words while others can run to 30 or more.

One other consideration in dealing with sentence length: different lengths have different effects on readers. Short sentences have punch. They emphasize. They hit hard. Longer sentences, on the other hand, can be useful in deemphasizing information that may be objectionable or unpleasant for your reader. They can also be used to subordinate less important information which you do not want to dwell on but which is necessary for understanding.

> ▶ *Keep sentences and paragraphs short unless de-emphasizing.* ◀

Building Efficient Paragraphs

Paragraphs should usually be short unless further de-emphasis is desired. People prefer to read information presented in manageable bits. When we receive a letter with very long paragraphs—even before reading the first words—we make a judgment about the message: This is going to be hard to read.

Grammatically, a paragraph should develop one theme. But we have considerable latitude in choosing when to break to a new paragraph. For functional writing, we recommend that paragraphs seldom exceed six lines. Figure 13-2 shows the visual effect of different paragraph lengths. Which letter would you prefer to read?

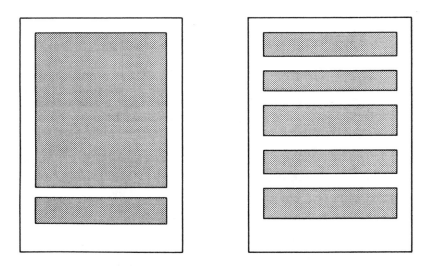

FIGURE 13-2 **Visual effect of long versus short paragraphs.**

Economy of Language

Economy of language should be a goal of the business writer. Many of the phrases that appear in business letters are there because "we've always done it that way." Typically, inexperienced letter writers check the correspondence files to see how others have written in the past. So they end up using phrases like the ones in the rhyme below:

> We beg to advise you and wish to state
> That yours has arrived of recent date.
> We have it before us; its contents noted.
> Herewith enclosed are the prices we quoted.
> Attached you will find, as per your request,
> The forms you wanted, and we would suggest,
> Regarding the matter and due to the fact
> That up to this moment your order we've lacked,
> We hope that you will not delay it unduly.
> We beg to remain, yours very truly.[3]

> *Don't bury the message under meaningless expressions.*

Although an exaggeration, this poem illustrates how the meat of a very simple message can get buried under these overworked expressions.

The most economical language results when we write pretty much the way we would talk in a planned, purposeful conversation. It is unlikely that, upon handing an envelope to a coworker in our office, we would *say,* "Enclosed herewith please find the report I've written." In conversation we'd be more likely to say "Here's the report I prepared on ..." So why not write that way? It gets to the point and conveys your message efficiently. The trend in written communication is to the less formal, more conversational tone.[4]

Here are some useful rules to encourage a conversational and economical style.

Use Simple Wording

> *Big words slow down the reader and the writer.*

Often a common word can do the job of a multisyllable jawbreaker.[5] There is a clear correlation between how many syllables are in a word and how difficult it is to read. Lots of big words slow down both the writer and the reader, and they usually don't communicate any more effectively, despite the increased effort. In the following examples, listen to the differences:

Long and Heavy Wording	*Short and Simple Wording*
Polysyllabic verbiage obfuscates comprehension.	Big words block clarity.[6]

Long and Heavy Wording	Short and Simple Wording
Our *analysis* of the *situation* suggests needed *experiential* training to *optimize* the job performance of our employees.	We think our people need more job training.
John *acceded* to the demands for *additional compensation.*	John agreed to pay them more.
My investment recommendations were *predicated* on *anticipations* of additional *monetary funds* being made available.	My investment recommendations were based on an expected increase in money available.
Ramifications of our *performance shortfall* included *program discontinuation.*	Since we didn't reach our goal, the program was discontinued.

Use Familiar, Conversational Words

Everyday language helps our reader understand what we are saying. Many business writers feel they must use technical or formal language to convey the appropriate image. We serve only our illusions of status with language so technical and stilted that it loses meaning for our receivers. Talk in terms that readers are sure to understand.

Unfamiliar, Stilted Words	Everyday, Conversational Words
ascertain	find out
terminate	end
endeavor	try
with all due dispatch	quickly
forthwith	soon
monetary transaction	sale or purchase
occupational position	job
financial obligations	debts
disproportionate	unfair

It's obvious, in our modern world of today theirs a lot of impreciseness in expressing thoughts we have.

—AN 18-YEAR OLD COLLEGE FRESHMAN

Use Concrete Words

Concrete terms paint word pictures.

Concrete words improve efficiency and hold your readers' interest by creating vivid mental images. Often these are short, familiar terms.

Abstract	*Concrete*
the leading student	top student in a class of 80
most of our people	87 percent of our employees
in the near future	by noon Wednesday
lower cost than …	$43 less than …
a sizable increase in sales	doubled in sales
low energy consumption	uses no more power than a 60-watt light bulb
the cost would be enormous	… would cost every taxpayer $286 per year

Use Active Verbs

Just as concreteness improves nouns and modifiers, use of the active voice adds impact to verbs. The grammatical term *voice* refers to whether the subject of a sentence acts or is acted upon. If it is *acted upon,* the passive voice is used; if it *does the acting,* the active voice is used. Active verbs make your sentences more

1. *Specific.* "The Board of Directors decided" is more explicit than "A decision has been made."
2. *Personal.* "You will note" is both personal and specific; "It will be noted" is impersonal.
3. *Concise.* The passive requires more words and thus slows down both the writing and reading. Compare "Figure 2 shows" with "It is shown by Figure 2."
4. *Emphatic.* Passive verbs dull action. Compare "The child ran a mile" with "A mile was run by the child."[7]

In active voice, the clearer relationship between subject and verb adds force and momentum to your writing. By closely associating the *actor* (noun) and the *action* (verb), we help our reader visualize more clearly what is happening. There are, of course, cases where the writer may intentionally want to deemphasize this association (or remove the actor entirely) by using passive voice. For example,

I just ran over your cat. (active)

Your cat has been run over. (passive)

The changes in emphasis caused by the selection of active or passive voice can be quite dramatic. For most business writing, the active voice is preferred because it adds vitality.

Passive	*Active*
Each tire *was inspected* by a mechanic.	A mechanic *inspected* each tire.
A gain of 41 percent *was recorded* for paper product sales.	Paper products sales *gained* 41 percent.
A full report *will be sent* to you by the supervisor.	The supervisor *will send* ... or, You *will receive* a full report from the supervisor.
All figures in the report *are checked* by accounting.	The accounting department *checks* all figures in the report.

Avoid Unnecessary Repetition

Although repeating an idea can be an effective teaching device (especially in oral communication), unnecessary repetition distracts the reader.

Needless Repetition	*Repetition Eliminated*
The *provisions* of the contract *provide* for a union shop.	The contract provides for a union shop.
The new rule will affect *each* and *every* employee.	The new rule will affect every employee.
In my opinion I think the plan is reasonable.	I think the plan is reasonable.

Avoid Surplus Words and Cluttered Phrases

Words that add nothing to the meaning of the sentence should be dropped. Phrases that can be replaced by a single word or shorter expression should be changed. Here are some examples:

Cluttered	*More Concise*
In the event that payment is not received ...	If payment is not ...
The report is *in regard to the matter* of our long-term obligations ...	The report is about ...
I have just received your letter and wanted to respond quickly.	I wanted to respond quickly to your letter.
The quality of his art work is so good that *it permitted us to* offer him a long-term contract.	His work was so good that we offered him a long-term contract.

QUICK SUMMARY OF MAJOR IDEAS

♦ Business writing is *functional* writing. It should always focus on a particular result. This desired result is the *big idea* of the message.

♦ Two questions should be answered before writing:

—Is this letter necessary (or useful)?

—Is this letter efficient?

♦ The BIF (big idea first) pattern of arrangement is best for routine or good-news messages, while the BILL (big idea a little later) pattern is usually better for messages that are likely to affect the reader's emotions. The latter situations include bad news and persuasive messages.

♦ Message efficiency is achieved through economy of language, simple conversational wording, active voice, and the like.

♦ Message effectiveness is determined by the degree to which the letter clearly conveys the message, projects a favorable image of the writer, and accomplishes the big idea.

♦ Content set creates appropriate expectations in the mind of the reader by previewing the message.

♦ Accessing adds verbal, visual, and psychological emphasis to important ideas in a message, thus helping your reader to get to the big idea.

QUESTIONS FOR FURTHER THOUGHT

1. Business communication is or should be more functional than other types of writing. Do you agree or disagree with that viewpoint? Justify your position.

2. Why does a conversational tone generally communicate more efficiently in business letters? Can you think of cases where tone should be more formal—even "stuffy"?

3. Take a look at some business letters or memos you have received at work or at home. What is the big idea of each? Where does the writer position this big idea? Is this the way you would write the letter? If not, what would you do differently? Why?

4. Why do active verbs and concrete nouns communicate more clearly?

5. Why is accessing important? Can you think of times when you may want to avoid accessing key ideas?

OTHER THOUGHTS ABOUT WRITING FUNCTIONALLY

IS THIS LETTER EFFECTIVE?

Every letter does two jobs. It attempts to *convey a message* and it *projects an image* of its writer. Sometimes one task is relatively more important than the other. Figure 13-3 illustrates how these functions could be plotted on a grid. As with the more famous "managerial grid," let's assume that each axis is calculated between 1 and 9 (low to high), with the vertical axis reflecting the degree of reader understanding—the *accuracy* with which the message has been received—and the horizontal axis reflecting favorableness of the impression created by the writer—his or her *image*. The ideal business letter would be a 9-9 (high accuracy, high image), while the total waste of paper and money would be a 1-1 (low accuracy, low image) letter. We may, however, get by with a 9-1 letter if the overriding task of the letter is to convey accurate information with minimal concern for image projected. A military directive or routine transmittal of some data may be efficient and fairly harmless as a 9-1. At the other end of the grid, a 1-9 letter, one whose message content is less than precise may be well received when it's the thought that counts. Inadequate but thoughtful expressions of sympathy or cheerful but rather vague notes of congratulations may be 1-9s.

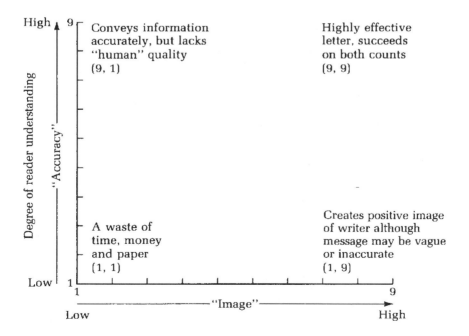

FIGURE 13-3   **The effective letter grid.**

In our letters we should normally be concerned with both information sharing and image building. Going back to our earlier discussion of word choices, the lawyer or stockbroker who insists on using professional jargon in an attempt to feed her sense of professionalism may convey a learned image but will soon turn off the reader who can't figure out what she is saying. Such impressive-sounding letters may stroke the writer's ego but only frustrate the reader.

Conversely, the writer who spits out cold, heartless, but fact-filled sentences with great precision may seem like a well-programmed android. Good business letters are more than pure information transfer. They also involve impressions and expressions of humanity. Even when mass printed by a computer, professional letters can sound like chat over the back fence with your neighbor. Letter effectiveness arises from both the informational and the human content of the message.

OTHER THOUGHTS ABOUT WRITING FUNCTIONALLY

THEY LAUGHED WHEN I SAT DOWN TO WRITE[8]
by Phil Theibert

Want to write compelling letters and memos? Want to write persuasive copy? Study your direct mail.

"You cannot bore people into buying." The years I spent writing direct mail copy drilled that classic David Ogilvy line into my head. That's why I love junk mail! It provides the best writing course in the world. Every word is designed to produce results. The pros have five seconds to hook you. If you don't call that 800 number, they're fired.

So they know how to use word and phrase cues like no one else in business: "Cent" is masculine; "penny" is feminine. "Take the quiz inside" beats "take the test inside" (people love quizzes, hate tests). "Postage-free" beats "postage-paid." With upscale customers use "complimentary," not "free." "Do you make these mistakes in English?" beats "Are you afraid of making mistakes in English?" And always include a 'P.S.'; 80% of all direct mail recipients read them.

You can use the same kind of psychology to make sure your own memos get read. Here are some corporate writing tops that can be found in your direct mail:

Emphasize control. "The Optima Card puts the right person in charge of your interest rate. You." People want to be in control of their lives. For a memo, "This seminar puts the right person in charge. You."

Tap into fear. A great headline: "I'll never lose my job. I'll never lose my job …" It tapped right into my sense of security (and fear of insecurity). In a memo, you could ask, "What is the one mistake that could ruin us?" Or simply begin by saying, "Protect yourself."

Promise to unlock a puzzle. "The Deaf Hear Whispers" compels you to read on. For a letter to your sales force: "How I doubled my client list in one evening."

Promise exclusivity. "Quite frankly, our credit card is not for everyone. And everyone who applies for membership is not approved." If it works for them, it can work for you. "I'm sending this to only a select few."

Tantalize. "Think how wonderful it would feel to walk without pain." This can be applied to most company problems. For a memo: "Think how wonderful it would be to reduce our inventory costs."

Show what's in it for me. "Save up to 60% on the books you order." For a letter: "Save up to 60% on our long-distance calls."

Use headline grabbers. "Golf pros banned from using new 'hot' ball; flies too far." To announce a training program: "Learn to use a computer in less than an hour."

Paint a picture. "Listen to 500 dolphins shrieking in panic as they gasp for air." For a memo: "Listen to 500 angry customers screaming for refunds unless you …"

Stress convenience. "Never waste another evening returning videos. We pick them up." Tell your employees how you can make their lives easier. To promote your travel desk, write: "Never stand in line for another ticket."

Emphasize the negative. "Are you making these seven common mistakes in your golf game?" In your office, ask: "Are you making these seven common mistakes in your entries?"

Play on underdog appeal. Remember the brilliant ad: "They laughed when I sat down at the piano"? People love underdogs who succeed. Use, "They laughed when I ordered 100 new …" or "They thought I was nuts when …"

Ask provocative questions. "When an employee gets sick, how long does it take your company to recover?" For a memo: "Are our pumps costing more to operate than they should?"

Use the "barker" technique. "Call your friends … check your fuse box … and get ready to rock … because we're bringing the world's loudest, most awesome …" Those people are excited! Show passion and excitement in your letters. "This company is about to take off like never before!"

Appeal to curiosity/greed. "If you think you could never get a boat, a car and a trip for $22.50, think again." For a memo: "If you thought we can't earn $100,000 with this new product, think again."

Elicit guilt; stress urgency. "In the 10 seconds it took you to open and begin to read this letter, four children died from the effects of malnutrition or disease." Ow! Right to the heart. Perhaps you could use: "In one week our company will waste $10,000 unless you …"

Use bullets. People skip-read. Pros bullet important points. For example, when selling driving glasses they write:

- ◆ Beat headlight glare.
- ◆ Drive through blinding rain.
- ◆ Increase vision and safety.

P.S.: Don't throw away that direct mail! It'll beat any writing course you ever took.

Mr. Theibert lives in Phoenix and is a speech writer for a large Western utility.

NOTES

1. Chapters 13 and 14 are overviews of techniques for improving your business writing. For a more detailed discussion, see Paul R. Timm and Christopher G. Jones, *Business Communication: Getting Results,* 2nd ed. (Englewood Cliffs, NJ: Prentice-Hall, Inc., 1987).

2. Al W. Switzler, a former professor at Brigham Young University, taught this exercise.

3. P. D. Hemphill, *Business Communications* (Englewood Cliffs, NJ: Prentice-Hall, 1976), p. 27. Reprinted by permission of Prentice-Hall, Inc.

4. Bill Repp, "Want Faster, Easier Business Writing? Talk on Paper!" September 1992, p. 7; and Greville Janner, "Towards a Readable Report," *Accountancy,* January 1993, p. 40.

5. John Leach, "Seven Steps to Better Writing," *Planning,* June 1993, pp. 26–27.

6. This example was taken from Bill Repp, "Want Faster, Easier Business Writing? Talk on Paper!" September 1992, p. 7.

7. Herta A. Murphy and Charles E. Peck. *Effective Business Communication,* 2nd ed. (New York: McGraw-Hill, 1976), p. 83.

8. Reprinted with permission from *Wall Street Journal,* April 11, 1994, p. B-28.

CHAPTER 14

FORMATS FOR BUSINESS LETTERS AND MEMOS

Different Situations– Different Approaches

▼

In this chapter you will find ideas that will help you:

♦ Apply the BIF format when writing routine or good-news letters

♦ Describe the options involved in writing a bad-news letter

♦ Cite three components of a persuasive letter

♦ Break the feature lists and build on benefits

♦ Understand the differences between letters and memos

♦ Use *informative* rather than *topical* subject lines for greater impact and content set

♦ Recognize and avoid some of the common failures in business writing

▼

"My style of writing is chiefly grounded upon an early enthusiasm for [Thomas H.] Huxley, the greatest of all masters of orderly exposition. He taught me the importance of giving to every argument a simple structure."

—H. L. MENCKEN[1]

Maria just started her new job as an office administrator at a local automobile dealership. One of her first tasks is to hire a new receptionist. Maria interviewed eight applicants and decided to hire Youchou Hu. She called Youchou and told him that he was hired for the position, and he was thrilled to be chosen. But now Maria must tell the other applicants that they did not get the job. She decides that she wants to write letters to the other applicants—but she doesn't know how to write the letters.

RECOMMENDED FORMATS FOR FUNCTIONAL BUSINESS LETTERS

About 90 percent of the letters written in a typical organization convey some sort of routine information. We send letters to report, to confirm, and to request information. These messages are factual, generally unemotional communications that generate predictable responses. Structuring these messages is easy.

There are, however, situations in which the reader of our letter is likely to get much more emotionally involved with the message we write. To be effective in such situations we need to be aware of psychological factors at work in our communication attempts. In a word, we need to be more reader-sensitive.

Most business communication writers agree that there are only a few basic letter types. The easy ones convey routine, nonemotional messages or good news for the reader. The trickier ones deal with the reader's emotions by conveying disappointment or refusing a request. A third type of letter attempts to get the reader to do something she or he would not normally do (e.g., buy something, pay an overdue bill). Fourth, a goodwill letter focuses on conveying image rather than content. We discuss each of these letter types, and then we'll talk about the difference between letters and memos, and common failures in business writing.

ROUTINE OR GOOD-NEWS LETTERS: USE BIF

Writers should consider the following principles when writing routine letters.

Be Direct

A writer can do little to destroy the effectiveness of a good-news letter. The intent is to tell readers something they are glad to hear, or, at worst, are neutral toward. Efficiency of communication should be an important consideration here. These letters are generally brief—although not curt—and to the point. A direct order of presentation (BIF) should normally be used. This means that the central point of the letter should come first. If you are writing to order 200 Disco-trimmers, start your letter with, "Please send me 200 Disco-trimmers."

The big idea of the letter may then be followed by other relevant subordinate information that clarifies details such as "I am enclosing a check for $1,000" and "Please ship them parcel post to our warehouse at...."

This may seem like a ridiculously simple issue, but many routine letters fail to get directly to the point. They might begin, "We are impressed with your advertisements for the amazing Disco-trimmer" or "We are interested in exploring the possibility of doing business with you." You simply don't need this stuff. Your reader isn't likely to miss the lack of pleasantries since the main thrust of your letter is good news.

Be Complete

> *Be sure that even the simplest letter is complete.*

The letter that is incomplete may fail to do the job. The following story illustrates this point.

Murphy and Peck tell this horror story about a company's direct mail sales campaign. A sales letter, personalized with typed inside address and personal salutation, was to be sent to 100,000 potential customers. The letter ended with the instructions that the reader "could take advantage of the offer" by simply initializing the letter and returning it in the prepaid envelope.

However, to save the expense of having typists insert the 100,000 inside addresses and personal salutations, a budget-minded official requested that the entire message be printed and that all inside addresses be omitted. And the salutation was changed to the general, printed, "Dear Customer." The result was that the company received over 11,000 of the letters back, but no one had had the slightest idea to whom the 11,000 initials belonged![2]

Don't Be Overly Assumptive

Another example of a good-news letter that flops is illustrated by this one received from the president of a university where one of Paul Timm's friends had applied for a job. The opening statement read: "You are hereby appointed Associate Professor ..." The letter sounded more like a coronation than an offer of employment. While my friend was pleased to be offered the position, the tone clearly assumed that he would jump at the opportunity. Instead, the presumptuous sound of the letter turned him off. He declined the job. Even in good-news letters, some sensitivity to tone is necessary.

BAD-NEWS LETTERS: USE BILL

Some business letters convey information the reader is not anxious to hear. Occasionally we need to refuse a request or give some other type of bad news. When this is the case, another cost decision must be made. Is maintaining goodwill with that reader important enough that you are willing to expend some *extra* effort in writing a letter? The alternative is simply to blurt out the bad news and let the public relations chips fall where they may. A tactful, carefully arranged bad-news letter costs more to produce but is likely at least to soften any negative impressions your reader has toward you or your organization. The payoff in maintaining goodwill may be worth the effort.

These are the options: (1) be blunt and organize your bad-news letter in the same direct manner as a routine letter, or (2) apply a pattern of organization that attempts to psychologically soothe the reader or at least create understanding of your viewpoint. If you decide on option 2, here is a way of going about it.

The organization of the indirect bad-news letter includes four ingredients. These are:

- ◆ A buffer
- ◆ The presentation of reasoning
- ◆ The actual refusal or bad news
- ◆ An optimistic close

A Buffer

The buffer sentences or paragraph presents neutral or positive information the reader is not likely to disagree with. Often we thank the reader for his or her interest in the organization. We may also make a general, rather abstract statement that anyone would be likely to agree with. This buffer is designed to get the reader into the rest of the letter—to avoid a premature turnoff before you've had a chance to explain the reasoning behind your refusal. It should cushion the blow. One caution: the buffer should not sound so encouraging that the reader is led to expect a favorable message. Keep it neutral or vaguely positive.

The Presentation of Reasoning

Next, there should be a natural flow from the buffer into the reasoning. Any refusal should be based in reasoning that makes sense to the manager writing the letter and, it is hoped, the reader. The task of this type of letter is in large part to convey that reasoning to the reader so he or she will either agree with the bad news or at least understand *why* you decided as you did. Ideally, the reader will say, "I'm disappointed but I'd probably make the same decision if I were in your shoes."

Your reasons should be logically and clearly presented. Avoid jargon or complexities that the reader may not comprehend. Also avoid the overuse of negative language or words that have undesirable overtones. These can be a real turnoff to your reader. If your decision was based on prudent reasoning, there is no need to sound judgmental in your tone—or to apologize. Be especially careful to avoid words and phrases that may imply a judgment of your reader. The following list illustrates the kinds of hidden meanings that may be conveyed to your reader.[3]

> **Listen for hidden meanings expressed by the tone of your words.**

WORDS AND PHRASE HAVING UNDESIRABLE OVERTONES

If you say	*You imply*
Apparently you are not aware	Not very well informed, are you?
Our records show	You can't be telling the truth.
We are not inclined to	We do as we wish.
We cannot understand your	You don't make yourself clear.
We differ from you	We must be right.
We do not agree with your	So you are wrong.

We question your	You're probably either wrong or lying.
We repeated to you	Must we tell you over and over?
Why didn't you?	You are so stupid, forgetful, negligent.
You apparently overlooked	You are careless.
You are misinformed	Somebody lied to you; it wasn't I.
You complain	Crybaby!
You are wrong	Arguing again, are you?
You contend	Carelessness!
You did not include	Stupid!
You do not realize	How dumb can you be?
You do not understand	Not efficient!

Get the idea? Even seemingly innocent phrases can convey a subtle accusation—and severely damage your message's tone.

In addition to choosing words carefully, we should try to avoid the use of but and however when these mark a direct shift in tone. The abruptness of the change can destroy any goodwill you've salvaged to this point. Here's a letter Paul Timm received several years ago which classically illustrates how *not* to write a refusal letter. Paul Timm had written to this individual requesting permission to do some interviewing and to administer questionnaires to employees in his organization. He began his response with a pretty good buffer, but look where he went from there.

Instead of moving from his fairly good buffer into reasoning, this writer shifted gears with the deadly "however." If Paul Timm had not recognized the value of this letter as a classic bad example to use in my classes, he would have been quite upset.

```
Dear Paul:

Thanks for your letter of November 10. Very happy to
hear from you and I'm delighted you are finishing your
graduate work.

I've been giving your proposal to do some research work
in the Orlando District a great deal of thought. Your
project sounds interesting and it is the kind of thing
I've personally been interested in for several years.
However, after having considered your request, I've
decided to decline your offer.

I hope you will be able to conduct your research else-
where without any difficulty and I wish you the very
best.


Yours very truly,

District Manager
```

The Actual Refusal or Bad News

Be tactful but conclusive. The actual refusal or bit of bad news should be carefully worded and strategically placed to avoid undue emphasis on it. At the same time it must be clear so that there is no misunderstanding on the part of the reader. He or she must see the matter as closed to further discussion—otherwise additional correspondence (and cost) may be generated and you may end up with a pen pal.

To soften the blow, phrase the bad news in the passive voice ("your request must be denied") versus active voice ("I am denying your request"). Alternatively, position the actual refusal so that it naturally receives less emphasis. The positions of strongest emphasis (which should normally be avoided for bad news) are at the very beginning and the very end of each paragraph or the total letter. The top positions are emphasized because they are the first words the reader sees in each paragraph. The end positions are phrases that tend to linger in the reader's mind and are thus emphasized.

> *Here's where passive voice can be useful.*

The two strongest emphasis positions in the whole letter are the first and the very last phrases written. Your refusal or bad-news phrase would be best positioned toward the *middle* of the letter for de-emphasis. Two other suggestions for this section of your bad news letter are: (1) offer a lesser alternative, and (2) don't hide behind policy.

Offer a Lesser Alternative

Often it is appropriate to offer the reader an alternative to the original request. The alternative should be explained in a positive tone conveying the assumption that it will be accepted. The letter on the following page illustrates such an effective refusal.

One final point about offering an alternative: make it easy for the reader to accept. We've seen dozens of letters that simply toss the ball back to the reader. Here is an example of the refusal-with-alternative section of such a letter.

"After checking my travel schedule for the remainder of the year, I find I will be out of town on the date you wanted me to visit your group.

If some other date would be acceptable or if another person from our company could be of help, please write to me again."

A letter such as this one fails to achieve closure—the problem remains unresolved. If your letter must refuse a request, do so in explicit terms so there is no misunderstanding. But if you offer an alternative, follow through on the new idea. Don't just give the problem back to the reader and start the whole letter and response cycle over again. Offering a lesser alternative should not be used as a way to avoid saying no. It should be used only when you genuinely want to offer an option to the reader.

Mr. Bob Gambrell, President
Young Businessperson's Federation
119 North Central
Hamburg, N.C. 28104

Dear Mr. Gambrell:

We are highly complimented by your interest in the
kinds of employee motivation programs we are developing
here at SYNECTIC-SYSTEMS. Your request that I speak to
your group in November is personally flattering and has
been considered carefully.

After checking my travel schedule for the remainder of
the year, I find I have a conflict with the November 19
date you mentioned. I will be attending a conference in
New York and will not return until November 22. May I
suggest an alternative?

Dr. Elliott Anderson has recently joined our organization. He brings excellent academic background and seven
years' industrial psychology experience with a major
manufacturing organization on the West Coast. He is
anxious to know more people in the area and has indicated a willingness to talk with your group on November
19.

Elliott is an excellent speaker and I'm sure you'll
enjoy his presentation. He will be calling you to confirm this early next week.

Again, we appreciate the opportunity to speak to your
fine group.

Cordially,

SYNECTIC SYSTEMS

George Bell

Don't Hide Behind Policy

If policy is the reason, explain the policy.

If you sincerely want to spare your reader's feelings, explain your reasoning as vividly as possible.
One quick way to aggravate your reader is to cite
"company policy" as *the* reason for a refusal.
Policy is, or should be, based on *reasons*. Simply
to cite policy without getting into the underlying reasons for that policy is like
saying "because" when asked why?—not a very satisfactory answer.

An Optimistic Close

Once the refusal has been clearly and tactfully conveyed, an optimistic close, which is similar in function to the buffer, should be written. Here we are interested in further repairing any damage to goodwill that may have occurred. Expressing confidence that a good business relationship will continue is one approach. It is important that you do *not apologize*. If, in fact, your decision has been based on sound, adult reasoning, there is no need to apologize. In fact, the effusive apology may cause your reader to question the reasoning. "The lady doth protest too much" implies underlying guilt for some imagined misdeed. Instead, confidently express a desire to maintain a favorable relationship with the reader.

As you can see, the bad-news letter requires more thought and effort than the routine informational letter. Its payoff lies in projecting a favorable, caring image to the reader.

NOT EVERYONE AGREES WITH THIS BAD-NEWS FORMAT

While the bad-news format just described is widely regarded as an effective way to deal with potentially sticky situations, some maintain that it's not worth the effort. One communication consultant, responding to an article that recommended careful use of this bad-news pattern when refusing job applicants, advocated "directness in 'no' letters—not rude bluntness, but straight-to-the-pointness." He went on to say, "I believe we patronize an unsuccessful applicant when, from whatever motivation, we lead him through a circuitous route to the core of our message." His alternative is to say something like this: "Dear Mr. Applicant: If it disappoints you to learn that we have selected another candidate to fill the position for which you applied, we want you to know that this reflects no unfavorable assessment of you or your excellent qualifications."[4]

This individual's view was primarily critical of the bad-news letter that sounds overly optimistic in the buffer section only to shift gears with the deadly "however" paragraph. Although we agree that the transition from buffer to refusal is sometimes too abrupt, we do not advocate throwing out this time-tested pattern in favor of the more direct one. We will concede, however, that some mature people could accept the more direct format without being offended. But some could not. Stick with the bad-news format to be safe.

PERSUASIVE REQUESTS: USE BILL

The persuasive business letter, like the persuasive oral presentation, is *action* oriented. It seeks to get the reader to *do* something he or she normally would not do without some prodding. The letter's effectiveness can often be judged by the action that results. The effective sales letter sells. The effective collection letter collects. By their fruits shall they be evaluated.

> *Resistance to change is a formidable competitor of persuasion.*

Persuasive communication situations presuppose some resistance to your proposals in the mind of your reader. Your message calls for action and action implies change. Change requires effort, and expending effort is something most of us would just as soon avoid. It's the writer's job to motivate the reader to expend the effort to change in the desired direction. To do so, we need to make some guesses about our readers' needs, wants, and motives.

Letters that persuade people normally require a slow, deliberate approach. They need to be phrased in terms of the reader's interests, not the writer's. They need to employ vivid language that conveys clear images. The underlying theme of the entire letter should be one of explaining the benefits of your proposal to your reader. And the letter should follow a systematic arrangement that leads the reader inevitably to the desired action. The three components of the persuasive letter are: the attention getter, the explanation of the proposal, and the action getter.

Getting the Reader's Attention

Just as in the persuasive oral presentation, it is crucial that we grab the message receiver's attention immediately. Remember, the very first line is a position of emphasis in your letter—so use it wisely. Lead with your strongest motivator and don't waste any words.

Success	Power and Status Enhancement	Self-Satisfaction	Curiosity
Positive Appeals Acting will lead to the reader's success in accomplishing goals. *Example:* "You can break into the million-dollar sales club…"	Acting will improve the reader's power and status. *Example:* "Want to get others to perk up and listen when you have something to say?"	Acting will lead to a sense of satisfaction for the reader. *Example:* "How would you like to be your own boss?"	Acting will answer questions the reader would like answered. *Example:* "How would you like to know your competitor's exact pricing tables?"
Negative Appeals Not acting will lead to the reader's failure to accomplish goals. *Example:* "Can you be satisfied with another average sales year?"	Not acting will cost the reader loss of power or status. *Example:* "Are other young executives passing you by?"	Not acting will lead to dissatisfaction or missed opportunity for the reader. *Example:* "How much longer can you take the drudgery of your your 8-to-5 job?"	Not acting will leave important questions unanswered. *Example:* "Is what you don't know about the competition killing you?"

FIGURE 14-1 **Attention-getting appeals.**

Attention getters can take several forms but all should appeal to the reader, not necessarily the writer. Joel Bowman and Bernadine Branchaw suggest four categories of appeals we can make to gain reader attention. We can appeal to the reader's needs for *health, wealth, pleasure,* and to his or her *curiosity.*[5]

In the organization we might add appeals to the need for *success, power* or *status enhancement,* and *self-satisfaction.* Such attention-getting appeals may be phrased positively or negatively. Positive appeals focus on what the reader stands to gain; whereas negative appeals accentuate what the reader might lose if he or she does not pay attention to your message. Examples of such appeals are presented in Figure 14-1.

Often the attention getter combines interest-creating information with a description of a problem. Television commercials typically follow this pattern, presenting an unpleasant situation in such a way that we can identify with the victim of, say, ring around the collar or indigestion or the restaurant hamburger with very little meat (Where's the beef?).

The intent is to depict a problem that can be solved by the product they want you to buy. Although TV spots are exaggerations, the persuasive pattern of attention, need development, and need solution is often an effective one. In this letter excerpt the persuasive intent is to get the reader to contribute to the university radio station. Here is the opening need-developing phase:

With the recent change of WBCY-FM to a rock music format, those of us who enjoy listening to stereo radio are stuck. There remains only one such station in our community. And because of this no-competition situation, that station has increased its advertising time and reduced the amount of beautiful music.

I still like the soft sounds of our one remaining station, WEZC-FM, and I suspect you do too. But is seems absurd that a city this size cannot offer more than one high quality station. What would we do if WEZC were to follow their competitor into the lucrative rock radio market? We'd all suffer the loss. Charlotte needs another FM station to play the kind of music discriminating adults enjoy.

Now you and I can play a part in filling that need and guaranteeing the continuation of our kind of music. The State legislature has pledged $70,000 in matching funds to WFAE-FM, the university radio station, if we can raise only $20,000.

Explaining the Proposal in Terms of the Reader

Once the opening appeal has succeeded in gaining the reader's interest, the writer's job is to explain how the need perceived can be satisfied. You need to show the reader what personal benefit is to be gained.

Many persuasive requests run afoul when the writer forgets the "you" attitude. The following letter illustrates what we mean. This letter was used by a political candidate to raise money for his campaign. It was printed on letterhead paper, personally signed, and was a generally attractive document. But let's consider the content:

$15,279.47

The figure above is the amount which I must raise in order to win election to the North Carolina House of Representatives.

You are one of 700 friends I feel that I can count on. I'm asking for your financial support in the amount of $21.83!!!

July 25th is the date we must have all money on hand!!!

Please make checks payable to: Alan Jones for N.C. House and forward to: John S. Fredericks, Treasurer, 2011 Doughton Road, Charlotte, N.C. 28207.

Thank you for you consideration.

Sincerely,

Alan Jones

Obviously the tone is I-oriented. The use of the dollar figure at the top of the page is fairly effective—it does spark curiosity in the reader. The use of exclamation points and underlining for emphasis seems out of place. Exclamation points give us the image of a circus barker.

Suppose you were working on this candidate's campaign. How would you rewrite this message to create a you orientation?" First, consider what the reader potentially has to gain by doing the desired action (sending in $21.83). We may want to appeal to the reader's need or desire to have good people elected to public office, assuming, of course, that they perceive this candidate to be a good person. But, more specifically, most people are likely to feel a sense of status enhancement in having a friend they supported get elected to office. A positive appeal may imply that their contribution will result in the candidate's election and that his election will give them some special influence in the legislature. Thinking along these lines, we might rework this letter, adding a you orientation, like this:

$15,279.47

The figure above is what it will cost to put your representative in the North Carolina House.

You are one of 700 friends I value deeply. Your past friendship and support have led me to believe that we share similar concerns for our state government and that I can effectively represent your interests in Raleigh. To bring this about, I'm asking for your financial help. Your contribution of only $21.83 puts us in a position where we can, and will, win the election on November 7.

To meet our campaign expenses, the money needs to be in the hands of John Fredericks, my Campaign Treasurer, by July 25. With your help, your voice will be heard in the upcoming legislative session.

Cordially,

Alan Jones

Explaining your proposal to the reader calls for action verbs and concrete nouns to create the vivid images people respond to. Often this calls for a longer letter, but without such detail, the persuasive appeal will fail.

Selling Reader Benefits, Not Product Features

As we explain our proposal, we should seek to gain the reader's interest and create desire. To accomplish this, you must clearly understand the distinction between the *features* of your product or proposal and the *benefits* to the reader. The skillful sales representative alludes to the product's features only as they

> *Features simply describe; benefits sell.*

relate to the benefits the customer will enjoy. The feature is some attribute of the thing you are selling. The benefit is what the feature means to the customer.

Paul Timm used to work with sales representatives for a large office products manufacturer. The copying machines the firm sold had a number of features not available on competing machines at that time. They could copy on both sides of the paper automatically, reproduce from light originals, reduce the original onto a sheet half the size, and so on. Time after time I heard sales reps sell these *features* but fail to sell the product. The successful persuader was the one who tied features to benefits: "This machine copies on both sides of a sheet (a feature). What this means to you, Mr. Customer, is that you can cut your paper costs significantly, reduce postage costs, perhaps even reduce the need for additional filing cabinets. This feature can save you a lot of money (the benefits)."

Let's apply this feature-benefit distinction to a persuasive request made to another department. The example on the following page is an effort to persuade one manager that another manager's suggestion is good enough that he should pay for it.

Helen is translating the features of her idea to the benefits by explaining "What this means to you...."

Features	*What This Means to You*
Gail majored in operations management.	Her training can be usefully applied to our problem.
Gail has been trained in business systems	She can trace orders through the system to pinpoint problems.
Gail is not yet permanently assigned	We can pay her out of our temporary budget and use her only as long as needed.

April 19, 1995
Jackson Gray, Manager
Installations and Repair
Central Telephone
Piedmont, Ohio 45701

Dear Jack:

Would you like to know why almost 15 percent of our orders are being worked later than the time agreed upon with the customer? And why both your service index and mine are among the lowest in the Division? I'd like to find out before we get a lot more heat from the Area manager.

Jack, we've talked about this ongoing problem for several months and neither of us seems to be able to pinpoint the problem. Here's an idea I'd like to share with you.

My District Manager has just hired a management trainee named Gail Engles. Gail is a recent Ohio State graduate with a major in business systems—exactly where we seem to be having problems. We could turn her loose with a stopwatch and some checksheets to see where our operations are fouling up. She could trace sample orders through the whole system.

Since Gail hasn't yet been assigned permanent duties, the only cost to us is that she'd have to be paid out of our temporary help or overtime budget. And we'd be obligated to use her only as long as she's needed. I think we should take advantage of this.

I'd appreciate it if you'd do two things. First check to see if you can swing one-half her salary costs for two or three weeks. Her base salary is $14,200. I'll pay the other half. Second, go with me to the DM's office to make the request. I think he'll be glad to see our interdepartmental cooperation on this.

I'll call next Monday the 23rd to confirm all this. I really think this will improve our customer service and help us avoid some future grief from the Area people.

Sincerely,

Helen Baker, Manager
Commercial Operations

Getting the Reader's Action

The third phase of the persuasive letter is specifying for the reader what action you'd like to see occur. In the example just cited, the writer requested two things: check the budget and go to the district manager's office with the writer. Often this action step is accompanied by a reminder of the benefits to be gained, a form of reselling the idea.

In addition to stating clearly what should be done and reminding the reader why, the action step should set a deadline or provide some other incentive to act soon. The promise of a follow-up call in the foregoing example does this. The action step should also make it easy for the reader to comply. Often a mail back reply card, a phone number, or promise of a follow-up call or visit alleviates some of the burden for the reader.

> *Action steps should be what- and when-specific.*

The tone of the action step should be assumptive. Assume that your reader has understood and agreed with your reasoning and now simply needs to be pushed a bit to obtain the benefits you promise. There is no need to be hesitant. Remember, what you're telling your reader to do is for his or her own benefit.

GOODWILL LETTERS

A goodwill letter is one you write even though you don't have to. Many managers, by failing to send goodwill letters, overlook an excellent opportunity to promote good feelings in their organization. Few things make an employee feel better than to receive from the boss a brief letter of appreciation, congratulations, sympathy, or concern. It only takes a minute, yet it can help to develop good employee relations.

As a manager for a telephone company, Paul Timm used to make it a point to send short letters to the homes of employees whose work was exemplary. The payoff for such a simple action is that: (1) the employee knows you recognize and appreciate their good work, (2) by sending the letter home, you allow the employee's family to share in the praise, (3) the letter can become a part of the employee's personnel file, and (4) by noting that copies have been sent to higher levels of management, the employee knows he or she is getting additional attention.

Opportunities for goodwill notes come up almost daily. In addition to on-the-job performance, personal and family accomplishments can be acknowledged. A daughter's wedding, an impressive bowling score, and recognition for community service can all be opportunities to show you care.

DIFFERENCES BETWEEN LETTERS AND MEMOS

Everything we've said about effective and efficient letters also applies to memos. A memorandum is essentially an "inside" letter. It serves to convey written messages *within* the organization. Because of this, a memo may differ slightly from a letter in that

1. It is less formal
2. Its writer is probably already known to the receiver
3. It normally conveys only one theme and is organized in a direct format
4. It frequently employs shortcuts that streamline the message, such as subject lines and enumeration of key ideas (often using incomplete sentences).

Subject Lines Create Content Set

A memo has two main parts, a heading and a body. The heading consists of four pieces of information at the top of the page: (1) the names of the intended receivers (the *To:* line); (2) the name or title of the writer (the *From:* line); (3) the date; and (4) the subject of the message. The subject line can be particularly useful in speeding the flow of information.

Two types of subject lines are commonly used: topical and informative. The *topical* subject line describes in a word or two the general subject matter of the memo. Although this may serve as a guide for filing, we strongly recommend using an informative subject line instead.

The *informative* subject line actually states the main point of the memo. Informative subject lines should be as specific as possible.[6] Since most memos convey routine, nonemotional information, placing the big idea in an informative subject line makes a great deal of sense. Your reader can grasp the main point immediately. If you need to get an idea to a busy executive who may only scan memos, this type of subject line will improve your chances of success. In the following list of topical and informative subject lines, note how much more information is immediately presented in the informative style.

> **The big idea can be quickly expressed in the subject line.**

Topical	Informative
Guest speaker	Bob Dole will be guest speaker at Kwanis Luncheon
Air travel on expense account	Reimbursement for business travel will be tourist class fare only

Advanced management program	You have been selected to participate in the Advanced Management Program on May 28
New policy on rental car insurance	Don't buy the dollar-per-day supplemental insurance when renting a car
Staff meeting	The entire staff will meet April 26 at 2 p.m. in room 374

Enumeration or Itemization

In memo format, itemizing a series of points is a common way to streamline the message. Compare the two memos below—one with itemization, one without. Which communicates more efficiently? Which has better *access*?

```
Date: April 16, 1994
To: Jean Kovatz, Assistant Supervisor
From: Pat Reynolds, Manager
Subject: Manager's Conference

Please contact the people at the Hilton in Greenville
to arrange for our upcoming conference. We will need
rooms for 30 managers (singles) for the nights of July
13, 14, and 15. Also arrange for a buffet dinner on
the 13th, a happy hour for the evening of the 15th,
and the conference room with tables and seating for 30
people from 9 a.m. to 5 p.m. all three days. Breakout
rooms for groups of 6 or 7 near the conference room
will be needed for the afternoon of the 14th. Be sure
they have a 35mm movie projector, overhead projector,
and flip charts. We should also have them bring in
coffee, juice, and doughnuts in the morning (about 10)
each day and soft drinks about 3 each afternoon.
Thanks for taking care of this.
```

Here is the same memo using an informative subject line and itemization. Notice how much easier it is to grasp the details. This memo could also serve as a checklist for those making the arrangements.

To: Jean Kovatz, Assistant Manager

From: Pat Reynolds, Manager

Date: April 16, 1994

Subject: ROOMS, SERVICES, AND EQUIPMENT NEEDED FOR THE
MANAGER'S MEETING, JULY 13,14, and 15.

Please arrange the following with the people at the
Hilton in Greenville.

ROOMS:

- 30 single rooms for the nights of July 13, 14, and
  15
- Conference room with tables and seating for 30 from
  9 a.m. to 5 p.m. on all three days
- Five breakout rooms for the afternoon of the 14th
  (six people per room)

EQUIPMENT NEEDED IN THE CONFERENCE ROOM ON JULY 13,
14, AND 15:

- 35mm movie projector
- Overhead projector for transparencies
- Screen
- Flip chart—tripod with paper

FOOD SERVICE:

- Buffet dinner the evening of the 13th
- Happy hour bar and snacks the evening of the 15th
- Coffee, juice, and doughnuts July 13, 14, and 15 at
  10:00 a.m.
- Soft drinks July 13, 14, and 15 at 3:00 p.m.

Thank you for taking care of this.

SOME COMMON FAILURES OF LETTERS AND MEMOS

If you were to analyze the letters and memos produced in your organization, you would be likely to find some effective letters and some that missed opportunities to create understanding and project a favorable image. Some common problems of written messages include the failure to:

♦ Eliminate noise from the message

♦ Sound human

♦ Conceal irritation

♦ Use creativity

♦ Give your letter clout

♦ Cool off before writing

Failure to Eliminate Noise from the Message

Anything that distracts the reader from the message can be considered noise. Among the most common sources of noise are unattractive paper or letterhead, smeared type, light type due to an old printer cartridge, margins too narrow, and coffee stains or finger smudges on the letter. In addition, misspellings and obvious grammatical errors create distractions and reflect on the credibility of the writer. The following letter is a replica of one that Paul Timm's friend received from his bank: a classic noisy note. He no longer banks there.

```
Dear Mr. Prewitt,

Since Milton Anderson insist on keeping a copy of the
deposit ticket that he sends us maybe if you would
give him these deposit that we have send you. Please
tell him to keep only one pink copy and send us all of
the other copies to us.

He has been tearing off the white copy which we need
to process to the deposit.

Sincerely,

Norwood Office
```

Failure to Sound Human

Most people resent getting a mechanical-sounding message. Here's an example of a mechanical message from a mortgage company:

```
IMPORTANT COMMUNICATION NOTICE TO ALL MORTGAGORS

WE ARE PLEASED TO ANNOUNCE THAT WE HAVE RECENTLY COMPLETED
A MAJOR CHANGE IN OUR ACCOUNTING PROCEDURES. WE FELT THIS
CHANGE TO COMPUTER PROCESSING WAS NECESSARY IN ORDER TO
PROVIDE ADDITIONAL SERVICES TO YOU IN RESPONSE TO MANY
REQUESTS RELATIVE TO ESCROW AND LOAN ACCOUNTING INFORMA-
TION. HOWEVER, IN ORDER TO FACILITATE PROMPT RESPONSES TO
YOUR INQUIRIES WHICH WE DESIRE TO RENDER AS SERVICER OF
YOUR MORTGAGE AND TO ASSURE PROMPT CREDIT OF PAYMENTS TO
YOUR MORTGAGE, WE REQUEST THAT YOU PLACE YOUR ACCOUNT NUM-
BER ON ALL CORRESPONDENCE AND CHECKS OR MONEY ORDERS COM-
MENCING JUNE 1.
          YOUR ACCOUNT NUMBER IS 01976328.
WE APPRECIATE YOUR USUAL FINE COOPERATION AND SUPPORT IN
OUR ENDEAVOR TO FURNISH ADDITIONAL SERVICES AND INFORMA-
TION FOR YOU.
```

Not only does this message sound machinelike, but it is terribly wordy and uses an indirect approach to convey a simple message: Put your account number on all correspondence and checks. It's bad enough to get a letter from a machine—but when it talks down to you, *it's downright maddening.*

Failure to Conceal Irritation

We all receive letters occasionally that are, frankly, a pain in the neck. The question we face is whether we should answer at all, and, if so, how much effort should we exert? Is the potential goodwill created worth the cost? One of our colleagues once wrote to a professional football team asking for information about their organization structure for a research paper she was doing. Two executives answered her request. Their replies show marked contrast in concern for goodwill. Here is the response from a vice president of the organization:

```
Dear M. McFarland:

In answer to your letter, I would be happy to discuss in
general terms the subject matter whenever it might be con-
venient to you.

It is a little too complex to answer in letter form as you
suggested.

We appreciate your interest.

Sincerely,
```

Here is the response from the president:

Dear Carol:

Thank you for you interest in the Buffalo Bills and in our organization.

Generally, pro football organizations are of two types: one with a head coach/general manager and the other with separate coach and general manager. Ours is the latter form with our general manager supervising our public relations, stadium operations, ticket and marketing departments. The Head Coach supervises his assistant coaches and works closely with the head of our player personnel (scouting) department.

The team physician is an independent contractor with a medical practice outside of his services to the Bills, while the trainers are employees of the Bills.

I appreciate your interest in our organizational set-up and your support.

With kind regards.

Sincerely,

BUFFALO BILLS

For a few additional moments of thought, this writer satisfied, at least in a general sense, the reader's request and conveyed a sense of goodwill.

Failure to Use Creativity

Many business writers feel bound to the traditional business letter format. For some reason we hesitate to set up the letter differently. The letter on the following page is an example of one who dared to be different. This letter, from a manager of an insurance agency, cleverly encourages the reader to respond—to establish a dialogue.

Failure to Give Your Letter Clout

If it deserves priority, send a copy to the boss.

One way to give a business letter clout is to let the reader know that others are also reading the letter. This can be done by simply "copying in" others. For example, suppose you are writing to

There are two sides to every question—one half of this letter is for your side.

THIS HALF IS MINE

You have been a valued policyholder for some time, but recently you neglected to pay your premium. There must be a reason for this, and I am writing you because I am sincerely interested in knowing that reason and wondering if we could be of assistance. Will you please use your half of this letter to tell me WHY? I can assure you that it will receive my personal attention.

Sincerely,

Manager

P.S. If you have already made arrangements to reinstate your policy, disregard this letter and accept our thanks. If you now wish to reinstate, please complete the attached form and return it with your remittance of $231.67.

Thank you.   THIS HALF IS YOURS

another division about a problem in receiving parts from them. By copying in an executive with authority over both divisions, you serve notice that others are being made aware of the problem. A simple "cc: John Robinson, Division Manager" adds clout.

Consumer advocates have long recognized the added power that comes from a complaint letter to, say, a local auto dealership, when the automaker's regional manager or even corporate president is copied in. The copy in technique must be done discretely and ethically, especially when communicating sensitive information.

By the same token, a goodwill letter of congratulations to an employee means more when others are copied in. And, of course, a notation indicating that the letter will go into the employee's personnel file also makes the recipient feel good.

Failure to Cool Off Before Writing

A final reason letters flop—or in this case, bomb—is that people write when they are hot under the collar. Many a blistering memo has haunted the normally thoughtful manager. Paul Timm once wrote a devastating reply to a message received from the personnel department that had advised him that some medical expenses he had incurred were not covered under his group insurance. He also expressed his conviction that the people working on his case were inept, unconcerned, and generally not too bright. No sooner had he mailed his missile, than the personnel manager called to explain that after considerable research effort they had found a loophole under which he was covered. One large crow was eaten.

Very few letters require an *immediate* response. When you get a maddening letter, go ahead and write the response, but then file it for a few days' cooling-off period. Just be sure your secretary doesn't mail it before you've reworked it.

A QUICK SUMMARY OF MAJOR IDEAS

- Routine and good-news letters should be direct and complete. Do not, however, assume too much.

- Bad-news letters generally should include a buffer, reasoning, the actual refusal or bad news, and an optimistic close. Be particularly sensitive to word tone, abrupt shifts from a buffer to the reasoning, clear phrasing of the refusal, and the offering of a possible alternative.

- Persuasive requests should begin with an attention-getter that appeals to the reader's needs. Need development and need solution should be clearly communicated, and features of the recommended solution (the big idea) should be phrased in terms of reader benefits.

- Informative subject lines can create content set and are generally preferable to topical subject lines.

- ◆ Some common problems of written messages include the failure to:
  - — Eliminate noise from the message
  - — Sound human
  - — Conceal irritation
  - — Use creativity
  - — Give your letter clout
  - — Cool off before writing

QUESTIONS FOR FURTHER THOUGHT

1. Do you agree with the recommended format for the bad-news letter presented in this chapter? If not, why not? How might your pattern of arrangement reflect your management style?

2. What are some key things to avoid when writing (a) routine messages, (b) bad-news messages, (c) persuasive requests?

OTHER THOUGHTS ABOUT FORMATS FOR BUSINESS LETTERS AND MEMOS

NOTE JOTTING MADE SIMPLE
by Jim Woodford

How many times have you found yourself scrambling for something to jot a note down on? And what were you in the middle of doing when you started scrambling? A business luncheon used to be my favorite place for doing this. I tore up more napkins at these functions, only to find a rolled up ball of napkin fragments in my pocket when my suit came back from the cleaners. I've also written on sugar packets, doggie bags, and newspapers—to mention just a few. I've often thought it would be interesting to conduct a survey on the most unusual things people have used as notepads.

I found a solution to my dilemma: three by five cards. They're perfect. You can write down quite a bit of information on one of these cards, and they fit right in your pocket or purse. Not only that, but when you get to the office you can easily file them for future reference.

NOTES IN THE OFFICE

You may find 3 × 5 cards quite handy when you're talking on the telephone. It's pretty simple to slip a card out of your pocket to jot something down. I've also found it helpful as I walk down the hall at work. I don't know about you, but normally I find myself in and out of several conversations between the time I leave my work station and the time I return. Sometimes I get distracted enough that I don't even remember what my original intentions were—the 3 × 5 card can be useful for directing efforts, too.

Before you leave your office to go talk with someone else, jot down what you need on one of your cards. As you get involved in side conversations heading to your destination, make pertinent notes for future reference. It's likely that you'll agree to get back to somebody on something, and if you jot down a reminder on a 3 × 5 card it will save you the embarrassment of later having to admit that you forgot. Then if you get to the point at which you forget what you originally set out to do, just glance at the 3 × 5 card before you start down the hall and you're back in business.

MORE HELPFUL HINTS

Another way you can use a 3 × 5 card is to jot down reminders of things you know you need to do (or maybe you remember something that you forgot to do) on your way home from work. Maybe you need to pick up a birthday card or some groceries. It may seem simplistic, but writing these things dow on a 3 × 5 card can make a difference in your own life.

You can use a 3 × 5 card as a bookmark and make notes on it about specific pages in the book you may want to refer to at a later date. I've also had success in using them to remind me of things I need to do in the heat of a busy day. Just jot down your reminder note on the bottom half of the card and fold it in half—it works just like a place card.

This little practice has served me well at times when I was interrupted by a phone call while I was in the middle of something important. I'd agree to do something for the caller, hang up the phone, and get right back into what I was doing before the phone rang. Invariably, I'd forget what it was I'd agreed to on the phone. But when I jot down this information on my 3×5 card and fold it, I have an instant reminder right on my desk. You can create a mini "to do" list this way as well.

If you happen to be partial to colors, 3×5 cards come in a variety of shades. I prefer white unlined cards because there's nothing to restrict creativity. And one final point: You may also find that at the end of a particularly hectic day or at the end of a particularly unpleasant task, chances are you'll get immense pleasure from ripping up those 3×5 cards. It beats $100 a pop talking to a therapist!

Jim Woodford is head of a management consulting firm in Xenia, Ohio. © 1992, Jim Woodford.

NOTES

1. Quoted in William H. Nolte, *H. L. Mencken: Literary Critic* (Middletown, CT: Wesleyan University Press, 1955), p. 33.

2. Herta A. Murphy and Charles E. Peck, *Effective Business Communication,* 2nd ed. (New York: McGraw-Hill, 1976), p. 80.

3. Robert M. Archer and Ruth Pearson Ames, *Basic Business Communications* (Englewood Cliffs, NJ:Prentice-Hall, 1971), pp. 391–392. Reprinted with permission.

4. Frederick W. Harbaugh in a letter to the editor of *The ABCA Bulletin,* September 1977, p. 23.

5. Joel P. Bowman and Bernadine P. Branchaw, *Effective Business Communication* (San Francisco: Canfield Press, 1979), p. 149.

6. The *Style Guide* by Shipley Associates (Sidney L. Jenson and R. Breck England (editors), *Style Guide* [Revised Edition], 1992) suggests that all subject lines should be informative subject lines.

CHAPTER 15

PLANNING AND PRODUCING EFFECTIVE BUSINESS REPORTS

In this chapter you will find ideas that will help you:

♦ Ask four key questions as you plan the business report

♦ Describe and use four basic ways to find information to be used in reports

♦ Be realistic about the time and costs involved in producing a report

♦ Write short reports as extended memos

♦ Begin longer reports with an effective proposal

♦ Apply a five-step procedure for organizing, writing, and editing individually prepared reports

♦ Apply an effective committee report-writing strategy

The following story illustrates a typical situation calling for a business report: During its first three years in business, Comatose Waterbed and Stereo, Inc., has enjoyed tremendous success. From a single 1,500-square-foot store on Bailey Avenue in Buffalo, Comatose has blossomed into a five-location business. Sales this year have increased by an astounding 560 percent over last year. The owners, Marge and Toni Bastioni, are delighted. But now they've set their sights even higher.

Last Tuesday morning, Tony Bastioni had a chance to visit with Chico Roberts, manager of the Tonawanda store. Their conversation went something like this:

Tony began, "Chico, your store is the best in the company. You've done a heck of a job, and Marge and I appreciate your efforts."

"Thanks, chief," said Chico. "This company has been good to me, too."

"That's why I wanted to talk to you," Tony continued. "I want to expand beyond Western New York. I'm playing with the idea of offering Comatose franchises nationwide. And I'd like your help."

"What can I do?"

"You've got a pretty solid degree in business administration, and my guess is you could pull together some information I need. What I'd like you to do, Chico, is take a few days off and put together a report for me. I need to know how to set up a franchising organization. I'd also like some suggestions about how to market the franchise, what locations would be most promising, where to advertise, and how much to charge."

"Sounds like a big order, Tony. Let me go over to the university library and see what I can dig up. I'll write you a proposal first before putting together a full-blown report."

"Great. Let me know how much time and whatever other help you'll need. And Chico, this is *really* important to our company...."

A GOOD REPORT GIVES ITS READERS
WHAT THEY NEED TO KNOW

> **Good reports are functional.**

Virtually every aspect of the manager's job revolves around having good information. Reports of various types, ranging from a simple computer printout to an extensive printed analysis running hundreds of pages, provide such data. In this chapter we are concerned with people-generated reports that gather a variety of types of information into a digestible format for managerial action. These reports may be routine, such as those that provide production figures, membership data, and sales results, or special reports (like the one Tony asked Chico for) that deal with specific organizational problems or issues and generally include more than just raw data.

THREE PURPOSES FOR BUSINESS REPORTS

When a report project is assigned, the person or group doing the work should be told their specific purpose—the extent and nature of the information-gathering task. There are three general purposes for business reports:

- ◆ Simply to supply data (an *informational* report)
- ◆ To make some analysis and integration of the data (an *interpretive* report)
- ◆ To specify a recommended action (an *analytical decision* report)

Regardless of the type and extent of the report, its emphasis should be on functional communication of ideas that will help solve organizational problems and keep the company on track, working toward its objectives.

Business communication professor Ray Lesikar defines a business report as *an orderly and objective communication of factual information which serves some business purpose.*[1] We've already talked about purposes, but there are two other key terms in that definition that deserve emphasis. First a report is *orderly*; it has been carefully prepared so that its contents are arranged in a predetermined fashion. More emphasis is generally placed on care in preparation of the written report than in other, less formal media.

A second key term is *objective*. A report should report, not express opinions. Special emphasis is placed on facts. The report writer should be especially sensitive to the problem of separating facts from inferences (see Chapter 2).

When opinion, guesses, hunches, or predictions are made, they should be clearly labeled as such so the reader will not mistakenly assume they are facts. Objectivity requires such clarification. It also demands that all relevant data or evidence be presented in such a way that we do not stack the deck in favor of or in opposition to a particular viewpoint.

The successful report gives its readers factual, useful information. It attempts to present such information in an unbiased, objective, and orderly manner.

FOUR KEY QUESTIONS FOR PLANNING THE BUSINESS REPORT

Careful thinking can save hours later.

Reports involve research, and research involves *planned inquiry*. One of the most important and time-saving steps in report preparation is to think through the research project along general lines before you dig in. Ten or fifteen minutes of concentrated thought may save hours of wheel-spinning effort later. This thinking-through process should focus on several questions:

- *Why is this report being prepared?* Usually because management needs specific information to make a decision.
- *How will I know when the purpose has been achieved?* When the boss' questions are clearly answered and a course of action is decided on.
- *Who will be reading this?* Often the intended audience will affect the way in which one chooses to present information in a report.
- *Where can I get the best possible information?* That's a tougher question. The university library is a good place to start. Perhaps interviews with other franchises, accountants, and lawyers would be useful. Marketing research through surveys or questionnaires may be needed. Answering this question is the most creative part of business report planning. Let's take a deeper look at this fourth question.

FOUR WAYS TO FIND INFORMATION USED IN REPORTS

A detailed discussion of research techniques would go far beyond the scope of this book. But it may be useful to consider the four basic ways to find out what we need to know: reading, interviewing, observing, and reasoning.

Reading

Many managers, on the day after graduation, promptly forget where the university library is. Yet libraries exist for the sole purpose of dispensing information. Become familiar with the library resources available in your area. You'll probably be amazed at what modern libraries have.

The term *reading* is used here in a general sense to include, not only graphic or printed matter, but also audiovisual materials such as films, tapes, and pictures. Most of what we'll ever need to know has been recorded somewhere at some time. The problem is in finding the right manuscripts, books, articles, statistical tables, computer data bases, and the like. Let a librarian help you.

Thanks to computer technology, it is possible to search through large amounts of information very quickly. An average computer search can go through 10 to 15 years of an index in just a few minutes. A computer search can also help you find items you would otherwise miss or give you access to materials that your library does not have. Current technology allows you to search several different libraries from a single location. If your library does not have the information you need, they can often retrieve it from another library across the nation.[2]

Interviewing

Interviewing an expert or source-person is a valuable way of gathering information. Any person who is intimately familiar with a specific problem or issue—who has firsthand knowledge—may legitimately be considered an expert. This means that the assembly line worker, the keypunch operator, or the building maintenance worker may be the person we need to talk with, even though their formal organizational position does not call for decision making. Many organizational problems are solved by going to those who are seldom sought after for managerial advice. When we have the opportunity to go to the people involved, we should use it. This is the strongest data-gathering approach for many problems.

Observing

When we can't find exactly what we need to know by reading or interviewing, we must sometimes observe for ourselves. Direct observation should *not* be *casual* observation—the observations should be planned in advance. If we simply go into an organization, look around, and draw conclusions from one or two observations, we run the risk of getting contaminated data—a distorted picture. Exactly *what* is to be observed and precisely *when* it is to be observed should be planned in advance. A reasonable number of different observations should be made and, where possible, the reliability of these observations should be established. Reliability is simply the likelihood that, on subsequent observation, essentially the same things will be observed. Using multiple observations and/or multiple observers helps improve reliability. In short, don't jump to conclusions based on one or two casual observations.

Planning exactly what you are looking for and knowing when you've found it also help improve reliability by reducing the amount of personal bias.

Usually it is helpful to design a data-gathering form or tally sheet to categorize events witnessed. The more thorough the preparation of such a form, the clearer your categories and the better your information.

Reasoning

The fourth general approach is reasoning from what we have learned. Drawing conclusions based on evidence gathered may be the most risky step in the research process. Our conclusions can be only as good as our evidence and our reasoning. There is no foolproof way to eliminate personal biases from this process, but it is important to be aware that our own point of view may prevent us from seeing other possibilities.

Organizational decisions are based on reasoning from the known (the information gathered) to the unknown (the predicted results of a course of action). If the reasoning processes are valid and the decision implemented, it should be an effective decision; this is the final test.

These, then, are four major ways to find out what we want to know for a written report: reading, interviewing experts, observation, and reasoning. Chapter 16 discusses research techniques in a little more detail.

FORMATTING REPORTS

These formatting guidelines represent a standard report format and are not the only way to format reports. Because of the wide variety of computer software available one may want to deviate from these suggested guidelines. Learn the various features available in your own software and use them to make your reports easier to produce and more creative.

Margins (see Figure 15-1)

In most cases, set your top margin at 1.5 inches on the first page and 1 inch for following pages. Set the right, left and bottom margins at 1 inch for all pages. If your report will be bound, add 0.5 inches to the left margin to allow for the binding.

Pagination (see Figure 15-1)

The first page is usually not numbered. All following pages should have page numbers either 0.5 inches from the top right, or 0.5 inches from the bottom center.

Spacing (see Figure 15-1)

Single-spaced reports can often be hard to read so use double spacing in most reports. The first line of each paragraph should be indented 0.5 inches from the left margin.

1"

XXXXXXXXXXXXXXXXXXXXXXXXXXXXXXXXXXXXXXXXXXX
XXXXXXXXXXXXXXXXXXXXXXXXXXXXXXXXXXXXXXXXXXX
XXXXXXXXXXXXXXXXXXXXXXXXXXXXXXXXXXXXXXXXXXX
XXXXXXXXXXXXXXXXXXXXXXXXXXXXXXXXXXXXXXXXXXX
XXXXXXXXXXXXXXXXXXXXXXXXXXXX

XXXXXXXXXXXXXXXXXXXXXXXXXXXXXXXXXXXXXXXXXXX
XXXXXXXXXXXXXXXXXXXXXXXXXXXXXXXXXXXXXXXXXXX
XXXXXXXXXXXXXXXXXXXXXXXXXXXXXXXXXXXXXXXXXXX
XXXXXXXXXXXXXXXXXXXXXXXXXXXXXXXXXXXXXXXXXXX
XXXXXXXXXXXXXXXXXXXXXXXXXXXXXXXXXXXXXXXXXXX
XXXXXXX

XXXXXXXXXXXXXXXXXXXXXXXXXXXXXXXXXXXXXXXXXXX
XXXXXXXXXXXXXXXXXXXXXXXXXXXXXXXXXXXXXXXXXXX
XXXXXXXXXXXXXXXXXXXXXXXXXXXXXXXXXXXXXXXXXXX
XXXXXXXXXXXXXXXXXXXXXXXXXXXXXXXXXXXXXXXXXXX
XXXXXXXXXXXXXXX   1"

XXXXXXXXXXXXXXXXXXXXXXXXXXXXXXXXXXXXXXXXXXX
XXXXXXXXXXXXXXXXXXXXXXXXXXXXXXXXXXXXXXXXXXXXX

##

FIGURE 15-1   **Margins, pagination, spacing.**

Headings (see Figure 15-2)

♦ *Title heading.* Should be typed in all capital letters and centered horizontally. Triple space after the title if there is no secondary heading. If using a secondary heading, double space only after the title.

♦ *Secondary heading.* Should have each major word capitalized and should be centered horizontally. Double space before and triple space after the secondary heading.

♦ *Tertiary heading.* Has each major word capitalized, is underlined and is left justified. Double space before and after the tertiary heading.

REPORT TITLE

Secondary Heading

Tertiary Heading

XXXXXXXXXXXXXXXXXXXXXXXXXXXXXXXXXXXXXXXXXXX

XXXXXXXXXXXXXXXXXXXXXXXXXXXXXXXXXXXXXXXXXXX

XXXXXXXXXXXXXXXXXXXXXXXXXXXXXXXXXXXXXXXXXXX

XXXXXXXXXXXXXXXXXXXXXXXXXXXXXXXXXXXXXXXXXXX

XXXXXXXXXXXXXXXXXXXXXXXXXXXXXXXXXXXXXXXXXXX

XXXXXXXXXXXXXX

Paragraph heading.

XXXXXXXXXXXXXXXXXXXXXXXXXXXXXXXXXXXXXXXXX

XXXXXXXXXXXXXXXXXXXXXXXXXXXXXXXXXXXXXXXXX

XXXXXXXXXXXXXXXXXXXXXXXXXXXXXXXXXXXXXXXXX

XXXXXXXXXXXXXXXXXXXXXXXXXXXXXXXXXXXXXXXXXXX

FIGURE 15-2   Headings.

♦ *Paragraph heading.* Has only the first word capitalized, is underlined, ends with a period, and is indented 0.5 inches from the left margin. Double space after the paragraph heading.

Quotations (see Figure 15-3)

If the quotation is longer than two lines, it is indented 0.5 inches from both left and right margins. Quotations are usually single spaced preceded and followed by a double space.

Listings (see Figure 15-4)

Listings are indented 0.5 inches from the left margin. Single space items longer than one line; indent second and following lines under the first word, not the number; and double space between items.

Documenting Sources Used

Many different styles can be used when citing sources used in preparing your report. Consult a reference manual for specific formatting possibilities. Regardless of which style you use, every source reference should include:

XXXXXXXXXXXXXXXXXXXXXXXXXXXXXXXXXXXXXXXXXXX

XXXXXXXXXXXXXXXXXXXXXXXXXXXXXXXXXXXXXXXXXXX

XXXXXXXXXXXXXXXXXXXXXXXXXXXX

XXXXXXXXXXXXXXXXXXXXXXXXXXXXXXXXXXX
XXXXXXXXXXXXXXXXXXXXXXXXXXXXXXXXXXX
XXXXXXXXXXXXXXXXXXXXXXXXXXXXXXXXXXX
XXXXXXXXXXXXXXXX.

XXXXXXXXXXXXXXXXXXXXXXXXXXXXXXXXXXXXXXXXXXXXX

XXXXXXXXXXXXXXXXXXXXXXXXXXXXXXXXXXXXXXXXXXXXXX

XXXXXXXXXXXXXXX

FIGURE 15-3   Quotations.

XXX

XXX

XXXXXXXXXXXXXXXXXXXXXXXXXXXXX

1. XXXXXXXXXXXXXXXXXXXXXXXXXXXXXXXXXXXXXXXXXXX
   XXXXXXXXXXXXXXXXXXXXXXXXXXXXXXXXXXX.

2. XXXXXXXXXXXXXXXXXXXXXXXXXXXXXXXXXXXXXXXXXXX
   XXXXXXXXXXXXXXXX.

3. XXXXXXXXXXXXXXXXXXXXXXXXXXXXXXXXXXXXXXXXXXX
   XXXXXXXXXXXXXXXXXXXXXXXXXXXXXXXXXXXXXXX.

FIGURE 15-4   Listings.

- ♦ author(s)
- ♦ date of publication
- ♦ source title
- ♦ where published
- ♦ publisher
- ♦ page number(s)

Internal Citations.   With internal citations, quoted material is cited directly within the report. Each citation is followed directly by the author's surname and year of publication, with page numbers included in the reference list that follows the report.

Footnotes/Endnotes.   Footnotes are numbered within the text with references located at the bottom of the page on which the number appears. Endnotes are like footnotes except the references are all located at the end of the report on a separate page labeled "Endnotes." It would be advantageous to learn how to use the automatic footnote function in your software package when using footnotes in your reports.

Reference List.   The reference list is located at the end of the report on a separate page and includes a title, such as References or Bibliography, followed by three spaces. Items in the list should be single spaced and in alphabetical order with double spacing between items. Begin the first line of each item at the left margin with following lines indented 0.5 inches.

GOOD REPORTS ARE REALISTIC ABOUT PURPOSE, TIME, AND COST

Virtually any topic can be researched to death. Anyone who has written a master's thesis, Ph.D. dissertation, or extensive term paper under the direction of an exasperatingly rigorous professor knows what we mean. At some point, of course, the cost of new tidbits of additional insight becomes prohibitive. Common-sense limits need to be placed on how much is spent on a report. It would be insane to spend $50,000 on research that will solve a $100 problem. The benefits must exceed the cost.

> *The cost of information must be considered.*

The magnitude of the problem's effects on the organization provides the key. A decision on what hours to open the cafeteria calls for a quick, short report at the most. An analysis of a problem on which the future of the organization hangs—say, how to fight off an unwanted takeover attempt, or how to combat a competitor's actions—would be a no-holds-barred research effort. Any reasonable expenditure would be justified.

> *Some reports are worth almost any cost.*

Budgeting Report Costs

How much can a person write in a hour or a day? It depends on the complexity of the material being written, the depth of the analysis, the familiarity the writer has with the material, and the writer's ability, motivation, alertness, and energy level. Analyses of these kinds of factors reveal that the professional writer *averages* from one to three hours of actual writing a day. Some writers can go for ten hours a day for a week but then run dry for a month.

> *A professional writer can average from one to three good writing hours per day.*

How much can be written in one to three hours? The average professional writer can complete at least one page a day. The one-page includes research, rough drafts, planning of illustrations, final drafts, and proofreading. That 3,000 words a week amounts to approximately ten typewritten pages of raw production—which in turn might convert into five final pages of original, creative writing.

Creative editing or the arranging of work contributed by several participating writers into a final report can take as long as original writing. So a team-written report of 30 pages would take about a month to prepare.[3]

So you can see that reports do cost. Nevertheless, there are times when there is no good substitute for a written report to meet information needs of an organization. As discussed in Chapter 3, there are several significant advantages to the use of this medium, including the capability of conveying complex information in an orderly fashion, the presence of hard copy for future reference, and the relative formality a report affords to important matters. A report can be used efficiently—read when most convenient and when the reader is particularly alert or motivated.

Report Length and Formality[4]

Because of the wide range and variety of shapes and sizes, business reports are often hard to define. We have chosen a wide definition by breaking all reports into two types—long and short. Typically, the longer the report, the more formal it is.

The long report is more traditional-bound and comprehensive than the informal report. The formal report is often bound, printed on quality paper, and implies an official source. It presents important information and often reaches readers outside the organization. The long report may be divided into several parts, which we discuss in the next section.

The short and usually less formal report covers less important information, such as progress reports, trip and expense reports, minor requests, and routine status reports. These reports can take the form of a letter or memo and can be handwritten—but are usually printed—typed on preprinted forms or sent electronically over E-Mail. The length of a short report is usually two or three pages. Informal reports seldom go outside the organization and usually stay in one division or department.

Formal (Long) Reports

Long Reports Should Start with a Proposal

> *Major reports are very costly and should begin with a proposal first.*

The proposal is one way to avoid the problem of spending too much on formal reports. *The proposal itself is a short report that lays out a working plan for the long report.*

First, the proposal crystallizes the writer's thinking and lets the reader know precisely what can be expected from the final report. Typically, it includes a clear statement of the problem or issue to be dealt with (including the background where appropriate), a description of what

> *The proposal helps both the writer and the person requesting the report.*

research steps will be taken to arrive at a conclusion, a statement of the goal of the report, and, in many cases, an estimate of the cost of preparing the report.

The proposal is helpful for the researcher because it:

1. Permits him or her to think out loud about the research steps to be taken
2. Provides an opportunity to discover a possible error or faulty thinking early in the project, where it's less likely to do serious damage
3. Serves as a guide throughout the investigation.

In addition, the carefully prepared proposal will include material for writing the introductory section in the final report.[5]

The report proposal should be addressed to the person(s) who will formally authorize the research project. Typically, it is presented in memo format and seldom runs longer than two or three pages. The parts of the proposal are discussed in the following.

Background. Before spending time, effort, and money, the decision maker should understand the conditions that gave rise to the problem or issue to be researched. This section puts the project into context and paves the way for a more specific definition of the immediate problem the writer will study. Although the background section may tell the reader things he or she already knows, it provides a chance for the writer and the person who authorized the report to be sure they are on the same wavelength. It is far better to catch any misassumptions here than after the research is in progress.

> *A good background statement puts writer and reader on the same wavelength.*

Statement of the Problem. Clearly defining the research problem is crucial to the ultimate success of the project. This section needs to include more than a one-sentence definition. Remember that your reader is likely to view the nature of any given problem a little differently than you do—our past experiences and unique viewpoints make that inevitable. So, in addition to stating your view of the problem, you'll need to explain why you see it that way. You must also convince your reader that yours is an appropriate view and definition of the issue.

> *The statement of the problem must be objective.*

Be careful of emotional language that may convey biases. An objective, unemotional statement should be your goal. The following examples illustrate this.

> *Be specific in stating the problem.*

Too Emotional or Judgmental	More Objective
First-line supervisors are incapable of writing good performance reviews for personnel files.	Most first-line supervisors are writing performance reviews that do not meet company standards.

A common error made in preparing this part of a proposal is to state the problem in terms that are too broad. When the problem is too grandiose or unusually wide in scope, the report loses focus. Here are examples:

Too Emotional or Judgmental	*More Appropriate*
This report will study the effects of foreign competition on our business.	This report will study the marketing strategy of the three foreign competitors that are having the most impact on our share of the market in cable television: Sony, Panasonic, and Mitsubishi.
This report will examine safety problems in our manufacturing operations.	This report reviews lost-time accidents reported in the past 12 months in our manufacturing plant and corrective actions taken to prevent recurrence.

The Goal of the Project.   Be sure the statement of your goal or objective fits the statement of the problem. The readers of your proposal should understand from this section exactly what they will be getting. You should state this in concrete, specific language. This section may include a list of goals rather than a single one. If a list is used, cite the most significant goal first. Supplementary objectives may follow. Avoid vague generalities.

> *Tell your readers what they can expect.*

Too Vague	*More Specific*
This report will suggest some ideas for changes to cope with rising labor costs.	This report will recommend a systematic approach to offset rising labor costs in the assembly plant via: 1. Upgrading of machinery 2. Training of supervisors 3. Changing the worker incentive plans

The Research Procedures.   In this section of the proposal, your methods for gathering and processing information should be spelled out. Since no research project is completely new, you may begin by citing previous work done in the area by others. As anyone who has ever written a major term paper will attest, this literature search is often tedious, but it does provide a sound foundation for the recommendations offered by the project.

> *Let the reader know how you will get the information.*

What your reader needs to know is how you are going to find the information needed to solve the problem posed. Your choice of methods is, of course, limited by the available resources (time and money, for example).

The Cost of the Project. The final section of the proposal tells your readers what the project will cost, so that they can decide if it is worth the expenditure. If the writer is on the organization's payroll, it is usually sufficient to estimate the number of work hours needed plus other material expenses such as computer time, printing, and postage. If the proposal is prepared by an outside consultant, a charge for professional services will also be included.

Although all this sounds like a great deal of information, the final version of the report proposal is seldom more than a few pages. Figure 15-5 shows an example of such a proposal.

INFORMAL (SHORT) REPORTS

Your readers will often need a detailed daily or weekly report on routine activities or answers to specific questions. Many organizations must submit reports to state or federal agencies in order to keep their accreditation or funding.

The skills necessary to write short reports are among the most important you can develop. You will be required to prepare short reports often on your job; business and industry would not be able to function without them. Although informal reports are brief, you should take the time and effort to plan and write them well. Below is a list of the various types of short reports you can write:

audit report	laboratory report	research report
compliance report	library report	research study
design report	manager's report	sales report
evaluation report	operations report	situational report
experiment report	periodic report	status report
feasibilty report	production report	task report
incident report	progress report	test report
investigative report	proposal	trip report
justification report	recommendation report	weekly report

From the foregoing list you can be sure we will be unable to discuss each of these reports in this chapter. Instead we concentrate on *five* of the most common reports you are likely to encounter in business and industry:

1. task reports
2. periodic reports
3. progress reports
4. meeting minutes
5. trip or conference reports

September 12, 1996

TO: Lynn McClurg, VP Training

FROM: Sharon Seamons, Staff Assistant

PROPOSAL FOR AN ANALYSIS OF AVAILABLE TRAINING SOFTWARE

BACKGROUND

Mr. McClurg, as you are aware, our company has recently diversified into two new areas of operation, fast foods merchandising and dairy products processing. Since this diversification, pressures to provide a wide range of additional training programs have mounted.

Our experiences in past expansions attest to the fact that computerized training packages are effective in developing a wide range of technical and managerial skills. In addition, a wide range of new software, now available, may meet our needs.

STATEMENT OF THE PROBLEM

The diversity of software poses opportunities as well as a problem. The problem is that the company lacks the information necessary to make an intelligent comparison among the many software packages. Information is needed to compare the content, costs, and potential usefulness of these packages in the light of our company's needs.

GOAL OF THE PROJECT

The goal of this project is to narrow the field of alternatives to three software packages for fast foods managers and three for the dairy people. Information will be gathered to support the selections. Each selection will be evaluated and ranked from most appropriate to least appropriate, based on findings of the research. Final recommendations will be made.

THE RESEARCH PROCEDURES

The information presented in this report will be gathered from three main areas:

1. Directories of software located in recent technical publications found in the local university's library will be reviewed. These directories include detailed descriptions of the type of material in each package.

2. Persons in management positions will be asked to suggest specific training needs they are experiencing or anticipate. Managers will also be polled as to their software preferences.

3. After a package has been recommended by a directory or by someone familiar with it, the vendor will be invited to demonstrate the product to our management and to sample groups of nonmanagement employees.

FIGURE 15-5   A proposal report.

4. A series of interviews will gather feedback from those sampling the software before a purchase is recommended.

Data gathering will be confined to our Chicago locations. No out-of-town travel is anticipated in this study.

THE COST OF THE PROJECT

Since this project is being done as a part of my normal job responsibilities, no special costs are anticipated. It is estimated that the study will take approximately ten workdays to complete. The following is a tentative breakdown of that time:

Preliminary library search	1 day
Interview of managers	2 days
Analysis of data gathered	1 day
Vendor demonstrations	3 days
Follow-up user interviews	1 day
Preparation of final report (including presentation to management)	2 days

Costs of secretarial services, paper, materials, photocopying, and the like will be absorbed by the Training Communication Department.

FIGURE 15-5   A proposal report *(continued)*.

Task Reports.   Many professionals are required to deal with a variety of tasks and assignments that require feedback through reports. These reports are often used to make recommendations, such as for buying new equipment, changing an existing policy, or creating a new program; or they could be used to report an inspection of a plant site, a program objective, or the effectiveness of firm personnel.

Periodic Reports.   These reports are often recorded on prepared forms and are the most familiar of short reports. As the name suggests, periodic reports provide readers with information at regularly scheduled intervals—daily, weekly, monthly, quarterly, yearly. They summarize regular activities and events performed during the reporting period, as well as irregular events that must be brought to the attention of the reader.

Progress Reports.   The progress report is used to inform the reader about the status of an ongoing project or assignment. These reports may be external (informing customers regarding the headway of a project) or internal (advising management of the status of activities). Progress reports are typically organized in either chronological or priority order. In your introduction specify the nature and purpose of the project, providing enough background to make your reader comfortable. Describe the work completed and the work in progress, including personnel, methods, activities, and locations. Anticipate possible

Report Component	Recommendation or Justification report	Inspection or Examination report	Information or Investigation report
Overview	introduce circumstances that necessitate the change	identify or define the subject being inspected	introduce circumstances that necessitate the investigation
Background	identify the criteria for selecting a change	describe the subject being inspected	identify the procedures, including method and materials, if necessary
Recommendation	recommend or justify a change	make recommendations, if necessary	make recommendations, if necessary
Evidence	provide data to support recommended change	present data from inspection or evaluation, noting discrepancies	present the results of the investigation
Discussion	explain the advantages or benefits of the change	discuss the impact of the discrepancies	explain the reasons for the results

(Burnett, 1994, p. 480)

FIGURE 15-6   Organization of possible task reports.

problems and offer solutions. Discuss future activities including the projected completion date.

Meeting Minutes.   Minutes are a record of meeting discussion and decisions. Meeting minutes often serve as official (sometimes even legal) records, which provide a review of the meeting for both those who attended and those who did not. When you are in charge of preparing minutes keep the following guidelines in mind:

a. Provide identification: date, time, location, meeting type, members attending, person presiding.

b. Maintain an objective tone: no editorializing or subtle slanting of statements.

c. Summarize where possible.

d. Express motions and amendments precisely: maker, seconder, margin by which motion passed or failed.

    e. Record time of adjournment and time and date of next scheduled meeting.

    f. Attach relevant announcements, agenda, or handouts.

Trip or Conference Reports. Most business professionals will have the opportunity to attend a convention or conference and will typically be required to submit a report when they return. The report should include new procedures, equipment, laws, and supply information affecting the products, operations, or service of the firm. The key to writing a good trip report is the ability to select the most relevant material and organize this material into a coherent report. Do not give a travel log, but instead concentrate on from three to five important topics that your reader will find interesting. Create an interesting introduction and closing and use the three to five important topics as your report body.[6]

Main Points To Remember about Short Reports

1. Short reports are generally organized in one of three different formats:

    ♦ *Memo format.* Internal short reports are often just two- to three-page memos.

    ♦ *Prepared form format.* Many short reports are routine and require a special form.

    ♦ *Letter format.* External short reports are usually part of a short letter.

2. Short reports are a few pages at most and get to the point quickly—don't beat around the bush.

3. You should anticipate the types of information your readers will need and how they will use it. The important information in a progress report is not the same as that in a periodic report.

4. Because your report is brief, you should organize the introduction, body, and conclusion clearly and logically.

5. Summarize and offer conclusions where possible.

INDIVIDUAL REPORT WRITING

One of the toughest steps in writing long or short reports is getting started. Getting your thoughts and the information you've gathered onto that ominous blank sheet of paper is a considerable chore. Yet worry no more. A simple five-step process will turn your mountain of raw data into a compact, effective report. Follow these steps and you'll end up with well-organized and even sensible written report.[7]

Organizing Your Reports

It makes no sense to jump into writing your report until you fully understand what's to be done. Be certain that you are on the same wavelength with the person who has authorized or requested the report. The proposal, of course, is designed to help you do just that. Your planning stage must include at least three phases, as described by Richard Hatch:

First, the problem on which the report will focus must be clearly defined, and the question to which the report will address itself should be specified. Second, the criteria that the decision makers will use to make a final decision must be spelled out; in other words, the factors that will decide the issue must be identified. Finally, sources of information and evidence must be identified, and methods of gathering the information selected.

Gather Preliminary Information

The most carefully planned research project involves a period of searching for useful data. Often this takes the form of leafing through books and periodicals

> *It's better to gather more data than you'll need than not to have enough.*

or conducting some loosely structured interviews with people familiar with the report topic. A common mistake for many is that they fail to write down this information because they're not sure it will fit into their final report. It makes sense to gather a little too much information rather than not enough—at least, at the early stages of the project.

Don't Be Too Selective at This Stage.   Reconcile yourself to the fact that you won't use every tidbit of information you gather. But getting anything that may prove useful onto paper or disk is important.

You may find 3 × 5 cards useful in gathering information. How many times have you found yourself scrambling for something to jot a note on? Often relevant information will come at the most inopportune times and places. It is pretty simple to slip a 3 × 5 card out of your pocket or purse to jot something down.[8]

You should never have to draft a common report completely from scratch.[9] If you or a colleague have completed a similar report in the past and it is retained on a disk, you could borrow parts for the current report you are writing. You must be careful in making sure the material contained in the past report is current, so keep an eye out for dated material and revise where necessary. Furthermore, the adaptation may mix two different writing styles and make the report difficult to read—be ready to adapt the writing style as well.

One final point about your early note gathering: Be sure to identify each quoted or paraphrased source. You will be taking three types of notes: *direct quotes, paraphrased quotes,* and your *own ideas.* For each type, the source can be identified in parentheses following the note. If you copy down a direct quote, use quotation marks and ellipses and brackets as necessary. When you omit words in quoted materials, you should use a series of three spaced periods—

called ellipsis points—to indicate the omission. And the omission must not detract from or alter the essential meaning of the sentence. Brackets are used to insert a word or phrase of your own to clarify the context of the quote for the reader.

An example of the use of ellipses follows:

Technical material distributed for promotional use is sometimes charged for, particularly in high-volume distribution to educational institutions, although prices for these publications are not uniformly based on the cost of developing them. (without omission)

Technical material distributed for promotional use is sometimes charged for … although prices for these publications are not uniformly based on the cost of developing them. (with omission)[10]

An example of the use of brackets:

Those who learn to write better reports tend to become more demanding in what they expect of the reports they receive. "When 800 people took my course at Standard of Ohio, says [Albert] Joseph [president of the Industrial Writing Institute], they began to ridicule the reports that still were written in the old style. The environment has changed."

Even if Joseph were introduced earlier in the article, without the brackets we would not know who he is.

> *Always cite the sources of the ideas gathered.*

Paraphrased material should convey the same thought as the original did, although in different words. Do not put quotation marks around such notes, but do cite the source of the idea.

One final type of preliminary note is often overlooked by researchers: *your own thoughts.* As you read and gather data, ideas are going to be triggered in your own mind. Don't let these get away. Jot them down immediately and identify them as your own simply by putting your initials in parentheses at the end of the note.

Here are examples of each type of note:

- ♦ *Direct quote:* "And unfortunately, the beginning report writers tend to overlook the preparation stage, sometimes even ignoring it completely, preferring to get into the more active job of gathering information."[11]
- ♦ *Paraphrased quote:* Beginning report writers tend to overlook the preparation stage, preferring to get directly into information gathering.[12]
- ♦ *Own idea:* One problem leading to our poor-quality reports may be that less-experienced writers are not spending enough time in preparation before they gather data. (PT)

Paul Timm's initials appear in the "own idea" example.

Review Materials and Create Preliminary Outline

Warning: This step calls for creativity. Keeping in mind your objectives, develop an outline showing a logical arrangement.

Get something down in writing and then rearrange it freely until each piece fits. Be sure to include the problem's definition and decision criteria. Based on your gathering of preliminary information, several issues and concerns should emerge. Let's say, for example, your report examines the feasibility of renovating an older shoe store in your city's downtown shopping district. Your preliminary research shows:

- *Fewer shoppers* use downtown stores than five years ago, but there has been a *slight uptrend* in the past two years.
- *Tax incentives* are available to companies that expand or locate new facilities downtown.
- Renovation of old stores is *less expensive* than a move to a new location.
- The Downtown Business Association is supporting a *redevelopment program* for the downtown area by recognizing the civic pride of companies who stay.
- *Shoppers* who do use downtown stores *spend less* than those who use our suburban mall stores.
- *The state legislature* is considering a bill to provide *low-cost loans* to businesses that renovate or relocate in urban areas.
- Many downtown shoppers are *elderly* and cannot travel to suburban stores.

How could this information be arranged? There are essentially three classes of information presented here:

1. Information about shoppers and potential profits
   - Fewer than in the past but improving
   - Spend less than in suburbs
   - Many are elderly
2. Information about costs
   - Less expensive to renovate
   - Tax incentives available
   - Possible low-cost loans in future
3. Information about public-relations benefits
   - Recognized by Downtown Business Association
   - Demonstrates service to elderly by renovation
   - Shows civic pride

Once these areas have been identified and numbered, each note or bit of data gathered should be examined to see where it fits best.

Refining Your Writing Style

Writing style is as crucial to writing a report as structure and content. Unfortunately, most reports are written with selfish disregard for the intended reader. By following some simple style guidelines your reports will be much easier to read and less likely to be dull, tedious, and patronizing.

1. Keep your sentences and words short. If you are writing on a complex subject, a reader can easily become confused and disinterested.

2. Use creative language such as similes and metaphors to add color and life to your writing. Avoid clichés and trite phrases that tend to annoy and bore your reader.

3. Avoid jargon unless the report is addressed to your colleagues. If your report will be read by those outside your immediate circle of colleagues, either avoid it or define it.

4. Use a dictionary and thesaurus to find the precise word you need to create a vivid analogy.

5. Use humor and wit, but do not hurt or humiliate. Remember that your words will reach unexpected eyes.[13]

Review and Proof the Final Version

Your report must be a quality product, both in appearance and in content. It is essential that it should be proofread by at least one other person. Check all figures and calculations more than once—this includes numbering and lettering of paragraphs for consistency throughout the document.

Your Finished Report

I could summarize this report-writing approach by listing a series of do's and don'ts.

DO	*DON'T*
◆ State the reason for writing in the first paragraph.	◆ Be overly selective in preliminary data gathering.
◆ Explain each key point simply and clearly.	◆ Forget to identify each source used and prepare a reference card for each.
◆ Maintain a "you" attitude: Write for your reader's benefit, not yours. Show that what you say will help the reader.	◆ Hesitate to be creative in developing your outline.
◆ Make it positive.	◆ Forget to edit several times when your mind is fresh.[14]
◆ Say exactly what you advise the reader to do.	

COLLABORATIVE REPORT WRITING

> **Collaborative writing has its advantages and disadvantages.**

Many of the most important reports used in business are written by a group of people—nine of every ten business professionals report that they sometimes collaborate or work as part of a team to create documents. Group writing may be necessary when:

1. A task is too large or complex for one person to accomplish.
2. A deadline is coming up and there is not enough time for one person to finish the task.
3. Many different skills and viewpoints are needed to to complete the task.
4. Agreement is needed from several people.[15]

Each member of the group has a specific role to perform, which capitalizes on each members' knowledge, experience, needs, skill, and influence. Team members also have self-centered roles that help them satisfy personal needs. These roles are listed in Figures 15-7 and 15-8.

An excellent approach to committee report writing was outlined by Joseph Allen and Bennet P. Lientz. Their step-by-step committee writing strategy is described in the following excerpt:[16]

Getting a Committee to Generate an Original Document

Take seven efficient businesspeople and set them down in a conference room. Be sure that each one is a good communicator. Ask them to write a document together—and watch nothing happen. They discuss the matter; they chew it up

---

Relationship—Positive
1. Shows solidarity, raises others' status, gives help, rewards.
2. Shows tension release, jokes, laughs, shows satisfaction
3. Shows agreement, shows passive acceptance, understands, concurs, complies.

Task Area—Neutral
1. Ask/Gives suggestions, direction, implying autonomy for others.
2. Asks/Gives opinion, evaluation, analysis, expresses feelings and wishes.
3. Asks/Gives information, orientation, repeats, clarifies, confirms.

Relationship—Negative
1. Disagrees, shows passive rejection, formality, withholds help.
2. Shows tension, asks for help, withdraws, defends, or asserts self.
3. Asks for suggestions, direction, possible ways of action. (Raspberry & Lindsay, 1994, p. 399)

FIGURE 15-7   Self-centered roles of committee members.

1. Leadership roles. In some informal groups no leadership is needed, but in teams the leader is usually designated because of position, knowledge or power. Leaders are expected to influence the decision making of the team, but they can also abuse their power by making decisions that favor their own personal goals.

2. Facilitator roles. Facilitators are the group problem solvers. They keep team members aware of group progress, help mediate between members in conflict, monitor work to make it consistent with team goals, and ensure participation of every group member.

3. Dysfunctional roles. Dysfunctional group roles can be classified into four general classes:
   a. The *Competitor* is one who attempts to control the group discussion or challenge the leader's credibility.
   b. The *Self-Confessor* uses the group as a personal ego boost in bolstering self-confi dence and gaining support.
   c. The *Non-participant* is one who chooses not to cooperate in group discussion and does not want to be a part of the group.
   d. The Dominator sidetracks team progress through arguing, attempting to force domi nating view on others, and redirecting discussion to unimportant tangent. (Raspberry & Lindsay, 1994, p. 400)

FIGURE 15-8   Team member roles.

again and again. You've never seen a more thorough analysis—but you have to stand over them with a gun to make them get down to writing. Why?

Since writing is viewed as a personal act, no one is willing to submit his or her writing to committee scrutiny until the committee reaches a point of des- peration. Then someone will finally be appointed to write a draft—which will, as expected, be torn to shreds when the draft is reviewed. Is that the only way to operate? In a word, no.

Objectives, strategy, tactics. A series of decisions must be made before pen is put to paper. They become overwhelmingly important in the committee envi- ronment. Because there are multiple minds at work—with multiple strengths and weaknesses—it's essential that all cards be laid on the table from the begin- ning. If there are irreconcilable differences in the objective phase, then that's the place to iron them out, not later on, when a draft has been submitted.

Objectives

The first thing any committee has to do in writing a document is make up a list of the particles of meaning it intends to convey. Most of the heated discussion takes place during this session. There are simply too many sets of particles of meaning to be dealt with easily. If you're to deal with them, you need a method. The following suggests such a method.

Memory: The First Step.   The largest problem with retrieving particles from a group is that they're stored in a number of different heads. So the first thing you need in your quest for consensus is a formal group memory. In a small committee, a note pad will serve the purpose. In a committee with more than three or four members, we recommend a chalkboard.

During the course of discussion, there'll be points brought up by the members that might lead to generally accepted particles of meaning. To keep them in the group's memory for future consideration, jot them down on your board (or pad). Be sure that what you jot down is a particle of meaning, not simply a piece of evidence, though. The following table gives some examples of particles as distinguished from evidence. Remember that most particles can be noted in very few words.

Particles of meaning as distinguished from evidence on the issue of instituting new equal opportunity incentives

Particles of Meaning	*Evidence*
1. Minorities are underrepresented at present.	1. Complaints from various social organizations 2. Statistics on current employees
2. Recruiting methods for minorities are inadequate.	1. Newspaper ads generate only WASP responses 2. College recruiters visit only large colleges with a majority of WASP students.
3. Company-wide goals must be set.	1. Government or judicial mandates 2. Social mandates
4. Company-wide goals must be met.	1. Federal contracts unavailable until goals are met 2. Corporate "good citizen" policy

Note that the particles listed in the table are broadly representative of attitudes and policies. They aren't weighed down with data, aren't narrowed by case studies. Any objections that committee members have to these particles must be made on the basis of philosophy or principle—which brings us to the subject of compromise.

Compromise. Many of us were brought up to believe that "compromise is defeat on the installment plan." Whether that statement is true or not, the defeat of a committee can easily be effected by a refusal to compromise. The essence of satisfactory compromise is knowing when it's inevitable. Anyone who has arbitrated agreements or negotiations can verify that all-important rule. And the next major step in committee writing is to flush out the essential compromises—before any writing (or decision about writing) is undertaken.

If you've faithfully noted all the major particles of meaning brought up by all committee members, you'll no doubt find that some of them conflict with each other. Look at the following list:

Particles of Meaning

1. Property tax relief is essential.
2. Government spending must be cut.

3. Essential services must be maintained.

4. No new taxes must be instituted.

5. Economic stimulus must be provided to business.

6. Schools must not be affected.

7. Employment must be kept high.

8. Renter relief must be included in property tax relief.

There are several areas of potential conflict. It's entirely possible, for instance, that numbers 2 and 3 of the list may appear mutually exclusive to the committee. The first step is to ask the committee members if any of them have irreconcilable differences with any listed particle. Take the particles one by one. Those that don't generate any nay votes can be allowed to survive for the moment. Obviously, then, some group discussion must be held on the particles for which there isn't immediate consensus. In the case of the list of particles, perhaps compromise can be reached by defining some of the following:

1. How much government spending must be cut?

2. Must that spending be across the board, or could whole programs be cut?

3. Which services are essential?

4. Can essential services be maintained by smaller budgets?

5. Can essential services be maintained satisfactorily at lower levels?

Obviously , there's no easy way around compromise. But issues must be met head on at the beginning. There's no point in shelving such disagreements for later consideration; the only possible product of such a move is trouble at a later stage of writing the committee's document. So you negotiate and discuss, haggle and plead with each other until the group is ready to agree that there are no longer any irreconcilable differences concerning any of the stated particles (however they've been amended). It's important to exclude discussions of evidence at this point because (1) it increases the areas of conflict, and (2) it may cloud the basic issues.

We may assume that, with a given amount of temper, smoke, and sweat, your committee will finally be able to complete a list of particles that's more or less satisfactory to all concerned. Then it's time to consider strategy.

Strategy

As you may recall there are seven decisions and one task in the strategy segment of your preparation for writing. Some will be made easily; others may call for some discussion. They are:

♦ Format

♦ Length (general)

♦ Method and organization

♦ Logic

- ◆ Direction
- ◆ Attitude to reader
- ◆ Personal impressions
- ◆ Outline

The outline is the first task the committee will have to perform that relates directly to writing the document. And in the best, most cooperative of committees, people will run for cover when it's time to outline. Nonetheless, there's a way to structure an outline discussion to produce results.

Generally, if you have made the *decisions* we ask you to make (format, length, method, etc.) before the outline is approached, the particles of meaning will fall almost automatically into their appointed slots. Remember that this outline will be a guide to the final document; it must be organized and worded so it is clear to every member of the committee—not just to the recording secretary. Once you have compiled an outline, we suggest a simple yea/nay vote to verify it. And from here on, the rest is cake. Even the writing chore will come relatively easily now.

Tactics

The group must now make a number of tactical decisions, such as which evidence should be used, what the report's tone and point of view should be, and the like. These decisions may be more time consuming than some of the strategic decisions—simply because they must deal with specifics. You'll find that making more detailed decisions here will make the writing that comes at the end much easier.

The only tough decision is the one we've called *evidence*. Despite the fact that the committee has now begun to pull together, there may be widely differing opinions on which evidence is the most potent, the least arguable. But this variation in opinions really represents a committee strength, rather than an organizational weakness.

A good committee is constituted of people from varying disciplines and responsibilities. A sample committee on equal opportunity incentives might include representatives from the following groups:

- ◆ Employee relations
- ◆ Government affairs
- ◆ Public affairs
- ◆ Manufacturing
- ◆ Financial management
- ◆ Administrative management

Each of these folks will have a distinct viewpoint and a distinct expertise in dealing with the issue. And even though they may be able to form a united front at outlining, they may tend to splinter over the issue of evidence.

The discussion of evidence must be shepherded carefully, and the committee must be persuaded to pick and choose among the many ideas. Why? Because if everyone's ideas were represented in the final document, the final document would be too long. It's as simple as that. A simple vote will suffice many times. You list all the potential data on a chalk board and vote on each piece of information separately.

One final hint on tactics: Allocate space specifically. If you're dealing with a lengthy document, set an arbitrary number of pages for each segment of the outline, and compromise from there. If the writing task is to be at all manageable, the members of the committee must agree on just how much space is to be devoted to each of the steps in writing.

Getting Down to It

If you've made all the decisions we've discussed—made them together—you're ready to write. There are two approaches to this task: one for short documents, the other for long ones. They are essentially the same process, though—a process of looking for a *base document* from which to work.

Short committee documents are likely to be sensitive. They frequently deal with subjects such as personnel policies, legal matters, and inquiries of various types. If they weren't matters of this nature, they wouldn't be subjected to the laborious committee process. And, since they're likely to be sensitive, it's practical to bring all the resources the committee has to bear on them.

Approach to Collaborative Writing

The customary approach to collaborative writing involves delegating and assigning tasks to each group member and following up on each task to make sure it is done. The greatest problem with collaborative efforts is spreading the work load evenly so one person does not end up doing all the work. The solution is to meet and discuss key issues at several points during the collaborative process.

You can divide the labor by many criteria—labor intensity, expertise, or willingness of volunteers. In *labor-intensive division* you estimate the total amount of work to be done in hours or by task and then assign each group member his or her "fair share" of work. With this approach the workload is distributed as evenly as possible—the main concern with this approach.

In *expertise division* you assign tasks according to member experience and training. Each member will have a different perspective toward writing—some will be interested in format, others in reasoning, and still others in research. The key to the expertise approach is to find the right person for each job. Unfortunately situations will almost always arise in which there is no expert for a specific task and someone must volunteer or the team leader will have to assign a team member to this task.

In *volunteer division* each group member decides which tasks they would like to work on and the group leader assigns the workload according to member preference where possible. The team must agree on an approach to assigning the tasks for which no one has volunteered.

No matter which division approach you take there may be disputes among group members about who is doing what, about who is doing more, or about who is getting credit for what. Each team member should participate to develop agreed-on procedures for resolving conflict. Each group should have a member who plays a mediator role in which the mediator controls discussion and helps solve disputes between team members quickly and efficiently using procedures accepted by the whole group.

After the workload has been divided and all have completed their assignments, the team meets together to integrate each part into the finished product. Revisions will be made as the group discusses each task and a final decision will be made before any one task is integrated into the whole.

The team should be concerned about transitions between tasks in writing the final report. Everyone has a different writing style and often the style of one team member will not follow smoothly after another. When writing the final report make sure that the writing style flows smoothly throughout the complete document.

A QUICK SUMMARY OF MAJOR IDEAS

♦ Reports should be planned with the reader in mind. Think about *why* the report is being prepared, *how* its success can be measured, and *who* will read it. Then seek the best possible information.

♦ The four basic ways to get information are reading, interviewing, observing, and reasoning.

♦ The costs of a report should be weighed against the potential value of the document. Generally, formal reports are expensive and should be used to deal with important organizational issues.

♦ Short reports can be extended memos. The format and approach are the same. Three key parts for most short reports are *introduction, information, and action.*

♦ Long reports should start with a proposal. Proposals should cover the *background* of the issues, a clear *statement of the problem,* the *goal of the project,* the *research procedures* to be used, and an estimate of the *cost of the project.*

♦ Individual report writing can be streamlined using a five-step process. The process begins with focusing the topic, and it ends with polishing the final draft.

♦ Committee writing calls for working out agreement about the report's objectives, strategies, and tactics before a base document and, ultimately, a final report can be produced.

QUESTIONS FOR FURTHER THOUGHT

1. What are the major advantages of using a direct order of presentation in a report? What are the disadvantages? When would a nondirect arrangement be more appropriate?

2. Review some reports you've received recently. Copy down just the headings used. Does the arrangement make sense? Are the headings informative or simply topical? If topical headings were used, change them to informative. How does this affect the report's readability?

3. Use the five-step method to prepare a report. Critique it as a method. What were its strengths and weaknesses? How can you improve on it to make it work better for you?

4. What advantages come from using committees to produce reports? List as many as you can.

5. Describe as many possible disadvantages to committee writing as you can. How might these be overcome?

OTHER THOUGHTS ABOUT PLANNING AND PRODUCING EFFECTIVE BUSINESS REPORTS

DESIGNING MANAGEMENT REPORTS[17]
by Sandra E. O'Connell

In these demanding times, HR departments can be bombarded with questions from management. The need for information and more importantly, analysis, on which to base business decisions has never been greater. Questions asked by executives may mask fundamental HR concerns such as affirmative action, or legal/tax implications for benefits. Merit-pay raises, layoff demographics, benefit costs and plan membership are some of the primary areas HR professionals are asked to report on.

REPORT REQUEST PROCESS

A process for defining reports helps get accurate data from your automated files efficiently, prevent rework and save time. In order to ask good questions of a computer system, you need to know the system's capability. Even though the HR manager may not plan on running the reports, it's a good idea to understand what data fields are in the system and how information gets into and out of the computer. And, there will come an afternoon when the president asks for the salaries and proposed merit increases for the vice presidents—by 10 a.m. tomorrow. At 5 p.m., it is only you and the blinking cursor on the screen.

   Person requesting information. What do you know about this person and the reason for the request? If confidential data is involved, is this person at the appropriate level? When is the report needed? Does the analysis have to be at the board's compensation committee for a 9 a.m. meeting, or available for review by next week? Assessing the request's priority helps decide what resources are committed to the project.

   The basis for the request. You must understand the purpose of the request before designing a report. This can prevent frivolous or merely curious requests from turning into a 10-hour project.

> *The responsibility of human resources is to examine the consequences of business decisions for the work force.*

   What HR questions need to be asked? The responsibility of human resources is to examine the consequences of business decisions for the work force. Consider questions concerning EEO, benefits implications and other HR consequences when responding to a request.

   What data manipulation will be needed? Must the information combine with data from another source such as payroll or the insurance carrier or have an HR application such as applicant tracking or a spread sheet analysis developed in your department?

   If the question concerns future salary or benefits costs, a multiplier is necessary. Is your HRIS able to perform the needed calculations or is further data manipulation needed? Describing the compa ratio for present job grades should be a standard exporting feature, however, looking at equity between grades is beyond the scope of most HRIS packages. Historical data is more complex and may prove difficult to retrieve and analyze.

What fields of information will be used? Define what fields from the HRIS or other package will be used. If necessary, identify the file name from the data dictionary.

How will the information need to be sorted? Department, location, job title and seniority are common indicators for grouping data in reports. Are the desired sorts easily available in your system or do they require extra effort? For example, when extracting information from a payroll system, the records may be limited to a sort by employee number. Sorting records by last name is usually needed, but not always available.

REPORT LAYOUT

How will the report need to look? Keep the audience and business purpose in mind when developing the columns, rows, pages and graphics, if needed.

♦ What are the column headings?

♦ Are totals and/or summaries needed? By what subgroup or grouping?

♦ Should information for different groups appear on different pages (important for some confidential decisions)? Make sure the reader can determine when the sort categories change.

♦ Is this request similar to any standard reports? It's often easier to edit a current report.

♦ Is the analysis or reporting of data sufficient, or do you need to provide text for interpretation? Very few HRIS packages or other HR packages produce graphs, although they provide the capability to download into a graphics package or a spreadsheet file that can produce the desired pie charts and graphs. Identify the steps needed to produce the desired output.

PRODUCING THE REPORT

Produce a draft report for review whenever possible. If your software allows an on-screen look at the report, you can quickly modify columns and lay-out. Mainframe systems commonly demand that you print the output first. If so, ask for a limited data set in the draft version so you are not buried with unnecessary paper. Take time to review for accuracy the output of a new or modified report. Inaccurate data from the HR department will, at the very least, jeopardize the perception of the integrity of your system.

Find out how the report was used. Did it provide the support needed for decision making? What additional analysis might have been useful? What steps were involved in producing the report? How might it have been done more efficiently? Make notes to the department for improvements next time. Once completed, be sure to file the requests and a copy of the report.

Record where the report format is saved so you are not searching for it the next time a similar request is made. TIP: To quickly access reports, put the file name in a page footer. The next time the phone rings at 5 p.m.—you'll be ready.

OTHER THOUGHTS ABOUT PRODUCING EFFECTIVE BUSINESS REPORTS

ALTERNATE APPROACH TO COLLABORATIVE WRITING

Once all the tactical decisions have been made, one approach to writing is for each member of the committee to tackle the job separately. The committee mandate must be followed by each member: Each draft must be the author's response to the decisions made in concert with the other committee members. Each draft should follow the outline closely, and each draft should be required to use the same pieces of evidence. If these guidelines aren't followed, all the work on consensus so far has been wasted.

After all members have completed drafts, they are asked to submit them *if they like* for the committee's considerations. Those who don't submit their drafts should hold on to them for use in the ensuing discussion. The drafts that are submitted should be either read aloud or distributed in photocopy to the members. A simple vote should be taken to determine which draft will serve as base document, a starting place.

From here on, the procedure is one of simple common sense. You prod the members for their revisions, suggestions, deletions from the basic document. You prod them until there are no more changes, then you send the final product to someone for a final draft. Viola! You'll find that, in most cases, the strongest draft will be the one chosen as a base document. The most glib of the members will work with the words and style, and the "thinkers" will be able to do what they do best as well. No one will become destructive, because each member had to think through the subject while writing his or her own draft. The writing process becomes a simple logical extension of the decision-making process. You probably won't believe that as you read this, but you'll discover it in time.

NOTES

1. Raymond V. Lesikar, *Report Writing for Business,* 5th ed. (Homewood, IL: Richard D. Irwin, 1977), p. 1.

2. Philip C. Kolin, *Successful Writing at Work,* 4th ed. (Lexington, MA: Heath, 1994), p. 327.

3. Adapted from Frederick C. Dyer, *Executive's Guide to Effective Speaking and Writing* (Englewood Cliffs, NJ: Prentice-Hall, 1962), p. 112.

4. R. W. Raspberry, & L. L. Lindsay,. *Effective Managerial Communication,* 2nd ed. (Belmont, CA: Wadsworth, 1994), pp. 339–340. M. E. Guffey, *Business Communication: Process and Product* (Belmont, CA: Wadsworth, 1994), p. 288. P. C. Kolin, *Successful Writing at Work,* 4th ed. (Lexington, MA: D. C. Heath, 1994), pp. 588, 624. R. E. Burnett, *Technical Communication,* 3rd ed. (Belmont, CA: Wadsworth, 1994), pp. 474–475.

5. Phillip V. Lewis and William H. Baker, *Business Report Writing* (Columbus, OH: Grid Publishing, 1978), p. 51.

6. M. E. Guffy, *Business Communication: Process and Product* (Belmont, CA: Wadsworth, 1994), p. 325.

7. Note: These five steps are offered for the writer who does not have access to word processing equipment. If you have a computer, you'll be able to streamline several of the steps by putting notes into a data base, using word processing routines to edit and rearrange material and so on. Nevertheless, the mental process is much the same with or without advanced technology.

8. J. Woodford, "Note Jotting Made Simple," *Supervisory Management*, 37, 10, October 1992, p. 6.

9. G. Janner, "Towards a readable report," *Accountancy*, 111, April, 1993, p. 40.

10. Charles T. Brusaw, Gerald J. Alfred, and Walter E. Oliu, *The Business Writer's Handbook* (New York: St. Martin's Press, 1976), p. 153.

11. Richard Hatch, *Communicating in Business* (Chicago, IL: Science Research Associates, 1977), p. 245.

12. Richard Hatch, *Communicating in Business* (Chicago, IL: Science Research Associates, 1977), p. 245.

13. G. Janner, "Towards a readable report," *Accountancy*, 111, April, 1993, p. 40.

14. B. Repp, "Want Faster, Easier Business Writing? Talk on Paper!" *Supervisory Management*, 37, 9, Sept. 1992, p. 7.

15. M. E. Guffey, *Business Communication: Process and Product* (Belmont, CA: Wadsworth, 1994), p. 104.

16. Adapted from Joseph Allen and Bennet P. Lientz, *Effective Business Communication* (Santa Monica, CA: Goodyear, 1979), pp. 121–29. Reprinted by permission of Goodyear Publishing Company.

17. Reprinted with permission of *HR Magazine*, May 1991.

PART SIX

AUDITING COMMUNICATION AND MANAGEMENT

CHAPTER 16

BUSINESS AND MANAGERIAL COMMUNICATION RESEARCH[1]

Getting the Answers You Need

▼

In this chapter you will find ideas that will help you:

♦ Understand the purpose for conducting managerial communication research

♦ Describe a model for conducting organizations research

♦ Cite several different techniques for conducting primary research

♦ Recognize some advantages and disadvantages of each type of data collection

♦ Identify the seven types of questions most commonly used in survey questionnaires

♦ Understand the difference between validity and reliability

♦ Become aware of the techniques involved in research interviews

♦ Describe three types of group processes used in organizational research

▼

If I made a decision fast, I was right 60 percent of the time. If I made a decision carefully, I'd be right 70 percent of the time, but it was always worth it.

—EDMUND C. LYNCH (OF MERRILL LYNCH)

Never have we needed a good crystal ball more than we do today. The success of today's organizations, more than ever before, hinges on information—ever new ideas and strategies for providing today's goods and services. Information, carefully cultivated and acted on, is the lifeblood of every successful organization. The managerial communicator plays a vital role in creating usable information.

To get such information, organization leaders need primary research skills. Research isn't just for professors and grad students. It is the key to good decisions and organizational effectiveness.

This chapter provides the keys to effective organizational research. With these keys, a manager can, indeed, keep his or her finger on the pulse as this book's subtitle promises.

The Purpose of Research

The purpose of research is to learn something we do not know and to provide managers with useful information to help solve problems. Children learn basic skills by trial and error—trying and failing until they get it right. There is no other way to learn how to walk or catch a ball.

> *Logic is a higher level of thinking.*

A higher level of learning however, uses logic that leads to conclusions based on previous generalizations and experiences. Logical thinking puts two different concepts together to form a new conclusion or concept. Research is simply a systematic way of linking information and forming conclusions. It incorporates data-gathering methods in order to advance our understanding—and to make better decisions.

Here is a simple example you may have experienced: If you decide to buy a new car, we doubt that you would just walk into the nearest dealer and grab the first car in sight. Instead, you would probably do some research. You might read stories in automobile magazines or consumer's guides to compare features. Perhaps you'll talk to friends who have recently bought new cars and ask about their experiences. You will want to test drive cars and you might even begin to count the number and type of new cars you see on the streets, assuming that if a lot of people are buying a certain model, it must be pretty good. See, you have been doing research all along.

It's not mysterious; it's not exceptionally complex. It can become a day-to-day activity that produces huge dividends in the form of good answers and good decisions.

For our purposes, the following definition will apply:
Research is the process of getting dependable answers to important questions using a systematic method of gathering, analyzing, and interpreting evidence.
Its end product is knowledge.

Research Can Be Classified as Exploratory, Secondary, or Primary

When we search through publications—books, magazines, newspapers, pamphlets, atlases, encyclopedias, etc.—looking for background information, we are doing what is called *exploratory research.* Exploratory research gives us a frame of reference or understanding of the issues and history of the industry we are researching.

Secondary research is the study of the primary research conducted by others that can be extrapolated to apply to our research topic. When you reviewed a copy of *Consumer Reports* before buying a car, you were using secondary research. The use of secondary research techniques allows managers to save their companies much time and money by avoiding unnecessary duplication; however, we must be careful using secondary research because the data may not perfectly fit our needs. The attitude here should be, "Why reinvent the wheel when it's so much easier to read about what others have already done?" Excellent sources of secondary research include trade magazines and government research reports.

Let's assume, however, that the secondary research effort has not yielded a solid answer to the question. You've read the car magazines but still aren't ready to make a buying decision based on this information. You want to be certain that you are buying the best car for your needs. You will find it necessary to do *primary* research—to collect primary data that must be obtained first hand from nonpublished information sources. Such information comes from four sources:

♦ observations

♦ surveys

♦ interviews

♦ experiments

In our car-buying example, you may well use all four. You will observe how well the car seems to be built, how it sounds, how it handles on the road. You may take an informal survey by interviewing some friends who have bought similar cars. You may even try an experiment where you'll try driving several cars over the same roads at the same speeds to see which handles better.

A RESEARCH MODEL

Models offer direction at the beginning of the project.

A model is a conceptual representation of the project—the plan. Just as a manufacturer wouldn't design a new product without first building several mockups (models), so the researcher should build a model first.

A model presents a framework from which to work. The structure is useful because it assures that researchers, in their excitement to implement a project, do not overlook important steps which, if not considered, might render the research worthless. If you write out a framework before conducting your research, you will be more focused and more efficient than if you do not build your model first. The following paragraphs explain the basic parts of a research model.

INTRODUCTION

Give a brief history of the research topic. Once the symptoms of an organizational problem appear, do some initial fact gathering that will help to determine the characteristics of the true problem. This fact gathering might include talking to others about the problem and conducting a library literature search on the topic. This fact-gathering process is aimed at refining the researcher's educated guess to a more accurate problem statement.

Objectives

The next step in doing any research is to define correctly the true nature of the research problem. What exactly do we want to know? Getting the right answers to wrong questions happens more often than you might think. Unless you are working directly on an *explicitly identified* problem, you really are not doing research, you are simply gathering data.

Write a Specific Problem Statement

The problem statement is exactly *what* we are researching. It is possible for researchers to get so wrapped up in acquiring new data that they forget to keep a specific research problem in the forefront of their minds. They go off on tangents and diversions from the primary purpose of the study, delaying the research findings and the business decision. During the initial investigation, the researcher must define the scope of the problem, and try to determine the cause-and-effect relationships between the *variables.*

In order to state a problem that can be researched, it is necessary to write it in a form that includes the following factors:

1. A *relationship* between two variables, or possibly among several variables, *is questioned.*
2. Each variable is *operationally defined,* either within the problem statement or in supplemental statements to it.
3. A *population* for the research is implied or identified.

Here is an illustration of the aforementioned factors as applied to a poorly worded research question: The question, "I wonder why our company's sales seem to be leveling off?" is essentially not researchable because it is inadequately defined. What relationships are described? How do we know sales are leveling off? Leveling off compared with what?

This research question suffers because the terms are not specifically defined. Do the sales refer to Product X or Products Y and Z? (Maybe X and Y are selling in record numbers but Z is pulling down the overall results.) Does *leveling off* mean that the growth of sales is slower that in the past or that there is no growth at all? Finally, what population is implied? Are we talking about all sales to all customers or only particular types of sales to a certain population of customers?

A better problem statement would be, "Has the cutback in print advertising for Product X [one variable] resulted in a decline in sales growth [another variable] for Product X over the last six months [time frame]?"

The new statement offers the hypothesis that the independent variable—cutback in print advertising—has made a change in the dependent variable—sales over the past six months.

The problem statement could be further improved by spelling out the relationship between the two variables and stating how the variables' advertising and sales were to be measured. An improved research question might become, "Has the 50% reduction in Product X's print advertising from January to December 1994 resulted in the low 1% sales growth of Product X for the six months of July through December 1994?" This statement is now correct and is researchable because all variables are *related, measured, and specific.*

Give a Purpose Statement

The statement should explain what you expect to gain by doing the research, or in other words, *why* you are conducting the research. The trick to writing good purpose statements is to not be so general that nothing really gets answered, and not so specific that some of the critical elements are overlooked.

Methodology

Methodology is a strategic plan of attack.

Once the research problem has been clearly stated, we can take the third step of the model, plan our attack. Remember to conduct secondary research first. Primary research can be time consuming and expensive, so finding answers to previously asked questions is always preferable—so long as it applies directly to your business question. In some cases, you will find such information through a thorough library search.

1.   *Determine what secondary information will be researched first.* Look for articles, books, trade publications, government documents, internal documents, and research done by other groups that address the issue you are studying. As we have mentioned, this level of research may provide the answers to our problem and we can stop here and not incur the additional cost of primary research. However, if secondary research is insufficient to answer the problem, then plan to do primary research.

2. *List what type of primary research must be done to solve the problem.* Will you conduct observations? Will you administer a questionnaire? Will you hold interviews or panel discussions? Describe each step thoroughly since *how* the research is conducted will make a significant impact on what kind of data you will receive from the research.

3. *Determine the appropriate sample size to survey.* The sample must be representative of the population if you wish extrapolate your findings to the population of your research. Gallup polls survey approximately 1,500 people to determine national sentiment on public issues and have confidence of plus or minus 3 percent in their findings. A sample of 300 to 500 people is a rule of thumb for most managers when conducting primary research. This size sample is large enough to apply the findings to a population between 2,000 and 10,000 people with a confidence interval of plus or minus 3 percent.

4. *Do Primary Research.* As you move into primary research, think through the following steps to ensure a systematic approach:

1. Establish limits on time and money to be spent
2. Determine whether a professional researcher is needed
3. Pilot test your research design
4. Gather the raw data
5. Analyze the collected data
6. Make a decision

♦ *Establish Limits on Time and Money.* How much time should reasonably be spent on researching this question? If the need is urgent, a limited "quick and dirty" study may be all one can do. If the problem has been identified early and the time is available to make a more thorough analysis, all the better.

    When figuring expenditures, remember to figure in costs of the researchers' time, printing and copying, computer time for data analysis, and hiring of outside experts as needed.

♦ *Pilot Test Data-Gathering Techniques.* Always test the tool on a group that is representative of the group you will be testing. A *pilot study* is the best way to test your research tool. A pilot gathers a small sample of data before spending a lot of money on large scale data collection. The pilot will quickly reveal any glitches in your methodology. Then you can get the bugs out before spending a great deal of time and effort on more extensive research.

♦ *Gather Data.* Details on gathering high-quality data are presented later in the chapter.

♦ *Analyze the Data.* Raw data is not the end product of research, it is an intermediate step toward a decision. To refine raw data into *information,* we must accumulate a sufficient amount, analyze it, and interpret it in order to draw conclusions.

♦ *Make a Decision.* The last activity in the basic model of primary research is making a decision based on the information gathered coupled with the manager's own good judgment. At some point you need to quit cutting bait and start fishing. When you recognize that additional information is providing marginal returns, it is time to quit researching and make a decision.

5. *Check the Outcomes.* Never act on the results of only one information-gathering technique. No matter how scientific the data-gathering technique is, findings should be checked by at least one additional research method. For example, a survey research approach might well be validated by personal interviews. Systematic observations of people may be checked against their productivity reports. The two technique approach is professionally known as the use of nonrepetitive, redundant measures. As the old carpenter used to say, "Measure it twice before cutting it once."

The ultimate proof in the pudding is whether or not the decision worked. After a reasonable amount of time, retest to see if the decision made has solved the original problem. If not, it's back to square one.

Once your model has been developed, analyzed, and approved, it is time to start collecting preliminary data. The next section discusses several observation techniques that you can use as you conduct research.

OBSERVATION TECHNIQUES

Perhaps you never thought of "just watching" as a research technique. It can be, but only if done with the purpose of satisfying stated research objectives. All people observe their environment to some degree. That is one reason observation is so frequently used to gather data. Although observation is so commonly used, it is also the most difficult technique to use correctly. Research observation involves much more than casual viewing and a haphazard absorbing of information. Things to be observed must be clearly decided before the observation is attempted. If the variables are not clearly defined, the observer might note one set of items during one observation and another set during another observation.

Advantages and Disadvantages of Observation

Observation data is real-world data, not data from a laboratory study designed to duplicate real life. Observations mirror situations as they really exist. Done correctly, the process reduces most bias and distortions.

Further, using observation techniques in connection with mechanical devices (such as rulers, time clocks, or gauges) can produce the most accurate possible data. Any system that produces hard data and consistent measurement will go a long way toward eliminating bias and interpretation errors from the study.

The last advantage of observation is that the results of the study can be verified readily. Managers can go down and check the results through similar observation techniques, and repeated observations can serve to validate the findings.

Do not be distracted by trivial observations.

A disadvantage of observation is that, if observers have not been carefully trained, the data may reflect observer biases. In addition, observers may spend a great deal of time and effort noting the routine, insignificant event. The unusual and potentially useful data are often hidden under a mountain of trivial observations.

Guidelines for Effective Observation

The person making the observations must have a clear understanding of the operational definitions being used for the study. In addition the researcher should:

1. Prepare the forms used to record the data in advance. Pretest these with a pilot study to be sure the observers know exactly how to record observations.

2. Use objective observers, not people who may have a bias. If, for example, you are observing work behaviors in a particular department, it would be best to use observers who do not work there (or better yet do not even know the people being observed).

3. Prepare a schedule of all observations in advance. Indicate who will observe, where to observe, and when to observe.

4. Make your observations methodical by carefully using the same methods of recording data. Although we often think of simply tallying observations on a clipboard, some situations may call for measuring devices such as counters, stop watches, computer monitoring, cameras, video recorders, and other mechanical devices.

5. The observer must minimize his or her presence in the observation process. If the observer is blatantly obvious in observing and recording data, the people being observed may act differently from normal, thus masking what really goes on in the company. Also, studies have shown that the very presence of the observer can lead to improved performance in the short run. This is called a Hawthorne Effect, named after a factory where it was first noted.

Specific Observation Techniques:

Time and Motion Studies

Time and motion studies can help managers determine the best way to do a job.

This approach has long been used to attempt to analyze specific actions needed to complete a task. Suppose that you have a few workers who produce substantially more output than the typical person in that job. You may want to use this observation technique to evaluate what the high producers do—specifically—and to compare their movements with those of the less productive workers. When you think you have figured out why the good workers are so good, you can teach other workers the same skills.

In addition to using a time and motion studies approach to increase productivity, it is also used to determine manufacturing costs of a new product and to develop work schedules.

Behavioral Frequency Counts

This observational approach focuses on how often particular behaviors occur in the people being studied during normal day-to-day actions. An example of this is a study that observed the behaviors used by top salespeople as compared with behaviors of the rest of the salespeople. The observers found, using behavioral frequency counts, that the best salespeople listened longer, asked more probing questions, and requested the order more often than the average salesperson.

Reports and Other Written Documents

Another way managers can use observations techniques is to review written documents. A great deal of data can emerge from a systematic study of records, reports, memos, letters, and so forth.

Telephone companies use this in connection with listening in on customer conversations. The conversations are recorded and any commitments or promises made by the service representative are noted. The service observer then goes through the company's records to see if those commitments were met.

Companies routinely maintain records that provide information on downtime, budget variances, absenteeism, tardiness, output, terminations, work stoppages, overtime, and many other factors. Systematic checking of such data using observational techniques can answer many business questions.

Tallying Observation of Behaviors

Use simple check sheets to record observations. A check sheet is an easy-to-understand form used to answer the question, "How often are certain events happening?"

Once you've determined what is to be observed and recorded, you'll need to decide how often and for how long observations will take place. Design the check sheet to be clear and easy to understand. A sample sales-rep-behaviors check sheet is shown in Figure 16-1.

SURVEYS

If a questionnaire is well-written, pretested, and administered properly, the study can yield a great deal of rich information about such things as organizational needs, problems, employee perceptions, and consumer attitudes. The sur-

	Greets Customer Promptly	Makes Small Talk	Asks Key Questions	Gives Info/ Assistance	Explains/ Clarifies Features	Asks for Order	Writes the Order
Salesperson 1							
Salesperson 2							
Salesperson 3							

FIGURE 16-1   Behavior observation check sheet.

vey approach has tremendous advantages for the business manager *if* designed and implemented properly.

Generally, the use of a questionnaire should be limited to research projects where information from other methods is not available. It could also be used to verify results generated from other methods.

Questionnaires are often mailed or otherwise distributed directly to the people who are asked to respond. They work best when respondents know their answers will be kept confidential. Mailed surveys are useful when collecting data from people who may be geographically dispersed, such as customers across the country. This spread out sample often rules out the use of interviews (except by telephone), observations, and experiments.

Advantages of Surveys

1. *They are inexpensive.* First, surveys are usually less expensive than interviews and experimentation. This is because the survey is not as labor intensive. Once designed, a questionnaire can gather a large quantity of data without requiring a great deal of employee time; therefore it costs less.

2. *They are easy to administer.* Since, by definition, the questionnaire is an instrument that requires a written response, the administrator does not have to be skilled in interviewing or observing techniques. Generally, a simple group explanation of the questionnaire purpose or an explanatory letter will suffice.

3. *Responses will have less bias.* The data in such cases may be more accurate since most respondents will be frank and honest when their answers are anonymous.[2]

4. *Management tends to be receptive to the questionnaire approach.* Data so gathered is usually seen as credible. (If handled correctly, it will be credible, but much depends on how well the survey is designed and administered. Garbage in, garbage out applies here.)

Disadvantages of the Survey Technique

1. *Survey questionnaires are impersonal and structured.* Questionnaire instruments are one-way communications that generally do not allow respondents to clarify answers. This forced-choice format makes for easy data processing, but if the researcher is asking the wrong questions or not allowing for a full range of all possible responses, the data will be contaminated. Survey questionnaires normally do not give people the opportunity to provide unstructured feedback or to elaborate on why they chose a particular rating.

2. *The questionnaire may be subject to overinterpretation.* Some people try to psychoanalyze every question. They read meaning into the question that was not intended and sometimes try to guess at how the researcher would like them to answer. For some people, the survey creates a "test" environment. They feel that they are being evaluated.

3. *The whole process can be time consuming, especially if the questionnaire is sent through the mail.* Allow ample time for people to respond. Put a due date on the survey but don't be surprised if responses dribble in well beyond that date.

4. Low response rates are common with mail surveys. Although many people can be reached at a relatively low cost with mail surveys, a major disadvantage is a low response rate. Many recipients simply ignore a mail survey.

Overcoming the Disadvantages

The impersonalization problems can be reduced by giving respondents clear oral instructions (if administering the survey personally) or using a conversational, friendly tone in written instructions. Overinterpretation can be reduced by instructing people to give their first impressions and not to attempt to analyze the questions. Time consumption can be reduced by administering the survey to larger groups of people (if possible) and by budgeting enough time to allow for mail delays if using mail surveys. Finally, response rates can be improved by rewarding the respondent with a token of appreciation. Some surveyors attach a dollar bill to a mail survey, others offer to make a donation to charity if the person will complete the survey. Be creative and you can overcome many, if not all, of these disadvantages.

> *A manager can do many things to improve response rates and decrease bias.*

How to Get a Random Sample

Randomness means that any member of the population has an equal chance of being selected for the survey. If your population is defined as people who bought Ford trucks during May of this year, all such buyers have an equal chance of getting your survey. To ensure randomness, use one of these methods:

1. Assign a number to each member of your population. If you have 173 truck buyers, number them from one to 173. Then, put slips of paper into a "hat" numbered 1 through 173. As your sample is drawn (suppose you decide to mail surveys to 50 people) check off each name and make your mailing list.

2. A better approach is to use a table of random numbers. Such a table is shown in Figure 16-2. This table is computer generated to ensure randomness. To use this table, determine that you will select every fifth number until you have a full sample. Close your eyes and point to the starting number in the table. Then go down five numbers at a time, selecting your sample. (Drop off digits as necessary. We'd use only three digits in our example because our population is 173 truck buyers.)

36137	42353	54264	01762	61844	70478
06511	50555	87031	32226	42361	48347
37411	30100	36383	78007	66760	02174
30546	17725	62862	63685	76105	46505
06835	07275	12563	43065	88713	15740
88566	78315	62044	77273	16241	42366
65011	14340	00533	77803	55314	37830
82448	66127	10637	62102	34488	50540
87276	62510	57557	61311	73472	71307
42334	88658	86130	87774	87348	76370
60030	05273	17186	18085	53333	81380
32731	43430	18565	15152	07581	23345
60056	28174	73801	16715	03554	50361
14280	52838	70656	28544	11240	47287
87108	68520	58574	13431	07222	70347
37816	84081	70116	86746	40372	78482
33137	37472	52371	28624	07705	50431
30067	87815	42464	43565	70036	74212
88452	32535	25765	28328	67145	05581
05657	73664	15566	25247	18880	35164
50001	86550	23353	38668	37308	05322
16084	13312	67676	13183	04768	76075
15010	07607	66471	20070	28838	66076
25056	85756	58287	27221	37367	31558
10851	53574	23084	00730	65464	28740

FIGURE 16-2 Table of random numbers.

Don't cheat on randomness.

Once you select a sample, stick with it. Substituting hurts randomness and a nonrandom sample is less reliable than a random one. If carefully selected, a random sample has the best probability of speaking for the whole population.

Questionnaire Design

Many of the drawbacks of questionnaire surveys can be overcome by using the ideas presented in this section.

Designing the Questionnaire

The following steps should be used in designing a questionnaire:

1. Determine the information wanted and types of questions needed.
2. Draft and develop the questions.
3. Test the questions.
4. Develop the complete questionnaire.

Step 1. *Determine the information and types of questions required.* Rule #1: Know What You Are Researching. Be sure you have a clear and specific picture of what information you want to get from the survey. Avoid the temptation to toss in a few extra questions that may be interesting but are not germane to your study. Keep it focused. The longer the survey is, the lower your response rate is likely to be.

Next, determine what types of questions would provide the most accurate data. Be sure to consider how the data will be tabulated and analyzed.

Seven types of questions are most frequently used in survey questionnaires. A questionnaire might have any or all of these types of questions:

1. *Close-ended questions.* This is a forced-choice question using an either/or or yes/no response.
   Example:
   ♦ I have good communications with my supervisor. ☐ Yes ☐ No
2. *Open-ended questions.* This type of question allows the respondent to give an unlimited answer. It should be followed by sufficient space for the response.
   Example:
   ♦ What problems are you having communicating with your supervisor? [followed by space to respond]
   WARNING: Open-ended responses are difficult to quantify. They can be used in surveys to get ideas, examples, and general feelings, but typically an interview is a better medium for this since it allows the researcher to probe and clarify responses.

3. *Checklist.* This type of question presents a list of items where the participant is asked to check those that apply to his or her particular situation.

   Example:

   ♦ Please check the following types of communications that you have with your supervisor.

   ☐ Informal meetings   ☐ After-hours discussions
   ☐ Formal meetings   ☐ Telephone
   ☐ Written report   ☐ Social gathering
   ☐ Letters   ☐ Committee meetings

4. *Multiple choice question.* This type of question offers a number of answer choices of which the respondent is asked to select the most correct one.

   Example:

   ♦ About how often do you communicate with your supervisor?

   > (a) once a day or less
   >
   > (b) two or three times a day
   >
   > (c) three or five times a day
   >
   > (d) six or more times a day

   For a question of this type to be effective, be sure that the choices presented *cover all possible options.* Responses for multiple choice questions should be *mutually exclusive.* Each choice is clearly different from the others. Respondents get irritated when their selection isn't one of the options. (You can add "none of the above" easily enough, but it won't tell you much.)

5. *Ranking scales.* This type of a question requires the participant to rank-order a list of items.

   Example:

   ♦ Of the following list of five types of communications that you might have with your supervisor, please place a 1 by the item that is most important to you, a 2 by the item that is second in importance, and so on. All five items should be ranked.

   ___Formal meetings   ___Letters or memos
   ___Informal conversations   ___Telephone discussions
   ___Written reports

6. *Likert scale.*[3] This type of survey item is generally used to measure attitude toward a concept or idea. It allows the respondent the opportunity to indicate the degree to which he or she agrees or disagrees (usually on a five- or seven-point scale) with a statement or idea.

Example:

♦ Please indicate the degree to which you agree or disagree with this statement: *I am satisfied with the amount of communication I have with my supervisor.*

Strongly Agree	Agree	Neither Agree nor Disagree	Disagree	Strongly Disagree
5	4	3	2	1

7. *Semantic differential.* This is used to measure attitudes by displaying pairs of opposite terms and asking respondents to check which term better describes their feelings toward the concept or topic. Each pair consists of a positive and negative adjective reflecting the extremes, such as, honest-dishonest, efficient-inefficient, powerful-weak, etc. The adjectives are placed at opposite ends of the line which is divided into an equal number of segments. Respondents can select the degree to which the adjective describes the topic.

Example:

♦ The following pairs of adjectives are to be considered as they apply to the *XYZ Corporation District Office.* Place an X in the space between the two terms that best describes how you see the words reflecting the situation in the District Office. Mark only one space between each pair of words.

```
            XYZ CORPORATION DISTRICT OFFICE
             Supervisor Performance Review
                  My Supervisor is:


Esteem-building: ___:___:___:___:___:___:___: Demeaning


Inefficient:     ___:___:___:___:___:___:___:Efficient


Not helpful:     ___:___:___:___:___:___:___:Helpful
```

Note: It is important to reverse some of the items so that people don't develop a response set, that is, the habit of marking the same column consistently. In the foregoing example, you see some positive terms on the left and some on the right column as well.

The advantage of using either the Likert or the Semantic Differential scales is that it is possible to begin to calculate a number that reflects attitudes and opinions. The values for each scale can then be added together to get a measure of a person's attitudes toward the subject (in our example, the subject is the District Office). Also, the researcher can calculate the mean attitude score for one group and compare it with another group or remeasure the same people at a later time to see if shifts in attitudes have occurred.

Step 2.   *Draft and develop the questions.* The two most important considerations in developing questions are validity and reliability. *Validity* is the degree to which the item measures what the researcher wants to measure. *Reliability* is the degree to which the item is likely to get the same results consistently.

> *Leading questions decrease validity.*

One method of improving validity is to ensure that the question will not produce a biased response. Emotionally packed words and questions that lead the respondent toward an obviously preferred answer should be avoided. Also, validity can be improved by including a number of differently phrased questions—each of which is aimed to solicit data about the same topic.

Questions that obtain reasonably consistent results when administered to similar samples (or the same sample at different times) are said to be reliable.

Step 3.   *Test the questions.* Pretest any questionnaire by administering the survey to a small group of people—people similar to those who will be asked to respond to the final version. Responses to the pretest will tell you how well people understand the questions. This feedback will help you refine the questions to eliminate misunderstandings and confusion in the final version.

Step 4.   *Develop the complete questionnaire.* Once the questions have been tested, they should be integrated into a clean, straightforward questionnaire that provides clear instructions on how it should be completed.

Numbering each question and all possible responses will help facilitate the coding process, especially if a computer is used for analysis. Spreadsheet programs are often sufficient for determining the results, although more sophisticated survey-processing software is readily available.[4]

The final version of the questionnaire should be psychologically attractive, leaving ample white space. Don't crowd the information, it'll look imposing to the reader and may reduce the number of responses.

The questionnaire should have as many questions as necessary, but as few as possible. Don't overburden the respondent with trivial items. Leave adequate space for fill-in answers. Nothing is more frustrating than trying to put a five-line response into a space where only several words will fit. (This is especially important when using open-ended questions). Consider the following complaint form:

Complaint Form

Write your complaint in the box below. Please write legibly.

☐

Administering the Survey Questionnaire

The method of administering questionnaires depends on the purpose of the research, the method of sampling, the availability of the sample, and resources available to the researcher. Below are some common administering options:

Group Administering

From the researcher's point of view, this is the most efficient. The instructions and introductory information are given at one time and the completed questionnaires are usually ready for coding within a matter of minutes. This works well when all the questionnaire participants are physically present in a local geographic area.

Mail

When the representative sample is geographically dispersed, mail questionnaires will have to be used. In such a circumstance, a good sales letter needs to be developed to motivate the targeted sample to spend the time necessary to complete the questionnaire. In addition, a self-addressed, stamped envelope should be included.

Using the mail almost always results in a low percentage of responses. People feel less obligation to respond to mailed surveys. Many procrastinate and ultimately fail to respond at all. You can improve mail survey response rates by:

1. Including a persuasive letter explaining the benefit to the reader if he or she completes the survey.
2. Attach a tangible reward such as a dollar bill, a valuable coupon, or a free booklet. This causes people to feel some obligation to complete the survey.
3. Make the mailout look personal. Use handwritten or individually typed names and addresses (rather than labels), a first class postage stamp (not metered mail), and a simple return address on the envelope that causes the reader to be curious about what's in the envelope.

INTERVIEW TECHNIQUES

The interview research technique combines observation and questionnaires to obtain a level of data that is deeper and richer than either of the two techniques can produce separately. Researchers who use interviews will not only be able to get verbal responses from the subject, but more importantly will also be in a position to observe the subject's nonverbal behavior. Many times the observed behavior of the interviewee will be more meaningful than the words alone.

Interview Design

Because interviews are so commonplace, some people underestimate the need for structuring and planning an interview in advance. Too many choose to fly without a preflight inspection, and the results can be disasterous.

A good interview process calls for the five C's:

1. Construct the interview.
2. Commence the interview.
3. Conduct the interview.
4. Conclude the interview.
5. Compile the data and analyze the results.

Each of these five steps applies whether you are interviewing one person at a time or a group.

Constructing the Interview

The first activity before all others is to *state in writing your purpose of the interview*. Be sure to understand what, specifically, you are trying to get from the interview. You will then be ready to construct a list of questions to be asked.

There are two types of interviews—structured and unstructured. A *structured* interview forces the interview process to follow a predetermined line of questioning; an *unstructured* interview allows participants to express freely thoughts important to them.

A structured interview is rather like an interrogation while an unstructured interview is more like a conversation. Structured interviews are clearly led by the interviewer, while in unstructured situations the interviewer takes the lead from the interviewee.

There are advantages to both types. The structured interview is more efficient and can produce needed data quickly. The unstructured interview can produce new insights into the problem that perhaps weren't even thought of by the interviewer. It can get to respondent feelings and qualitative data more effectively.

The big difficulty with the unstructured interview is that responses may be hard to record, compile, and analyze. Themes usually do emerge, but these are subject to the researcher's interpretation. A disadvantage to the structured interview is that the interviewee often feels like he or she is being interrogated and can become uncomfortable, which can bias results.

Another aspect of interview preparation is pretesting the newly designed interview outline. Just as with survey questionnaires, an interview guide should be tested to determine if respondents are confused about questions. Two groups of individuals should be asked to respond to the proposed interview guide. The first group should be people just like those who will ultimately be sampled. Use this group to determine whether the questions are understood and the desired information can be obtained.

> *Always pretest the instrument before operating.*

The second group to pretest is other managers. Solicit the comments of fellow managers or other business people who might be able to respond on the instrument's validity. Ask specifically if these questions seem to be getting at the information needed.

Commencing the Interview

Begin with a greeting to help establish rapport. Since people often form their basic impressions of one another during the first few minutes of contact, the interviewer should always take the time to create a positive rapport and alleviate nervousness on the part of the interviewee. This can be accomplished by doing the following things:

◆ Introduce yourself.

◆ Use enthusiastic nonverbal welcoming messages like a smile and a handshake.

◆ Make an informal, neutral comment about the weather, a positive comment about the person's appearance, or brief chit-chat about a noncontroversial current event.

◆ Use humor to break the ice.

After the initial contact, the researcher must *motivate the interviewee* to cooperate positively during the interview process. Any rewards that might result from the interview should be mentioned. Rewards may range from something tangible to simple appreciation for their participation.

Stress the importance of the interviewees' answers, letting them know that what they say will be carefully considered and will have a critical impact on the problem being studied.

Explain how the interviewees were selected in order to avoid any suspicion that they are being singled out for some sort of special inspection. This is especially important in cases where employees are being interviewed regarding some company-wide problem. As with surveys, random selection is an excellent and easily explained process that will put people at ease. Another option for some situations is to interview every member of a particular group (say, a department).

Give the interviewee an orientation to the interview. Explain the purpose of the interview, the interviewee's role in the interview, and how the information is going to be used.

Conducting the Interview

> *Confrontation will distort information.*

During the interview process, the interviewer must be mentally *alert to the feedback.* If the questions are not clearly understood, ask them in a different way. If the response misses the point or is confusing, probe for clarification in a nonthreatening way.

Also, during the interview, *avoid disagreement.* If you feel the respondent is saying something out of line or inconsistent with what you know to be true, don't confront. Use careful, probing questions to ask for clarification. Be careful of tone of voice here. Don't put the interviewees in a position where they feel defensive. The interviewer should at all times *be neutral,* assuming the role of a careful but nonjudgmental listener.

The researcher needs to *manage the interview time* efficiently. This can be accomplished by skipping over trivialities, changing the focus when the interviewees develop a monologue, shifting the topic when interviewees start selling their opinions or pressing the interviewer for agreement, and, finally, by keeping the small talk to a minimum, but sufficient enough to maintain rapport.

As the interview progresses, capturing the data being generated becomes very important. This can be accomplished either by *efficient note taking, tape recording or both.*

Here are some tips that can help you improve your note-taking abilities:

1. Do not try to record word for word what is said. Jot down key information such as names, dates, ages, percentages, and relevant figures.

2. Don't bury your head in your notes while the respondent is talking. Note only major points, and follow up key facts and figures.

3. Don't be bound to linear, textual notes. Develop a personal shorthand. Use symbols instead of words, circle key thoughts, use color pens to highlight repeated or emphasized ideas.

4. Slow the pace when necessary. Tell the respondent that you want to be sure to get his or her ideas clearly. Most people are flattered by your efforts to record what they say carefully.

Audio or video taping of the interview provides an excellent opportunity for detailed data verification. Exact information is recorded rather than interpretations of it. This information then can be stored indefinitely and referred to as needed.

There are two major disadvantages, however, to the use of recording equipment. First, the presence of recording devices may bias the data by caus-

ing the subjects to behave differently than they normally would. This may be overcome by allowing the subjects to get used to the recording device before the important parts of the interview are covered.

The second disadvantage is that the data must still be interpreted by the human listener after it is recorded. This means that the whole interview process requires at least twice as much time as the nonrecorded interview.

In actual practice, most professional interviewers prefer note taking with taped backup that can be reviewed to clarify specific points.

Concluding the Interview

Stop the interview when both people have run out of things to say. When this occurs, the interviewer should summarize what was learned, express what he or she intends to do with the information, and what actions may be precipitated from the findings. After this, the interviewer should sincerely thank the interviewee for his or her time and contributions.

Compiling the Data and Analyzing the Results

The data from closed questions can be easily summarized and analyzed using a form much like a questionnaire. Open-ended question data is another matter. With open-ended information, frequency counts and *content analysis* should be undertaken.

A frequency count simply notes the number of times the same or closely related comments have occurred. Content analysis identifies common themes. Be sensitive to subtle nuances and common threads that run through the respondents' answers. If several respondents verbally or nonverbally refer to a product or person with apparent disdain, you may conclude there is a less-than-positive feeling toward that product or person.

Three Interview Formats

Three interview formats are used for business research: face-to-face individual interviews, telephone interviews, and group interviews. Advantages and disadvantages of each are described in the following.

Face-to-Face

The face-to-face or personal interview technique is used most often when complete and comprehensive replies are needed. Since interpersonal communication is made up of words, mannerisms, and voice modulation, face-to-face contact provides feedback to the interviewer from all three sources.

ADVANTAGES OF FACE-TO-FACE INTERVIEWS:

1. The technique may be the only way to obtain accurate data on complicated or sensitive questions.
2. You get fewer refusals and premature interview termination because the respondent is one-on-one with the interviewer.
3. The questioning process is generally more thorough.
4. You can build stronger rapport and better respondent cooperation in this more personalized format.
5. The interviewer can get fuller explanations and clarifications through probing (follow-up questions) and observations of nonverbal behaviors. Because of the aforementioned advantages, personal interviews by skilled individuals is normally credited as being the most accurate data-gathering research method.

DISADVANTAGES OF FACE-TO-FACE INTERVIEWS:

1. Cost. One-on-one interviewing is definitely the most expensive and time-consuming way to gather information.
2. The interview process requires skilled interviewers to eliminate interview bias.
3. Personal or sensitive information may be withheld because of the recording device or a poor chemistry between interviewer and interviewee.
4. If the researcher is perceived to be the interviewee's boss, people may not level with him or her.

Telephone Interviewing Technique

We have all been subjected to telephone interviews, especially by polling organizations or market research groups. The telephone allows data gathering without the cost of actually getting together face to face.

ADVANTAGES OF TELEPHONE INTERVIEWING:

1. Difficult-to-contact people who are unwilling to give you the time in person may be open to a telephone call, especially a long-distance call.

2. It is much easier to take notes, tape the interview, and use a script without the interviewee being distracted.

3. The telephone commands attention and privacy, which minimizes interruptions that can occur in a face-to-face interview.

4. The telephone allows for the interviewer to come quickly to the point and establish a businesslike climate without the interviewee feeling rushed.

5. In many instances, people tend to be more candid over the phone than in a face-to-face interview.

DISADVANTAGES OF TELEPHONE INTERVIEWING:

1. Telephone interviews tend to be shorter than face-to-face interviews, usually not lasting more than 10 to 15 minutes. Because of this, research projects that require gathering a large amount of data per contact are not suitable for telephone interviewing.

2. The interviewer cannot use props, samples, or illustrations as part of the questioning process. This rules out complicated questions that require a demonstration or some type of visual device.

3. The telephone interview is limited to those having phones. For research within a company, for example, this would probably eliminate assembly line workers or those who work outside.

4. The telephone does not allow for personal observations of mannerisms which are one of the best sources of information during interpersonal communications.

Group Interviews

Two types of group interviews are used successfully to collect good research information: panels and focus groups. We look at the pros and cons of each of group interview format next.

Panels are groups of 7 to 12 people who share some organizational *expertise*—say, for example, a manufacturing company might assemble a quality control panel composed of employees who play roles in the quality process. The panel group is brought together for a few hours and asked questions. The group atmosphere relieves a lot of pressure from each member, allowing a natural flow of opinions based on each member's expertise. This form of research is particularly helpful when we are learning about a new topic. We expect to gather a lot of *new* information from panels of experts.

Panels

ADVANTAGES OF PANELS:

1. The major advantages to a panel is that the accuracy of information gathered is high. If the panel has been structured, established, and instructed properly, information generated by the panel will be usually better than any information that can be obtained from a single panel member. The combined expertise is better than the ideas of any one member. You achieve synergy.

2. A second advantage is that panels can be reassembled time and time again and asked similar questions to test if opinions change over time due to test variables.

DISADVANTAGES OF PANELS:

1. Panels can be expensive to establish and administer. Taking a group of high-paid experts away from their other work, for example, can be disruptive and costly.

2. It is often difficult to organize a representative panel that reflects the concerns and input of all relevant groups.

3. An ongoing panel may develop groupthink—their own biases that can damage the integrity of the inquiry process. This can happen in panels where group cohesiveness and internal harmony become more important than making tough decisions.

Focus Groups

This is a consumer research technique that has been used since the 1950s to enable market researchers to draw out consumer feelings and opinions of products and services. A focus group is normally a randomly selected group of customers (they typically do not have expertise in the organization) who are invited to share their observations and ideas with organizational leaders.

> *Focus groups foster open opinion flow.*

This group interview process is an unstructured group discussion between the interviewer and a group of 8 to 12 people. Because the interviewer does not ask questions or record answers in a traditional sense, he or she is free to act as a discussion leader or group moderator whose purpose is to direct and focus the group discussion toward the issues being researched. A focus group is like a group of friends who talk about a subject, with one friend who keeps the group on the topic.

ADVANTAGES OF THE FOCUS GROUP:

1. The focus group typically brings in outside ideas from the end user of an organization's goods or services.

2. As the focus group discussion begins to evolve, a spontaneous interchange of ideas will hopefully result in a wide variety of insightful and useful data.

DISADVANTAGES OF THE FOCUS GROUP:

1. Cost and time consumption. Typically participants are paid to participate or, minimally, are given a free dinner.

2. Assembling a random sample of participants may be difficult. Some customers don't have the time or inclination to participate.

3. Qualitative data received may be difficult to interpret, especially when opposite recommendations are offered by people within the group.

1. Hold the group on neutral grounds—a conference room or an off-site hotel.

2. Notify participants where, when, and why the meeting will take place.

3. Provide a relaxed atmosphere with refreshments and allow participants to interact to break the ice before starting.

4. Seat everyone around the table and explain the purpose, why and how the participants were chosen, and how the results of the session will be used.

5. Have all members introduce themselves to loosen up the group and give you feedback on how well each person meets the selected profile.

6. Direct the discussion in a consistently deductive manner, moving from general ideas or impressions to more specific ones.

7. Avoid discouraging novel or unusual ideas. Sometimes these can be very useful.

8. Provide equal opportunity for all members to contribute; passive members should be encouraged to interact.

EXPERIMENTS AND TESTS

The foremost rule of effective marketing applies for many other business functions. Simply stated, it says, "The three most important marketing activities are testing, testing, and testing." Never assume that what has always worked will continue to work. Business success is a constant process of evaluation and improvement. Testing is the research technique that can best help you keep a finger on the pulse of all aspects of organizational success.

Experiments can be the most reliable and accurate of all the research procedures. They are not used to solicit opinions or ideas from people; rather, they are used actually to determine results of organizational decisions. They don't measure what is said, believed, or felt but what *happens* when a change is introduced into the equation.

Effective experiments yield hard facts, produce actual results, and deal in reality. Because of the type of information generated by experiments and tests, they are the most powerful business research method to project future results.

The Game Is to Control the Variables

The secret in putting together a successful experiment is to keep all the variables—or anything that could possibly be a variable—constant, except the one being investigated. For example, let's say you are interested in determining the cost effectiveness of a new direct mail advertising piece. This new mailout includes a different call-to-action incentive for the customer. Let's say that it offers customers who respond within 10 days a buy-one, get-one-free deal.

The important thing that needs to be done here is to control all extraneous variables and to make sure that the only difference being measured is the buy-one, get-one-free incentive. This sounds easy, but can be a difficult thing to do. To effectively test this offer, we would need to keep the following variables constant:

1. The sales message
2. The document layout
3. Printing and paper quality
4. The mailing schedule (pieces would have to be mailed on the same days of the week or month)
5. The postage amount
6. The mailing lists used (each approach would be equal and any one prospect in the target market would have an equal chance of receiving either offer.)

In Search of Validity and Reliability

You'll want your experiment to have both validity and reliability. An experiment is valid when the results actually measure what is supposed to be measured. In our example, we would be interested in the different effects of the incentive offer. By carefully controlling variables, you can be reasonably sure that a result from a test is due to the test variable. Such a result would be valid.

Reliability is the probability that you would get the same results if the experiment were repeated in the same way. Our experiment would have reliability if the results could be duplicated consistently, i.e., every time we use the buy-one, get-one-free offer the results will be the same as the results of our experiment.

It's All in the Design

Taking our example of testing a new incentive offer, let's look at a number of design approaches we can use to build reliability and validity into our experiment on the new mailer.

Let's Give it a Try

The first and most common test method used is what might be called the "Let's Give It a Try" (LGIT) approach. Rearranging a display in a store or putting impulse buy items near a cash register are examples of LGIT tests.

The problem with the LGIT design is that the experimental variable was introduced without a control (comparison) group or without any specific prior knowledge about the individuals who received the mailer. This does not allow us to evaluate the effectiveness and make a valid comparison between two offers.

When the risk of poor results is potentially costly (say our mailing example costs tens of thousands of dollars and will be repeated regularly), a more carefully designed experiment is appropriate.

Before and After (B/A)

The before-and-after experiment design is often seen as an improvement over LGIT. This experiment design would have us send two mailings—one with the incentive and one without—to the same individuals at different times. The results could then be compared. This is an improvement over LGIT, but not that much! The timing really gums things up. All kinds of errors can creep into the experiment. Change occurs over time and introduces factors that will contaminate the results. One obvious possibility is the customer who accepts the nonincentive offer and then gets a better offer for the same product a few months later. How is he or she likely to feel?

ADVANTAGES OF USING THE EXPERIMENTAL RESEARCH TECHNIQUE

1. Experiments and tests are the most reliable and accurate of all research methods.
2. The use of control groups greatly reduces errors from outside, unforeseen factors.
3. A variety of factors or variables may be tested at the same time.

DISADVANTAGES OF THE EXPERIMENTAL RESEARCH TECHNIQUE

1. Cost.
2. Need for expertise in research design in order to isolate variables and create comparable situations.

Naturally, we realize that one chapter is not going to cover all the techniques and hints of effective researching. Our intent with this chapter is to give a few guidelines so that future research that you conduct will be well organized, with a specific purpose and clear direction. If you implement the hints that we have offered in this chapter, you will improve your time efficiency and the relevance of your data to the problem you are researching.

Also, we realize that the word *research* strikes fear in many peoples' hearts. This is usually because they are inexperienced with research or they are ineffective researchers. We hope that this chapter offers a framework for those who fear research, because research is both rewarding and fun.

A QUICK SUMMARY OF MAJOR IDEAS

♦ The purpose of organizational research is to learn something we do not know and to provide managers with useful information to help solve problems.

♦ The basic parts of a research model are the introduction, objectives, and methodology.

♦ Primary research can be conducted using observations, surveys, interviews, and experiments.

♦ Researchers can use panels, focus groups, and nominal groups to collect data.

♦ Researchers must be careful to make sure the information they collect is both valid (when the results measure what is supposed to be measured) and reliable (when the same results can be obtained if the same results can be duplicated consistently).

♦ A focus group is an unstructured interview between the interviewer and a group of 8 to 12 people.

QUESTIONS FOR FURTHER THOUGHT

1. What are the differences between exploratory, secondary and primary research? When is each to be used? What kind of data do each provide?

2. What ways can you think of to overcome low response rates from the people you survey by mail? How will you overcome the bias associated with personally administered surveys and interviews?

3. What are the research techniques that managers can use to keep a finger on the pulse of their organizations?

OTHER THOUGHTS ABOUT BUSINESS AND
MANAGERIAL COMMUNICATION RESEARCH

AUDITING ORGANIZATIONAL COMMUNICATION

The term "audit" is commonly used in the accounting profession, but it can accurately describe systematic analyses of virtually any aspect of an organization. The objective of an audit is to determine to what extent functions within an organization are being performed optimally. The major question of an audit is, "Are appropriate procedures being followed?"

To be systematic, a process like the one described in Figure 16-4 should be followed when auditing (that is, diagnosing) communication.

SO WHAT HAPPENS AFTER THE AUDIT?

A communication audit, taken alone, will not solve any communication problems. Changes in the way an organization communicates can come about, however, by means of what specialists in organizational development call "interventions." An *intervention* is a managerial action taken to bring about improvement in group functioning. Listed in ascending order of difficulty, managers may

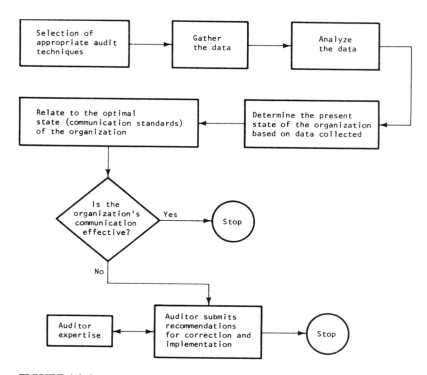

FIGURE 16-4

intervene in organizational communication behaviors:*

- ◆ Increasing awareness and sensitivity to the way individuals "come across" to others.
- ◆ *Teaching principles* and standards of appropriate communication behavior.
- ◆ Inducing *changes in individuals' attitudes* toward communication and interpersonal relations.
- ◆ Inducing *changes in group attitudes* toward communication and intergroup relationships.
- ◆ Creating a "safe" environment in which individuals can try on new communication behaviors.
- ◆ Reinforcing any improvement in communication behaviors as soon as it occurs.
- ◆ Developing an organizational culture based in trust and support conducive to effective, ongoing communication.

*The latter interventions are more difficult than the earlier ones because they call for long-term, ongoing emphasis from management.

OTHER THOUGHTS ABOUT BUSINESS AND MANAGERIAL COMMUNICATION RESEARCH

DIAGNOSING COMMUNICATION "BREAKDOWNS" USING CRITICAL INCIDENTS

In Chapters 1 and 2 we treated the problems of creating understanding and how our personal communication style can complicate that process. A generic research technique that can be applied to communication breakdowns after the fact is the critical incident method. This analysis tool seems simple, but, if used carefully, it can yield meaningful information.

The inventor of the critical incident method, John C. Flanagan, was a World War II military psychologist faced with the problem of improving military flight training. Specifically, too many trainees were cracking up training planes. Someone in the War Department suggested that perhaps the training wasn't emphasizing the right things.

Flanagan did something deceptively simple. He asked pilot trainees who were able to walk away to describe—in terms of behavior—what exactly they had done incorrectly. This technique of illiciting "war stories" is the core of the critical incident process.

Critical incidents are reports or descriptions of behaviors enacted by the people being studied. These incidents are recorded and classified as effective or ineffective in achieving the desired job (or communication) results. The descriptions can take the form of stories, anecdotes, reports, and observations related—verbally or in writing—by supervisors, peers, subordinates, or any other observers qualified to judge the performance.

To be simple, critical incidents must address four questions:

1. What was done that led to effective communication or job performance?
2. What was done that detracted from effective performance or that led to ineffective job performance?
3. What, if done differently, would have been more effective?
4. What attitudes, values, abilities, knowledge, or skills (present or absent) *seemed* to lead to success or failure?

Some ground rules for collecting critical incidents should be presented to your data-gathering team. Sample directions are show in Figure 16-5, along with a sample of a written incident.

Here are examples of both effective and ineffective communication incidents:

Observed Behavior:

Customer service clerk identified a billing error on customer statement. Explained error to customer in a clear manner and initiated paperwork to correct statement.

Outcome:

Upset customer was pacified by clear explanation and immediate corrective action.

Observed Behavior:

Customer service clerk accused a customer of trying to avoid paying his bill when customer was upset and could not understand billing payment.

Outcome:

Customer left office angry at clerk and vowed to quit doing business with company.

After many such incidents are collected, a panel of management employees sorts them into groups identifying major concerns. The first example may go into a stack called "explaining billing," while the second may be categorized as "tone of customer communication." These categories can be named anything you want, but the labels should identify areas of commonality among incidents. Sometimes the incidents need to be categorized several times until satisfactory classes can be identified.

Once categories are determined, corrective actions such as training programs can be implemented to correct common communication problems. Training modules may include topics such as:

♦ How to "keep cool" when your customer is angry.

♦ How to clearly explain our billing.

♦ How to pacify the customer.

♦ Etc.

Don't forget to include *positive* critical incidents in your audit. Often the people who have developed exceptional skills can be useful in training others. Informal exchanges of "war stories" can give others ideas on how to better handle future communication incidents.

In a sense, the critical incident technique is an application of Alfredo Paredo's Law of Disproportionate Distribution. Italian mathematician Paredo originally discovered that 80 percent of the wealth of Italy was controlled by 20 percent of the population. This principle also applies to other situations: Twenty percent of a company's salespeople make 80 percent of the sales; 20 percent of the sales generate 80 percent of the profits; and 20 percent of the effort yields 80 percent of the output.

The critical incident approach tries to point out what that critical 20 percent of effort, which yields 80 percent of the performance, looks like.

Directions:

1. Identify specific *examples* of effective communication you have seen on the part of employees. (Don't limit your recollection just to superstar performance. We're interested in competence, not world records.)

2. On the form, write down what you *observed* and what the *outcome* of the performance was.

3. Write out as many of these scenarios as you can observe.

4. Limit your stories to incidents you have observed in your assigned group of employees.

What I Observed the Employee Doing

This sales rep started the meeting by finding out what each person in the room was responsible for and how each was using computer printouts or terminals. During the presentation, he mentioned a benefit of three responsibilities and areas of need.

The Outcome of What They Did

The client team decided to let us design a system plan and make a bid.

Typical instructions to auditors using the critical incident technique.

Typical incident written by a critical incident auditor.

FIGURE 16-5   Instructions and sample incident.

NOTES

1. This chapter is adapted from Rick C. Farr and Paul R. Timm, *Business Research: An Informal Guide* (Menlo Park, CA: Crisp Publications, 1994). Used with permission of the authors.

2. Technically, questionnaire responses are anonymous only if there are no identifying marks on the survey which could be associated with the respondent. If the surveys are numbered or request respondent's name or other identification, the person should be told that his or her identity will be confidential. This means that what they say will not be associated with their name, except possibly by the researcher. The most sensitive issues are better handled via *anonymous* surveys.

3. Named after it's creator Rensis Likert.

4. The following names are titles of sophisticated statistical software programs: SPSS, SAS, SYSTAT, and STATISTICS.

INDEX